THE Which? BOOK OF MONEY

THE Which? BOOK OF MONEY

Published by Consumers' Association

The Which? Book of Money is edited and designed for the publishers, Consumers' Association, by Frances Lincoln Publishers Ltd.

First edition, first revise
Copyright © 1980 **Consumers' Association** and **Frances Lincoln Publishers Ltd.**

ISBN: 0 340 25049 6

Printed by Butler & Tanner Ltd
Frome and London

Acknowledgements

Editors	**Kathryn Cave and Helena Wiesner**
Designer	**Howard Dyke**
Verifier	**Helena Kania**
Art Director	**Sally Smallwood**

Contributors	**Janice Allen, Lorna Bourke, Vera di Palma Adrienne Gleeson, Brian Guthrie Rosemary Hartill, W. E. Pritchard Ronald Pullen, Mark Rowland Sarah Williams, John Willman**
Illustrators	**Howard Dyke, Tony Hatt, John Ireland Paul Izard, David Mallott, Paddy Mounter, Nigel Osborne Derek Parnell Associates**

The Editor of 'Money Which?', its staff and consultants provided valuable assistance throughout the production of this book

Contents

PART ONE

Your work

I What you bring home

Something most of us learn from our first payslip (if not before) is that there is a big difference between *gross pay* – what you earn – and *net pay* – what you take home. It makes no difference how you are paid (by cash or direct to a bank account) or when (by the week or month). Once your earnings go above a certain minimum level (about £100 a month or £23 a week in the 80/81 tax year) a gap is likely to develop between your earnings and your net pay. And the more you earn, the larger the gap is likely to be.

In Fig. 1.1 we take a look at one person's payslip, to show how the gap arises.

The person in our example, Mary Jacobs, is a newly qualified computer programmer, earning £5,400 a year. She gets paid by the month, so every month she earns £450. But before she gets her hands on this, her employer has to deduct:
- tax due under PAYE ($\triangleright$ below)
- her National Insurance contributions.

With Mary's agreement, he may also knock off amounts ($\triangleright$ Fig. 1.1) for things like the following:
- the firm's pension scheme
- trade union subscription
- subscription to things like the firm's sports or social club or savings scheme
- repayments for a company loan.

The deductions made should be shown on the payslip she gets each month. In Fig. 1.1 you can see one of her payslips with notes on what the most important entries mean. Your own payslip may look rather different – for example, it may be made out manually rather than on a computer – but it should show broadly the same details, though perhaps with different headings or abbreviations.

The PAYE system
The heftiest deduction on Mary's payslip – and possibly on yours too – is for the tax her employer collects under Pay-As-You-Earn (PAYE). You pay tax this way all through your working life, unless you are self-employed ($\triangleright$ ch. 3), not at work ($\triangleright$ ch. 2), or earn too little to pay any tax at all. When you retire, a pension from your former employer may also have a slice taken out of it under PAYE.

If you pay tax under PAYE, the system may be used to collect tax on other income which is *not* taxed before you get it – eg interest earned on a bank deposit account, regular freelance earnings, your State pension (though this will be taxed before you get it from 1982).

You won't pay tax at all if your income is below a certain level, since everyone is entitled to some pay free of tax. How much depends on which *allowances* you can claim (eg for supporting a needy relative, or for being married) and what *outgoings* you have which qualify for tax relief (eg interest on a mortgage). Even single people, with no dependants and no outgoings can claim the single person's allowance – this means that in the 80/81 tax year you can earn at least £114.95 a month free of tax. For more details of allowances and outgoings $\triangleright$ pp. 220–3. Tax is charged on the part of your income which is taxable at increasing rates. The first slice of your income (the largest for most people) is taxed at the *basic rate*; successive slices are taxed at a series of increasing *higher rates*.

The taxman tells your employer how much of your pay should be free of tax by giving him a *PAYE code* for you. He sends this to your employer at the beginning of the tax year, together with a tax deduction card and two sets of tax tables – one for working out free-of-tax pay, the other for working out how much to deduct from your taxable pay. With these your employer can calculate how much to deduct from your gross pay each month (or week).

Your employer fills in on your card your gross pay for the month/week (after deducting any contributions you make to an approved pension scheme, $\triangleright$ p. 55). He turns to the appropriate month/week in the Free Pay Tables and looks up the amount

Figure 1.1
Mary Jacobs is unmarried, and earns £5,400 a year. She gets paid £450 each month and pays 5 per cent of her salary into her firm's pension scheme. This year she can set mortgage interest of £850 against her tax bill (▷ p. 223) and get the dependent relative allowance because she started supporting her elderly mother this year. (▷ p. 221).

a Period ending
This shows the month for which Mary is getting paid — the month of October 80.

b Gross pay
This is the figure for Mary's monthly salary (£5,400÷12). It would include any holiday pay, overtime or bonus payments, if these are paid. They would have been entered in the appropriate boxes further along the line.

c Basic pay
This is the same as gross pay in Mary's case because she has no holiday pay, overtime or bonus payments.

d Hol/Sick
Depending on your company's policy, it may list here your pay while on holiday or off sick, or it may list only exceptional payments (eg pay in lieu of holidays).

e Expenses* (non-taxable)
Payments for non-taxable expenses you have to incur for your job would be entered here — eg to cover protective overalls you have to buy for your job. Special rules may apply for the higher-paid — those earning £8,500 or more a year in the 80/81 tax year.

f Allowances* (non-taxable)
Non-taxable payments (eg for an evening meal or travelling allowance) are entered in this box. As with Expenses (see previous column) special rules may apply for the higher-paid.

g Total ded.
This is the total of the tax, NI contributions and so on deducted from Mary's pay — ie the gap between what she earns and what she gets.

h Tax
This is the figure for tax deducted under PAYE. Mary gets $\frac{1}{12}$ of her free-of-tax pay (▷ opposite) each month. Her employer knows how much free-of-tax pay she is entitled to from her PAYE code. Mary pays tax on her earnings *less* her contributions to her company pension scheme *less* her free-of-tax pay.

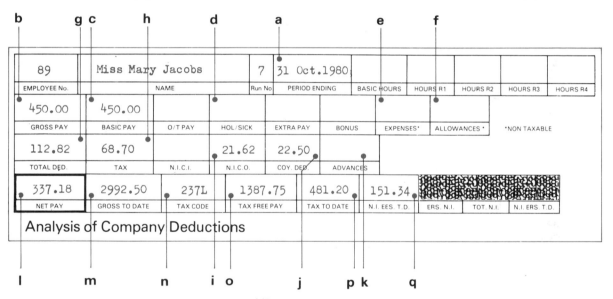

89	Miss Mary Jacobs		7	31 Oct.1980						
EMPLOYEE No.	NAME		Run No	PERIOD ENDING		BASIC HOURS	HOURS R1	HOURS R2	HOURS R3	HOURS R4
450.00	450.00									
GROSS PAY	BASIC PAY	O/T PAY	HOL/SICK	EXTRA PAY	BONUS	EXPENSES*	ALLOWANCES*	*NON TAXABLE		
112.82	68.70		21.62	22.50						
TOTAL DED.	TAX	N.I.C.I.	N.I.C.O.	COY. DED.	ADVANCES					
337.18	2992.50	237L	1387.75	481.20	151.34					
NET PAY	GROSS TO DATE	TAX CODE	TAX FREE PAY	TAX TO DATE	N.I. EES. T.D.	ERS. N.I.	TOT. N.I.	N.I. ERS. T.D.		

Analysis of Company Deductions

i NICI/NICO
National Insurance contributions are entered here. Which box they are entered in depends on whether the firm is in (entered in the NICI box) or out (entered in the NICO box) of the State pension scheme (▷ p. 54). Mary's scheme has contracted out — and her NI contributions work out at £21.62 (compared with £30.37 if the scheme were not contracted out). (Details of the different contribution rates are on p. 52.)

j Coy. ded.
This is Mary's monthly payment to the company pension scheme. Her employer will deduct this figure from her salary *before* it is taxed.

k Advances
If Mary were repaying a company loan — for a season ticket, or a cheap mortgage, perhaps — her repayments would be shown here. So too would payments she made to her employer's medical insurance scheme.

l Net pay
This is what is left of Mary's gross pay after the figure for total deductions has been subtracted. This is Mary's take-home pay.

m Gross to date
This is the figure for Mary's gross pay less pension contributions from the start of the tax year. It is made up of 7 payments of £427.50 (ie her monthly salary from April to October of £450 *less* her monthly payment of £22.50 to the firm's pension scheme).

n Tax code
This is Mary's PAYE code number. For how this is worked out, ▷ p. 14.

o Tax free pay
This is the total to date of Mary's pay which is free of tax because of the allowances she can claim, and the outgoings on which she gets tax relief (*not* including her payments to the company pension scheme).

p Tax to date
Mary has paid this much in tax since the beginning of the 80/81 tax year.

q N.I.EES.T.D.
This is the amount Mary has paid in NI contributions since the beginning of the 80/81 tax year.

of tax-free pay indicated by your PAYE code. The tables are worked out so that every month/week you get a proportion of your yearly free-of-tax pay ($\frac{1}{12}$ if you are paid monthly, or $\frac{1}{52}$ if you are paid weekly).

Next he deducts your free-of-tax pay from your gross pay; on the income that remains you have to pay tax. To find out how much tax to deduct, he turns to the Taxable Pay Tables, which give details of tax payable at basic and higher rates.

If rates of tax change (eg in a Budget), the taxman sends your employer a new set of tables and tells him the date from which he should use them. Although the new rates will generally apply from the beginning of the tax year (6 April), he won't normally get the new tax tables until somewhat later. Until then, you may be paying more (or less) tax than you should. If you're entitled to a tax rebate, you'll get it automatically as soon as your employer starts using the new tables, but you don't normally have to pay any additional tax you owe until later.

Out of work, off sick, on strike?

If you are out of work for a time, or if you are off sick or on strike, and your employer stops paying you, you will be missing the tax-free allowances you are entitled to during that time, and so will have paid too much tax when working.

But if you go back to work again in the same tax year, the tax tables used by your employer automatically ensure that you are given the allowances you missed. On the first pay day after returning to work, you should get a tax rebate in your pay packet.

If you are out of work for more than 4 weeks, and want your overpaid tax back before you start work again, apply to your tax office for a tax rebate (ask for form P50). If you are off sick or on strike, ask your employer to pay you your tax rebates on your normal payday.

Starting or leaving a job?

When you first start work

If your earnings rise above a certain level (£114.50 a month in the 80/81 tax year) your employer will tell the taxman and – until the 81/82 tax year – you will then be sent a Tax Return.

Until the taxman gets your Tax Return back, he doesn't know what allowances and outgoings you can claim, and so can't give you your correct PAYE code. And until he sends a PAYE code to your employer, the latter has to deduct tax on an *emergency code*,

which gives you a single person's allowance ($\triangleright$ p. 220) and nothing more. Emergency code is applied on a *Week 1* or *Month 1* basis, which assumes you have been working all through the tax year and have already had the benefit of the free-of-tax pay you are entitled to in the earlier part of the year.

From the 81/82 tax year, it's proposed that people just starting work (eg school leavers) whose earnings go over the limit, should automatically get a single person's allowance, and that a *Week 1* or *Month 1* basis won't be used. So the tax deducted in your first pay packet will allow for the fact that you haven't yet used up the free-of-tax pay due to you since the start of the tax year. You won't be sent a Tax Return unless (from your answers to a short questionnaire from the taxman) it seems that your PAYE code is incorrect – eg because you can claim other allowances or outgoings.

Whichever procedure is used, once you get your correct PAYE code, you should automatically get any refund of tax owed to you.

If you change jobs

Make sure you get a P45 form from your old employer and give it to your new one. The form shows your PAYE code and your gross pay so far this tax year. Your new employer needs this information to start deducting the correct amount of tax each week or month.

Notice of Coding

The taxman uses a Notice of Coding ($\triangleright$ Fig. 1.2), to show in detail how your tax-free allowances are worked out, what outgoings are included in your code, and whether any extra income is being taxed under the PAYE system (eg income not taxed before you get it) and any other adjustments the taxman makes. Notices of Coding are generally sent out in January or February and apply for the tax year starting on 6 April. But you should get one any time your circumstances change (eg you claim a new allowance, or incur a new outgoing).

● Check your Notice of Coding carefully Make sure you are getting all the allowances and outgoings you are entitled to. For help in checking, see Mary Jacobs' Notice of Coding on p. 14, where we explain what the different parts of the notice show. If you think you aren't getting the allowances and so on you're entitled to, write to your tax office, enclosing the Notice of Coding.

And if your circumstances change during the tax year – if you marry, for example, or buy a home on a mortgage – write to your tax office and tell them about your change in circumstances at once. Send in your most recent Notice of Coding too, if you still have it. Unless you get your code put right before the end of the tax year, you will pay the wrong amount of tax under PAYE. And you'll either have to claim a rebate, or be faced with more tax to pay in a later tax year. For how to get your code changed ▷ p. 224.

If you are dissatisfied with the taxman's verdict on your code, you can appeal against it to the General Commissioners (▷ p. 225). Against their decision, however, you can't appeal.

If your PAYE code goes up

If your PAYE code goes up, more of your monthly (or weekly) pay will be free of tax, so the amount of tax deducted each month (or week) will go down.

Getting a higher code means that, since the beginning of the tax year, you've had too little pay free of tax each month or week – so you will have been paying too much tax. The first time your new code is used, you'll automatically get a tax rebate in your pay packet.

If your PAYE code goes down

If your code goes down, less of your monthly (or weekly) pay will be free of tax, so you will have been paying too little tax. But the taxman may tell your employer not to deduct the backlog of tax you owe in one go, if this would lead to a sharp drop in your take-home pay the first time your new code was used. The taxman might, instead, tell your employer to apply your new code on a *Week 1* or *Month 1* basis – ▷ opposite. This would mean that each pay day you'd get the correct proportion ($\frac{1}{52}$ or $\frac{1}{2}$) of your new, lower free-of-tax pay. The backlog of tax you owe would be collected over a later tax year by adjusting your code for that year.

Code	Rate of tax
BR	30%
DO	40%
D1	45%
D2	50%
D3	55%
D4	60%

PAYE code letters

The letter at the end of your PAYE code depends on the allowances you can claim. It will be:

L   if you get the (lower) single person's or wife's earned income allowance

H   if you get the (higher) married man's allowance or the additional personal allowance for children

P   if you get the full age allowance for a single person

V   if you get the full age allowance for a married man

T   under certain circumstances, eg if you ask the taxman not to tell your employer what personal allowance you're getting, or you get less than the full age allowance

The letters L, H, P and V allow Budget changes in personal allowances, age allowance or additional personal allowance for children to affect your PAYE deductions more quickly. The taxman can tell your employer to make changes automatically (eg to give all people with the H-code extra free-of-tax pay). It will take longer for your PAYE code to be adjusted if you have a T-code. T-codes have to be reviewed one by one when there is a tax change, and that takes time.

There may in certain circumstances be a letter at the beginning of your PAYE code rather than at the end. It will be F if you have a taxable national insurance pension which is higher than your tax-free allowances. If so, the taxman has to tax you at a single, higher-than-normal rate on the whole of your earnings (or pension from a former job) to cover tax due on the NI pension.

More than one job?

If you have more than one job, and the code for the second is one of those shown left, all you earn from the second job will be taxed at the rate shown. (Rates are for the 80/81 tax year – these may change, so check with your taxman.)

If the code for your second job ends in T (eg OT), the first chunk of taxable earnings from that job will be taxed at the basic rate (£11,250 in the 80/81 tax year), and successive slices at higher rates of tax.

Figure 1.2 Mary Jacobs started supporting her elderly mother in July 80. She let the taxman know, and was sent a new Notice of Coding, telling her her new PAYE code. Mary checked the Notice of Coding carefully to see that she was getting all the allowances and outgoings she was entitled to. To help you do the same for your Notice of Coding, we take you through the entries on the Notice step by step.

These notes refer to form P3(1980) (PAYE Coding Guide) enclosed or sent with a previous notice of coding ▼

YOUR ALLOWANCES	£	See note	
Expenses, etc.		**3**	a
Death and Superannuation Benefits		**4**	b
Building Society interest payable	850	**5**	c
Loan, etc. interest		**6**	d
Personal	1375		e
Age (estimated total income £ ....)			f
Wife's earned income		**7**	g
Additional personal			h
Dependant relative	145		i
....			j
....			
....			
TOTAL ALLOWANCES	2370		
LESS: Allowances given against other income		**9**	k

TRUSTEE SAVINGS BANK INTEREST *See Note 9* ▶

Untaxed interest			
Occupational pensions			
National Insurance benefits ...			
....			
....			
NET ALLOWANCES			
LESS: Tax unpaid for earlier years		**10**	
19 - £ *equivalent to a deduction of*			
1979-80 £ *(estimated) equivalent to a deduction of*			l
Other adjustments		**11-14**	m
ALLOWANCES GIVEN AGAINST PAY	2370		n
			o
			p
YOUR CODE FOR 1980-81 ▶	237 ⋮ L	**1**	

This form is for the 80/81 tax year — it may change from year to year, but the principles remain the same.

a This covers any expenses — like professional subscriptions, for example — that the taxman agrees are allowable for tax.

b You get tax relief on half the amount you pay towards pension, funeral, or life insurance benefits via a trade union or friendly society subscription.

c If the taxman knows you have a mortgage, he includes the amount of interest he estimates you will pay in the relevant tax year.

Note that if mortgage interest rates change in the tax year, the taxman may wait until the end of the tax year to see whether you've paid too much or too little tax. If too much, you'll normally get a tax rebate after the end of the tax year. If too little, the taxman will normally lower your PAYE code in a later tax year.

d This covers interest paid to banks and lenders other than building societies on loans which qualify for tax relief — a bank loan for improving your main home, for example.

e The married man's or single person's allowance comes here (£2,145 and £1,375 respectively in the 80/81 tax year). If the wife's earnings are taxed separately (▷ p. 127) both get the single person's allowance. Note that for the majority of Notices of Coding (sent out in January or February) the taxman will use the allowances for the previous tax year — if these change in the Budget, your code will be changed automatically (▷ p. 13).

f If either you or your wife is 64 or over before the start of the tax year, you may benefit by getting age allowance (up to £1,820 for a single person, £2,895 for a married couple in the 80/81 tax year). The *estimated total income* is included in your Notice of Coding because age allowance is scaled down if your 'total income' (▷ p. 216 for what this means) is over a certain limit (£5,900 in the 80/81 tax year) — but it won't be reduced to below the level of personal allowances in **e**

g Working wives get the wife's earned income allowance (up to £1,375 in the 80/81 tax year) unless the wife's earnings are taxed separately (▷ p. 127).

h This is an additional allowance for single-parent families (▷ p. 221 — £770 in the 80/81 tax year).

i You can claim this if you support a needy relative (▷ p. 221). The allowance was £100 for the 80/81 tax year, £145 if claimed by a single woman or wife whose earnings are taxed separately.

j The taxman might use this gap to enter allowances not specifically mentioned on the Notice of Coding, eg blind person's allowance. Check pages 220 to 222 to see that you've got all the allowances you're entitled to. If you haven't, be sure to let the taxman know as soon as possible.

k The taxman may use the PAYE system to collect the tax on some income which was not taxed before you got it

(eg State retirement pension, interest from a bank deposit account, taxable fringe benefits). He does this by reducing your tax-free allowances by the amount of the untaxed income.

l If you have paid too little tax under PAYE in earlier years, you will normally have your tax-free allowances for the current year reduced, so that your tax repayments catch up with what you owe. If you pay tax at the basic rate, a deduction of about 3 times the tax you owe will bring in the tax required; if you pay tax at higher rates, a smaller deduction will do the trick.

Note that your Notice of Coding for the 81/82 tax year will normally be sent to you before the end of the 80/81 tax year — so if the taxman reckons you've underpaid tax for the 80/81 tax year, his figure can only be an estimate.

m This is where the taxman can make any other adjustments necessary to collect the correct amount of tax from you. He might make an adjustment here if, for example, you pay tax at higher rates and have investment income which has been taxed at the basic rate only. You'll have to pay extra tax on this income. And the taxman might decide to collect the extra tax through the PAYE system, by making a *'taxed' investment income* deduction on your Notice of Coding. (But you can ask him for a separate bill if you don't want to pay the extra tax through PAYE.)

If a husband and wife pay tax at higher rates on their joint

earnings, the taxman might make an *excessive basic rate* deduction. This is normally made from the husband's code as far as possible, any balance from the wife's.

This deduction is made because the tax tables used by employers would charge tax at the basic rate on the first £11,250 (for the 80/81 tax year) of both husband's and wife's taxable incomes (whereas they should, in fact, pay higher rate tax on anything over £11,250 of their *joint* taxable income — unless they've chosen to have the wife's earnings taxed separately, ▷ p. 127).

If you deduct tax at the basic rate from payments you make under a court order, the taxman might make a deduction if you are not entitled to the full amount of tax relief you've given yourself. On the other hand, there might be an addition if you're a higher rate taxpayer, and entitled to extra tax relief.

n This is the total amount of pay which you can have free of tax in the tax year.

o Ignore the last digit of your total allowances and you get the number part of your PAYE code. So if the total is £2,370, the code number is 237. Note that if the total is between £1 and £19 the code is 1.

You might think that by knocking off the last figure you would lose tax-free pay equivalent to that number of £££. But you don't — because if your code is 237, as in our example, your employer's tax tables give you tax-free pay of £2,379, *not* £2,370. So the rounding works in your favour.

p For the letter part of the code ▷ p. 13.

2 Not at work

Great Britain has a working population of around 26 million men and women. If all of them worked a basic 5-day week, 48 weeks a year, they could put in more than 6,000 million working days each year. But each year, getting on for 700 million or so days are lost through unemployment, illness and strikes.

Figure 2.1 (below left) shows roughly how many days each year an 'average' employee would lose from those three causes.

Don't be misled into thinking the 'average' worker exists. The days lost are not spread evenly among the working population: some industries and regions lose more than others. And some people *never* get ill, while others are less fortunate. Nonetheless, unless you're very lucky the chances are that sooner or later *you* may need the kind of help available for people who are off or out of work. The aim of this chapter is to explain the different kinds of help you can get and how to go about claiming them.

Where possible, we give the titles of official leaflets about the State benefits in question. You can get them from your local social security office (listed in the phone book under *Health and Social Security, Dept of*). We have also tried to give an idea of the scale of benefits by quoting the latest available figures. These figures are updated (normally in November each year) to keep up with inflation. When we say for example, 'in November 79, the amount was ...' we mean the rate that applied for the year beginning in November 1980 – ie ending in November 1981. To get the current rates, see DHSS leaflet NI 196 *Social security benefit rates.*

A guide to the organization of the chapter is set out on the right.

National Insurance contributions

Much of the State help we talk about in this chapter is paid for by National Insurance contributions. This means that what you

are entitled to in the way of benefits can crucially depend on the amount you have paid in NI contributions. There are complicated rules for the different benefits. There are additional complications for many married women and widows who have chosen to pay lower-than-normal rates of contributions and to get a more limited range of benefits. For details of these complex rules ▷ p. 237.

In practice, you needn't worry too much about contribution conditions if you have been working full-time for an employer over the past 3 years or so – you almost certainly qualify for most benefits. But you need to consider your contribution record if:

● you have recently started work
● you have had a long spell off work in the past 3 years or so
● you are a woman who pays lower-than-normal contributions (▷ p. 237)
● you have recently worked abroad.

Your local social security office should be able to advise you if you are in doubt.

Figure 2.1
Estimated number of working days lost each year by the average worker through sickness, strikes and unemployment

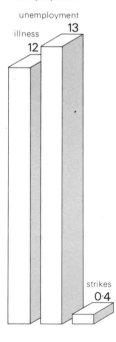

unemployment

illness

13

12

strikes

0·4

Off sick

As Fig. 2.1 shows, the average employee is off work through illness for 12 days each year. Nowadays, illness does not spell destitution, as it might have done a hundred years ago. The State helps people who can't work because of illness, and many employers help too.

The result is that if you are off sick for less than 3 to 6 months, you may not lose out – until 1982, you may even take home slightly more pay. For details of the help offered by employers ▷ p. 20, and for why you can be better off after-tax when sick ▷ Fig. 2.2, p. 20. If you are interested in taking out insurance to provide an income should you have to stop work for a long time through illness, see the section on *sick pay insurance* beginning on p. 142.

Help from the State

Sickness benefit

This currently has two parts: a flat-rate benefit and an earnings-related supplement (but ▷ p. 19 for changes on the way). We give details of each separately.

Flat-rate benefit

● Who qualifies?
People who have paid enough Class 1 or 2 NI contributions and are incapable of work.
● How long is it paid for?
Up to 28 weeks (after that, if you are still off work through sickness, you can claim invalidity benefit ▷ p. 18).
● When does it start?
The first 3 days (not counting Sundays) you are off sick are called *waiting days*, and you get no sickness benefit for them. But if you have a second spell of more than 3 days off sick less than 6 weeks after the first, the second spell counts as part of the first and there are no waiting days.
● How much?
In November 80 the basic rate of sickness benefit was £20.65 a week – this might be reduced if your NI contribution record (▷ p. 235) is incomplete. But you may be able to get extra amounts, called *increases*, for children you support, or for an adult dependant (▷ pp. 227–8). For example, a married man getting increases for a wife and for 2 children could have got up to £35.90 in November 80 (again, depending on his contribution record). Sickness benefit is currently tax-free.

Note that if the person claiming earns more than a certain amount (£15 a week from November 80) while off work his sick-ness benefit may be reduced. An increase cannot be paid for a wife or adult dependant if their earnings go over a certain amount (£12.75 a week in November 80).

Earnings-related supplement

● Who qualifies?
People getting *full* flat-rate sickness benefit may get this after 2 weeks off work. But you can't get it if:
● you are self-employed (only Class 1 contributions count)
● you are over pension age (65 for a man, 60 for a woman).
● How much?
The maximum was £17.67 in January 80. The amount depends on how much you paid in Class 1 NI contributions in the *relevant tax year* – normally the last or last-but-one complete tax year (▷ p. 235). To get the maximum in January 80, you would have had to be earning £120 or more each week in the 78/79 tax year. The earnings-related supplement is currently tax-free.
● How to claim sickness benefit
Get a doctor's statement as soon as you become unable to work through illness. You can get one from your doctor, or your hospital (if you end up there as an outpatient). If you are an inpatient, you should ask for a hospital certificate.

Make your claim on the doctor's statement or hospital certificate and send it in to your local social security office within 6 days (21 days if it's the first time you have claimed).

If you can't send a doctor's statement in within that time, write to the social security office to say that you are claiming the benefit. Give your name, address, date of birth, and (if possible) your NI number.

If you are still unable to work at the end of the period specified on your doctor's statement, get another doctor's statement. You can lose out if there is a gap between statements, so keep a note of when your current doctor's statement runs out, so that you remember when to get a new one.
● After you claim
You will be told in writing how much benefit you will get and when it is to be paid. If you are going to appeal against this decision, you usually have to do so within a certain time – normally 21 days.

● Further information
NI 16 *Sickness benefit*
NI 155A *How your earnings-related benefit is worked out*
(Both available from social security offices.)

When and how you get paid
You normally get the first payment 7 to 10 days after the first doctor's statement reaches your social security office, and then weekly or fortnightly.

Benefit is paid by National Girobank cheque, which you should cash at a post office or pay into a bank account within 3 months of the date on it. If you can't leave your home, you can authorize someone else to cash the cheque for you.

With long-term illnesses, you may get a book of orders which you can cash weekly at any post office, normally within 3 months of the date stamped on them.

If your circumstances change
Tell your local social security office at once of any changes which could affect your benefit — eg if you or any of your dependants go abroad or into hospital, or you change your address, or a child leaves home.

Getting a job will probably affect your entitlement to benefits. Check this at once with your local social security office.

Invalidity benefit

This has three parts: invalidity pension, invalidity allowance, and an earnings-related additional pension.

● Who qualifies?

People who qualify for sickness benefit or industrial injury benefit and are off work for more than 28 weeks get an *invalidity pension*. Men who were under 60 or women under 55 on the first day of their illness can get *invalidity allowance* as well. Those who have paid enough in Class 1 NI contributions since April 78 also get an *additional pension*.

● When does it start?

As soon as sickness benefit runs out.

● How long for?

Invalidity pension is paid until you can return to work or draw a retirement pension. Additional pension continues after retirement, and so does invalidity allowance, provided that:

● you qualify for a retirement pension on your own NI contributions

● you are getting invalidity allowance on any day within 13 weeks of retirement.

● How much?

In November 80, the basic rate of *invalidity pension* was £26.00 a week. But you may be able to get extra amounts called *increases* for children you support, or for an adult dependant (▷ pp. 227–8). For example, a married man getting an increase for his wife and for 2 children would have got £56.60 a week in November 80. Invalidity pension is currently tax-free.

The size of the *invalidity allowance* depends on the age of the person claiming on the first day of the illness. In November 80, a person under 40 when their illness began would have got £5.45 (the maximum) a week, and so would someone who fell ill before 5 July 48. Invalidity allowance is currently tax-free until retirement age – after this it is taxable.

The size of the *additional pension* (taxable) depends on how much the person claiming earned in his 20 best earnings years after April 78 (p. 53). So far, very little additional pension could have been built up. In November 80 the maximum was £3.45 (will go up again in April 81).

● How to claim

You get it automatically when sickness benefit stops. But you still need to go on getting doctor's statements to send to your social security office.

● Further information

NI 16A *Invalidity benefit* (available from social security offices).

Non-contributory invalidity pension

For more details ▷ p. 233.

● Who gets it?

Anyone of working age (16 to 65 for men, 16 to 60 for women) who has been off sick for a continuous period of at least 28 weeks and who did not qualify for the full flat-rate sickness or invalidity benefit because of a poor NI contribution record. A married woman claiming (in addition to being incapable of paid work) must also be unable to do her normal household duties for a continuous period of at least 28 weeks.

● How long for?

As long as you remain unable to work.

● How much?

In November 80, the basic rate was £16.30 a week. But you may be able to get extra amounts, called *increases*, for children you support, or for an adult dependant (▷ pp. 227–8). For example, a married man getting an increase for his wife and for 2 children could get £41.10 a week. This pension is currently tax-free.

● How to claim

Claim on the form in leaflet NI 210 (leaflet NI 214 for married women), available from social security offices.

● Further information

NI 210 *Non-contributory invalidity pension*
NI 214 *Non-contributory invalidity pension for married women*
(Both available from social security offices.)

Industrial injuries scheme

This is a scheme to compensate people disabled (mentally or physically) while working for an employer. Qualifying for this benefit does not depend on your NI contribution record. If you're involved in an accident at work which you think might qualify, get it declared an *industrial accident* – ask your local social security office for form BL 95 to report the accident to them. Inform a senior person at work at the time.

There are two main benefits under the scheme: *industrial injury benefit* and *industrial disablement benefit*.

Industrial injury benefit

● Who qualifies?

Most employees who become incapable of work as a result of accidents caused through their work, or because they are suffering from one of the specified industrial diseases. An earnings-related supplement may be paid – the conditions are the same as for sickness benefit (▷ p. 17 and p. 19).

If your disease is not one of the specified ones, you may be able to claim sickness benefit instead.

● How long for?

Benefit is paid for a maximum of 26 weeks from the date of the accident, or start of the disease. After this the person claiming may be able to get industrial disablement benefit.

● How much?

Generally more than you would get under sickness benefit. For example, a married man getting an increase for his wife and for 2 children would have got £38.65 a week from November 80. The earnings-related supplement was a maximum of £17.67 a week from January 80. The benefit is currently tax-free.

● How to claim

If you become incapable of work, ask your doctor for a doctor's statement, fill it in and send it within 6 days to your local social security office.

● Further information

NI 5 *Injury benefit for accidents at work*
NI 2 *Prescribed industrial diseases*
(Both available from social security offices.)

Industrial disablement benefit

● Who qualifies?

Any employee who is injured permanently (mentally or physically) as a result of an industrial accident or disease – even if he doesn't have to stop work. If he *does* have to stop work, industrial injury benefit could provide more money during the first 26 weeks (he can't get both at the same time).

● How long for?

As long as the disability lasts. It can be paid in addition to any other NI benefits you are entitled to – eg sickness or invalidity benefit or retirement pension.

● How much?

Assessment of your disability (▷ How to claim, below) is made on a percentage scale. For 100 per cent assessment (eg loss of both hands or sight) and no extra allowances (▷ below) the rate in November 80 was £44.30 a week. For an assessment of less than 20 per cent, you get a lump sum – eg £2,950 for 19 per cent. This benefit is currently tax-free.

Extra allowances may be paid in addition for those who are severely disabled – eg if the person can't go back to their old job, or as good a one, or if they need constant care and attendance. To qualify, their disability must be assessed at 100 per cent.

● How to claim

Ask your local social security office for Form B1 100A (accidents), B1 100 (Pn) (pneumoconiosis and byssinosis), B1 100 (OD) (occupational deafness), or B1 100B (other diseases). Your degree of disablement is decided by an independent medical board. In certain circumstances, you can appeal against their decision to a medical appeal tribunal. Your social security office will provide details.

● Further information

NI 6 *Disablement benefit and increases*
NI 3 *Benefits paid for pneumoconiosis and byssinosis*
NI 207 *Benefits paid for occupational deafness*
PN 1 *The pneumoconiosis, byssinosis and miscellaneous diseases benefit scheme*
(all available from social security offices).

Changes on the way

The Government has put forward proposals to make employers responsible for paying employees a flat-rate benefit for the first 8 weeks off work. The proposals have been set out in a consultative document for discussion by interested groups – and no final decision had been taken when this book went to press. The changes are planned for 1982, so the procedures set out in these pages should be followed until then.

Another important proposal for April 1982 is to make sickness benefit, invalidity benefit and industrial injury benefit taxable. And by January 1982, the Government plans to have abolished the earnings-related supplement paid with sickness benefit and probably that paid with industrial injury benefit. As a first step, earnings-related supplement will be reduced from January 1981 onwards.

Help from your employer

White-collar workers are likely to go on getting a full salary from their employer for a time when off sick – for 3 months, say. Even after this, many employers pay half salary for a time – a further 3 months, say. One of the most generous arrangements is offered by the civil service, local authorities, and the NHS: 6 months' full pay, followed by 6 months' half pay.

Manual workers, however, are likely to be worse off: only around half of them get any sick pay from their employer. And any sick pay they do get is normally related to their basic wage (ignoring regular overtime, bonuses, etc, which could make up a large proportion of normal pay).

Your employer will normally deduct from your sick pay an amount equal to whatever State benefits you can claim. So even if you are covered by a sick pay scheme at work, you should still claim sickness benefit and any other State benefits you are entitled to.

People who get full salary while off sick often find themselves better off financially than before under the current tax rules. The sickness benefit paid by the State is tax-free, so that only the amount the employer pays is taxable – ie less than the full salary itself (▷ Fig. 2.2). If sickness benefit becomes taxable as planned (▷ p. 19), this state of affairs is unlikely to continue.

Some employers provide a group *sick pay insurance scheme* – which will go on supporting employees after normal sick pay arrangements end.

Figure 2.2
What you get while off sick

There are three different types of income you may currently get when you are off sick (other than through industrial injury – ▷ p. 18).
● sickness benefit
● earnings-related supplement
● employer's sick pay.

Figure 2.2 shows how much Fred Foster with earnings of £6,000 a year would get when off sick in December 80. (Note that from January 81, his earnings-related supplement would go down under present Government proposals.) Figure 2.2 also shows how he is currently better off while sick: he loses less from his wallet in tax then.

It's worth noting how little Fred would have to live on if he had to rely on flat-rate sickness benefit alone, as he would have to if his employer did not give sick pay and he couldn't claim the earnings-related supplement. Most self-employed people (who don't qualify for earnings-related supplement) would be in this position. So sick pay insurance (▷ p. 142) is particularly important for them.

Note that anyone who is unable to work through illness may qualify for *supplementary benefit*, and other benefits for people with low incomes (▷ p. 230).

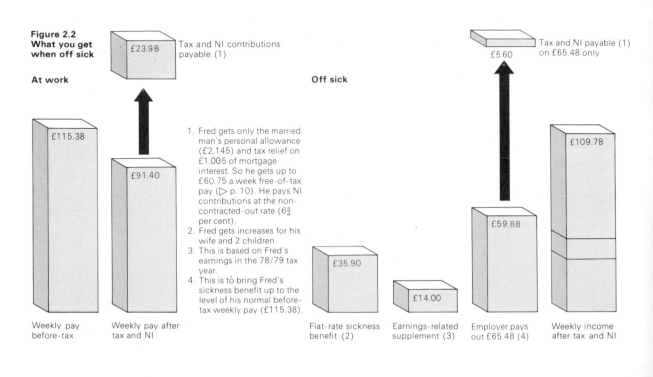

Figure 2.2 What you get when off sick

At work

£115.38 — Weekly pay before-tax

£91.40 — Weekly pay after tax and NI

£23.98 — Tax and NI contributions payable (1)

1. Fred gets only the married man's personal allowance (£2,145) and tax relief on £1,005 of mortgage interest. So he gets up to £60.75 a week free-of-tax pay (▷ p. 10). He pays NI contributions at the non-contracted-out rate (6¾ per cent).
2. Fred gets increases for his wife and 2 children.
3. This is based on Fred's earnings in the 78/79 tax year.
4. This is to bring Fred's sickness benefit up to the level of his normal before-tax weekly pay (£115.38).

Off sick

£35.90 — Flat-rate sickness benefit (2)

£14.00 — Earnings-related supplement (3)

£59.88 — Employer pays out £65.48 (4)

£5.60 — Tax and NI payable (1) on £65.48 only

£109.78 — Weekly income after tax and NI

Group sick pay insurance

Sick pay insurance pays out an income after a certain period off sick until the person insured can return to work or reaches retirement age. You can take out this type of insurance cover yourself (for details ▷ p. 142). But there can be advantages in getting sick pay insurance through an employer's group scheme.

First, you won't have to pay any tax on the premiums your employer pays on your behalf. If you take out this sick pay insurance yourself, you have to pay the premiums out of your after-tax income.

Second, the income paid out through employers' schemes is normally a proportion of the employee's salary, less anything paid out by the State. This means that the amount of cover rises automatically with salary. If you take out sick pay insurance yourself, your premium normally buys you a set amount of income if you fall ill (or one that increases – but by amounts that don't guarantee to match current inflation rates). This means that you need to regularly review your cover to cope with inflation and increases in pay through promotion.

Finally, these schemes are normally arranged so that your employer carries on paying you a proportion of your salary when you are off sick, and claims the money back from the insurance company. The income you get is taxed as *earnings*. Income from sick pay insurance you take out yourself is taxed as *investment income* – ie may be more highly taxed if it raises your investment income over a certain limit (£5,500 for the 80/81 tax year – ▷ p. 194 for further details).

One *disadvantage* of getting sick pay insurance through your employer is that you could find yourself without cover if you change jobs and your new employer does not offer it as a fringe benefit. If your health has deteriorated while you have been a member of a group scheme, you could find that the premiums for a policy of your own are particularly high – or even that you can't get insurance at all.

Coping with long-term illness

No-one likes to face a future which holds out the prospect of long-term illness. But if you find yourself in this position, it is more than usually important to be as financially secure as possible:

● make sure you claim all State benefits you are entitled to – both those described in this chapter and those for people with low incomes (▷ p. 230) and for the disabled (▷ p. 232)

● find out what help you can get from your local authority – for example, meals on wheels, laundry service, home helps (for more details ▷ p. 234)

● examine your finances – budgeting of the type described on p. 28 will be essential if your income is to be restricted for some time.

People suffering from long-term illness can often do some sort of work even if they can't go back to their old job. Disablement resettlement officers specialize in helping such people find jobs – they can be contacted through jobcentres or employment offices. And employment rehabilitation centres run courses to help people improve their capacity for work. But it's worth noting that extra income you may get while on these courses can affect the amount you get from State benefits (or replace them altogether). It may also affect the income you get from sick pay insurance. Check on these points before you start counting on being a lot better off with a job. Your local social security office will tell you what the effect of working will be on State benefits; the insurance company will tell you how any income you get from a sick pay insurance policy will be affected.

Brian Brew stopped work at the end of 80 with searing back pains. His doctor advised him to stay off work for a week, and gave him a doctor's statement. Brian filled in the back of the statement, and sent it off to his local social security office to claim sickness benefit. He got no benefit for the first 3 days he was off sick: but from then on he got £35.90 a week sickness benefit – this included extra benefit for his wife Mary (who does not work), and his 2 children, aged 6 and 4. (His firm has no sickpay scheme, so he got nothing from them.)

Brian's backache showed no sign of improvement after a week, so he went back to the doctor when his first doctor's statement was due to expire. The doctor signed him off work for another 2 weeks and gave him another doctor's statement, which Brian posted off to the social security office.

One week later, Brian's earnings-related supplement came through, as he had been off work for 2 weeks. His earnings-related benefit was £9.57 a week, bringing his sickness benefit up to £45.47 a week – still a drop on the £100 he was earning each week before falling ill.

He'll be able to claim some supplementary benefit – ▷ p. 26.

To help tide him over, Brian asked his employer to pay him his tax rebate each week (it worked out as £19.50) rather than having it all in one go when he went back to work. Even this amount left him feeling rather broke, and Brian was most relieved when his doctor pronounced him fit after 5 weeks off work.

Out of work

Twenty-five years ago, the threat of unemployment probably didn't loom too large in the thoughts of most working people. In the sober light of the early 80s, with up to $1\frac{1}{2}$ million signing on each week, optimism has become less easy to justify. More and more people face a spell of unemployment at some time in their working lives.

Of course, some people will be out of work for short spells only – between jobs, say, or while they retrain for a new career. But for some, loss of a job can lead to a lengthy period of unemployment. Figure 2.3 shows how long the people who were registered as unemployed in July 78 had been out of work. 93 out of every 100 had been out of work for more than a week – ie 7 per cent had become unemployed within the previous week. But 16 out of every 100 people unemployed in July 78 had been out of work for between 6 months and a year, and 22 for more than a year. These figures are a lot higher than those of 10 years ago – so not only are you now more likely to be unemployed, you are also likely to be out of work for longer.

Redundancy

Getting a redundancy notice is a depressing business. But there's a lot you can do to soften its financial impact, and to maximize the speed at which you leave the dole queue.

Bear in mind that redundancy need not be the end of your working life: the chance that you will be out of work for less than 3 months is 50/50. And unless you live in a region where work is especially hard to come by, the likelihood of your being out of work for more than 6 months is much less than Fig. 2.3 suggests: the averages include the unemployed living in such hardcore unemployment areas as Tyneside or Clydeside.

There is a lot of financial help available for those who can find their way around the system:
- statutory redundancy payments – tax-free lump sums which are yours as of right if you have worked for your employer for more than 2 years and meet the other qualifying conditions ($\triangleright$ p. 23)
- unemployment benefit – yours as of right if you have paid enough full Class 1 NI contributions and meet certain other conditions
- supplementary allowances – to top up your income so that it doesn't fall below official subsistence levels.

The next part of the chapter looks at each of these subjects, the amounts payable, how they are taxed, and how to get the most out of each.

At first sight, redundancy can seem something of a windfall: tax-free payments, possible tax rebates, and normally entitlement to a range of social security benefits. But while it's unlikely that you will be out of work for more than 12 months, it makes sense to assume that your resources may have to hold out for some time, and conserve them accordingly. So if you are newly unemployed:

**Figure 2.3
Unemployment – how long might it last?**

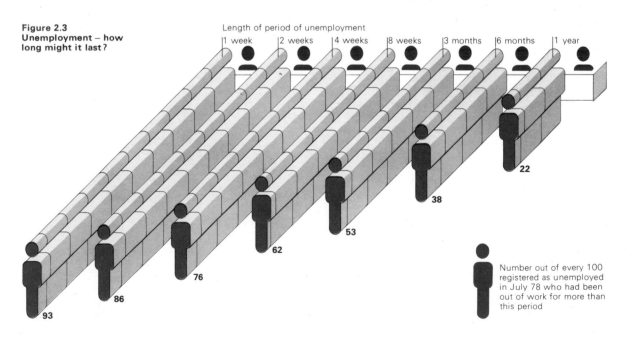

Length of period of unemployment

| 1 week | 2 weeks | 4 weeks | 8 weeks | 3 months | 6 months | 1 year |

93 86 76 62 53 38 22

Number out of every 100 registered as unemployed in July 78 who had been out of work for more than this period

- take a careful look at your finances –
▷ pp. 28–9 for some tips
- invest your capital to its best advantage.
You are likely to need to look for an income
from it – this is not the best time to make
long-term savings plans. For advice on investing ▷ the Route Maps on pp. 188 and
190.

Redundancy payments

If you are made redundant you may be
entitled to a lump sum (which is tax-free)
under the State Redundancy Payments
Scheme. And your employer may add to
this legal minimum – what he pays may also
be partly or wholly free of tax.

The State Redundancy Payments
Scheme

- Who qualifies?
An employer is, in most circumstances, legally obliged to pay a minimum lump sum
in redundancy money to any employee who
is made redundant after working for that
employer continuously for at least 2 years.

You are likely to count as *redundant* if you
lose your job because your employer:
- closes down his business, or cuts his staff
- moves to another place of work
- changes his line of business.

You may also get redundancy money in
certain other circumstances – eg, if your
employer can only offer you work that is
'unsuitable' (▷ p. 25) or you leave your job
because of frequent lay-offs or continual
short-time work. If you are in one of these
less straightforward situations check with
your local jobcentre or employment office.

You won't get redundancy money under
the State scheme in any of the following
cases:
- you are of pensionable age (65 for men,
60 for women) or over
- you are under 20 years old
- you lose your job because you can no
longer do it properly
- your job is due to end anyway *after* you
leave it (unless your employer agrees in
writing to bring forward the date of dismissal and not to replace you)
- you have finished a fixed-term contract
of 2 years or more and agreed in writing to
forgo your right to redundancy money
- you are on a fixed-term contract drawn
up before 6 December 65
- you work for an organization – like the
civil service or the NHS – which is excluded
from the State scheme (though they have
schemes of their own).

And if you are going to get a pension or
lump sum from your ex-employer within

90 weeks of being made redundant, he may
offset these payments against your redundancy money – so that you end up with less.
- How much?
The amount you get depends on
- your weekly pay
- your age
- how long you have been working for your
employer.

Weekly pay does not include overtime,
unless your contract fixes a working week
which includes overtime work. There is a
maximum amount which can be counted as
a week's pay: £120 in April 80.

The amount you get in redundancy
money is:
- 1½ weeks' pay for each complete year you
have worked for your employer since your
41st birthday
plus
- 1 week's pay for each complete year you
have worked for your employer between
your 22nd and 41st birthdays
plus
- ½ week's pay for each complete year you
have worked for your employer between
your 18th and 22nd birthdays.

Only the last 20 years you have been
with that employer count for redundancy
money. So the highest redundancy money
would go to a male employee, aged between
61 and 64, who had worked for the same
employer for at least the past 20 years. If
his weekly pay was at or over the £110 maximum, he would get:

$$20 \times 1\tfrac{1}{2} \times £120 = £3,600$$

Men aged 64 and over, and women aged
59 and over, have their redundancy pay cut
by $\frac{1}{12}$ for each complete month by which
their age was over 64 (for a man) or 59 (for
a woman) on the Saturday of the week in
which they left their job.

Extra redundancy money from
employers

Most employers add to the amounts payable
under the State Redundancy Payments
Scheme – so that employees get more than
the legal minimum.

If you aren't in a position to negotiate
extra payments, it's worth asking your
employer to help you get the maximum
benefit from the favourable tax rules on
redundancy payments. For example, pay in
lieu of notice – provided getting it is not included in any service agreement – is tax-free
if paid *after* an employee has left a job. So
if your employer is prepared to allow you
to take pay in lieu (rather than work out

Harry Hawkins was
made redundant at the
end of 1980 after 24
years working for the
same employer. At the
time of his redundancy,
he was earning around
£115 a week. Harry
works out what
redundancy payment
he is entitled to.

First, he works out
his *week's pay*.
Although he makes
around £115 most
weeks, his basic pay
for a 40-hour week is
£103 – the other £12 a
week comes from
regular overtime. It is
on his *basic weekly
pay* of £103 that his
redundancy money will
be based.

Next, Harry works
out how many times
his week's pay he will
get in redundancy
money. Harry is 47,
and started work with
his employer when
aged 23. So he has
worked for the firm for
more than 20 years,
but it is only the last
20 years which count
towards his redundancy
payment. Harry will
get:
- 1½ weeks' pay of
£103 for each of the 6
complete years he has
worked for his
employer since his 41st
birthday – ie 1½ × £103
× 6 = £927, *plus*
- 1 week's pay of £103
for each of the 14
complete years before
that – ie 1 × £103 × 14 =
£1,442.
This comes to a total
redundancy payment of
£927 + £1,442 = £2,369
– all of which will be
tax-free, as it comes to
less than £10,000.

your notice), you could save a considerable amount in tax on what you get. But note that you can't get unemployment benefit for the notice period.

Tax on redundancy and other leaving payments

The following payments are *free of tax*:
● lump sums for injuries or disabilities which caused the loss of the job
● usually, compensation for loss of a job outside the UK
● gratuities from the armed forces (but if for *early* retirement, the balance over £10,000 may be taxable)
● certain lump sum benefits from approved pension schemes
● normally, allowances under the Job Release Scheme for those retiring early.

If an employee is leaving a job before retirement age, and gets a refund of some pension contributions, the trustees of the fund deduct any tax due – there is no extra tax to pay, even if the employee is liable for tax at the higher rates.

The following are *free of tax if they do not, in total, come to more than £10,000*:
● payments made under the State Redundancy Payments Scheme
● any other payments made to an employee after leaving a job – so long as they are not payments for work done, not part of a service agreement, and – technically at least – unexpected. This would normally cover extra redundancy money from employers, and pay in lieu of notice.

If the total of these payments comes to more than £10,000, there may be tax to pay on the excess. But if you are going to get more than £10,000 there are ways of keeping the tax to a minimum – get advice from your trade union, or see an accountant.

Note that any payments for work done (eg wages, salary, commission or bonuses) paid when or after leaving a job are taxable. So, too, is pay in lieu of holiday.

How to claim redundancy money

All redundancy money is claimed from employers. But 41 per cent of the amount paid by employers under the State Redundancy Payments Scheme can be claimed back from the Redundancy Fund – which gets its money from the NI contributions paid by all employers.

If you can't agree with your employer on the amount of money you ought to get, you could get help from your trade union or staff association. If you aren't a member of either of these, get help from a jobcentre, an employment office or a Citizens' Advice Bureau (address in the phone book).

If you still can't agree on how much you ought to get, you will have to make a formal claim. Write to your ex-employer, giving details of your claim, within 6 months of leaving (if you leave it later than 6 months, you normally lose your claim by default. Keep copies of your letters, and send them by recorded delivery.

If your ex-employer still doesn't pay up, you can within a further 6 months take your claim to an industrial tribunal. Ask for the relevant forms at your local jobcentre or employment office.

If your employer goes bankrupt, and can't pay, you will still get the redundancy money you're due under the State scheme. The money will be paid out of the Redundancy Fund – apply though an employment office or unemployment benefit office.

● Further information
Department of Employment leaflet:
RPL6 *The Redundancy Payments Scheme* (from jobcentres and employment offices).

Help from the State

Unemployment benefit

This is for anyone who normally works for an employer and pays full Class 1 NI contributions. So you can't normally get it if:
● you are self-employed (unless you have worked for an employer recently, and paid enough Class 1 NI contributions in the right year).
● you are a married woman who has chosen to pay the reduced NI contributions (▷ p. 237).

People who retire on a pension from their employer can sign on as unemployed so long as they don't draw their State retirement pension. From April 1981 onwards, it is proposed that the unemployment benefit paid to such people who are over 60 will be reduced by £1 for every £1 of pension they get from their employer over £35 a week.

Unemployment benefit currently has two parts: a flat-rate benefit and an earnings-related supplement (but ▷ p. 27 changes on the way).

Flat-rate benefit
● Who qualifies?
Anyone out of work who has paid enough full Class 1 NI contributions (▷ p. 235), provided they are willing and able to work.

People on short-time work may be able to get it too (for details ▷ p. 26).

● When does it start?

No benefit is paid for the first 3 days (not counting Sundays) off work. These are called *waiting days*. But if you have a second spell of more than 3 days off work (either unemployed or sick) not more than 6 weeks after the first, the second spell counts as part of the first and there are no waiting days.

You may have to wait longer for benefit if your employer gives you pay in lieu of notice or compensation for losing your job, or if you leave your job voluntarily for no good reason, or are fired for misconduct.

● How long for?

Up to 312 days (equivalent to 52 working weeks) in one stretch. Once you have claimed 312 days, no further benefit is paid until you have worked for at least 16 hours a week for 13 weeks for an employer. This 13 weeks need not be in one stretch, or for the same employer.

● How much?

In November 80 the basic rate of benefit was £20.65 a week. But you may be able to get extra amounts, called *increases*, for children you support or for an adult dependant ($\triangleright$ pp. 227–8). For example, a married man getting an increase for his wife and for 2 children would have got £35.90 a week in November 80. Unemployment benefit is currently tax-free.

Earnings-related supplement

● Who qualifies?

People under pension age (65 for men, 60 for women) on *full* flat-rate unemployment benefit after 2 weeks off work.

● When does it start?

Not paid for the first 12 days off work. As with flat-rate benefit, a second spell of more than 3 days off work not more than 6 weeks after the first counts as part of the first spell, and the waiting days don't apply.

You may have to wait longer to claim if you had to wait longer than usual before getting the flat-rate benefit ($\triangleright$ above).

● How long for?

For up to 156 days (equivalent to 6 working months) in one stretch. After this time runs out, you have to clock up 13 continuous weeks of employed work before you can claim again (working for at least 16 hours a week).

● How much?

The maximum was £17.67 a week in January 80. The amount depends on how much you paid in Class 1 NI contributions in the *relevant tax year* – normally the last or last-but-one complete tax year ($\triangleright$ p. 235). To get the maximum in January

80, you would have had to be earning £120 or more a week in the 78/79 tax year.

The earnings-related supplement is currently tax-free.

● How to claim

Claim at your local unemployment benefit office (address in phone book, under *Employment, Department of*). You should claim on the first day of unemployment – no benefit can normally be paid for days before it is claimed.

When you go to claim your unemployment benefit, take the P45 form you got from your last employer – or, if you have not got a P45, take a note of your NI number.

You will be asked if you want to claim for any dependants (eg wife, children). If you do, you will get a claim form. Fill this in as soon as possible afterwards.

● After you claim

People claiming unemployment benefit usually have to visit the unemployment benefit office regularly each fortnight to make their claims. But this requirement is waived for people who live more than 6 miles from their nearest unemployment benefit office – and may be waived in certain other circumstances (eg if it would cause undue hardship because of an illness or disability, or because the journey is difficult).

You can't get unemployment benefit unless you are willing and able to work – so you have to register for work at your local jobcentre or employment office. You should do this as soon as you have put in your claim for benefit. Young people who have left full-time education within the last 2 years can register as unemployed at their local careers office if they prefer.

Once you are getting benefit, you should tell the unemployment benefit office if you want to claim for a new dependant (eg a new child, your wife who stops working). If a payment comes through from your old employer (eg pay in lieu of notice, compensation for loss of a job), the rules say that you should tell the unemployment benefit office about it. The same applies if you do any work, paid or unpaid – you can lose your benefit if you earn more than 75p a day, or if the job would stop you taking on full-time work if you were offered it.

People getting unemployment benefit can be disqualified from benefit for up to 6 weeks if they refuse the offer of a 'suitable' job in their normal line of work. A job would not be regarded as 'suitable' if it offered pay and conditions which were worse than the going rate, or worse than those paid by good

On the first day he was out of work, Harry Hawkins went to the unemployment benefit office to get unemployment benefit. He claimed extra benefit for his wife, who doesn't go out to work, and his 2 children aged 9 and 10.

When his benefit came through, Harry found that he got £35.90 a week, which includes the extra benefit for his wife and children. After 2 weeks out of work, Harry got another £10 in earnings-related supplement – bringing his total benefit up to £45.90 a week. He can claim supplementary benefit ($\triangleright$ p. 26 for how much he got).

After 4 weeks out of work, Harry claimed a tax rebate; he got £57.30 – and he got this much every 4 weeks from then on to the end of the tax year.

Harry had, of course, registered for work at his local jobcentre after claiming unemployment benefit. There seemed to be no suitable jobs in the area, but Harry did not expect to be unemployed for long. However, the months ticked by, and still no suitable job came along. After 6 months, Harry stopped getting earnings-related supplement, so was left with £35.90 in unemployment benefit. His supplementary benefit went up, though ($\triangleright$ p. 26).

Six months later, when he had been unemployed for a year, Harry's unemployment benefit ran out. He now had to depend entirely on supplementary benefit – and his fast-dwindling savings (now less than £1,000).

employers. After a 'reasonable' time, benefit can be stopped if the person getting it turns down any suitable job – even if it isn't in their normal line of work.

These (and other equally complex) conditions mean that the success of a claim can often rest on how words like 'reasonable' or 'suitable' are interpreted. If you disagree with a decision to stop or reduce your benefit – or you are getting less benefit than you think you should – you can appeal. But you must do so within 21 days of being told of the decision you are unhappy about. You can get a form to appeal on from an unemployment benefit office.

● Further information
NI 12 *Unemployment benefit*
NI 155A *How your earnings-related benefit is worked out*
(Both available from unemployment benefit offices and social security offices.)

Short-time workers

You may be able to get flat-rate benefit if you have paid enough Class 1 NI contributions, provided you are off work for 2 or more days out of 6 days running (not counting Sundays). Days which are normally holidays don't count towards your 2 days. And the 3 waiting days (▷ above) before benefit is paid, still apply.

If you are getting paid under a guaranteed wages agreement with your employer, you don't qualify.

To start qualifying for earnings-related supplement, you have first to be laid off for 6 days running (not counting Sundays and holidays). Then you have to build up the 12 waiting days (▷ above) before you can claim the earnings-related supplement. It's unlikely, therefore, that a short-time worker would get earnings-related supplement.

Other social security benefits

People on unemployment benefit or sickness benefit may still be below the official poverty line – if their *resources* fall short of their *requirements* according to official definitions. In this case, they can get help from supplementary benefit. Indeed, once their entitlement to unemployment benefit runs out – normally after a year – most unemployed people must rely on supplementary benefit for their income. Unemployed people with incomes above the level qualifying for supplementary benefit may be able to get help from the State in the form of free or cheap prescriptions, glasses, dental treatment, and so on.

Supplementary benefit
(For full details ▷ p. 229.)

Anyone aged 16 or over with *resources* less than *requirements* according to official definitions can get supplementary benefit (called *supplementary allowance* for people below pension age). In the case of a married couple (or an unmarried couple living together), only the husband can normally claim. The amount payable is normally the amount needed to bring the resources of the person claiming up to the level of their requirements.

Broadly, *resources* are all the part-time earnings of the person claiming (and any income of his wife). Certain amounts can be left out, though – eg deductions for tax, NI contributions, pension contributions, expenses connected with working (eg trade union subscriptions, travelling costs), the first £4 a week of wife's earnings and the first £2 a week (£4 from November 1980) of any part-time earnings of the person claiming, if unemployed. Any NI benefits and pensions (including child benefit) are added to resources. Income from investments can be left out, but if the value of your savings and investments (including redundancy payments) comes to more than £2,000 you will get no benefit.

Requirements are assessed according to the circumstances of the person claiming, but the following normally count:
● rent or, if you own your home, mortgage interest payments, ground rent, and a sum for repairs and insurance for the house
● rates and water rates
● an allowance to cover normal living expenses on a fixed scale – in November 80, for example, a single person could get £21.30 a week, a couple with 2 children aged 6 and 8 could get £49.20
● an allowance to cover unavoidable additional requirements such as heating, dietary and laundry bills where the person claiming meets certain conditions to qualify for them. For example, in November 1980, a claimant with a child under the age of 5 could get an extra £1.40 a week to cover heating costs.
● How to claim
If you're unemployed, claim on form B1 (available from your local unemployment benefit office) – any benefit is normally paid together with unemployment benefit on a single National Girobank cheque. If you don't get unemployment benefit – because your entitlement has run out, say – you still have to register for work and go to the unemployment benefit office to get supple-

Harry Hawkins can get supplementary benefit if his resources fall below his requirements (according to the official definitions). Using the figures for November 80, Harry works out that his requirements are approximately as follows:
● £4.83 a week rates and water rates
● £6.42 a week mortgage interest payments
● £49.20 living allowance for himself, his wife and children.
Total requirements therefore, are around £60.45. Harry's resources when he is first unemployed are his unemployment benefit (£45.90 a week with earnings-related supplement) and child benefit (£9.50 a week altogether) – a total of £55.40. He can get supplementary benefit of £60.45−£55.40= £5.05.

After 6 months, when he loses the £10 a week of earnings-related supplement, his total resources fall to £45.40 and he can get supplementary benefit of £60.45−£45.40= £15.05 a week. When his unemployment benefit runs out altogether, Harry has only the £9.50 a week of child benefit, so he'll get £60.45−£9.50= £50.95 a week in supplementary benefit.

mentary benefit (although some people, such as single parents and some blind and chronically sick people, are excused this).

Note that if you don't qualify for supplementary benefit when you first become unemployed, it could pay to apply again later – when your earnings-related supplement has run out, or your savings have begun to dwindle away.

● Further information
SB 1 *Cash help: how to claim supplementary benefit*
SB 2 *Supplementary benefit and trade disputes*
SB 9 *After you've claimed supplementary benefit – when you're unemployed*
(All available from social security offices.)

Low-income welfare benefits
This group of benefits includes free NHS prescriptions, free or cheap NHS dental treatment and glasses, and free daily milk and vitamins for children under school age and expectant mothers. For further details ▷ pp. 231–2.
● Who qualifies?
Anyone getting supplementary benefit automatically qualifies. Schoolchildren and expectant mothers may also qualify; and so may people whose income is slightly higher than the level which qualifies for supplementary benefit.
● Further information
M11 *Free milk and vitamins, glasses, dental treatment and prescriptions* (available from post offices and social security offices).

Miscellaneous benefits
You may also qualify for some of the help below.
● help with the cost of housing – rate rebates, rent rebates and rent allowances (▷ p. 231)
● free school meals – for some or all children at school (▷ p. 157)
● help with the cost of education – for example, help with the cost of uniform, and education maintenance allowances (▷ p. 158).

Changes on the way
The Government plans to abolish the earnings-related supplement part of unemployment benefit by January 1982. As a first step, the earnings-related supplement will be reduced from January 1981 onwards. The Government also plans to tax the benefits paid to the unemployed (ie flat-rate unemployment benefit and supplementary benefit) from April 1982. Additions for

children and money paid to cover rent and rates are likely to be left non-taxable.

Help from a trade union
Some trade unions provide some form of unemployment pay – although normally only to full members who have kept up their subscriptions. This kind of help is tax-free, and won't affect the amount of unemployment benefit you get. But it counts as part of your resources for the purposes of supplementary benefit – and is likely to reduce the amount of supplementary benefit you are entitled to get.

Trade unions may also be able to help unemployed members to find a new job – sending them lists of jobs available in their trade, or by providing an introduction to an employer who employs only members of the union.

For details of what help your trade union (or professional association) offers, contact the head office, or local office if there is one.

Finding a new job
You may be able to find a new job through your own efforts – by writing to employers or answering newspaper advertisements, say – but don't ignore the help offered free by the State. You will have to register for work at your local employment office or jobcentre in any case, if you want to get unemployment benefit or supplementary allowance.

Help with job-hunting
Jobcentres work partly on a self-service basis. Details of jobs available are displayed on cards on the walls, and you can look among these for work that suits you.

When you register for work for the first time after losing a job, you normally see an employment adviser. He will talk over job opportunities with you, and arrange interviews with prospective employers when the time comes. He may be able to give you advice about special problems too – eg if you are disabled – or suggest some kind of occupational guidance. You don't have to pay for this service, and you can use it whether you are unemployed or not.

Help with retraining
The training services division of the Manpower Services Commission (MSC) offers various forms of free training under the *Training Opportunities Scheme* (TOPS). You can train to get a new skill or just brush up one that's rusty.

Trainees get a tax-free weekly allowance – normally well above the level of unemployment benefit – and may be able to get travel and other expenses repaid too.
● Further information
Details of the courses in your area and of the allowances paid to trainees will be at your local jobcentre or employment office.

Help with expenses
You may in certain circumstances get help with the cost of travel, and a subsistence allowance through the *Job Search Scheme* if you have to go to job interviews (or look for work) away from your home area. There are also various grants and allowances available through the *Employment Transfer Scheme* for some people who are unemployed (or under threat of redundancy) and who find jobs away from home.
● Further information
You can get details of both these schemes at jobcentres and unemployment offices.

On strike
If you're on strike, you will have to depend on two sources for cash (in addition to your own savings):
● strike pay from your union – if any is paid. If the union is not paying strike pay, there may be a hardship fund from which it can make payments to strikers in dire financial straits. Strike pay from a union is tax-free.
● supplementary benefit – but this is paid for your family only.

In addition to these two sources, you may also be entitled to a tax rebate (▷ right).

Supplementary benefit for strikers' families
In general, anyone involved in a strike or any trade dispute is not entitled to get supplementary benefit for his own requirements. This means that a single person can't normally get supplementary benefit at all, and a married man will get benefit only for his family. From November 1980, the amount of benefit paid to strikers' families will be reduced by £12 a week (on the assumption that the striker is getting at least that amount of strike pay – even if the strike is unofficial or the striker does not belong to a union). The first £12 of any strike pay will be disregarded in working out the striker's *resources* – but any tax refunds due will be taken into account in full. And you won't be able to get any supplementary benefit to help with hire purchase commitments, fuel bills, or any other debt during a strike.

In practice, single strikers might get help from supplementary benefit if in 'urgent need' – if, for example, he or she would be evicted from lodgings and there is no-one else to turn to.
● Further information
SB2 *Supplementary benefits and trade disputes* (available from social security offices).

Tax rebates
People who pay tax under the Pay-As-You-Earn system (PAYE), whose pay stops in the middle of the tax year because they are out of work, off sick, or on strike, can normally get a tax rebate – even if they are married and the husband or wife still works. For details of why this is so and an explanation of how the PAYE system works ▷ pp. 10 and 12.

Note that even if you don't claim your rebate as described below, you should get it automatically either after the tax year ends, or in your first pay packet after you go back to work again.

How to get your rebate
● Off sick or on strike?
Some employers automatically pay any rebate that's due, on each pay day that you're off work. If your employer doesn't do this, tell him you'd like your rebates as they arise, rather than when you go back to work. You should then get your tax rebate on your normal pay day.
● Unemployed?
Wait until you have been off work for 4 weeks, then get form P50 from your tax office. Once you have returned it, you

should get a rebate fairly swiftly. Any further rebates will be paid at 4-weekly intervals.

Changes on the way

The Government proposes to tax benefits paid to the sick, the unemployed and strikers' families from April 1982. This is likely to mean a drop in the size of tax rebates when off work – which, for the unemployed and people on strike, will then not be paid until after they return to work.

The exact details of these changes will not be announced until nearer the time.

Paying the bills

It makes sense for most people to keep track of their spending – but a period off work often makes some sort of budget essential. If you are off sick, your income may not drop for some time – indeed your household income may even rise somewhat because sickness benefit is not taxed (▷ p. 20). But it's prudent to bear in mind the possibility of a delayed return to work and a drop in income when your employer's sick pay (if any) ends.

If you are unemployed, budgeting is even more important. Redundancy payments and tax rebates are one-off phenomena, and they offer at best a temporary respite from the inevitable drop in income for most people who depend on unemployment benefit.

The principles of drawing up a budget for someone off work are no different from those described in chapter 14. But certain possibilities need to be built into the assumptions you make when you draw up the budget – the likelihood that the period off work will last a year or more, for example. If these assumptions turn out to be over-pessimistic, then nothing is lost – but they ensure that the budget is drawn up with a realistic outlook from the start.

If you're off sick, and there's a good chance you will be back at work before your employer stops paying full pay, then perhaps you can budget on the assumption that there will be no drop in income over the next 12 months. But it would still be sensible to avoid entering into further financial commitments (eg large HP or credit card debts) until your future income is secure.

If you suddenly become dependent on social security benefits for income, it is essential to draw up a new budget. Savings or redundancy money can be used to pay off outstanding debts, or invested to give a regular income to cover any gap between household income and expenditure (▷ p. 183). It would be unwise to commit yourself to new long-term savings plans. If you are already committed to some form of regular savings plan, it could be worth reviewing your investments and even investigating what you would get back if you wound up the plan now. The last course is not to be taken lightly: the return to an investor who winds up his investments is usually poor. But if you think your chances of working again quickly are slim, you may want to pare your financial commitments to the bone.

Keeping up with payments on the mortgage, bank loan and so on

Many people off work face the worry of various debts they took on when their income was higher – HP debts, bank loans, building society mortgage, and so on. This worry is often needless – it may, for example, be possible to rearrange debts to reduce the monthly payments needed to cover them. And some of the people owed money may be prepared to allow interest-only payments for a while, or even no payments at all for a short period.

If you have a mortgage and face a period of reduced income, let the lender know as soon as possible about your changed circumstances. Don't just fall behind with the payments. The building society (or local authority, with local authority mortgages) will prefer to help you keep up with your mortgage payments, rather than face the prospect of evicting you and selling off your home to get their money back. And a sympathetic lender may be prepared to help you pay off a loan (eg from a bank) for home improvements and add the debt to your mortgage if this means lower monthly payments.

Once you have sorted out just what you have to pay, you might be able to get help with some hire purchase payments from supplementary benefit, if your resources are less than your requirements (▷ p. 229). Mortgage *interest* payments are included as part of your requirements in working out what you can get. The capital part of the repayments (or the life insurance premiums, with endowment mortgages) will not be included in your requirements – so if you can't pay for these yourself, try to negotiate an arrangement to pay interest only until your income recovers.

3 Working for yourself

You can work for yourself in so many different ways that, in the space available, it isn't possible to give information that would be generally useful from the *business* angle. Instead, this chapter concentrates on the aspects of working for yourself that have most impact on your *personal* finances. It considers:

● the pros and cons of being self-employed
● the legal side – for many people who work on a small scale, there may be little distinction between their personal and their business assets
● tax – the rules both for what you pay and when you pay it will be different if you work for yourself
● protecting yourself – the amounts you can claim from social security if things go wrong are generally lower if you are self-employed than if you are an employee.

Some of the topics dealt with here are also covered elsewhere in the book – and are cross-referenced accordingly.

Self-employed – the pros and cons
The life of the self-employed is not all wine and roses. There are, however, advantages to working for yourself.

Advantages
● Psychological advantages
A *Money Which?* survey carried out in 1976 indicated that the self-employed were more satisfied than average with their jobs. And being self-employed means that you can, to a certain extent, make your own decisions about things like the kind of jobs you take on, the kind of environment you work in, and so on.
● A higher chance of making a lot of money
According to the survey above, the earnings of the self-employed were, on average, nearly 50 per cent higher than those of employees. And Inland Revenue statistics show that a higher proportion of self-employed than employed people earn a lot of money – over £10,000 a year, say.

● Tax advantages
With the right advice you should be able to cut your tax bill by claiming as business expenses part or all of the cost of some of the things you'd spend money on anyway – a house or car, for example (▷ p. 33). If you sell your business on retirement, you're likely to pay less capital gains tax on the gain you make than you would on a gain from selling such things as shares or a valuable work of art (▷ p. 37). The same goes for capital transfer tax – there's likely to be less to pay on a business when you die than on other assets of equivalent value (▷ p. 38).
● Freedom from incomes policies
If your business can afford it, you can give yourself a bumper pay rise at times when rises for employees are restricted by government incomes policies.

Disadvantages
● Psychological disadvantages
You're on your own and there's no employer to fall back on if you are sick or injured. Time off – for holidays, sickness, or training – is paid for out of your profits. You may worry about the honesty and competence of your employees, especially while you're away. You could find yourself working long hours – and the pressures of owning your own business, and perhaps being responsible for the livelihood of the people who work for you, can be heavy.
● Greater risk
There's no employer to pay your wages when business is poor. If your business doesn't succeed, you don't qualify for unemployment benefit or for a redundancy payment. And if your business collapses you could end up losing all your possessions (including your home) to pay off your debts. When you retire you'll get only the flat-rate pension from the State – the self-employed aren't entitled to get the new earnings-related additional State pension. And the only non-State pension you can get is one

you pay for yourself – with most employees' schemes, the employer contributes a substantial amount too.

● A poorer deal from social security
For example, the self-employed can't normally claim unemployment benefit. And with most other benefits, the self-employed get only the flat-rate amounts of benefit – they aren't entitled to the earnings-related amounts currently added to many social security benefits for the employed.

● Paperwork and red tape
Once you start your own business, you're likely to have to keep accounts to satisfy the taxman (▷ p. 37), make regular VAT returns (▷ p. 38) and answer questionnaires from local authorities and government departments. You could pass much of this work on to an accountant – but you have to pay for this help and you'd still be left with a certain amount of paperwork. If you start to employ other people, more problems arise. You'll need to cope with employees' tax and NI contributions, employment laws, the Health and Safety at Work Act, maternity leave, and so on (▷ right).

Verdict?

If you're concerned about security of income, prefer to leave your work behind when you go home in the evening or just don't rise to the thought of running your own show, then self-employment is unlikely to be a sensible choice for you.

But if you can cope with the drawbacks, the attractions of self-employment seem fairly powerful. Whatever the ups and downs of running your business, you have the satisfaction of being your own boss and undoubtedly more opportunity to make a pile – and keep it.

If you're not too sure about going into business on your own, consider starting up a business in your spare time, while going on working for an employer. This would give you a trial run, the chance to get used to the paperwork and legal hassles and the opportunity of claiming some of your costs as business expenses – without risking all (▷ p. 32 for some help in setting up). But check that spare-time work wouldn't break your contract of employment.

Could you count as self-employed?

With some jobs, you've no choice about whether you count as self-employed or employed. If, say, you're a doctor in general practice you always count as self-employed; if you're a tax inspector, you always count

as employed. But the distinction between self-employed and employed isn't always hard and fast. With some jobs, you may be able to arrange your affairs in such a way as to be able to choose whether to be employed or self-employed.

For example, if you're an architect working as an employee for a firm of builders and doing some freelance work in your spare time, you might be able to reorganize your work so that you could count as a self-employed architect. You would do much the same work as before – provided your former employer didn't mind you going it alone – but be working for yourself rather than someone else.

If you want to set up as self-employed while doing much the same work as you did for your employer, you might have to convince the taxman and your local social security office that you are not an employee. These are some of the things they are likely to look at to decide which category you fall into:

● whether you are running a business with its own accounts, and are responsible for any losses it makes, as well as taking any profits

● whether you are in charge of your own work, providing your own equipment and tools and employing other people to help you, or whether you work under the direction of someone else

● whether you're independent of the organization which pays for your services or whether you're an essential part of it

● what sort of contract you work to – whether it's a contract *for* services (eg to design a certain building) or a contract *of* service (eg to design anything which your employer asks you to design).

Having more than one job won't automatically mean that you count as self-employed. If, say, you're a lecturer with part-time jobs at several technical colleges, each of your jobs is likely to count as working for an employer – because the work you do in each job is clearly not under your own direction.

If you are trying to establish yourself as self-employed, and the taxman or a DHSS official rules that you are employed, you can normally appeal against their decisions. But if you're likely to be a borderline case, it could pay you to get advice on how to arrange your affairs from a solicitor or accountant.

Employing other people
If you employ other people in your business, you'll face a new set of problems. Here are some examples:
● collection of tax and NI contributions from your employees' pay
● payment of employers' NI contributions for each employee
● employer's liability insurance – compulsory type of insurance to compensate employees who are injured at work (eg trip up on a loose stair carpet) and successfully sue you
● redundancy payments – legal minimum payments for employees you make redundant
● legal procedures to follow when dealing with trade unions or sacking employees
● maternity rights for female employees
● guaranteed pay (up to a maximum of £6 a day for up to 5 days in any 3-month period) for employees if you can't provide work for them
● health and safety at work regulations
● laws against discrimination on grounds of sex or race
● minimum rates of pay and conditions of employment laid down by wages councils for certain types of work.

For more information about tax, get leaflet P7 *Employer's guide to PAYE* from your local tax office. Leaflet NP15 *Employer's guide to National Insurance contributions* (available from social security offices) will tell you more about National Insurance. Your local jobcentre or employment office (under *Employment Services Agency* in the phone book) should be able to provide leaflets about employment law.

And the Small Firms Service (▷ p. 39) publishes guides to taking on people.

Starting in business

As soon as you begin working for yourself (full-time or part-time), you should inform the following:

● the taxman (in the phone book under *Inland Revenue*).

● the local social security office (in the phone book under *Health and Social Security, Dept. of*)

● the local VAT office (in the phone book under *Customs and Excise Department*) if you want to register for VAT or your takings are likely to be more than a certain amount a year (▷ p. 38).

The next step is to choose your business name – for many self-employed people, this will be their own name (eg Miles Martin). If you want to call your business anything other than your own name (eg Catering Unlimited), you must register the name with the Registrar of Business Names (for address ▷ p. 39). There's a fee for doing this (£1 in mid-80). The registrar can turn down the name you've chosen if it's 'misleading or undesirable'.

If you're going to employ people and pay them more than a certain amount (£26.50 a week or £114.50 a month for the 80/81 tax year), you'll need to tell the local tax office and arrange to deduct tax from their wages under PAYE. You'll also have to contact the local social security office about National Insurance contributions for any employees earning more than the lower earnings limit (£23 a week or £99.67 a month for the 80/81 tax year).

If you're using your home for business, and this means that the use of your home (or part of it) is changing from being a place of residence to a place of work, you might need to get planning permission from your local authority planning department. If part of your home officially becomes a place of work, your rates are likely to go up – you'll pay the higher rates for business or commercial property on that part of your home (and you may be liable for some capital gains tax on selling the home – ▷ p. 37).

It makes sense to keep accounts from the start, making records of money you pay out and money you get in. Keep receipts, bank statements and so on as proof of the figures you enter in your records. If you use a car (or van) partly for business, partly privately, keep a record of your business mileage – these records will make it easier for you to persuade the taxman that your accounts are correct.

It might also be sensible to discuss your business ideas with your bank manager – especially if you want to borrow some money. A separate bank account for your business helps keep track of your income and expenditure. The bank is also likely to offer special services for businesses, like help with paying wages, night safes, and so on.

The legal side

From the legal point of view, there are three basic ways of being in business as a self-employed person:

● on your own (known technically as being a *sole trader*)

● as a member of a *partnership*

● as a *company*.

It's important to be clear about the way you operate – it may have very direct implications for your personal finances if the business goes through a bad patch.

● If you operate on your own

You are the only owner of the business, and solely responsible if things go wrong. You have to find capital for your business from your own resources, or borrow it – and it may be difficult to persuade lenders to lend to you. There's no distinction between your business assets and your personal ones, so far as the law is concerned. If the worst came to the worst, your personal possessions (like your car, home, and so on) might have to be sold to pay your business debts.

Technically, when a sole trader dies, his business ceases (even if his wife or children, say, carry on what is effectively a new business). If there are employees, they could be entitled to redundancy money – some of which would have to come out of the dead person's estate. Unless you protect yourself to some extent (eg by life insurance) it may come as a nasty shock to your heirs. They might even have to sell the home to settle up.

● If you are in partnership

If you want to go into business with someone else, or with more than one other person, going into partnership is one way of doing it. Partnerships can be set up informally, or by a legal deed – if you want advice on how to go ahead, a solicitor should be able to help you.

Each partner is separately liable for the debts of the partnership (including the tax bills). If one partner decamps leaving unpaid bills, the other partners have to stump up to pay them – so it's sensible to satisfy yourself that prospective partners are trustworthy before you go into partnership. Note that some partners may be able to limit their liability for debts (▷ Limited liability, opposite).

Further information
Inland Revenue leaflet
IR 28, *Starting up in business*, available from your tax office.

Limited liability
If you are in business on your own you have *unlimited liability* for your business debts. This means that if your business owes money which it can't pay, you will be faced with bankruptcy – and your possessions can be sold off to pay your debts. You may find it difficult to start up in business again. (This is why many self-employed people transfer some of their assets to their husband or wife.)

But a company can go for *limited liability*, so that if it goes bust, the shareholders can lose only the money they have invested in the company.

In return for this concession, a limited company must put 'limited' or 'ltd' after its name to warn people who are lending it money. And it must send its audited accounts each year to the Registrar of Companies – anyone can look at these if they are thinking of doing business with the company.

If your business is a partnership, some of the partners can go for limited liability if they are 'sleeping partners' (ie they supply some of the cash, but don't take part in the day-to-day running of the business). But at least one of the partners *must* have unlimited liability – and be fully responsible for the partnership's debts.

Note that banks and suppliers who are lending money to a small limited company often ask the directors for personal guarantees that the loan will be repaid. This means that if the company can't repay the loan, the directors will have to pay up – despite the limited liability.

● If you operate as a company
(For details about forming a company ▷ below.) You may or may not be liable for the debts of a business, depending on whether or not you have limited liability (▷ left).

Forming a company can have advantages other than limited liability – eg it could cut your tax bill if you pay high rates of income tax, it could give you the chance of providing yourself with a good pension more cheaply. But if you set up a company to run your business, you will no longer be self-employed. Directors of companies are treated as employees, are liable for Class 1 national insurance contributions and have to pay tax under PAYE.

An accountant or solicitor should be able to tell you whether forming a company could be worthwhile for you – and help set it up.

Forming a company

A company is a business organization which is separate from the people who provide the cash to set it up. If, say, a group of people decide to set up in business together, they will each contribute something towards the setting up of the company (eg cash, equipment or goodwill), in return for a share in the company's profits. The company will be run by directors elected by the shareholders. With a small company – set up by a few friends, for example – they might all become shareholders, and all directors.

If one of the shareholders wants to get out of the business, his share in the company can be sold to the other shareholders or to somebody outside the business. And when he dies, his share can be passed on to his heirs, or sold (subject to the company's rules).

Setting up a company is fairly complicated – you must draw up certain legal documents, have a registered office, and register with the Registrar of Companies (▷ p. 39). One way of saving time and bother is to buy a company, which has been set up already, 'off the shelf'. Buying or setting up a company might cost £100 or so plus at least £20 a year in formalities to keep going. If you're thinking about setting up a company, it would certainly make sense to get professional advice first. A solicitor or accountant can advise you about the legal requirements.

Tax for the self-employed

We deal first with income tax. For capital gains tax ▷ p. 37, for capital transfer tax and VAT ▷ p. 38.

Income tax

Your taxable profit is your takings *less* certain costs you incur and deductions you can make:

● allowable business expenses – including, for example, rates and electricity bills on business premises, the cost of raw materials and things you buy for resale (▷ below)
● stock relief – to allow for increases in the value of your stocks, such as raw materials and goods waiting to be sold (▷ p. 35)
● capital allowances – for the cost of machinery and plant (eg car, office equipment) which you use in your business (▷ p. 35)
● losses – any business losses from earlier years which haven't been set off against other income (▷ p. 35)

Allowable business expenses

If you're self-employed, the main income tax advantage is much wider scope for claiming expenses in connection with your work than if you work for an employer.

If you work for an employer, the only expenses you can claim are those which are incurred *wholly, exclusively and necessarily* in the course of your duties. *Necessarily* in this context means that anyone doing your job would have to incur the expense – ie that it is necessary in relation to the job. The self-employed can claim expenses which are incurred *wholly and exclusively* for the purpose of the business – ie the expenses don't have to be necessarily incurred. So the self-employed don't have to prove that anyone in their line of business would have to pay out the expenses they claim – and can claim a wider variety of things (▷ Fig. 3.1).

For example, if you're self-employed, you can claim a proportion of the costs of running your home (ie rent, rates, electricity, gas and so on) as business expenses if you use part of your home exclusively for business – but beware of capital gains tax (▷ p. 37). If you work for an employer, you can claim these expenses only if anyone doing your job would have to work at home.

Note that the *wholly and exclusively* rule doesn't mean that you can claim nothing if, say, you use your car sometimes for business purposes, sometimes for private purposes, or you use part of your home for business. You can normally claim a proportion of those costs attributable to business use.

Figure 3.1 Business expenses if you're self-employed

	Normally allowed	Not allowed
Basic costs and general running expenses	Cost of goods bought for resale and raw materials used in business (▷ opposite for how to work out how much to claim). Advertising. Delivery charges. Heating. Lighting. Rates. Telephone. Rent of business premises. Replacement of small tools and special clothing. Postage. Stationery. Accountant's fees. Bank charges on business accounts. Relevant books and magazines.	Initial cost of machinery, vehicles, equipment, permanent advertising signs – but ▷ Capital allowances, opposite. Cost of buildings. Expenses incurred more than a year before initial launching of business.
Use of home for work	Proportion of telephone, lighting, heating, cleaning and insurance. Proportion of rent and rates, if use part of home *exclusively* for business – but claiming these may mean some capital gains tax to pay if you sell your home (▷ p. 37).	
Wages and salaries	Wages, salaries, and leaving payments paid to employees. Reasonable pay for your wife, provided she is actually employed. Pensions for past employees and their dependants.	Your own wages or salary, or that of any partner.
Taxes and National Insurance	Employer's National Insurance contributions for employees. VAT on allowable business expenses if you're not a registered trader for VAT (and, in certain circumstances, even if you are).	Income tax. Capital gains tax. Capital transfer tax. Your own National Insurance contributions.
Entertaining	Reasonable entertainment of overseas trade customers and their overseas agents (and normally your own costs on such an occasion). Entertainment of own staff – eg Christmas party.	Any other business entertaining – eg entertainment of UK customers.
Gifts	If to advertise your business (or things it sells), gifts costing up to £2 a year to each person. Gifts (whatever their value) to employees.	Food, drink, tobacco, or vouchers for goods given to anyone other than employees.
Travelling	Hotel and travel expenses on business trips. Travel between different places of work. Running costs of own car; whole of cost if used wholly for business, proportion if used privately as well.	Travel between home and business. Cost of buying a car or van – but ▷ Capital allowances, opposite.
Interest payments	Interest on overdrafts and loans for business purposes.	Interest on capital paid or credited to partners.
Hire purchase	Hire charge part of payments (ie the amount you pay *less* the cash price).	Cash price of what you're buying on hire purchase (but you may get capital allowances, opposite).
Hiring	Reasonable charge for hire of capital goods, including cars.	
Insurance	Business insurance – eg employer's liability, fire and theft, motor, insuring employees' lives.	Your own life insurance.
Trade marks	Fees paid to register trade mark or design.	
Legal costs	Costs of recovering debts; defending business rights; preparing service agreements; appealing against rates; renewing a lease, with the landlord's consent, for a period not exceeding 50 years (but not if a premium is paid).	Expenses (including stamp duty) of acquiring land and buildings. Fines and other penalties for breaking the law.
Repairs	Normal repairs and maintenance.	Cost of additions, alterations or improvements.
Debts	Bad debts and, in part, doubtful debts.	
Subscriptions and contributions	Payments which secure benefits for your business or staff. Payments to charities, and to societies which have arrangements with the Inland Revenue (in some cases only a proportion).	Payments to political parties, churches (but small gifts to *local* churches may be allowable).

● **Stocks**

You can claim as an allowable expense the cost of raw materials you use in your business, and the cost of things you buy for resale. But you can claim only the cost of business materials which you actually *sell* during your accounting year – ie the value of your stocks of these things at the start of the year, *plus* anything spent on buying more during the year, *less* the value of your stocks at the end of the year.

An *increase* in the value of stocks will normally increase your taxable profit for the year. A *decrease* in the value of stocks, on the other hand, reduces your taxable profit for the year. If your stocks increase in value you might qualify for stock relief (▷ right).

Capital allowances

You can claim capital allowances for buying machinery or plant – things like vans, cars, typewriters and other equipment. Special rules apply for buildings – check with your Tax Inspector.

As with business expenses, capital expenditure must be *wholly and exclusively* for the business. And again, on anything used partly for business, partly privately, you get a proportion of the capital allowances, depending on the proportion of business use.

A *first-year allowance* of up to 100 per cent of the cost of machinery or plant (excluding cars, ▷ right) can be claimed for the accounting year in which you buy it. If you claim less than 100 per cent, the remainder of the cost (the *written-down value*) is added to your *pool of expenditure* at the start of the next accounting year. Your pool of expenditure is the total written-down value of all the bits of machinery and plant you've claimed capital allowances on in the past.

You can claim a *writing-down allowance* of up to 25 per cent of the value of your pool of expenditure at the end of each accounting year. Your pool is then reduced by the amount you claim.

If you sell something you have claimed capital allowances on, the proceeds must be deducted from your pool of expenditure *before* working out your writing-down allowance for the accounting year in which you sell it. If the proceeds of sales come to more than the value of your pool of expenditure, the difference (the *balancing charge*) is added to your profit. There are special rules for working out capital allowances in the early and closing years of a business – ask your tax inspector for details.

Remember that, for any accounting year,

you don't have to claim the maximum in capital allowances. Don't claim more in allowances than is needed to keep your tax bill to a minimum.

● **Cars**

Lorries, vans and so on are treated like other machinery and plant, but there are special rules for cars (including estate cars). There's no first-year allowance: instead, the cost of the car goes straight into your pool of expenditure, and you can claim a writing-down allowance of 25 per cent for each year – including the last – that you own the car.

The writing-down allowance on a car costing more than £8,000 is restricted to a maximum of £2,000 in any year. Allowances on each car costing more than £8,000 – and on any car used partly for private purposes – have to be worked out separately from those on other machinery and plant.

Losses

If your allowable business expenses, together with stock relief and any capital allowances you can claim come to more than your takings, you will have made a loss. This loss will normally be carried forward and set against future profits from the same business. But you can ask the taxman to set the loss off against any other income you have for the tax year in which you incur the loss (which – because profits are normally taxed on a preceding year basis – includes last year's taxable profit). If your loss is greater than your other income for the tax year, the balance is set off against other income for the following tax year.

Since 6 April 78, if you make a loss in any of the first 4 tax years of a new business, you can set the loss off against any other income (including earnings from a job) you had in the 3 tax years *before* the year in which you made the loss. This rule means that if you make a loss in the 80/81 tax year, you can set the loss against taxable income from as long ago as the 77/78 tax year.

The detailed rules for working out how much tax rebate you're entitled to are complex – ask your tax inspector for details.

You might save tax (or save tax sooner) by choosing to set a loss off against other income rather than future profits. You have 2 years from the end of the tax year in which you make a loss to make the choice.

When you close down a business which has made a loss in its final 12 months, you have no option but to set off the loss against the profits of the last 3 complete tax years – against the last year first, and so on.

Stock relief
Inflation means that the value of your stocks at the end of your accounting year is likely to be higher than it was at the start – even if the quantity of stocks you keep stays exactly the same. This means you might have to find more cash to buy the same amount of stock. Because of this, stock relief was introduced.

If the value of your stocks increases during the year, you can claim stock relief equal to the amount by which your stocks have increased in value, *less* 10 per cent of your profit (15 per cent if you operate as a company) after deduction of allowable business expenses and any capital allowances you claim. If your stocks have increased in value by less than 10 per cent of your profit (15 per cent for a company), you get no stock relief. Stock relief is deducted from your taxable profit, so reducing your tax bill.

If you get stock relief and then over one of the following 6 complete accounting years the value of your stock falls, you may in certain circumstances lose some of the stock relief you've had.

Once 6 years are up, stock relief you've had can no longer be 'clawed back' if the value of your stock reduces. Check with your tax inspector for details.

You can claim stock relief at any time up to 2 years after the end of the tax year in which your accounting year ends. So if you tell the taxman before 6 April 1981, you can claim stock relief for your accounting year which ended in the 78/79 tax year.

There are special rules for new businesses and for the year in which a business closes down – ask your tax inspector for details.

● Debts
Money owed *to* your business at the end of your accounting year counts as part of the income of the business – even though you haven't in fact received it. Money owed *by* your business counts as an allowable business expense – even though you haven't in fact paid it. So don't include amounts you've received, or amounts you've paid, to settle debts from earlier years – because these debts were included (or should have been) in your accounts for those years.

You can claim bad debts and (in part) doubtful debts as business expenses. As debts you are owed count as part of your business income, this simply cancels out income you never got.

Self-employed people (such as builders and architects) who have contracts which involve progress payments must count these payments as part of their income for the accounting year in which they should have been paid – even if the payments have not been made.

If you normally have to wait some time for your fees (eg if you're a solicitor or an accountant) the taxman may agree to let you run your business on a 'cash basis' – ie count as income only money actually received. The taxman won't agree to this for the first 3 accounting years of a new business.

When your profits are taxed

If your business is just occasional freelance work, it is normally taxed on a *current year basis* – ie your tax bill for 80/81 is based on your profit during that year. Note that this makes it convenient for your accounting year to be the same as the tax year.

The tax will either be collected under PAYE, from your earnings in your main job, or have to be paid in 2 equal instalments – on 1 January 81 and 1 July 81 for profits made in the 80/81 tax year.

If you run a business on a larger scale, things get more complicated. Once the business has been going for 2 whole tax years, tax is normally charged on a *preceding year basis* – ie your tax bill for the 80/81 tax year is based on the profit you made in your accounting year ending in the 79/80 tax year. This tax will have to be paid in 2 equal instalments on 1 January 81 and 1 July 81. Note that in the first 3 years or last 3 years

of the business's existence, special rules apply (▷ Fig. 3.2).

Paying tax in arrears has disadvantages – it's easy to spend today's profits now, and find yourself with no ready cash to pay the tax bill tomorrow. And it can make life very difficult if you stop being self-employed and go back to work for an employer. Tax bills for the business profits will go on arriving after the business is wound up, when your income from your employer is also being taxed.

Keeping accounts

Not all accounts are complicated – see the example below – but if you don't feel up to doing them on your own, you can pay an accountant to do so. (He may be able to give you other help too – ▷ right.) The fees you pay him normally count as an allowable business expense. After a couple of years,

Figure 3.2   What your tax bill is based on in early and closing years of business

	Tax initially based on	But for some years, there's a choice
First tax year you are in business	*Actual profit* (1) in that tax year	No choice this year
Second tax year	Profit in your first 12 months of operation	Your choice: you can choose to have your tax bills for the second and third tax years (but not just one of them) based on the *actual profit* (1) for each of those tax years. Do so if this would make the total tax bill for the 2 years less
Third tax year	Profit in your accounting year ending in the preceding tax year (or, if your first accounting year hasn't ended, normally your first 12 months' profit)	
Fourth tax year (and subsequent tax years)	Profit in your accounting year ending in the preceding tax year (ie a *preceding year basis*)	No choice for these years
...UNTIL your last-but-two tax year	Profit in your accounting year ending in the preceding tax year	Taxman's choice: when you tell him that you've closed down the business, he can choose to base your tax bills for the last-but-two and the last-but-one tax year (but not just one of them) on the *actual profit* (1) for each of these tax years. He'll do this if it makes the total profits (and the total tax) for the 2 years more
Your last-but-one tax year	Profit in your accounting year ending in the preceding tax year	
Last tax year you are in business	*Actual profit* (1) that year	No choice

1. Your actual profit for any tax year is the proportion of your profits attributable to that tax year. Profits are normally attributed to tax years on a time basis. So, for example, if the first 4 months of an accounting year falls in a tax year, then $\frac{4}{12}$ (ie $\frac{1}{3}$) of the profit of that accounting year is attributable to that tax year. In this case, if your business has been going for some years, $\frac{8}{12}$ of the profit for another accounting year is also attributable to that tax year.

if your affairs are straightforward, you may feel confident enough to handle the accounts yourself.

Special enquiries

In recent years, the Inland Revenue has decided to do 'in-depth' investigations into the books of a small proportion of the self-employed each year – rather than spend its time making rather superficial, routine enquiries into everyone's accounts. This means that you may hear little about your accounts for several years – but suddenly find yourself being the subject of rigorous enquiries, involving personal interviews with your tax inspector. For example, if your profits seem to be much below the average for your line of business the taxman

will want to know why. Or, if you work in a business where there is ample opportunity to pocket cash payments without entering them in your accounts, the taxman might be interested in where you got the money to pay for your new car, colour TV or whatever.

If you are enquired into in this way, an accountant's advice and experience could prove very valuable.

Capital gains tax

If you sell or give away some of your assets (eg shares, a second home) on which you have made capital gains, there may be some capital gains tax (CGT) to pay (details in ch. 18, p. 195). The same goes if you sell or give away a business. But there are two concessions for businesses:

● if you buy another business at the time you sell your existing one (or within 3 years) you may be able to defer the payment of CGT until you finally stop your business activities.

● if you're at least 60, and you sell or give away a business you have owned for at least a year, some or all of the gain you make may be tax-free – up to a maximum tax-free amount of £50,000. If you sold a second home and made a taxable gain of £50,000, there'd be £15,000 to pay in capital gains tax.

● Capital gains tax and your home
If you use part of your home exclusively for your business, you will be liable for some CGT when you sell it (a gain on your only or main home is normally free of CGT ▷ p. 195).

● Capital gains tax and gifts
If you give away your business – eg to your children – there could be some CGT to pay. There are special rules (called *roll-over relief*) under which *your* CGT bill can be reduced to zero – though this could mean more CGT eventually for the person who gets the gift. Check with your taxman.

Using an accountant
An accountant should be able to advise you on your business finances, VAT returns, PAYE and so on. He will also advise you on how to keep your accounts, draw up your accounts at the end of your financial year, and negotiate with the taxman on your behalf to agree your income tax bill.

If you intend to use an accountant, it probably makes sense to contact one before you start up in business. A good accountant should be able to advise you about the feasibility of the business you want to go into, the amount of cash you're likely to need to get it off the ground, how best to arrange your accounts for the taxman (particularly important in the first few years), and so on.

You may well depend on your accountant's advice and services for many years – so choosing one is an important step. The best way to find an accountant could be to ask a business friend if he knows anyone he could recommend. Failing this, a professional adviser (eg solicitor or bank manager) might be able to recommend an accountant.

Accountant's fees (which you can normally claim as a business expense) depend on the amount of work involved in handling your business accounts, and on the amount the accountant charges for each hour of his time. Hourly rates can be as little as £5 – but they go up to £50 an hour or more for some accountants in central London. Ask for an estimate of your likely bill for the first year when you are choosing your accountant.

Fees for freelance editing	£	£
		3,750
Allowable business expenses		
Travel	310	
Telephone	45	
Stationery and postage	50	
Books, subscriptions	35	
Typewriter service	9	
Sundry expenses (eg photocopying, typewriter ribbons)	20	
Business use of home (rates, heating and so on)	60	
Which comes to		529
So profit after deduction of allowable business expenses		3,221
Stock relief	0	
Capital allowances		
First year allowance (100% claimed) for a new typewriter	135	
First year allowance (100% claimed) for new bookshelves	45	
Losses from previous years	0	
Which comes to		180
So *taxable profit is*		£3,041

Figure 3.3 Fiona Philip's business accounts
Fiona Philip is in business as a freelance editor. Here are the accounts she sends to the taxman for the year ending 30 April 80.

Capital transfer tax

Capital transfer tax (CTT) is a tax on gifts you make during your lifetime, and on things you leave when you die (▷ ch. 15).

If you own a business, the chances are that much of your wealth will be tied up in it. But with most types of small business there are special rules for valuing the business for CTT. A business which qualifies for special treatment will have its value (broadly, the value of the business assets, including goodwill, less any debts the business owes) reduced by 50 per cent for the purposes of CTT. So a business worth £200,000 would be valued for CTT at only £100,000.

These rules mean that there is much less CTT to pay on a small business than on gifts of houses, shares, unit trusts and other investments. For example, if you make no taxable gifts in your lifetime, and die leaving £120,000 worth of shares to your children, there would be £28,500 of CTT to pay. But if the £120,000 were tied up in a business, there would be only £3,000 to pay in tax.

Another CTT concession for businesses is that tax can, in certain circumstances, be paid in instalments over 8 years (instead of having the time limit of up to a year which applies to most other taxable gifts). This could make it easier to find the money to pay the tax without having to sell the business to raise it.

Value added tax (VAT)

If you sell more than a certain amount of goods and services a year (▷ left), you have to register for VAT. It could make sense to register even if you don't have to (there can be advantages in registering if you sell things abroad, supply businesses which *are* registered, or sell things which are zero-rated for VAT).

VAT is likely to mean tedious and time-consuming paperwork – eg keeping records which will satisfy the VATman. And you must allow VATmen to visit your business premises, give them information about how you run your business and show them documents they ask to see (all within reason, of course).

For more details of VAT, get leaflet no. 700 from your local VAT office. There are also leaflets for special types of business (eg exporters, second-hand dealers).

You must register for VAT if your *taxable turnover* (broadly the value of goods and services you sell) exceeded £4,000 in the past 3 months or £13,500 in the past year *or* if your taxable turnover is likely to be more than £13,500 in the next year.

Do you need extra protection?

If you work for yourself (and don't work for an employer too), you'll pay Class 2 (and maybe Class 4) NI contributions rather than the Class 1 contributions paid by people who work for an employer. Some social security benefits aren't open to those who pay only Class 2 or 4 contributions: principally unemployment benefit and the earnings-related parts of other benefits (▷ p. 236 for details). The self-employed may need extra protection for themselves and their dependants.

There are four questions to consider:
● What happens if I'm off sick?
You won't get the earnings-related supplement currently paid with sickness benefit. Your partnership or company may make some provision for paying you an income if you're off sick. But if you aren't in this position (or if the income provided would be too low), consider taking out *sick pay insurance*, which will guarantee you an income while you are unable to work through illness. For more details of how this works ▷ ch. 12, p. 142. If you already have sick pay insurance, make sure that self-employed people are not excluded – you may have to pay an extra premium to get the cover you need.
● What happens when I retire?
The self-employed don't qualify for the additional (earnings-related) part of the State pension so would get just the basic pension from the State when they retire (for details and current rates ▷ ch. 4, p. 51). This may not worry you too much because you may feel you could make up for this by selling the business for a large enough lump sum to give you plenty of income to live on when you stop work. Or you could plan to get extra income by acting as consultant to the business after you reach retirement age. But you need to bear in mind the possibility that your plans won't work out as you hope: the business may go through a bad patch and be worth much less than you'd counted on when the time comes to sell up. Your health may stop you carrying on for long with consultancy or part-time work. Either way, you could find yourself worse off than you'd bargained for in retirement.

It may be wise to make some further provision for your retirement.

One way for you to do this is by making payments into a personal pension scheme. You'll get tax relief on the payments you make, up to the limit allowed (in the 80/81 tax year this was up to 17½ per cent of your earnings from self-employment). That means that if you pay tax at a top rate of 40 per cent, say, every £100 you pay into the pension scheme, costs you only £60. In addition to tax relief on the payments you make, the fund in which your money is invested pays no capital gains tax on gains it makes by buying and selling the assets in the fund, nor does it pay income tax on income earned.

Of course, you could provide for your old age by investing your regular savings some other way (for investments that might suit you ▷ the Route Map on p. 190). But because of the favourable tax treatment received by personal pension schemes, you may find them the best way to save.

● What would happen to my dependants if I died?

Many people get some life insurance cover from their employers (▷ ch. 11, p. 137). It's possible that you'll get this kind of cover if you work for a partnership or company (and, within limits, will get full tax relief on any payments you make for it – ▷ p. 221). Whether you get this cover or not, check that you have enough life insurance. Guidelines on how to work out how much life insurance you need are in chapter 11.

● Are my business assets fully insured?

If you use your home as an office, as many self-employed people do, make sure that the things you use to carry on your work (like typewriters, calculators, and other pieces of equipment) as well as your other possessions are fully covered by insurance against theft or other damage (▷ ch. 6).

And if you work from home, be particularly careful to keep the buildings insurance up to date (▷ ch. 6, p. 86). You'd be doubly hit in the pocket by under-insurance: you'd have to foot part of the bill for rebuilding costs and at a time when you might find it hard to carry on business (having lost the place you work from), let alone pay hefty bills.

With any insurance policy you have, make sure you tell your insurance company you're self-employed – if you don't, it may invalidate your policy. You may have to pay an extra premium if the company thinks that being self-employed increases the likelihood of you claiming.

National Insurance
Men and most women whose earnings from being self-employed (part-time or full-time) are above a certain amount (£1,250 for the 80/81 tax year), have to pay flat-rate Class 2 National Insurance contributions: in the 80/81 tax year these were £2.50 a week. Some married women and widows may have chosen not to pay Class 2 contributions at all – ▷ p. 237.

If your profits come to more than a certain amount (£2,650 a year for the 80/81 tax year), you'll also have to pay Class 4 NI contributions. For the 80/81 tax year these are 5 per cent of your profits between £2,650 and £8,300 a year – ie a maximum of £282.50 in Class 4 contributions.

Class 2 contributions have to be paid weekly – either by banker's order, or by buying stamps at a post office. Class 4 contributions have to be paid to the Inland Revenue along with your tax bill for the year – ie for the 80/81 tax year, on 1 January 81 and 1 July 81.

Note that if you work for an employer as well as being self-employed, you might have to pay Class 2 and Class 4 contributions in addition to the Class 1 contributions you pay on your earnings from employment. But there are special rules to prevent you having to pay more than a certain amount of all classes of NI contributions.

For the 80/81 tax year, you won't have to pay more than £591.66 in Class 1 and Class 2 contributions, or more than £415.50 in Class 1, 2 and 4 contributions (somewhat less if you belong to a pension scheme which is contracted out of the additional State pension scheme).

Help for the self-employed
As well as the organizations listed below, you might be able to get help from your local councillor (especially if you face difficulties with the local council), the local Chamber of Commerce, or a professional body set up for people in your line of work (eg Institution of Mechanical Engineers, Booksellers' Assoc.).

Small Firms Service – 10 regional centres run by the Department of Industry, Small Firms Division (Abell House, John Islip Street, London SW1P 4LN). Free information, advice, publications, contacts. Also runs the *Small firms counselling service*, staffed by recently retired businessmen offering very cheap advice on problems faced by small businesses.

Jobcentres and employment offices (address in phone book, under Employment Services Agency). Free advice and help with employing people. Training courses for you or people you employ – including courses on business management.

Industrial and Commercial Finance Corporation, 91 Waterloo Road, London SE1 8XP. Finance for small and medium-sized companies, with free help and guidance for the smaller firm.

Council for Small Industries in Rural Areas, Queen's House, Fish Row, Salisbury, Wiltshire SP1 1EX. Help, advice, loan facilities, training courses and so on for people running manufacturing or service industries in rural areas or small towns, employing not more than 20 people.

Organizations for the self-employed
Alliance of Small Firms and Self-Employed People, 279 Church Road, London SE19 2QQ. A pressure group which represents people running their own businesses, and helps them if they get into difficulties with the authorities.

Association of Independent Businesses, World Trade Centre, London E1 9AA. Represents the interests of the small and medium-sized business to the UK and EEC governments.

Institute of Directors, 116 Pall Mall, London SW1Y 5ED – more than 30,000 members, including many directors of small businesses.

National Federation of Self-Employed; 52 Shaftesbury Avenue, London W1V 7DE. A campaigning pressure group for people who are either self-employed, or own their own businesses.

Small Businesses Bureau, 32 Smith Square, London SW1P 3HH. The Conservative Party's organization for keeping in touch with and advising owners of small businesses.

Other useful addresses
Registrar of Business Names, 55–71 City Road, London EC1Y 2DN.

Registrar of Companies, Companies' Registration Office, Crown Way, Maindy, Cardiff, CF4 3UZ.

Institute of Chartered Accountants in England and Wales, Moorgate Place, London EC2 6EQ.

Association of Certified Accountants, 29 Lincoln's Inn Fields, London WC2A 3EE.

4 Planning for retirement

If you're looking forward to retirement, you probably don't need much urging to make plans for it. Even if you dread retiring, however, it's worth sitting down with pen and paper and making as detailed a forecast as you can of what the following will be when you stop work:
- your likely income (from pension, investments, help from relatives, and so on)
- your likely spending needs.

It's sensible to do this well before you retire – 20 years before is not too soon – and then revise your estimate regularly (each year, say) to keep it up to date.

Both your income and your spending needs are likely to change when you retire.

How your income may change
Almost certainly your income will fall. Instead of your salary/wages from work, you will get:
- a basic pension from the State (currently well below half the average full-time wage)
- possibly an addition to your State pension related to what you earned while at work
- possibly a pension from your employer
- the income from any savings you managed to build up while you were at work.

It's unlikely that all these added together will be as much as your take home pay in your working years. So from the time you retire you'll probably have less (maybe much less) money to spend than you have now.

Later on in retirement, you may find yourself increasingly badly off. Your State pension should approximately keep pace with inflation, but the pension from your employer may well fail to do so. So the immediate drop in income upon retirement is likely to be followed by a steady subsequent fall in real income (what you can buy with your money).

How your spending needs may change
Around the time you retire, a shift in your spending pattern is very probable. You may be able to predict some of this change fairly easily, especially the part that relates to simply stopping work. You won't have to pay for fares to and from the office, for example, or for lunches at work. And you may also know that you'll spend more on particular hobbies – golf, gardening, or painting, say – when you have the time to give to them. You may also know that some of your current financial commitments – the mortgage, or school fees, for example – will have ended by the time you retire.

It's less easy to take into account the effects of simply growing older. In your late sixties, you may well want to spend more than you do now on, for example, staying warm, transport, labour-saving appliances, holidays (you may not want to rough it any more).

Giving realistic weight to this kind of age-related spending change is very hard – particularly if you're trying to look 20 or 30 years into the future. But it's still worth trying to allow for it when you work out your future spending needs: that way you stand a better chance of coming close to the truth than you do if you assume you'll spend your money the same way in your sixties as in your thirties or forties.

Where to look for information
This chapter is designed to help you assess for yourself how well you are likely to be able to manage financially when you retire. It looks in detail at the changes in your income and spending needs in the next few pages, and at ways of improving your prospects. The second half of the chapter looks in very much more detail at how your State pension and employer's pension are worked out – not vital for planning, but useful to sort out how much *you* will get from these sources.

A guide to the organization of the chapter

is below. But you may also find useful information in chapters 16 to 18 (on planning your investment strategy) and 21 (social security).

Guide to chapter 4

What you'll get

If you won't reach retirement age (65 for a man, 60 for a woman) for a good many years, it's just not feasible to try to work out what you are going to get in money terms. It is hard enough to guess what the rate of inflation will be over 12 months, let alone 12 years. The best solution is to base your forecast on the level of prices and pensions today, with the hope that in the future both pensions and earnings will rise more or less in line with prices. This way your calculations should give an answer that's roughly right in terms of what your pension etc can buy.

As a first step towards working out what you'll get, make a list of income from various sources (the State, previous employers, your own savings), which you can rely on after you retire (for example ▷ p. 42).

What you'll get from the State

One of the most important sources of income you are likely to have is a State retirement pension.

Anyone who has worked for long enough (and paid enough full Class 1 or 2 NI contributions – ▷ p. 51) is entitled to a basic flat-rate pension (£27.15 a week for a single person, £43.45 for a married man, in November 80). Those who retire after April 79 and are *not* self-employed may (if their employer's scheme is not contracted out of the State scheme, ▷ p. 54) get an *additional retirement pension* on top of their basic pension. This additional pension is related to what they earned (and replaces

the graduated pension – ▷ p. 53 – which operated between April 61 and April 75). Both the basic pension and any earnings-related addition are increased each year in line with changes in the Retail Price Index (RPI). So these pensions should have roughly the same buying power in the future as they have now. For full details of how the State retirement pension works ▷ pp. 51–4.

As well as a pension, you may get other help from the State: rent/rate rebates (▷ p. 231), free or cheap services (▷ p. 231), local authority help (▷ p. 234) and other social security benefits (▷ pp. 232–3). And you will also get a higher personal allowance for tax purposes than you do before retirement (▷ p. 44).

What you'll get from your employer

If you belong to an occupational pension scheme (around half the working population of Britain did in April 80) you may get a pension from your job as well as a basic pension from the State when you retire. The way your occupational pension is worked out varies from scheme to scheme, but most commonly, it is related to your pay at the time you retire and the number of years you've belonged to the scheme. The most an employer is allowed to pay out is $\frac{2}{3}$ of final pay. You may, with some schemes, be able to get a lump sum in addition to your pension or in place of part of the pension if you choose. Details of occupational pension schemes begin on p. 55.

● Warning

If you change jobs, you may lose out on your entitlement to an occupational pension – for details ▷ p. 59.

What you'll get from your savings

If you have money saved already, or plan to save in the future, you can add on to what you get from the State and your employer any income you'll get from investments. But remember:

● if you invest your money for maximum safety, its value is not likely to keep pace with inflation – its buying power, and that of the income it can give you, will fall with time

● if you accept some degree of risk in the attempt to safeguard the buying power of your money, you stand the chance of losing at least some of it.

Unless you can count on being able to top up your savings so that they retain their buying power, it's sensible to make a pessimistic estimate of the income they are likely to give you in, say, 20 years' time. (If you are close to retirement, of course, your position may be clearer – but you still need to take inflation into account when working out the likely buying power of your investment income in the years after you retire.)

What you'll need

If you are doing your planning well in advance, bear in mind that your spending needs may look quite different when you retire from the way they do now. Look at your current budget (▷ ch. 14 for how to draw this up) and try to see where the changes are likely to occur. It may help to think of how your situation may change in the following areas.

Family circumstances

Your children will probably have left home, and may be completely financially independent by the time you retire. So you may need to spend less on food, clothing and general household expenses than when they were younger. But on the other hand, you may have taken on new responsibilities (elderly parents, for example) which may cancel out your savings so far as your children are concerned.

Example

Paul and Pippa Price sit down together to try to work out what they can count on as income for their retirement. Paul is now 55 and earns £8,500 a year. His current take-home pay is £492 a month (about £5,900 a year) after tax, NI contributions, and pension scheme contributions. He began work in 1945, and has had 4 different jobs altogether.

From the first he'll get no pension – there was no occupational pension scheme for it. From the second he'll get a preserved pension (▷ p. 59), based on his pay in 1965 – the year he left his job. This pension won't rise. From his third job he gets no pension: he took a refund of his contributions instead (▷ p. 59). From the fourth (his present job), he'll get a pension based on his final pay: $\frac{1}{60}$ for each year he's been with this employer. When he retires he will have been with the employer for 17 years.

He'll also get a basic pension from the State, but no additional pension because his firm contracted out (▷ p. 54) of the State scheme. He'll get graduated pension based on his earnings between 1961 and 1975. Pippa won't get a pension in her own right.

At current rates, he would get:

State retirement pension	£2,259 a year
Graduated pension	£150 a year
Pension from	
Job 1	Nil
Job 2	£512 a year
Job 3	Nil
Job 4 (if he stays until retirement)	£2,408 a year

Paul knows that by the time he retires, his preserved pension from Job 2 will have a much lower purchasing power than it has now. He thinks 10 per cent is a realistic guess at the likely rate of inflation over the 10 years before he retires and he calculates that his frozen £512 will be worth only about £200 by 1989.

So his pensions in the year he retires will add up as follows: £2,259 + £150 + £200 + £2,408 = £5,017 (in terms of buying power today).

Paul has no savings yet, and doesn't know if he will manage to save before he retires, so he can't add on any income from investments. His wife Pippa looks after the home, and can't claim any pension of her own.

Paul sees from p. 44 that – assuming the tax rules stay the same – when he retires, less of his income will be taxed, because he'll be able to claim the age allowance instead of the married man's personal allowance. He works out how much tax he'll have to pay on the £5,000 or so (in buying power) he'll get – it works out at £630. So in the first year Paul retires, they'll have an income of around £4,370 a year (around £365 a month), substantially less than he takes home at the moment (about £5,900 a year or £492 a month after tax, NI contributions and payments to his firm's pension scheme).

Regular financial commitments
You'll probably be free of your mortgage by the time you retire. School fees, too, should be a thing of the past – so should payments into a personal pension scheme (▷ p. 46).

Lifestyle
It's very likely that the lifestyle you'll want in your sixties won't be the same as the one you enjoyed in your thirties. You may want to spend more money on holidays, for example – and pay for 3 weeks in Majorca rather than 2 weeks camping in Scotland. You may want to spend less time on, say, cooking, more time on gardening – either

way, you may end up spending more money. You can only try to guess what your priorities are likely to be after you retire.

Extra expenses
As people get older, they often incur heavier expenses than they had when young. After you retire you may want a warmer house, warmer clothes. If you don't have a car, you may not be prepared to walk to do the shopping in the pouring rain, or wait for an erratic bus service in the February gales – so you may pay out more for taxis, or for bus rides over distances you are now happy to walk. In old age, you may also want to

Example
Paul and Pippa Price draw up a list to show what items in their budget they expect will change after Paul retires (by which time their son Peter, 17 now, will have left home). They do their sums using today's prices – they hope that inflation will affect their spending *and* their income in broadly the same way.

Some items – rates, telephone, insurance, for example – they expect won't change much. On other items – like clothes or meals out – the fact that they may wish to spend more should be balanced by the fact that they won't be paying out for Peter. They leave these items out of their calculations.

Paul takes home around £490 a month at the moment. When he retires this will fall to around £365 (▷ opposite). They will have about £125 less each month to spend, but their spending needs only look like dropping by £88.50 − £32.50 = £56. To keep their present style of life, they will need to find an extra £70 or so a month (after deductions).

These are likely to go up	by about this many £££ a month
Gas	2.00
Electricity	2.00
Gardening	4.00
Golf	4.00
Books, records	4.00
Stamps, stationery	1.50
Entertaining	5.00
Help in the home	10.00
Total	£32.50

These are likely to go down	by about this many £££ a month
Life insurance	6.00
Fares to work	20.00
Meals at work (compared with eating at home)	2.50
School meals (Peter, their son, is now 17)	7.00
Holidays	10.00
Petrol	8.00
Peter's allowance	10.00
Food (Peter will have left home)	25.00
Total	£88.50

be in the position to pay for help with heavy housework, or for someone to do the shopping for you. And to make sure you can get medical treatment for minor complaints quickly, you may want to spend more on private medical treatment – or medical bills insurance (▷ pp. 146–9).

Again, even if you can't put a precise figure on this kind of new spending need, it's worth thinking roughly how much the items mentioned would cost today, and budget for at least some of them after you retire.

Fewer work-related expenses
Once you retire you shouldn't have to spend money on some of the expenses you had while you worked:
- NI contributions
- trade union dues
- payments to an occupational pension scheme
- fares to and from work
- meals at work.

You may also find less need to spend money on smart clothes, or subscriptions to trade magazines.

And don't forget that after you reach pension age, different tax rules apply, which may mean less tax to pay.

See p. 43 for how one couple try to work out their likely spending needs in retirement.

What to do if there's going to be a gap between income and spending needs in retirement
If it looks as if you'll need more money than you're going to have in retirement, you can try one (or all) of the following tactics.
- plan to spend less in retirement (move to a smaller home, choose cheaper hobbies, get rid of the car, and so on – ▷ p. 47)
- plan to spend less *now* so that you can save up for retirement while you still have time (▷ p. 46)
- plan ways of increasing your income after retirement – by reorganizing your investments to give income later (▷ p. 47) or taking part-time work, if you can find it.

If the gap is very large, you may have to try all three tactics. Which is a good reason for doing your planning early enough to leave you some flexibility.

Tax after retirement
The over-65s pay tax in just the same way as everyone else (▷ chs. 1 and 20). But they can claim a higher personal allowance.

Age allowance
Anyone who is 64 or over before the start of the tax year (or whose wife is) can claim age allowance – whether or not they have retired – instead of the ordinary single person's or married man's allowance. Age allowance is higher than the ordinary personal allowances (for the 80/81 tax year the full age allowance was £1,820 for a single person, £2,895 for a married man). But age allowance is reduced if the person's 'total income' (▷ p. 216) is above a certain limit (£5,900 for the 80/81 tax year). Age allowance is reduced by $\frac{2}{3}$ of the amount by which 'total income' exceeds £5,900. But it's never reduced below the level of the ordinary personal allowance, no matter how high 'total income' is. For the 80/81 tax year, this meant that an elderly person with an income of not more than £6,567 if single or £7,025 if married could benefit from age allowance.

Note that if a couple choose to have the wife's earnings taxed separately (▷ p. 127) both husband and wife get the single person's allowance, however old they are – neither can get the age allowance.

Married women and tax on pensions
If you're a married woman, a pension for which you qualify on your own contributions (whether National Insurance or a company scheme) counts as your own earned income. This means that you can claim the wife's earned income allowance (£1,375 for the 80/81 tax year) on it. So up to £1,375 of pension you earned in your own right (together with any other earnings you have) would have been tax free.

If you get a pension based on your husband's NI contributions, it normally counts as your *husband's* earnings, and wife's earned income allowance cannot be set against it. If you're entitled to a NI pension of your own but choose to get a pension based on your husband's contributions because this is higher, you can count as earnings the amount of pension you were entitled to on your own contributions.

How pensions are taxed
Certain pensions are tax-free. The most important tax-free pensions for the elderly are supplementary pensions and the £10 Christmas bonus. War widows' pension is tax-free too.

Tax on investment income
Many elderly people who get investment income which has tax deducted before they get it (eg interest on local authority loans, share dividends) and who pay little or no tax may be able to claim a tax rebate. For details ▷ p. 225.

Investment income surcharge
People with large amounts of investment income have to pay a special tax called the *investment income surcharge*. In the 80/81 tax year you may have had to pay investment income surcharge if your investment income was over £5,500 a year.
Details of how this tax works are on p. 194.

The following pensions are *taxable* – and normally count as earned income:

● State retirement pension (including any graduated pension, additional pension, and invalidity allowance you get)

● old person's pension (or non-contributory retirement pension)

● pension from former employer – paid to you or your widow or widower

● self-employed pension – provided you got tax relief on the payments you made into the personal pension scheme (if you didn't get any tax relief, the pension counts as investment income)

● partnership retirement annuity – provided you retired through old age or ill health, and the income from the annuity comes to no more than half your average yearly share of the profits in the best 3 years of the last 7 years during which you were involved virtually full-time in the partnership (anything over this counts as investment income).

● Pensions from abroad

You are normally liable for tax on $\frac{9}{10}$ of any pension from abroad, whether or not it is brought into the UK. Pensions from abroad are generally taxed on a *preceding year basis* – so your 80/81 tax bill will be based on $\frac{9}{10}$ of any pension you got from abroad during 79/80. Ask your tax office for leaflet IR25.

How tax is collected on pensions

Although the State retirement pension is taxable, tax isn't deducted before the pension is paid. If the State pension is all the income you get, you won't have to pay any tax – because the pension comes to less than age allowance. But if your State pension, added to any other taxable income you get (eg a pension from your former employer, or investment income), comes to more than your total outgoings and allowances, there will be some tax to pay on your income.

If you get a pension from your former employer, the tax due on the *whole* of your income will, until April 82, be collected under PAYE from your employer's pension – for how the taxman adjusts your PAYE code to do this ▷ note **k**, p. 15. This way of collecting tax on the State retirement pension puzzles many elderly people – because it makes it look as if their employer's pension is being taxed at a higher rate than their earnings were before they retired (see Fig. 4.1 left).

Tax on your part-time earnings

If you have a job after you retire, and your combined income (from the job, your pension, and investments) makes you liable for tax, your employer will usually deduct the income tax that's due under the PAYE system (▷ p. 10). So the tax deducted under PAYE will cover any which has still to be paid on your investment income and on your State pension, as well as the tax due on your earnings alone. It may look to you as if you are losing too much from your pay-packet in tax, but if the tax due on the other parts of your income were not collected under PAYE, you'd have to pay up in a lump sum at the end of each year.

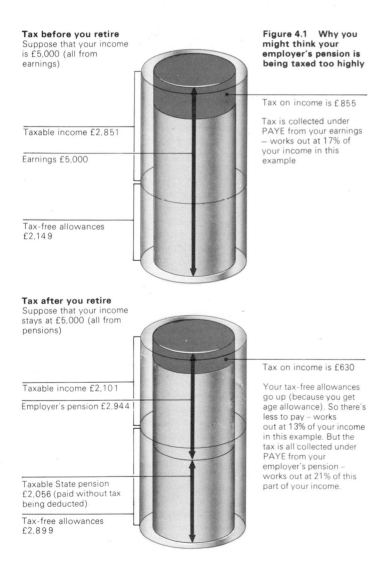

Tax before you retire
Suppose that your income is £5,000 (all from earnings)

Taxable income £2,851

Earnings £5,000

Tax-free allowances £2,149

Figure 4.1 Why you might think your employer's pension is being taxed too highly

Tax on income is £855

Tax is collected under PAYE from your earnings – works out at 17% of your income in this example

Tax after you retire
Suppose that your income stays at £5,000 (all from pensions)

Taxable income £2,101

Employer's pension £2,944

Taxable State pension £2,056 (paid without tax being deducted)

Tax-free allowances £2,899

Tax on income is £630

Your tax-free allowances go up (because you get age allowance). So there's less to pay – works out at 13% of your income in this example. But the tax is all collected under PAYE from your employer's pension – works out at 21% of this part of your income.

Saving for retirement

If you foresee that you're going to need more income when you retire than you are likely to get from your pension and current savings, then – provided retirement is far enough ahead of you – saving now is one way for you to bridge the gap. If you will be retiring soon (within the next 5 years, say) read Too late to save? (opposite) with particular attention.

If you are looking ahead some way to retirement, you need to be thinking in terms of ways of protecting your long-term savings against inflation until the time comes when you'll actually need them.

You can consider either or both:
● investing your regular savings yourself
● putting them into an *occupational pension scheme* or a *personal pension scheme* (▷ below), both of which have considerable tax advantages.

If you take the first course, you should read chapters 16–18, particularly the information on long-term saving.

Warning

Your calculations may show that your income when you first retire should cover your needs – but unless they show a healthy surplus or your employer's pension is both adequate *and* index-linked, you would be wise to try to save now as well. If inflation runs at 10 per cent a year, an income of £5,000 at the start of retirement will be worth only around £3,100 after 5 years, and only around £1,930 after 10 years.

Occupational pension schemes

With some jobs, you don't have any choice whether to belong to the firm's occupational pension scheme: you *have* to be a member. In other cases you may be able to decide when you first start work for the employer whether you want to belong to the scheme or not. If you have this choice, or are in a job where there's no occupational pension scheme, ▷ below for details of personal pension schemes.

Occupational pension schemes may be *contributory* (you have to pay a proportion of your salary into the scheme each month – 5 or 6 per cent is common) or *non-contributory* (you pay nothing). If the scheme is contributory, you won't have to pay tax on the part of your income that goes in payments to the pension scheme – which makes this way of saving for retirement relatively cheap. Your employer pays the balance of the cost – how much this is will vary from year to year. You pay no tax on the amount contributed by your employer.

There's another tax advantage with occupational pension schemes. Generally all the contributions (both yours and your employer's) go into a *pension fund* – along with income from investments belonging to the fund and gains made by buying and selling these investments. The pension fund pays no income tax or capital gains tax.

These tax advantages, together with the fact that your pension is often linked to your pay when you leave the job (so giving some protection against inflation) could make joining an occupational scheme a good way of saving for retirement.

But belonging to an occupational scheme may not be such a bargain if:
● the benefits the scheme offers are poor (▷ pp. 55–8)
● you change jobs frequently – and so don't build up a long run of pension contributions with one employer (▷ p. 59)
● you stop working for the employer some years before you retire – either because you take a different job, become redundant, or have to give up work through ill-health (▷ pp. 58–9).

Additional voluntary contributions

Some occupational pension schemes allow members to make additional voluntary contributions (over and above those they have to make to belong to the scheme) in order to get a higher pension on retirement. Your employer doesn't normally match your voluntary contributions by paying extra contributions on your behalf. What you get for your extra contributions is usually some fixed amount of pension at retirement age – which *won't* be increased as time passes.

The extra contributions you pay are treated the same way as ordinary ones for tax purposes (ie you get tax relief on them), provided you keep them up for at least 5 years and that the total you are paying into the occupational scheme is not more than 15 per cent of your earnings from that job.

Again, this is a good way to save for retirement unless your occupational pension scheme offers poor benefits, or you don't want this part of your savings tied up completely until you retire.

Personal pension schemes

You can get tax relief on payments into a personal pension scheme if:
● you are self-employed or have some freelance earnings.
● you have earnings not covered by an occupational pension scheme.

There are rules about how much you can pay in each year and still get tax relief. The amount depends on your *non-pensionable earnings* – ie your earnings from being self-employed, or from jobs in which you do not belong to a pension scheme. In the 80/81 tax year, you could pay in up to 17½ per cent of your non-pensionable earnings and still get tax relief. You get tax relief at your top rate of tax.

Personal pension scheme funds also pay no tax on the income they get, or on gains they make. So they may be a good way to save – particularly so for the self-employed. If you're employed and have the choice of whether or not to join your employer's scheme, bear in mind that your employer will also be making contributions for you.

Note that with personal pension schemes it will be as impossible for you to get money out of the scheme before you retire as it is for those who contribute to pension schemes run by their employer.

Too late to save?
If you are due to retire within the next 5 years or so, there's not much time for you to build up extra savings while you're still at work. Check the Route Map on p. 190 for investments which might be suitable. But unless your budget for retirement shows a healthy surplus or your pensions are fully index-linked, your position in retirement may go downhill rapidly unless after you retire you can do one or both of the following:
● cut down on expenses
● boost your income.

We look at both these strategies in the next section of this chapter.

Cutting down on expenses
The first step to take is to make sure you're not spending more than you need on items where the State may offer help to the hard-up or elderly. You may be able to get dental treatment, prescriptions, home help and other things free or at reduced rates. More details on pp. 231–2. Make sure, too, that you are not paying out more in tax than you should be. Details of allowances and outgoings you may be entitled to are on pp. 220–23.

Next, take a look at your budget (▷ p. 164) – it should show the way you spend money at the moment. You may be able to see at once areas where you could cut back spending relatively painlessly. One expensive item you might be able to get along without is a car – but you may have to re-

organize the way you spend your free time if you do (▷ p. 112). Better to economize now (and build up some savings while you still can) than have the shock of a big change in lifestyle when retirement comes.

Third, think whether it might make sense to move to a smaller house which is cheaper to run – lower rates and fuel bills, better insulation, closer to public transport, for example. It may not be as difficult to make the move when you're 60 as when you're 70 – and moving to a smaller house may well release some capital which you can invest. Remember, though, to allow for all the expenses you'll incur in moving home (▷ checklist on p. 79).

Finally, if you've managed, one way or another, to cut down your expenses, decide how you'll use the extra money. You could:
● save it (in which case ▷ p. 190 for investments to consider)
● spend it in a way that will cut costs when you retire (eg by making repairs to the house or car, by buying a new washing machine, or by paying for a thicker layer of loft insulation or better draught exclusion now rather than in 5 years' time).

Investing your savings in the second way may not bring you an immediate financial return, but knowing there'll be fewer large bills to meet when you're retired may be worth it in terms of peace of mind.

Boosting your income

More income from investments
The first thing to check is that your investments are working as well for you as they can. You should be looking for investments that stand a chance of maintaining your buying power – either through an increasing income as time passes, or as capital growth, with the possibility of withdrawing regular amounts to use as income. No investment can fully match these needs, but see the Route Map on p. 188 for some possibilities you can consider.

If you have already retired, your reduced income as a pensioner and the special tax rules which apply to the over-65s mean that you are probably paying less tax than you did while you were working (or maybe none at all). Make sure, then, that the investments you chose before retiring are still suitable for your current tax situation.

In particular, if your income is too low for you to pay any tax (▷ p. 10) don't invest your money in any kind of building society account. Building society interest counts as if basic rate tax has already been paid on it before it is paid to investors. This may be fine for taxpayers – but if your income is too low for you to pay tax you will not be able to claim back the tax deducted from the interest before you received it. Check the Route Map on p. 188 for some alternative investments which may be more attractive.

One particular investment – National Savings Index-linked Retirement Certificates – will protect at least part of your capital against inflation. This investment is available only to people of retirement age (65 for a man, 60 for a woman). The certificates pay no interest as such, but the value of your investment is guaranteed to rise in line with the official retail price index – so it won't be overtaken by inflation. After you've invested your money for a year, you can cash part of your investments (to give you an income) without losing out on the index-linking.

The main drawback to this investment is that there's a limit to how much you can put into it: £1,200 for each person investing, in April 80. This means that it can be a home for only a rather limited amount of your savings. You need to look into some of the other investments discussed in chapters 16–18 as well.

Taking an extra job

If you foresee a large gap between your needs in retirement and your income, you could try to boost your income by taking a part-time job – as long as you are fit to work. People who are over retirement age don't have to pay NI contributions – so you should lose less in deductions from your pay. This is true whether you have postponed retirement (to build up a bigger pension – ▷ p. 52 for details) and are not yet drawing the State pension, or whether you are drawing the State pension and working part-time as well.

So when you work out the benefit of taking work after you retire, you needn't budget for NI contributions.

If you earn more than a certain amount from a job in the first 5 years after you retire, and are drawing your State pension, you may find that it is reduced because of your earnings (this is called the *earnings rule*). In November 80, for every 10p you earned between £52 and £56 a week you would have lost 5p a week of your State pension and for every 5p you earned above £56 a week, you would have lost 5p a week of State pension. If the husband is getting an increase in his pension for his wife, the earnings rule starts to bite if her earnings are £45

a week or more. If you're in the age band affected (65–70 for a man, 60–65 for a woman), and if your earnings are likely to be substantial, it makes sense to check what the current earnings rule is. It may be to your advantage to defer drawing your State pension for a couple of years (building up a bigger pension too, ▷ p. 52).

Note that the earnings rule applies to the self-employed too.

For details of how part-time earnings are taxed ▷ p. 45.

Income from your home

You may be able to use your home to raise extra income in retirement.

One way of doing this is simply to sell it and move to a smaller one, chosen with an eye to low running costs. This should leave you with a lump sum to invest to help improve your position when retired. Especially if your home is very large, expensive to run, far from local amenities and poorly placed for public transport, it may well be sensible to move early in retirement (or even before) rather than later, when the upheaval of moving house may be less easy to cope with. Moving from a home of which you have happy memories may be a wrench, but if you foresee the place will become too much for you to manage later on, it makes sense to make the move as early as possible. But beware of moving too far from the area where your friends, clubs, social life and so forth, are.

If your home is of a convenient size and easy to run, there is no need for you to move – you could consider getting extra income from your home by taking out a special kind of annuity – called a home income plan – which is specially designed for the elderly (the over-70s, say). See p. 50.

An alternative way to use your home to raise money – without moving out – is to take in a lodger. Before you decide to try this, however, get up-to-date information on your rights (and duties) as a landlord – in particular, what your rights are if you find having a lodger is not to your liking. The Department of Environment has 2 leaflets, *Landlords and the law* and *Rooms to let* which are useful reading – you can get them from your local council offices or Citizens' Advice Bureau. And remember that when you take a tenant you are going into business on a small scale: you should keep careful records of income and expenses, and keep an eye on changes in the law which may affect you.

Example

Colin Carter has worked most of his life as a self-employed builder, on a small scale. But in 1977 he had a bad year, and decided to take work with a local builder's firm instead. He's now only 3 years away from retirement, earning £5,420 a year (around £70 a week after tax, NI contributions, and pension scheme contributions). Until now he has pushed out of his mind thoughts of how he'll manage when he has to stop work.

In the years when he worked for himself, he paid Class 2 NI contributions, but put nothing into any personal pension scheme (▷ p. 46). So (at current rates) all he will get as pension after he retires is the flat-rate State retirement pension of £27.15 a week and his pension from 6 years with the firm (which gives 1/80 of final pay for each year of service) – which works out at £7.80 a week.

He works out what he'll get when he retires using the 80/81 figures, realizing that if he ignores inflation's effect on his earnings and on State benefits until he retires and on prices too, the answer he'll get will be roughly right in terms of what his £££ will buy when he retires.

He was recently left £1,000 which is currently in a building society ordinary share account. If left there it will bring him – at mid-80 rates – £105 a year (around £2 a week) and with no tax to pay. He has no other assets. Taking this investment income into account, Colin's income after he retires will be around £27.15+£7.80+£2 = £36.95. After tax of about 60p a week this will leave him with just over £36 – a drop of around £34 a week compared with what he takes home now. And although the pension from his job may go up from time to time after he retires, it's not index-linked, so his situation is likely to get worse as he gets older.

The real cause of Colin's poor prospects is his failure to make proper provision for retirement while he was self-employed (and had the chance to make payments into a personal pension scheme – which would have qualified for tax relief). It's now too late for him to improve things much by saving on his own (and anyway, he seems to have little to spare out of his £70 take-home pay each week).

He takes a careful look at the way he's spending his money at the moment and decides:
● he can cut his expenses by around £7.50 a week by giving up his car and using the bus instead, and save another £6 a week by taking sandwiches for lunch at work (in-stead of going to the pub). Altogether he could cut expenses by £13.50 a week
● since his rent and rates are £15 a week he'll be able to get £5.20 a week supplementary benefit (▷ p. 229 for the rules on this)
● he may be able to boost his income by reorganizing his investments. (He will add to the £1,000 the £500 he expects to get from selling his car.) In future he'll leave no more than £500 as an emergency reserve in his building society ordinary account, and will invest the rest with an eye to getting the highest possible income, without running too many risks (for possible choices ▷ Route Map on p. 188). But he doesn't count on ending up that much better off than he is at the moment.

After his calculations, his retirement budget looks like this:

Needs	£70−£13.50=	£56.50 a week
Income	£36.00+£5.20=	£41.20 a week
Gap		£15.30 a week

Colin has no chance to save money by moving home. Nor (since he rents his home) to go for a home income plan. He's loathe to dip into his small amount of capital, as he'd end up with no emergency reserve to fall back on. Either he'll have to economize severely after he retires, or try to take on part-time work (he is a fair carpenter) to boost his income. Luckily he has every chance of being able to work occasionally for his present employer – and if that falls through he'll advertise in local shops for work as a carpenter.

He will have to give up his supplementary benefit if he takes this work (and he may also have to give up the idea of doing without a car) – but Colin feels he won't be able to make ends meet without more income. Provided he stays fit enough to work part time, his retirement shouldn't be too grim. But if he survives into his eighties, he will probably find managing a great struggle.

How a home income plan works

Briefly, you get a loan from a life insurance company, based on the security of your home; the loan is used to buy an annuity from the company. While you live you receive the income from the annuity, from which basic rate tax and interest on the loan have been deducted. When you die, the loan is repaid out of your estate *before* capital transfer tax is worked out.

If you pay tax, you can claim tax relief on the full amount of the interest payments. This means that if, for example, you pay tax at the basic rate (30 per cent in the 80/81 tax year), you save 30p tax for each £ of interest you pay (▷ Fig. 4.2 for how this works out).

● Pros and cons

The value of your home is likely to go up year by year, after you've taken out the loan. This increase in value all goes to *you*, not to the insurance company. And you may be able to use the increase in value to get a further loan – up to a maximum loan of £25,000 – and buy another annuity. In this way you might be able to increase your income in line with inflation.

With an ordinary annuity, inflation reduces the buying power of your fixed income, and there's not much you can do about it. With these schemes, inflation still reduces the buying power of your fixed income, but it correspondingly reduces the value of your debt to the insurance company. So rising prices don't wholly work against you.

On the other hand, you'd be almost certain to get a better after tax increase in your income by paying cash for an annuity (if you could do so) rather than mortgaging your home. And if it's likely you'll have to sell your home (to move in with relatives or into an old people's home, say) you shouldn't go for a home income plan. If you do move later on, you'll have to repay the loan, and you'll be left with a rather low fixed income annuity.

● Other points

You generally have to be at least 65 (and generally older) to be eligible for this kind of annuity. And the most you can usually borrow is a percentage (commonly 75 or 80 per cent) of the market value of your home.

Verdict

Worth considering as *part* of your investment strategy, provided you're at least 65 (or preferably older), and a taxpayer. But it isn't wise to expect the income from one home income plan to see you through your old age – and it's particularly rash to commit yourself to this kind of scheme if you can foresee having to sell your home in the near future (the next few years).

Figure 4.2
How a home income plan works

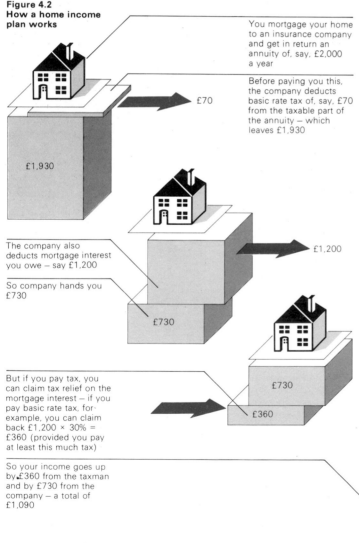

You mortgage your home to an insurance company and get in return an annuity of, say, £2,000 a year

Before paying you this, the company deducts basic rate tax of, say, £70 from the taxable part of the annuity – which leaves £1,930

£70

£1,930

The company also deducts mortgage interest you owe – say £1,200

£1,200

So company hands you £730

£730

But if you pay tax, you can claim tax relief on the mortgage interest – if you pay basic rate tax, for example, you can claim back £1,200 × 30% = £360 (provided you pay at least this much tax)

£730

£360

So your income goes up by £360 from the taxman and by £730 from the company – a total of £1,090

£1,090

A pension from the State

A person's State retirement pension may be made up of three parts:

- a basic flat-rate pension
- an additional pension, based on earnings since April 78, and payable from April 79
- a graduated pension, based on NI contributions while the scheme was in operation (1961–75).

Basic pension

- **What is it?**

A flat-rate pension available to those employed in a job, the self-employed, and even those not employed at all – so long as the contribution conditions for qualifying are met (▷ right). An addition may be paid for an adult dependant (eg a wife with little or no earnings, and no pension of her own).

- **How you qualify**

You qualify by paying enough full Class 1 or Class 2 NI contributions (▷ right). Married women over 60 can qualify for a pension on their husband's contribution record if their own has gaps, or if they have chosen not to pay contributions that will build up their own pension. In addition, there are now special rules (▷ p. 236) to make it easier for those who have to spend some years at home (to care for children or a disabled relative, say) to qualify for the basic pension in their own right.

- **How much**

Pensions are reviewed each year to try to maintain their buying power. The basic pension is increased in line with the increase in prices (measured by the Retail Price Index). For the year from November 80 the rates were:

Single person	£27.15 a week
Married couple	£43.45 a week
Married couple if wife qualifies for full pension too	£54.30 a week

But if you (or your wife or husband) have more than a certain level of earnings, your pension may be reduced (▷ The earnings rule, p. 48). Information on how pensions are taxed is on pp. 44–5.

- **Further information**

Ask at your local social security office (address in phone book under *Health and Social Security, Dept. of*) if you have any problems – as a first step, they should be able to provide a number of leaflets about pensions.

Contribution conditions

To get the full basic pension, you have to have paid a certain minimum amount of NI contributions over most of your 'working life' – which, roughly speaking, refers to the years between the ages of 16 and 64 for a man, between 16 and 59 for a woman. For those who were born before 5 July 1932, however, the span of time may be slightly different – so if you are in doubt about whether you qualify for a pension (or any other problems with your contribution record), you should check with your local social security office.

Your 'working life' is looked at to see whether it passes what's known as the *contribution test* (▷ below for details).

However long or short your working life, you have to pass the contribution test for about 90 per cent of it.

This means that you can have some years of your working life – about 10 per cent of it – when you have not passed the contribution test, and still get a full flat-rate retirement pension.

Note that any years for which you've worked abroad, taken a rest or a degree, dropped-out or whatever, will normally be included as part of your 'working life'. The only gaps allowed – ie for which you are considered to have paid the necessary contributions when you in fact have not – are those in which you were registered sick or unemployed, or got invalidity, or maternity benefit. But ▷ p. 236 for special rules for those who stay at home to care for children or a disabled relative.

The contribution test

For any tax year during your *working life*, you pass the *contribution test* if you have paid at least a certain minimum in contributions.

What this necessary minimum in contributions is depends on the year:

- for each tax year you work after 5 April 78 (when the new State pension scheme started) the minimum is what someone who earns just enough each week to have to pay any contributions at all, would have to pay in contributions for a full 52 weeks' work
- for each tax year you worked from 6 April 75 to 5 April 78 the minimum was what someone who earned just enough to pay any contributions at all, would pay in contributions for 50 weeks' work
- for any time you worked before April 75 – when NI contributions were two-tier, a flat rate and a graduated rate – the total number of flat-rate contributions you paid

Special rules for married women
If you pay full Class 1 or Class 2 NI contributions, you qualify for a basic pension (and – with Class 1 contributions only – the earnings-related addition) in your own right in the same way as everyone else (▷ this page and p. 53). And if you have had to spend time at home (caring for children for example) you can qualify with a shorter contribution record. For details ▷ p. 236.

However, if you pay the lower Class 1 contribution or no Class 2 contribution (only possible for those married on or before 5 April 77 and who had chosen to pay lower or no contributions) you can only qualify for a pension on your husband's record. You will only get a pension when *your husband* reaches retirement age (rather than when you do). The pension you get will be smaller than one based on your own contributions – around $\frac{3}{5}$ the basic rate.

Widowed?
If the husband paid enough NI contributions his widow gets some or all of the benefits listed beginning on p. 135. All but the State retirement pension stop if she remarries or lives with a man as his wife.

All widows benefits increase in the same way as the basic retirement pension.

- **Over 60?**

You'll normally get the basic retirement pension. But if your husband was *not* getting a retirement pension at the time he died, you can normally get the (higher) widow's allowance (▷ p. 135) for the first 6 months after his death, instead.

during that time are divided into lots of 50. Each lot (or part of a lot) is then treated as a tax-year's worth of contributions, regardless of whether each lot of 50 happened to fall in a complete tax year.

Note that it's only full Class 1 (for the employed) or Class 2 contributions (for the self-employed) that help build up your rights to a pension. Class 2 contributions (which are flat-rate amounts) count in the same way as contributions at the level of earnings at which contributions start having to be paid.

With the rules that now apply, clearly the more you earn over the level at which people have to pay contributions, the more easily you'll be able to pass the contribution test, even if you work for only part of the year.

For current rates of Class 1 NI contribution ▷ Fig. 4.3 (for what contracting out means, ▷ p. 54).

What happens if you haven't paid enough contributions?

If you pass the contributions test for less than 90 per cent of your working life, your basic pension will be scaled down. And if you pass the test for a lot less than 90 per cent of your working life, you may get no basic pension at all. Use the rough guide below to work out how a pension is scaled down. If you don't know how many years you have already passed the test for, ask at your local social security office.

How the basic pension is scaled down

% of working life for which you pass the contribution test	Approx. % of full flat-rate pension you will get
90 or more	100
75	84
$66\frac{2}{3}$	75
50	56
$33\frac{1}{3}$	38
25	28
Less than about 22% or less than 7 years' full contributions	None

Earning extra pension

One way to increase the size of State pension you get is to put off your retirement by not drawing your retirement pension.

How you can earn extra pension

For each 6 days you postpone drawing your pension, your total State pension (basic plus earnings-related additional pension plus graduated pension) will be increased by $\frac{1}{8}$p a week for every £1 a week of State pension you were entitled to at retirement age. But you have to put off your retirement for at least 7 weeks to start increasing your pension. Note that if you go on working during the period that you put off drawing your pension you won't have to pay any NI contributions – though your employer will.

How much extra pension?

For each year you postpone drawing your pension after retirement age, the pension you get will be increased by $7\frac{1}{2}$ per cent. If you put off retirement for 5 years, your pension from the State will be increased by $37\frac{1}{2}$ per cent of the amount of pension you would have got had you retired at the normal time.

How long can you postpone retiring?

You can go on boosting the State pension you are entitled to in this way for 5 years. Once you are more than 5 years over retirement age (ie 70 for a man, or 65 for a woman) your State pension is paid out even if you go on working.

A wife can't claim a pension on her husband's contributions until *he* starts drawing the State pension, so if he postpones retiring, she has to agree to postpone getting her part of his pension too. Her pension too will increase – but by only half the percentage increase earned by her husband for himself.

What to do

You have to let your social security office know *before* you reach retirement age that you are postponing retirement.

The earnings rule

For details of how earnings you have after you've started *drawing* your State pension may affect how much you get ▷ p. 48.

Figure 4.3
NI contributions

	Employees	Employers
Class 1 contributions Standard not-contracted-out rate	6.75%	13.7%
Standard contracted-out rate (1) on first £23 a week (or monthly or other equivalent)	6.75%	13.7%
plus (2) on earnings between £23 and £165 a week (or monthly or other equivalent)	*plus* 4.25%	*plus* 9.2%
Reduced rate for married women and widows who have elected to pay lower contributions (▷ p. 51)	2%	13.7% not-contracted-out rate or 13.7%+9.2% contracted-out rate
Men over 65 and women over 60	Nil	13.7%
Children under 16	Nil	Nil
People earning less than £23 a week (or monthly or other equivalent)	Nil	Nil

Additional retirement pension

● What is it?

A supplement to the basic pension, for those who pay NI contributions on earnings above a certain minimum. The size of what you get and what you pay depends on your earnings.

Note Between April 61 and April 75 you may have contributed to the earnings-related graduated pension (▷ right). If you are retiring in the next few years, most of the earnings-related part of your pension will be the graduated pension rather than the new additional retirement pension which is discussed below.

● How you qualify

By paying enough full Class 1 NI contributions in your 'working life' (▷ p. 51). Note that neither Class 2 and 4 contributions (which you pay if self-employed) nor Class 3 contributions (which are voluntary) help you qualify for this part of the pension. If you belong to an occupational pension scheme which has *contracted out* of this part of the State scheme, you get no additional retirement pension from the State – your employer provides the equivalent or more instead (▷ p. 54 for what contracted out means, and how your pension is made up).

● How it works

People earning below a certain level (£23 a week in April 80) pay no contributions – so *none* of these earnings count towards the additional pension. If you earn over this lower limit you pay NI contributions on the *whole* of your earnings up to a given ceiling (£165 a week in April 80). NI contributions on earnings up to the lower limit count towards your basic pension. Contributions on earnings over the lower limit count towards your additional retirement pension.

The Department of Health and Social Security calculates for each year you work, how much of your earnings counts towards the additional pension. The amount of additional pension is related to the earnings recorded for all these years. But of course, inflation might make your earnings of 25 years ago almost worthless – so these earnings are *revalued* each year. This means that they are increased in line with the way average earnings have increased between the year you earned the money and the year you retire.

When your earnings for each year have been revalued, the best 20 years of earnings are picked out (if you haven't been earning for 20 years, you make do with those you

have). The additional pension you get is $\frac{1}{80}$ (ie $1\frac{1}{4}$ per cent) of each of the best 20 years of revalued earnings.

So, if you clock up 20 years' earnings after 5 April 78, your additional pension will be $\frac{1}{4}$ of your average revalued earnings. But note that you won't be able to clock up 20 years' earnings before retirement age unless you were born after April 1933 (for a man) or April 1938 (for a woman).

● How much

The amount you get depends on how many years you clock up after 5 April 78 before retiring and on how much you earn (though up to a ceiling). Maximum in November 80 was £3.45 (will go up again in April 81). Figure 4.4 below shows how this works out for someone due to retire in 1983 (with 5 years' earnings counting towards his additional pension). Figure 4.5 (p. 54) looks at how much additional pension you could get if you had 25 years to go to retirement after 5 April 78. Note that if inflation continues, someone retiring in 25 years' time will find his revalued earnings – *and* additional pension – much higher than in our example. But the actual buying power of the pension will be the same.

Finally, look at Fig. 4.6 for how your State pension (basic *plus* additional) is likely to compare with your earnings in your last year at work. Note that the more you earn, the bigger the drop if you have to rely on the State scheme alone when you retire – so the more important it may be for you to belong to an occupational pension scheme or to top up your pension by saving in other ways for retirement (▷ p. 46).

Figure 4.4 How your additional pension is worked out

Suppose you have only 5 years of earnings which count towards your additional pension:

Revalued earnings	Additional pension (1/80 of first column)
£ 4,000	£ 50
4,150	51.88
4,450	55.63
4,750	59.38
5,000	62.50
Total additional pension in year you retire	£279.39 a year ie £5.37 a week

Graduated retirement pension

In addition to your basic pension and additional pension, you may also get a *graduated pension* when you retire. Only people who were at least 18 and employed in a job between 1961 and 1975, and who earned more than £9 a week during that time, qualify for this type of State pension. The graduated pension scheme has now been abandoned – but you'll still get the meagre pension that your past contributions have earned.

Between April 61 and April 75, NI contributions were of two kinds: a flat-rate one paid by almost everyone in employment, and a graduated one paid by people who earned more than £9 in any one week.

For each £7.50 he has contributed, a man gets a pension of 2½p a week. If you're a woman, it will have taken £9 of contributions to earn that 2½p a week (the rules were set this way because women retire earlier than men, and live longer).

Your graduated pension is increased in step with rising prices after April 78. But it's still likely to be a small part of your total pension.

At most, a man's graduated pension worked out at £2.88 a week in November 80, a woman's at £2.40 a week – and it's unlikely that many people will have earned even this much.

The Department of Health and Social Security keeps records of how many *units* of pension each person has earned (each unit producing a pension of 2½p a week) – check with your local social security office for details.

Figure 4.5 Additional pension if you retire in 25 years

Suppose you have 25 years of earnings which count towards your additional pension

Revalued earnings	Best years (max.20)	Additional pension (1/80 of second column)
£	£	£
3,840		
3,870		
3,915		
4,086	4,086	51.08
4,052	4,052	50.65
4,071	4,071	50.89
4,005		
4,089	4,089	51.11
4,262	4,262	53.28
4,065	4,065	50.81
4,049		
4,335	4,335	54.19
4,368	4,368	54.60
4,415	4,415	55.19
4,656	4,656	58.20
4,787	4,787	59.84
4,896	4,896	61.20
4,941	4,941	61.76
5,169	5,169	64.61
5,463	5,463	68.29
5,498	5,498	68.73
5,613	5,613	70.16
5,894	5,894	73.68
5,762	5,762	72.03
5,946	5,946	74.33
Total additional pension in year you retire	£1,204.63 a year ie £23.17 a week	

1. Includes the flat-rate pension and any additional retirement pension, but not the graduated retirement pension.
2. Husband and wife each earn half the amount shown in the second column.

What 'contracting out' means

When the new State pension scheme started in April 78, employers who ran pension schemes for their workers (occupational pension schemes) could arrange either to belong to the new State additional pension scheme or not to belong ('contracting out').

If you belong to an occupational pension scheme which is contracted out, you pay lower NI contributions but do *not* get the additional pension from the State. Your pension scheme takes over from the State the job of providing the additional pension. In order to be allowed to contract out, your employer's scheme must provide you with at least as good a pension as the additional pension from the State. This guaranteed pension is called the *guaranteed minimum pension* (GMP). So you won't be worse off than if your scheme was not contracted out — indeed you may be better off. However, with the State scheme, once the additional pension is being paid, it is increased in line with rising prices. Contracted-out schemes aren't expected to foot the bill for increasing the GMP part of your pension in the same way. Instead, the State will pay out any inflation increases to your GMP after you retire.

If your employer decided *not* to contract out, you pay NI contributions in full (▷ Fig. 4.3, p. 52), and get the additional retirement pension in the normal way.

Figure 4.6 Your State pension as a percentage of earnings (1)

Tax year in which you'll be retiring	Your typical yearly earnings in today's money	Single person %	Married couple %	Married couple if both qualify for own pension (2) %
1983–84 with 5 years of additional pension	3,000	51	79	95
	4,000	40	61	73
	5,000	33	50	60
	6,000	29	43	51
	7,000	25	37	44
	8,000	23	34	40
	10,000	19	27	33
	12,000	16	23	29
	15,000	12	18	24
1988–89 with 10 years of additional pension	3,000	55	83	97
	4,000	44	65	76
	5,000	38	55	63
	6,000	34	48	55
	7,000	31	43	49
	8,000	28	39	44
	10,000	23	32	38
	12,000	19	27	34
	15,000	16	21	29
1993–94 with 15 years of additional pension	3,000	58	87	98
	4,000	48	70	78
	5,000	43	59	66
	6,000	39	53	58
	7,000	36	48	53
	8,000	34	44	48
	10,000	28	36	43
	12,000	23	30	39
	15,000	19	24	35
1998–99 with 20 years of additional pension	3,000	62	90	99
	4,000	53	74	81
	5,000	47	64	70
	6,000	44	58	62
	7,000	41	53	57
	8,000	39	50	53
	10,000	33	41	47
	12,000	27	34	44
	15,000	22	27	40

A pension from your job

A good pension from your job may make all the difference between a reasonably comfortable retirement and a hand-to-mouth existence. If you're in an occupational pension scheme, it makes sense to understand how it works and what you can get from it.

Who pays?

Your employer, and usually you too (if your scheme is a *contributory* rather than a *non-contributory* one). If you make contributions to an occupational pension scheme, you'll get tax relief on the payments you make.

Maximum benefits allowed

There are complicated tax rules which a scheme must meet in order to get the favourable tax treatment outlined on p. 46. There are also limits on the maximum benefits which can be paid out by occupational pension schemes. Your scheme may, of course, provide *less* than these maximum benefits.

Examples of maximum retirement benefits the taxman will allow

Pension at normal retirement age	$\frac{2}{3}$ final pay after 10 years' membership. Less than this if lump sum is also paid – for example, if tax-free lump sum is $1\frac{1}{2}$ times final pay, maximum pension is $\frac{1}{2}$ full pay
Cost-of-living increases	Up to the rise in cost of living as measured by Retail Price Index (or, if the taxman agrees, any other suitable index)
Tax-free lump sum on retirement at normal retirement age	$1\frac{1}{2}$ times final pay after 20 years' membership

There are also limits to what the schemes can pay out in other benefits ($\triangleright$ right for what these benefits are). For a discussion of the life insurance you might get from your pension scheme (or separate from it) $\triangleright$ p. 137.

What you'll get from your pension scheme

To work this out you need to know what kind of scheme you belong to. There are four main kinds – the commonest is a *final pay* scheme ($\triangleright$ pp. 56–7 for summaries of the less common schemes).

Final pay schemes

With a final pay scheme, the number of years you've been a member of the scheme, and the yearly amount you're earning at the time you retire – or in the few years before then – normally decide the size of your pension. Many schemes pay $\frac{1}{60}$ of your final pay for each year of membership. Other schemes pay, for example, $\frac{1}{80}$ of final pay.

The maximum pension you can get at normal retirement age is $\frac{2}{3}$ of your final pay – otherwise the scheme falls foul of the taxman. There's a lower maximum if you get a tax-free lump sum.

So if you reach normal retirement age after 40 years' membership of a scheme which pays $\frac{1}{60}$ of your final pay for each year, you can retire on $\frac{2}{3}$ final pay (and you still retire on $\frac{2}{3}$ final pay if you reach normal retirement age after 45 years' membership). By contrast, schemes which work on eightieths would give only half final pay ($40 \times \frac{1}{80}$) after 40 years' membership.

If your employer can afford it, the scheme is allowed to provide the full $\frac{2}{3}$ for members joining the scheme so late that they'll have only 10 years' service before they reach retirement age.

Clearly, the higher your final yearly pay, the higher will be your pension from a given scheme.

It's important to realize that what counts as final pay for working out your pension can be very different from what you actually earn in your last year at work. Different schemes have different rules, but most schemes are based on one of the following definitions of *final pay*:
● average of the best 3 consecutive years' pay in the last 13
● basic salary in the last year before you retire (or last-but-one year), plus average of overtime, commission and bonuses during the last 3 years
● average yearly pay over the last few years (commonly 3 or 5).

Some schemes work on variations of these methods – check with your employer about your scheme.
● Taking account of the State pension
Some final pay schemes make a deduction *either* from the final pay used to work out

Other benefits a pension scheme can provide
Pension schemes can provide other benefits besides a retirement pension for you. They may also provide:
● a pension for you if you are forced to retire early because of ill-health
● a pension for your wife if you die first. Or if you are a married woman, a pension for your husband
● pensions for children or other dependants you leave on death
● an income for you if you have a long spell off work as a result of sickness or disablement (this starts to be paid when your employer *stops* paying you your normal pay). Note that with some employers, this may be provided for all employees – even those not in the employer's pension scheme
● a lump sum for someone you nominate, should you die *before* leaving your job or retiring. (Again, this may not be part of the pension scheme, and may be provided for all employees, whether they belong to the employer's pension scheme or not.)
These benefits are mainly of importance when you are working out how much life insurance you need ($\triangleright$ pp. 133–7).

your pension, *or* from the pension itself, to allow for the fact that you'll be getting some money from the State.

How much your pension is reduced depends on the scheme. Some schemes haven't altered the amount they deduct for years – and it can be as little as £1.70 for each year of membership of the scheme. Other schemes don't specify an amount in £££, but deduct a proportion of whatever the basic single person's State pension amounts to at the time you retire (in November 80 it was just over £1,400). Commonly, the deduction is $\frac{1}{40}$ of the State pension for each year's membership of the scheme.

If your scheme has a deduction of one sort or another for the State pension, and if the normal retirement age in your job is earlier than 65 (or earlier than 60 if you're a woman), the deduction should not apply until you reach the official retirement age for the State pension – but this is something you should check. It's particularly important that it does *not* apply if you're forced to retire early through ill-health.

● Warning.

A scheme which makes little or no reduction to allow for the State pension isn't necessarily better than a scheme which makes a large deduction. What matters is the total amount of pension you end up with.

Tax-free lump sums

You can normally choose to exchange part of the future income from your pension for a tax-free lump sum. But with some schemes, you automatically get a pension *and* a lump sum (part or all of which you may be able to exchange for extra pension).

Men retiring at 65 can expect a lump sum of around £9 for every £1 of pension they forgo. Women retiring at 60 can expect around £11 for every £1 they forgo (women get more per £1, because their pension is expected to be paid for longer – so they're sacrificing more).

The most you can normally get as a lump sum in this way is $\frac{3}{80}$ of your final pay (however defined) for each year in the scheme. So for a full career of 40 years or more in the same scheme, this works out at $40 \times \frac{3}{80} = \frac{120}{80}$ or $1\frac{1}{2}$ times your final pay. (A lump sum of $1\frac{1}{2}$ times your final pay is the most a scheme can pay out without falling foul of the taxman's rules – ▷ p. 55.) If you've less than 40 years' service in the scheme, and if your scheme can afford it, you can still get the maximum lump sum of $1\frac{1}{2}$ times your final pay after only 20 years.

● If you have a choice, should you go for a tax-free lump sum or for a pension? If your pension is inflation-proofed (▷ p. 58) this is so valuable that you should be wary of exchanging any of it for a lump sum. On the other hand, if you don't expect worthwhile increases in your pension after retirement, it could pay you to exchange as much as possible of your pension for a lump sum. If you then use this lump sum to buy an annuity, your after-tax income from the annuity may be more than the pension that you've given up. It would be worth your while to check up close to the time you retire on what income you'd get from an annuity.

Earning extra pension

For details of how you can make extra contributions to your occupational pension scheme (and earn extra pension) ▷ p. 46.

Other, less common ways of working out pensions

Average pay schemes

With average pay schemes, your pension is based on your pay in each year you belonged to the scheme.

The schemes are usually based on a graded scale of earnings. For each year that your pay is in a particular earnings band, you get a fixed amount of pension. As you move up the earnings scale, the amount earned in pension will rise (as will any contributions you pay). The yearly pension you're eventually paid will be the total of all the little bits of yearly pension you've earned in each earnings band.

For example, suppose the scheme uses a very simple graded scale like the one in Fig. 4.7 below:

Fig. 4.7   Example of average pay scheme

	Earnings band	Yearly pension for each year with earnings in this band
Earnings Class A	£1,500 to £2,999	£40
Earnings Class B	£3,000 to £3,999	£50
Earnings Class C	£4,000 to £4,999	£60

Someone with 30 years' service, of which 10 years were spent in each of the 3 earnings classes, would have earned the following pension: $10 \times £40 = £400$, plus $10 \times £50 = £500$, plus $10 \times £60 = £600$, giving a total yearly pension of £1,500.

The drawback with average pay schemes of this type is that by the time you retire, the amount you were earning in the early part of your career – and on which part of your pension is based – will probably bear very little relation to your final pay, because of inflation and promotion. These schemes are therefore likely to give lower pensions than the final pay type, unless the amount of pension earned each year is *revalued* in line with inflation.

Flat-rate schemes

Flat-rate schemes provide a fixed amount of pension – say £5 a year – for each year's membership of the scheme.

Money purchase schemes

The pension from a money purchase scheme is the income that the contributions of you and your employer, added together, will buy. Unlike final pay schemes, both sets of contributions are fixed as a percentage of your earnings, so your employer has some control over the total cost. People joining these schemes late in their working lives won't get much, because the contributions will have had little time to grow, and there won't be many of them anyway.

On the other hand, if you belonged to a money purchase scheme for the whole of your working life you *could* end up with a higher proportion of your final pay as pension than someone in a final pay scheme (subject to the normal $\frac{2}{3}$ limit).

But such a result hinges on several things:

● the rate of return on the money invested for you must keep up with (or overtake) your pay rises. And unfortunately the rate of return on investments may not keep pace with pay rises (and for a number of the past years has failed to do so)

● you must *not* get startlingly high pay rises (through inflation or promotion), particularly if these come late in life. People in this situation are likely to do better with a final pay scheme

● the contributions must be set high enough.

Money purchase schemes should come into their own for people who – like many of us – change jobs several times during the course of their working lives. If all schemes were of the money purchase type, then no matter how frequently you changed jobs you wouldn't normally lose out. The money in each scheme would continue to earn interest right up until the day you retired. By contrast, changing from one final pay scheme to another normally results in a final pension much lower than if you'd had one job all the time ($\triangleright$ p. 59).

However, as most pension schemes are *not* money purchase type, the theoretical advantages of money purchase schemes cannot often be put into practice. In fact, if you ended your career in a money purchase scheme, with previous spells in final pay schemes, you'd get the worst of both worlds. If you were to move from a money purchase scheme to a final pay scheme later in life, you'd be able to cash in on the advantages of both kinds of scheme.

Example

Lucy and Diana are each due to retire next year, after 20 years' membership of their firms' pension schemes. Each of them works out what she will get after retiring.

Lucy is now earning her highest salary ever: £4,950 a year. Her pension scheme uses the average pay rule, and her pension will be made up like this:

For the 3 years when she earned between £1,500–1,999 a year she will get a yearly pension of $3 \times £20 = £60$.

For the 6 years when she earned between £2,000–£2,999 a year she will get a yearly pension of $6 \times £35 = £210$.

For the 7 years when she earned between £3,000–£3,999 a year she will get a yearly pension of $7 \times £55 = £385$.

For the 4 years when she earned between £4,000–£4,999 a year she will get a yearly pension of $4 \times £75 = £300$.

Her yearly pension from her job will be £60 + £210 + £385 + £300 = £955.

Diana, currently earning the same as Lucy, belongs to a pension scheme that uses the final pay principle. She will get $\frac{1}{80}$ of the average of her last 3 years' pay for every year she belonged to the scheme, *plus* a lump sum of $\frac{3}{80}$ of her average final pay for each year she belonged to the scheme. Over the last 3 years her pay averages out at £4,500 (though her pay at the moment is the same as Lucy's), so her yearly pension will be $\frac{1}{80} \times £4,500 \times 20 = £1,125$ and she will get a lump sum of $\frac{3}{80} \times £4,500 \times 20 = £3,375$.

So even though Lucy and Diana have the same length of service behind them, and the same salary upon retiring, one will be considerably better off than the other, because of the way their pensions are worked out (though, of course, they may well have contributed different amounts).

Inflation-proofing

Retirement can last a long time, particularly for women: on average, men retiring at 65 have 12 years of retirement, women retiring at 60 have 20 years. And you'll want an adequate pension not just at the time you retire, but when you're in your seventies. If you still need convincing about the devastating effect of inflation on a fixed income, consider the facts in Fig. 4.8 below:

Figure 4.8 What £1,000 will be worth

	Yearly rate of inflation				
	5%	10%	15%	20%	25%
After 5 years	£783.53	£620.92	£497.18	£401.88	£327.68
After 10 years	£613.91	£385.54	£247.18	£161.51	£107.37
After 15 years	£481.02	£239.39	£122.89	£64.91	£35.18
After 20 years	£376.89	£148.64	£61.10	£26.08	£11.53

A pension of only half your final pay, but inflation-proofed, can soon overtake an apparently better pension of $\frac{2}{3}$ final pay which has no protection against rising prices – ▷ Fig. 4.9.

But not many schemes can promise that pensions will be fully inflation-proofed, because the cost of such a promise cannot even be guessed at. Schemes whose benefits are insured with insurance companies would not get the insurance companies to agree to such a limitless risk. Schemes which are privately run dare not promise more than their resources allow.

Many schemes, however, do promise to increase pensions by a certain percentage each year – because a known increase can be budgeted for. Commonly, an increase of 3 per cent a year is promised – and though better than nothing, this falls far short of today's rate of inflation.

While few schemes can *promise* to increase pensions in line with unknown future inflation rates, some schemes – particularly those run by large companies – have in practice given increases which don't fall far short of inflation. This has been paid for, in the main, by special payments from the company's profits into the pension fund. But how far companies can continue to do this – particularly if inflation takes another turn for the worse, and if companies' profits fail to improve – is uncertain.

Unless your pension is guaranteed inflation proof, you should make some allowance for a fall in its purchasing power while you are retired. You may need to boost your income from non-pension sources as retirement continues – a point to bear in mind when deciding how much you need to save off your own bat for retirement.

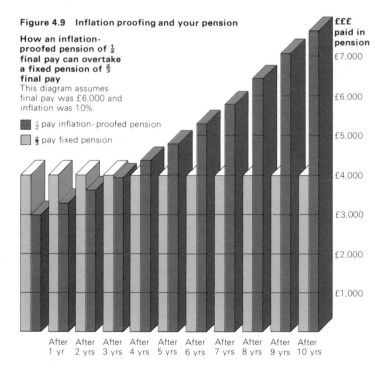

Figure 4.9 Inflation proofing and your pension

How an inflation-proofed pension of $\frac{1}{2}$ final pay can overtake a fixed pension of $\frac{2}{3}$ final pay
This diagram assumes final pay was £6,000 and inflation was 10%.

■ $\frac{1}{2}$ pay inflation-proofed pension
☐ $\frac{2}{3}$ pay fixed pension

£££ paid in pension
£7,000
£6,000
£5,000
£4,000
£3,000
£2,000
£1,000

After 1 yr | After 2 yrs | After 3 yrs | After 4 yrs | After 5 yrs | After 6 yrs | After 7 yrs | After 8 yrs | After 9 yrs | After 10 yrs

Late retirement
Retiring late is something you shouldn't count on too much in advance – even if your employer normally allows it, your health may not permit it, or your views on it may have changed by the time you reach retirement age.

If you do retire late, you'll usually get a higher pension when you eventually retire – but the rules for working it out may be extremely complex. Check with your employer, when the time comes, how your scheme works.

Note that in certain circumstances (and with lengthy periods of service with the same employer) you can increase your pension above the taxman's normal maximum of $\frac{2}{3}$ final pay.

Early retirement
You may be forced to retire early – if ill health, say, cuts your working life short.

But if you *plan* to stop work early (because you like the thought of more leisure for example), bear in mind that you'll end up with a lower pension than if you had worked up to retirement age.

Your pension is likely to be worked out as $\frac{1}{80}$ (or whatever percentage your scheme works on) of your final pay for every year you belonged to the scheme. There may be a reduction to take account of the fact that you are retiring earlier than normal – so are likely to be getting your pension for longer.

If you're thinking of retiring early (for whatever reason), check how your scheme will calculate your pension.

Changing jobs

Unless you stay in one job all your working life, you need to know what happens to your pension rights when you move from one pension scheme to another. And what generally happens ($\triangleright$ examples in Fig. 4.10) is that you lose out.

At the time you change jobs you can choose:

● to take a *preserved pension* ($\triangleright$ right) from your old job – this means that the scheme will pay you the pension you've earned during your membership of the scheme, when you reach normal retirement age for your job

or

● to make a *transfer payment* ($\triangleright$ p. 60) into the pension scheme of your new employer (if the schemes of both old and new employers allow this).

If you changed jobs before April 1980, you could also have chosen:

● to take a refund of all the contributions you had made into the scheme, and get no pension from that job at all.

But now you will only be able to get a refund of contributions you paid up till April 75, *plus* a preserved pension running from that date until the time you changed jobs.

But note that if you're under 26 when you change jobs, or have less than 5 years' membership, your scheme does not have to provide a preserved pension for you nor make a transfer payment to your new employer's scheme. So you may have to take a refund of your contributions.

Preserved pensions

When pensions are worked out on a final pay basis, a preserved pension is likely to be pretty low, for two main reasons.

● the pension will be based on your pay (and years of membership of the scheme) at the time you left the job. For example, if you belonged to a scheme for 20 years and it paid $\frac{1}{60}$ of final pay for each year, your preserved pension would be $\frac{20}{60}$ (ie $\frac{1}{3}$) of *your pay at the time you left*. Your pay at that time may well be very much lower than your final earnings on retirement.

● the pension is unlikely to be increased in line with inflation between the time you leave the job and the time you retire – so the earlier on in your career you change jobs, the less your preserved pension will turn out to be worth. If your employer's scheme is *contracted out*, there are some safeguards ($\triangleright$ right).

For these two reasons combined, the final pension of someone who changes jobs a fair amount is likely to be much lower than someone with the same level of earnings over his working life, but who stayed in one job instead of moving. Figure 4.10 shows the effect on your pension of changing jobs, and of accepting a preserved pension each time. The lower the rate of increase in your pay (we've used 10 per cent), the less you forfeit by changing jobs; the higher the rate, the more you forfeit.

As you can see, someone who changes jobs 4 times ends up with a total pension of around $\frac{1}{4}$ his final pay. But someone with the same year-by-year earnings who works for one employer throughout can end up with a pension of $\frac{2}{3}$ final pay.

Safeguards
If your employer runs his own pension scheme, it can contract out of the new State scheme (which started in April 78). This means that it takes over from the State the job of providing the equivalent of the additional pension ($\triangleright$ p. 53). Broadly, a contracted-out scheme must guarantee that the pensions it pays (including preserved pensions) will not fall below the additional pensions members would have got from the State for their years of membership if the scheme hadn't been contracted-out. This guaranteed minimum pension (GMP) will go up to take account of inflation. So although your preserved pension from a job you leave may start off higher than the GMP you're entitled to for your years of membership, this GMP might eventually catch up with the preserved pension. If that happens, your preserved pension must, from then on, be increased in line with the guaranteed minimum pension.

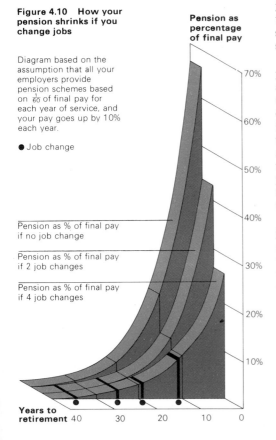

Figure 4.10 How your pension shrinks if you change jobs

Diagram based on the assumption that all your employers provide pension schemes based on $\frac{1}{60}$ of final pay for each year of service, and your pay goes up by 10% each year.

● Job change

Pension as percentage of final pay

70%
60%
50%
40%
30%
20%
10%

Pension as % of final pay if no job change

Pension as % of final pay if 2 job changes

Pension as % of final pay if 4 job changes

Years to retirement 40 30 20 10 0

Transfer payments

You may be able to arrange for the pension scheme of your old employer to make a payment – called a *transfer payment* – into the pension scheme of your new employer (which will then take over responsibility for your pension rights from your old job).

In return for this payment, your new employer will either:

● agree to pay you extra pension from retirement (the amount will normally be fixed in £££ and won't increase in line with future pay increases)

or

● give you a credit of a number of years membership of his scheme. This will almost certainly be fewer years than you had been in your old employer's scheme – because the transfer payment will normally be based on your pay today, whereas your new employer's scheme will eventually pay you a pension based on your pay when you retire (after inflation and promotion have pushed your salary up).

So even if you get a transfer payment, you're likely to lose out on pension as a result of changing jobs.

There's one important exception to this rule. If you're changing from one job to another in the public sector (eg from teacher to civil servant) a transfer payment normally includes an allowance for future pay rises – and your new pension scheme will credit you with years of membership. If the two schemes offer similar benefits, all your years of membership of the old scheme will normally count as years of membership in the new scheme – so there'll be no loss of pension rights when you change' jobs.

If you have to choose between taking a preserved pension or making a transfer payment in the future, the step-by-step guide ($\triangleright$ below) may help you decide which course is best.

What to do when you change jobs

Step 1 Ask the employer you are leaving how much your *preserved pension* will be in £££ a year.

Step 2 Ask him how much the *transfer payment* to your new employer would be. Unless you are very young the transfer payment is likely to be bigger than the answer to Step 1, since it is one single payment, whereas your preserved pension is likely to be paid for a number of years.

Step 3 Now ask your new employer how much yearly pension your old employer's transfer payment (Step 2) will buy. The answer will usually be a fixed addition (in £££ a year) to whatever pension you earn from the years you work in your new job.

Step 4 Better still, ask your new employer how many years of membership he will credit you with in exchange for the transfer payment.

If the answer to Step 3 is greater than the answer to Step 1, you may well benefit from getting a transfer payment rather than accepting a preserved pension. But note that this holds good only if the normal retirement age for the two schemes is approximately the same, and if the schemes' benefits are approximately the same. If the schemes are very different, weighing up the pros and cons gets more complicated.

If you can get an answer to Step 4 which is not too far short of the years of membership in your old employer's scheme, you're likely to benefit from a transfer payment if the two schemes are similar – and provided you don't leave the new job after just a few years.

In fact, getting years of membership credited can work out better than a preserved pension, even if you move to a slightly inferior scheme. This is because, with final pay schemes, extra years will increase the proportion of final pay you will ultimately get in pension – and final pay is likely to be a lot higher on retirement than at the time you changed jobs.

PART TWO

At home and away

5 Buying a home

This chapter concentrates on the procedure for buying and selling property in England and Wales. Parts of the process are different if you are doing so in Scotland or Northern Ireland (▷ pp. 76–7). For more detailed information, check with a local estate agent or solicitor.

Once you start to think about setting up home, you'll realize that the arguments for and against buying need to be weighed particularly carefully – buying a house or flat is likely to be the biggest single investment you make. And once you get involved in actually trying to buy a home it becomes pretty clear that the process of buying is always complicated, and often subject to unnerving set-backs and delays.

That so many people go ahead anyway (owner-occupation in Britain has risen from just under a third of all households to over half in the last 25 years or so) is an indication of the strength of the arguments for buying.

Why buy?
There are really two different kinds of arguments for and against buying: ones that depend on your own particular circumstances (which we call *personal* reasons) and those that are straight financial ones.

Personal reasons
Ask yourself these questions:
- how long do you expect to live in the home? If you have to move quite soon – within 2 years, say – it may not be worth your while to buy. Buying can take a long time, and the incidental expenses are high
- what size of home do you need, and are such homes available to rent/buy in your area?
- do you think your job will mean you have to move from time to time? If so, you'll have more freedom of action when you move if you are already on the ladder of owner-occupation. The supply of rented homes may be good where you live at present but poor in the area to which you'll have to move later on
- what is the supply of rented/owner-occupied homes like in your area? Particularly if you live in the south-east, or close to a large city, you may find rented homes extremely scarce.

Financial reasons
- buying a home is a form of long-term saving. Rent gets you a place to live, but mortgage payments get you this *and* a real asset which you can, if you wish, turn into money in the bank
- it's a form of saving on which you can get tax relief (for details ▷ p. 73). This makes what it costs you to buy a home much less than it looks at first sight
- you should not normally have to pay capital gains tax if you sell your only or main home at a profit
- you should be able to borrow money to buy a home at a very favourable rate of interest (even before allowing for tax relief). In the past, borrowers have generally been able to get money for house purchase much more cheaply than any other form of long-term credit (except, possibly, cheap loans from their employers)
- at a time when the purchasing power of the pound is falling, the purchasing power of what you have borrowed will be falling too. Assuming inflation continues, the £££ you pay back to the building society will (in terms of what you can buy with them) be worth much less than the £££ you borrowed in the first place
- if you buy, you'll end up with one of the very few investments the value of which has, over the long term, more than kept up with inflation. As you can see from Fig. 5.1 on p. 63, house prices have risen faster than prices generally over the past 20 years.

Assuming you can afford the monthly payments, the financial arguments are strongly in favour of buying rather than renting. The force of personal arguments depends, of course, very much on your own particular circumstances.

Keep your options open

Even if you don't want to buy now, it may be wise to start saving with one or two building societies in case your circumstances change later.

Building societies give priority to people who have been saving with them for some time (6 months, say) and have built up a reasonable amount in their account (enough for the deposit, for example).

If you are planning ahead, it's sensible to check with the societies with which you are considering saving. Find out:

● how long you're likely to have to save for and how much you need to have in an account before the society will consider an application for a mortgage

● how much money the society is likely to lend you (▷ p. 66)

● whether it will lend you money to buy the type of home you are likely to want (▷ p. 66)

● what proportion of the price of the home the building society will lend you, assuming the price is in line with the society's valuation

● whether a charge will be made if you pay off the mortgage early

● if you'll want a large mortgage – eg over £15,000 – whether a higher-than-normal interest rate will be charged (▷ p. 73)

● what you can do about your repayments if the mortgage interest rate goes up (eg with a straightforward repayment mortgage some building societies allow you to keep your monthly payments the same but increase the number of years the mortgage lasts).

Choose the societies which seem most likely to be liberal.

If you're going to be a first-time buyer, be sure to join the *Homeloan Scheme*. Under this, if you meet certain conditions, you can top up your mortgage with a loan of £600 from the government (interest-free for 5 years), plus a cash bonus of up to £110 (June 80 figures).

Homeloan Scheme

We give below details of how this scheme worked in June 80 – but the rules may have changed since then and you'll need to check up again for yourself. You qualify for the £600 loan and the £110 cash bonus if:

● you have been saving for at least 2 years, putting your money into an account which qualifies (▷ below for details of qualifying accounts). Your savings must amount to £600 when you apply for your mortgage

● you are at least 18, and buying your first home with a mortgage of at least £1,600 and at least ¼ of the purchase price

● you have had at least £300 in the qualifying account throughout the 12 months before you apply for your mortgage

● the price of the property you want to buy does not exceed a certain limit (which depends on the area the property is in).

Qualifying accounts are run by most of the building societies, and by the High-Street banks. National Savings Bank accounts and Save As You Earn also qualify. When you open your account, ask for and fill in the form provided for prospective members of the scheme. This registers your savings under the scheme.

Figure 5.1 House prices and inflation over the past 20 years

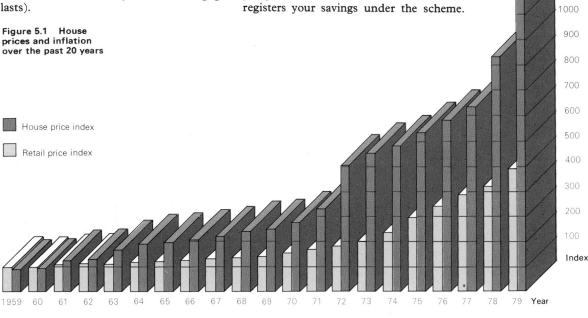

House price index

Retail price index

Action plan for first-time buyers

Jane, a nurse, earning £4,000 a year, and Tim, a teacher, earning £5,500 a year, are planning to marry and buy their own home. This is how the year passes for this pair of first-time buyers.

January

Jane and Tim get engaged.

They start thinking about buying a home.

They go to three local building societies to check up on their lending policies (▷ p. 66).

They start saving (lump sum plus regular monthly deposits with the two that gave the best answers to their questions).

February

They contact their bank manager and tell him what their plans are. He agrees to advance up to £500 to help with furnishing, removals and legal costs.

They start looking at homes in three areas they're interested in.

They study advertisements and estate agents' windows.

They discard one area as too expensive. They take a good look around in the other two (looking at shops, transport, etc – ▷ p. 68).

March

They contact three estate agents in each area to say they are looking for a home. They reckon (taking their savings into account) that the most they can afford to pay is £20,000.

Estate agents' details start flooding in. They sift out the possibles and start looking at property in the price range they reckon they can afford: (£18,000 to £20,000).

They shop around for a solicitor to handle the legal side for them. They ask for an estimate of the fees for doing this (saying they expect to buy a home costing between £18,000 and £20,000).

They check with their local authority whether or not they would qualify for a mortgage, but are told there is little chance of a loan in the near future.

April

They call in at the estate agents' offices again, to say they are still looking. They tell the agents they're interested in anything under £22,000 (they know they couldn't afford that much, but they could always try an offer).

More looking at homes.

May

They find the home of their dreams.

They work out how much it would cost to get it into reasonable shape, and decide they can't afford it.

They carry on looking.

They ginger up the estate agents, who are flagging after 10 weeks with no sale.

June
Find another house, asking price £21,000, owned by Bob and Mary Green. They offer £18,500 subject to contract and survey — ie provided the survey they intend to have done turns out OK and that neither buyer nor seller withdraws from the sale. The offer is turned down.

They try another offer: £19,250. The Greens accept. Jane and Tim contact the Slagthorpe Building Society. The manager says he will lend, subject to the society's valuation of the house (▷ p. 77) They fill in an application form and send it off with the fee of £41 for the building society's valuation. They contact the solicitor they chose in March and ask him to act for them. They contact their own surveyor and ask him to do a structural survey (▷ p. 78). This costs them £90.

Reading between the lines of the survey, they decide the house is fairly sound and won't cost *that* much to put right. They decide to go ahead, provided the Slagthorpe Building Society will lend them enough.

Jane and Tim stand by the letter box all week waiting for the letter from the Slagthorpe.

July
The Slagthorpe offers 75 per cent of their valuation of £18,500, ie £13,875. Not enough. Jane and Tim have only £3,700 saved up. They fill in a form for the Brickport Building Society, and send it off with the valuation fee.

More waiting.

At last, the Brickport offers 85 per cent of valuation of £18,500, ie £15,725, with an indemnity policy (▷ p. 80) to cover the top 5 per cent. Jane and Tim take a careful look at their finances and decide to go ahead. They turn down the Slagthorpe offer and accept the Brickport's. They tell their solicitor to go ahead with checking on the legal side (▷ p. 76). Since the house is registered (▷ p. 76), he says the legal side should not take more than 6 weeks (with luck).

They start planning their wedding for the second week in September. They pay their surveyor, and ask the bank manager to make £500 loan available.

August
Frequent trips to look at 'their' house from the outside — and once or twice to measure for curtains and carpets. They haunt the junk shops for furniture.

The Greens have problems with the house they will be moving into, and say they cannot complete (▷ p. 76) before second week in October.

Jane and Tim decide they'll have to put off their wedding until late October.

September
They get quotes for removals from two firms. Since they're counting pennies now, they decide they'll have to move themselves, to save money.

They exchange contracts (▷ p. 76) with the Greens and arrange house buildings insurance to start right away. They pay 10 per cent of the house purchase price — ie £1,925. They arrange to complete 4 weeks later.

They arrange to have their mail forwarded by the post office for 6 months from 25 October.

October
They tell the gas and electricity boards and the post office when they will be taking over the house so that they can get the meters read and the telephone transferred to their name.

Completion. They hand over to their solicitor the money needed to make up price: they've paid a deposit of 10 per cent (ie £1,925), the mortgage is £15,725, so they still have to pay £1,600 (ie £19,250 minus £15,725 minus £1,925). They pay the solicitor's bill of £370, which includes the fees for searches, registration charges etc. Since the house costs less than £20,000 there's no stamp duty (▷ p. 77) to pay. The house is now theirs.

They move their furniture in. (They tell their house contents insurance company they're moving.)

Wedding and honeymoon.

November
Honeymoon continues.

Jane and Tim move in and start redecorating.

December
Their first Christmas at home.

Harriet Hall earns £6,500 a year. One of the building societies with which she is saving applies the yearly income rule, and is prepared to lend her up to twice her salary – ie up to £13,000. The other uses the monthly outgoings rule, and restricts her outgoings (mortgage repayments) to £125 a month. The result is they will agree to lend her only up to £10,000.

John Vane earns £4,500, and his wife Linda £3,500. The first building society they approach for a mortgage is prepared to lend them up to twice their joint income – ie up to £16,000. The second society is prepared to lend only 2¼ times John's salary, plus once Linda's – ie £10,125+£3,500= £13,625.

Your rights
● Sex discrimination It is illegal for the lender to insist on applying the larger multiple to the husband's income alone. In cases where the wife earns more, it is *her* income which should be used for the higher multiple.

How much can you borrow?

As soon as you've decided you're going to buy your own home, you need to start saving with at least one building society (if you aren't doing so already). You also need to establish how much you'll be able to spend (your price range).

To work out how much you can spend, start from whatever money you have already, and add on the amount you can borrow. What you can borrow depends partly on how the lender regards *you* (▷ below) and partly on the view he takes of the property you're hoping to buy (▷ right). At this preliminary stage you may not have too clear an idea about the kind of home you'll end up wanting to buy. All you may be able to establish is what a lender would be prepared to lend you in principle – ie assuming the home you choose meets whatever the lender's criteria happen to be.

The lender's view of you

What you can borrow depends, in the main, on three factors:

● your regular income (overtime, bonuses, etc, don't normally count unless you can prove that they come in regularly)
● your prospects – lenders tend to look with less favour on those whose income prospects are uncertain (eg because they work in a trade, like building, where lay-offs are common, or because they are in a job where career prospects are uncertain)
● your commitments – these generally are less important than income and prospects, but if you're very heavily loaded with debts already you may find the amount you can borrow restricted. Lenders are also likely to want to know about your family circumstances.

Lenders generally determine how much you can borrow by taking a multiple of your income. They are likely to use either the *yearly income* or the *monthly outgoings* rule.

The yearly income rule

According to this rule (applied by most building societies) you can borrow a multiple of your yearly before-tax income – probably between 2 and 2½ times, depending on the lender's policy.

A married couple, both working, can usually borrow the normal multiple of the larger income, and a lower multiple of the smaller (eg 2¼ times the larger, and once the smaller). Some lenders allow a couple to borrow a multiple of their joint income (eg twice the two incomes combined).

The monthly outgoings rule

Many local authorities apply this rule. It restricts what you can borrow so that your monthly outgoings on your home don't exceed your weekly before-tax income. Monthly outgoings are generally taken as mortgage payments before tax relief. Some lenders also count rates and ground rent as outgoings. A married couple, both working, can generally take as their before-tax weekly income the higher of the two incomes plus a proportion (say, a half) of the other.

Rules for the self-employed

If you're self-employed the lender will generally want proof of your income over the last 3 years. The best proof you can give is annual accounts for that period (or if possible longer), prepared by a professional. Most lenders take your income to be the average of the last 3 years (not so good if your income has risen rapidly over that period, either because of inflation or because business has gone particularly well). Some lenders base the loan on your income for the last year.

If your income fluctuates very sharply from year to year, you'll probably have to resign yourself to the loan being calculated on a lower than normal multiple.

The lender's view of the property

When someone lends you money to buy property, the safety of the loan depends on your ability to repay (▷ left) and their ability to sell the property if you can't keep up the repayments at a price which should give them their money back.

With this in mind, most lenders take two precautions:
● they make their own valuation of the property – this is normally lower than the price you are paying, because it's supposed to be an indication of what the home could be sold for in a hurry
● they make you find some of the money (the deposit) yourself.

They aim to ensure that, even if the property has to be sold at a lower price than they valued it at, the money they have lent you will probably be safe (because they'll actually have lent you less than their valuation). It is you who will carry the loss (just as you will pocket the profit if the property is sold at a higher price than you paid for it).

The size of *deposit* you are asked for will vary according to the lender's estimate of his ability to resell the property quickly, easily and at a good price. However, that estimate will vary, not just from lender to lender, but even from branch to branch of the same lender. So to be quite certain of the society s policy on the sort of property you want to buy, you'll have to ask at the branch to which you intend applying for a loan. However, here are some broad guidelines on the kind of home lenders may not be too keen on.

Property whose value is likely to fall over time

You're most unlikely to be able to get a mortgage at all, if the home comes under this heading. It covers:
- a home at or near the point of collapse – eg a house on a crumbling cliff
- a home on a lease likely to run out within a certain time (25 years, say) after the mortgage ends – eg for a mansion flat on a 25 year mortage, a lease of less than 50 years
- a home subject to a demolition order or likely to become subject to such an order. This partly explains why some building societies are chary about lending in rundown inner city areas. If you do find a lender willing to give a mortgage on this kind of property, you may have to take out an indemnity policy ($\triangleright$ p. 80)
- a home that's very dilapidated. Societies tend to look carefully at homes built before the 1920s, and even more so at homes built in the 1800s. But it shouldn't be impossible to get a loan on an old home in a good condition.

Property which might be difficult to resell

You'll probably have to hunt around for a building society prepared to lend at all. You might have to go to one of the smaller societies which charge above-average rates. Homes that might be hard to resell fast include:
- flats with only one bedroom
- houses with no garden
- converted flats and maisonettes (these should be all right in urban areas, provided the conversion has been done to a reasonable standard)
- property with a sitting tenant
- freehold flats or maisonettes (the problem here is who pays for the repair and maintenance of the building).

Property without basic amenities

If the home has no lavatory or bathroom, for example, or is in very bad repair, the building society may turn your application down flat. Or it may offer only a low propor-

tion of the valuation, or withhold part of the loan until you make certain specified repairs to the building. They might take the last course if, for example, the home needs an inside bathroom or lavatory, major repairs (like a new roof) or rewiring. If the repairs needed are less important – like repointing a wall or repainting outside woodwork, for example – the society may just ask for an undertaking that you will get them done within a specified period – say 6 months.

But don't count on your loan too soon

Even though you've avoided the pitfalls of a property a lender may not go for *and* the lender has agreed in principle that you can borrow a certain amount, you may find that when you apply for the loan it may not be available at all, or it may be much smaller than you bargained for.

There could be several reasons for this:

The building society may be short of money

The money that the building society lends you has been borrowed from other members of the public. If building society rates for savers become uncompetitive, those savers will put their money elsewhere (and new savings will not flow in at the usual rate). Building societies generally deal with this by putting their rates up to both savers and borrowers. But in the meantime they may turn your application down flat, or tell you that you have to join a queue for it, or impose a lower-than-normal limit on the amount that you may borrow.

Government intervention

Many people argue that house price movements partly reflect the availability of money. When house prices threaten to rise very rapidly, the government may put pressure on the societies to 'voluntarily' restrict their lending – eg a building society may put a limit on the amount which it will lend to any one applicant.

What to do

If you find that one particular lender is not prepared to give you as much as you want, don't despair. It's worth trying to borrow more from a different lender, or it might be possible to top-up the first loan with other funds ($\triangleright$ p. 74). Think, too, about trying to renegotiate a lower price with the seller; he may accept less than he wanted originally rather than lose a buyer.

Finding property

Remember three things when property-hunting:

- take estate agents' descriptions with a pinch of salt. They are acting for the seller, not the buyer: their facts will probably be accurate, but you should form your own opinions. And don't expect them to point out the property's defects
- be prepared for the business to go on for months (you might be lucky and find your dream house in the second batch of estate agents' literature, but most people don't)
- never, never rush into a purchase.

Talk to the neighbours, if you see them. Look round the area carefully, remember that a pub or restaurant next door can be a drawback as well as an advantage. Don't make decisions on the strength of a Sunday or bank holiday visit – on weekdays the place may seem quite different (especially if there's a school or a factory nearby). When you do make an offer, make it 'subject to contract and survey' (things work differently in Scotland and Northern Ireland – ▷ pp. 76–7).

What to look for

Before you commit yourself to buying, there are matters other than whether or not you like the property and the area to consider.

How much will it cost you to live there?

- Rates

These vary widely from area to area, and in urban areas there can be striking differences from street to street. Even spread over the year (▷ p. 99) rates can make a fair hole in your budget. Ask about the level of water and sewerage rates, too.

- Service charges

These are likely to be a significant drain on your resources if you are buying a flat or maisonette. Grill the present owners, not just on the current level of charges and what they cover, but also on what has happened to the charges over the past few years. Bumping up the service charge is one way for an unscrupulous ground landlord or his agent to make a little extra.

- Fuel costs

Ask the present owners about the size of their fuel bill – and check while you're there what form of heating they use, and how good their draught insulation is.

- Commuting costs

These may take you by surprise – particularly if you'll have to switch from one form of transport to another (from bus to car or train, for example). If you're going to have to pay much more than you are used to for travel to and from work, you want to know about it in advance. Find out before you buy.

What will you have to pay for repairs, and so forth?

You may well want to redecorate and buy new curtains and carpets. You may also need to make substantial repairs – like damp proofing, rewiring, treating rot or woodworm, or doing up the bathroom or kitchen. If you aren't an experienced handyman, you'll need professional help for some of these jobs. Take a careful look at the home before you decide to buy it. See Fig. 5.2 for things you should watch out for.

Make sure you go and look at the property in daylight – and try to see it when it's raining if possible. Try to find out what repairs have recently been carried out. If you find anything that looks suspicious raise it with the sellers.

- But don't overestimate your own expertise in spotting defects. It could well pay you – if only in peace of mind – to have a structural survey done (▷ p. 78). If there are obvious repairs that need doing, get estimates of what the work will cost (your surveyor should be able to help).

What about local amenities?

- Public transport

How far is it to the nearest train or bus stop? How reliable is public transport in the neighbourhood?

- Shops

Are they far away? Are they adequate? How easily can you get to them (particularly important for those with young children or elderly relatives in the household)?

- Schools

How easy are they to get to, and what are they like?

- Leisure and cultural facilities

What are the libraries like? The parks, pubs, adult education centres, cinemas, sports clubs?

How easy should it be for you to resell?

You had better give some thought to this, just as your lender will.

Look at the general appearance of the houses near yours. If they look neglected, it could be that the area is going down rather than up in the world, and this will affect you when you try to resell later.

Find out if there are plans in the pipeline – for a block of flats or a new road, say –

Figure 5.2 What to watch out for

Faulty roof
What to look for
Damp stains on upstairs walls (inside or out) and ceilings, missing or broken tiles, bumpy top to flat roof
When not to worry
If there's only one small damp stain, it may be just a few missing tiles or a blocked or broken gutter – check
When to worry
If there are many damp stains, or signs of damp (eg mould) – especially if the property is old or the roof is flat

Damp-proof course bridged, damaged or missing
What to look for
Damp stains on down-stairs walls, starting near skirting boards
When not to worry
If staining is localised, look outside to see if damp-proof course is bridged – eg covered by earth. If so, you may only need to remove whatever's bridging it. If the property is old, the damp-proof course may have broken
When to worry
If there is staining in a lot of places it may mean a broken damp-proof course, or none at all – could be expensive to put right

Leaking water pipes, old plumbing
What to look for
Damp stains on ceilings or walls. Pipes (inside or out) which have been replaced, or which are made of lead but repaired with copper
When not to worry
If there's only one stain, it may have been caused by a burst water pipe – not too expensive a repair
When to worry
If there are many damp stains and property is old, or some of the pipes have been replaced, plumbing may need replacing. Lead pipes repaired with copper are unsatisfactory

Damp penetration/ walls
What to look for
Damp stains on inside walls, or mortar between outside bricks soft or loose
When not to worry
If damp isn't extensive (eg if only small amount of mortar needs replacing)
When to worry
If damp is widespread (eg if it looks as if you need to repoint the whole building)

Condensation
What to look for
Water on inside of walls and windows. Mould on walls, window frames
When not to worry
Certain amount of condensation is normal – especially in kitchen and bathroom
When to worry
If walls are always damp, it may cause mould or wet rot. Curing severe condensation can be expensive

Wet rot
What to look for
Damp in the wood – the fibres will break apart. Look particularly at floorboards, skirting boards, and around window frames
When not to worry
If rot isn't extensive, it can be cured by replacing the affected timber
When to worry
If a lot of timber is affected, may be expensive to repair

Dry rot
What to look for
Thrives in damp, unventilated conditions. Look particularly at floorboards, and in cellar and loft. Signs of dry rot are dry, cracked, powdery wood and musty smell. If the house has wooden

floors downstairs, there should be air-bricks low down in outside wall – check they're not blocked
When not to worry
Dry rot is always worrying
When to worry
Any house affected by dry rot will need expensive repairs

Woodworm (or beetle)
What to look for
Thrives in the same sort of conditions in which dry rot thrives. Look for tiny holes in wood
When not to worry
Woodworm may have been treated. If only small amount of wood affected fairly cheap to treat
When to worry
If large areas of home are badly affected. Wood may have been weakened – and need replacing

Faulty window frames
What to look for
With wooden frames, look for wet rot. With metal window frames, look for rust
When not to worry
If only 1 or 2 window frames are affected
When to worry
If the window frames have all rotted or rusted badly they will need to be replaced – an expensive repair

Settlement, subsidence
What to look for
Cracks, both inside and out, in the brickwork and plaster, particularly around window and door frames. Gap between floor and skirting board. Trees close to house can cause subsidence
When not to worry
If cracks are hairline and haven't moved for several years
When to worry
If there are signs that the building is still moving – eg, a sign that the cracks have been repaired and cracked again. Serious subsidence could be expensive to repair

Faulty or old wiring
What to look for
Look at electric sockets to make sure they take square-pin plugs. Check that wiring in roof space, under floorboards and around fuse box and meter doesn't look old, worn or untidy – as a rule, wiring can be expected to last for 25 years
When not to worry
If the electric sockets take square-pin plugs and wiring looks reasonable
When to worry
If there are old-fashioned sockets or the wiring looks worn, untidy or is more than 25 years old

Leaking water pipes, old plumbing

Damp penetration/walls

Woodworm (or beetle)

Faulty roof

Wet rot

Dry rot

Faulty or old wiring

Faulty window frames

Condensation

Settlement, subsidence

Damp-proof course bridged, damaged, or missing

which may lower the value of your home when they are carried out. Your solicitor will carry out a *search* with the local council which should reveal plans for putting up a block very near by, but distant blocks or plans at a very early stage may slip through the net. So talk to the local council planning department, check with the local papers and ask your prospective neighbours.

Examples

Sam and Sandra Smith have just moved into a sixth-floor flat in a modern block on Property Street. They have borrowed up to the hilt from the building society to do it, and have in addition borrowed from the bank and on Access to pay the incidental costs and the cost of furnishing the flat. They have allowed for the rates (£180 a year, which they'll pay in 10 instalments of £18) and for the fact that they have to redecorate. But they haven't allowed for the service charge, which is a stiff £300 a year. Of their joint monthly income of £260 after tax, National Insurance and the mortgage payments, they now have the following tied up in regular outgoings:

Rates	£18
Service charge	£25
Bank and HP repayments	£44
Access repayments	£14
Electricity	£20
Telephone	£12
Insurance (house, contents, mortgage protection)	£5
Commuting	£40
Total	£178

This leaves them with just £82 a month for food, living expenses, clothes, entertainment, holidays, and further purchases for their new flat. Obviously life is going to be tough for the Smiths for a while: and certainly neither of them can afford to be out of work for the moment.

Anthony and Anthea Alton bought one of the big 1930s houses halfway down Property Street 6 months ago, largely because they have 3 growing children to accommodate.

They planned to send the children to the local comprehensive; but the eldest was unhappy there, and after one term they took him away. He now goes to a private day school, which is pricey. They're very happy with their house and like the area, but the move has proved very much more expensive than they anticipated; they might have done better staying where they were before and extending that house instead.

Joseph and Judith James have bought one of the Victorian cottages at the far end of Property Street. They succeeded in getting it at a lower price than they were prepared to spend, borrowing 60 per cent of the valuation from the local authority. Once they moved in it was apparent that – as their survey had pointed out – there was a great deal of work to be done. Estimates came to:

Part replacement of roof	£500
Some replumbing	£200
Damp course installation	£420
New windows in three rooms	£180
Treatment for dry rot	£90
Total	£1,390

This is before allowing for doing up kitchen and bathroom, or any redecoration.

They may be able to get a grant from the local authority towards the cost of some of the work that needs to be done (▷ p. 82), but will have to borrow the rest from the bank or find it elsewhere. What's more, after 6 months of sharing the place with the builders, they say that if they'd realized that things would be this bad, they wouldn't have gone ahead in the first place. (In a year's time they may love it.)

Types of mortgage

Which type to go for

In Fig. 5.3 we give details of what different types of mortgage might cost. Below we give a summary of how each type works. As you'll see from the verdicts, the best buy for most people will be either a repayment mortgage, or a lower-cost endowment mortgage.

If you want to keep your costs down to a minimum in the early years, go for a repayment mortgage. The lower-cost endowment mortgage costs more early on, but will leave you with a lump sum when the mortgage is paid off. If it suits you to make this kind of long-term investment at the same time as you're paying off the mortgage, this scheme is worth thinking about. But with any sort of endowment mortgage, you *have* to increase your monthly payments if the interest rate goes up while you're still paying off the loan. You might not have to do this with a repayment mortgage ($\triangleright$ right).

Repayment mortgage

● Who lends the money?
A building society or local authority.
● How you pay off the loan
By regular – normally monthly – payments. Part of each payment is interest on the amount you still owe, the rest goes towards paying off the loan.

In the early years, most of each payment is interest, and only a little goes towards paying off the loan. With a 25-year mortgage, for example, you'll have paid off only $\frac{1}{10}$ of the loan after 10 years if the interest rate is 15 per cent.

But as the amount you owe goes down, the proportion of each payment needed to pay the interest goes down, and the proportion that goes towards paying off the loan goes up.
● What you pay out
Depends on the size of the mortgage, the interest rate, and the length of the mortgage. The black figures in Fig. 5.4 (overleaf) give the monthly payment for each £1,000 you borrow for a range of different interest rates and lengths of mortgage.

If the mortgage interest rate goes up, most building societies will allow you to extend the length of your mortgage, rather than insist on you increasing your monthly payments. Note that a large increase in the mortgage interest rate (2 per cent, say) can mean that your payments *have* to go up – otherwise they might not be enough to pay the interest on what you owe.

With this type of mortgage, you might also want to pay for a *mortgage protection policy* – a type of life

---

Figure 5.3. What the different types of mortgage cost (1)

Monthly after-tax-relief cost of a £10,000 mortgage for 25 years

		If you pay tax at the basic rate only £	If you pay tax at top rate of 60% £	Do you get a cash sum at the end?
Repayment mortgage (2)	1st year	89	56	
	5th year	94	57	
	10th year	96	62	No
	15th year	100	70	
	20th year	109	87	
With-profits endowment mortgage (3)		120	82	Yes – £20,000 plus, say
Lower-cost endowment mortgage (3)		103	65	Yes – £2,500 plus, say
Non-profit endowment mortgage (3)		108	69	No
Option mortgages —*monthly cost the same whatever rate of tax you pay*				
Repayment type (4)		97		No
Lower-cost endowment type (5)		106		Yes – £2,500 plus, say

1. For a healthy, 30-year-old man. Basic rate of tax 30 per cent.
2. Including £2 a month mortgage protection policy. Rate of interest 15 per cent.
3. Rate of interest $15\frac{1}{4}$ per cent.
4. Rate of interest effectively $10\frac{1}{2}$ per cent.
5. Rate of interest effectively 11 per cent.

insurance designed to pay off the mortgage if you die ($\triangleright$ p. 140). For a healthy 30-year-old man, this would add an extra 15 to 20p or so a month to the cost of a mortgage for each £1,000 borrowed.
● Tax relief
For general rules about tax relief $\triangleright$ opposite. You get tax relief on the interest part of each payment at the highest rate of tax you pay. The amount of tax relief you get falls over the years, as the proportion of each payment which is interest falls. So the after-tax-relief cost of a repayment mortgage rises over the length of the mortgage. (Note that because of inflation, the buying power of what you pay out after tax relief may actually fall over the length of the mortgage.) The blue entries in Fig. 5.4 show the after-tax-relief cost of each £1,000 of mortgage to a basic rate taxpayer in the first year of the mortgage.

Verdict
Worth considering:
● cheapest in early years if you pay enough tax
● flexible if interest rate rises
● best buy for tax-payers whose finances will be strained by taking out a mortgage.

With-profits endowment mortgage

● Who lends the money?
A building society or insurance company.
● How you pay off the loan
With the proceeds of a with-profits endowment insurance policy. The policy guarantees you enough to pay off the loan at the end of the mortgage – plus whatever bonuses the insurance company adds. This means you should get back very much more than you need to pay off the loan. At present bonus rates, you could expect to get more than 3 times the amount you need to pay off the mortgage – leaving you with a large lump sum at the end (though, because of inflation, it may not be that large in terms of buying power).
If you die before the end of the mortgage, the insurance policy pays out enough to pay off the loan (plus the bonuses already added to the policy).
Note that many lenders won't let you link your mortgage to a *unit-linked* life insurance policy. With this type of policy your premiums are invested in a fund of shares or property, for example, and what you get back

at the end depends on how well the fund does.
● What you pay out
Interest on the full amount of the loan for the period of the mortgage. Most building societies charge a rate of interest which is $\frac{1}{4}$ or $\frac{1}{2}$ per cent higher than the rate they charge on a repayment mortgage. Insurance companies normally charge a higher rate of interest than building societies – often around 1 per cent more.
You also pay premiums for the insurance policy. For a healthy 30-year-old man taking out a 25-year mortgage, the monthly premium is around £3.10 for each £1,000 borrowed.
● Tax relief
You get tax relief on the interest at the highest rate of tax you pay.

Verdict
Not recommended:
● costs more each month than any other type of mortgage – but leaves you with a lump sum at the end
● not flexible if interest rate rises
● really a way of investing as well as a means of buying a home.

Lower-cost endowment mortgage

● Who lends the money?
A building society or insurance company.
● How you pay off the loan
With the proceeds of a special type of insurance package – sold under names like *Build-up House Purchase Plan* and *Mortgagemaster*. Basically, the package is a combination of a with-profits endowment policy and term insurance. The with-profits policy normally guarantees just under half the amount you'd need to pay off the loan at the end of the mortgage, *plus* whatever bonuses the company adds. At present bonus rates, you should get back more than 3 times the amount that's guaranteed. This would be more than enough to pay off the loan – leaving you with a lump sum worth about a quarter of the amount of the mortgage.
If you die before the end of the mortgage, the loan will be partly paid off by the with-profits policy. The rest of the loan will be paid off by the term insurance included in the package.
● What you pay out
Interest on the full amount of the loan, for

the period of the mortgage – normally at the rate being charged for a with-profits endowment mortgage ($\triangleright$ left).
You also pay premiums for the insurance package. For a healthy 30-year-old man taking out a 25-year mortgage, the monthly premium is around £1.40 for each £1,000 borrowed.
● Tax relief
You get tax relief on the interest in the same way as for a with-profits endowment mortgage.

Verdict
Worth considering:
● costs more than repayment mortgage in early years – but likely to leave you with a lump sum at the end
● not flexible if interest rate rises
● really a way of investing (on a smaller scale than with a with-profits mortgage) as well as a means of buying a home.

Figure 5.4 Repayment mortgage: monthly cost (in £££) for each £1,000 of mortgage (1)

Black figures: payment before allowing for tax relief
Blue figures: after-tax-relief cost to a basic rate taxpayer during first year of mortgage (2).

Length of loan in years	Rate of interest							
	10%	11%	12%	13%	14%	15%	17%	19%
15	10.96	11.59	12.24	12.90	13.57	14.25	15.66	17.10
	8.46	8.84	9.24	9.65	10.07	10.50	11.40	12.35
20	9.79	10.46	11.16	11.86	12.58	13.31	14.81	16.34
	7.29	7.71	8.16	8.61	9.08	9.56	10.55	11.59
25	9.18	9.90	10.63	11.37	12.12	12.89	14.46	16.05
	6.68	7.15	7.62	8.12	8.62	9.14	10.20	11.30
30	8.84	9.59	10.35	11.12	11.90	12.69	14.30	15.92
	6.34	6.84	7.35	7.87	8.40	8.94	10.04	10.17

1. Excluding cost of mortgage protection policy.
2. Basic rate of tax 30 per cent. For rules about tax relief $\triangleright$ opposite.

Non-profit endowment mortgage

● Who lends the money?
A building society or insurance company.
● How you pay off the loan
With the proceeds of a non-profit endowment insurance policy. The policy guarantees you just enough to pay off the loan at the end of the mortgage – with no lump sum left over.

If you die before the end of the mortgage, the insurance policy pays off the loan.
● What you pay out
Interest on the full amount of the loan for the period of the mortgage – normally at the rate being charged for a with-profits endowment mortgage (▷ opposite).

You also pay premiums for the insurance policy. For a healthy 30-year-old man taking out a 25-year mortgage, the monthly premium is around £1.85 for each £1,000 borrowed.
● Tax relief
You get tax relief on the interest in the same way as for a with-profits endowment mortgage.

Verdict
Worst buy:
● costs more than a lower-cost endowment mortgage – but leaves you with no lump sum at the end
● not flexible if interest rate rises

The option mortgage scheme

This is a government-run scheme to help people whose tax bills aren't large enough for them to benefit fully from the tax relief available on mortgage interest. With an option mortgage, you pay a lower rate of interest instead of claiming tax relief, and the government pays a subsidy to the lender. The subsidy is supposed to be roughly equivalent to the amount of tax relief a basic-rate taxpayer would get if the lender charged him the normal rate of interest. So an option mortgage would benefit people who do not pay tax at the basic rate (or higher rates) on at least as much of their income as they'd pay in interest with an ordinary mortgage.

With a repayment mortgage, the subsidy means that you pay 10½ per cent interest if the mortgage rate is 15 per cent. The rate you have to pay depends on what the basic rate of tax is at any particular time. Check with a building society or other lender at the time you want the loan. Because there's no tax relief, the cost of your monthly payment is the same over the whole period of the loan.

With an endowment mortgage under the option mortgage scheme, you pay interest at 11 per cent if the lender normally charges 15¼ per cent for endowment mortgages.
● Joining and leaving the option mortgage scheme
Most lenders will let you have an option mortgage – you are normally asked if you want to join the scheme when you apply for a mortgage. If you've already got a mortgage and – because of the rate of tax you now pay – you think it would pay you to change to (or from) an option mortgage, check with your lender whether you can change and what notice you need to give.

You're unlikely to be able to change to, or from, an option mortgage unless your present mortgage has been going for at least a year. And you can't keep swapping backwards and forwards – for each mortgage, you're normally allowed just one change – either to an option mortgage, or from it.

Verdict
Best buy for non-taxpayers
● cheapest if you can't benefit fully from tax relief on mortgage interest.

Tax relief

You can get tax relief on the interest you pay on up to £25,000 of loans to buy (or improve) your main home.

For each £ of interest that you get tax relief on, you escape paying tax on the most heavily taxed £ of your income. For example, if you pay tax at 30 per cent you save 30p tax for each £ of interest. So each £ of interest costs you £1 *minus* 30p = 70p. If you pay tax at higher rates, or the investment income surcharge, you save even more tax.

If you move home, you can normally get tax relief for up to 12 months on the interest you pay on up to £25,000 of any bridging loan, too – so long as it is a loan, and not an overdraft.

Note that you get a subsidy from the taxman automatically on the premiums you pay for any life insurance policy to do with your mortgage (▷ p. 222 for details).

Where to go for the money

Although building societies are the main source of money for home purchase in this country, they are not the only one. It may also be possible to borrow from a local authority, or from your employer (generally at a lower-than-normal rate of interest), or from an insurance company or bank.

Borrowing from a building society

When building societies receive applications for mortgages, they give priority to people who have been saving with them for some time and have built up a certain amount (enough, say, for the deposit on a home), or to people who have loans from them already.

Since you'll have to put the savings for your deposit and the many other expenses of buying (▷ p. 75) somewhere, it's sensible to try to try to take advantage of this policy by placing them with the societies to which you intend to apply for a loan.

Even if you do save with a building society, you may still need extra help when money is tight (▷ p. 67). Then you may have to enlist the services of a mortgage broker (▷ p. 75). In normal circumstances, however, you should apply directly to the society for your money (otherwise you may have to pay the broker a fee).

When you apply, the society will send you a form to fill in, asking for details of:
● your age, occupation and employer, income, dependants, and the names of referees
● the amount of money you want to borrow, and the period for which you want to borrow it (generally between 15 and 25 years, though some societies will, in exceptional circumstances, lend for as long as 35 years)
● the property you want to buy: whether house or flat, freehold or leasehold; the number of bedrooms, reception rooms, etc; whether there is a garden, garage, etc
● the price you have agreed to pay.

This application form has to be returned, with the building society's valuation fee (▷ p. 77), and you should hear fairly quickly (within 3 weeks or a month, say) whether your application has been accepted.

Points to watch
● Large loans
Many societies increase the rate of interest charged on large loans (commonly inter-

preted as £15,000 and over). Some simply add on another ¼ or ½ per cent, others operate a sliding scale – they charge an extra ¼ per cent, say, for loans over £15,000, an extra ½ per cent over £20,000, and so on. Each society has a different policy, so if you know you will need a large loan, it's worth asking before you decide where to put your savings.

● Early repayment
Some societies make an extra charge – it can be as much as an extra 3 months' interest – if you pay off your mortgage in the early years. However this charge is often waived if you take out another mortgage with the same society within 6 months.

● Interest rates can vary
They may go up as well as down. Check whether, with a repayment mortgage, the society will allow you to increase the number of years, and keep the monthly payment the same.

Borrowing from a local authority

If you can't get a loan from a building society, either because your income is too low, or because the house or flat you want does not suit them (eg because it's too old, or in a run-down inner city area), you could try the local authority in whose area the home is. But don't rely on getting a loan from the local authority:

● their ability to lend may be restricted by central government cut-backs in spending
● the interest rates they charge are generally higher than those charged by building societies.

The advantage of local authority loans are that they may lend where building societies (or insurance companies, ▷ right) won't, and that they'll give mortgages of up to 100 per cent of the valuation.

Borrowing from your employer

If you work for a financial organization (like a bank, building society or insurance company) you are almost certain to be able to get a loan from your employer at a lower-than-normal rate of interest. Even if your employer doesn't lend money for mortgages, it's still worth asking him what help he can give you. He may be able to give you an introduction to a building society or local authority to help you get a mortgage.

If your employer can't help, your trade union or professional association might be able to.

Borrowing from an insurance company

A few insurance companies give full-scale mortgages for home buyers, although generally speaking their lending policies are stricter than than those of the building societies.

You repay by taking out an endowment policy on which you pay premiums at the same time as paying interest (it may be variable or fixed). The insurance company may insist that you take out a non-profit endowment mortgage – the *worst buy* (▷ p. 73).

You might *have* to go for a non-profit endowment mortgage from an insurance company if you want a very large mortgage (£25,000 or more, say). Other lenders (apart from banks – ▷ below) are usually reluctant to give such large loans.

Borrowing from a bank

Some banks are making full-scale loans for buying homes. Check with the bank on restrictions – eg it may be only for large loans (greater than £25,000, say) or for relatively short periods of time (less than 10 years).

Other lenders

You might be able to arrange a private mortgage through a solicitor, or the person you're buying the home from, for example. Terms vary and it makes sense to get your own solicitor to check the mortgage deed for you.

Warning: If the seller offers to give you a mortgage himself – beware. It may mean that none of the usual lenders will give a mortgage on the home – and you'll have problems when you come to sell it.

Topping-up loans

If a building society has offered you an inadequate loan, you may be able to top it up to the level you need by borrowing more money from some other source. Note that if you can't get a big enough mortgage because your income is too low, or the home you want to buy is old or unusual, you're not likely to be able to get a topping-up loan from a bank or insurance company. They tend to have stricter lending policies than the building societies.

From a bank

These loans are generally arranged on much the same basis as a 5-year ordinary loan (▷ p. 210). You generally pay back the loan in instalments, and you pay whatever the current interest rate on your outstanding debt may be.

From an insurance company

These loans are generally repaid from the proceeds of an endowment policy over the same period as the mortgage. The company will insist that you take out endowment policies to cover both the loan from the building society and the loan they make. And they will probably insist that one of the endowment policies should be non-profit. The interest you pay on the topping-up loan is normally at a higher rate than that for a building society loan.

Through a broker

A broker is likely to arrange a loan from an insurance company. But he may go to a finance house, and loans from finance houses tend to be very pricey. So if you go through a broker, it's worth checking where he is getting the money from and what it will cost. And ▷ p. 207 for your rights as far as broker's fees go.

Points to watch

Some building societies won't allow you to take out a topping-up loan. So ask before you arrange one – and be prepared to argue. And you may find it difficult to get a topping-up loan if you need less than £1,000 (though your bank may help) or you want a top-up of more than your original building society loan.

Bridging loans

If you find yourself in a situation where your long-term borrowing is satisfactorily arranged, but an awkward gap has developed in the short term, you need a *bridging loan*.

This could happen if, for example:

● you arrange a building society mortgage on an old and picturesque cottage, but the society retains part of the money until essential repairs are done

● you arrange to sell your house and to buy another. You need to have 10 per cent of the purchase price of your new home available for the deposit when you exchange contracts, but at that stage you have received nothing on the sale of your existing home.

You can almost certainly arrange bridging finance from your bank, although – since the amounts involved are apt to be large – they might want some sort of security for their money: generally an irrevocable authority to your solicitor to pay them back when your long-term funds come in will be enough. The loan works like an ordinary loan (▷ p. 210), but there will

be a charge for arranging it – around 0.3 per cent of the amount you borrow, or a flat charge of £40, say. You have to pay this even if you decide not to use the bridging loan you've arranged.

Note that you can normally get tax relief on interest you pay on a bridging loan – ▷ p. 73 for more details.

Other expenses

Over the long term, it is vital for you to sort out the right kind of mortgage to get. But when you are at the point of buying, incidental expenses are likely to seem a much more pressing problem. The cash you need mounts up in an alarming way, particularly for the first-time buyer – and the second-time buyer has the expense of selling his existing home to consider too.

Try to get as much cash together as possible – preferably by saving, but failing that by borrowing – before you venture into the property market. And take fully into account the expenses listed below. The checklist on p. 79 may help you work out the likely overall cost of the move.

The deposit

Unless you can get a local authority mortgage, or money is very plentiful, you had better assume you will need to provide something like 20 per cent of the purchase price as a deposit.

Second-time buyers score when it comes to finding the deposit, because their existing home is likely to have risen in value since they bought it. The Homeloan Scheme (▷ p. 63) now exists to help first-time buyers.

Legal fees and taxes

When you buy a home, the legal fees come in all shapes and sizes. It's well worth shopping around to see whether you can reduce the size of your bills. And you'll need to take account of any land registry fee or stamp duty you have to pay.

Solicitor's fees

A solicitor charges for the work involved in the transfer of ownership of property from one person to another – known as *conveyancing* (▷ overleaf for what's involved).

By law, solicitors and notaries public are the only people who are allowed to charge for drawing up documents for transferring property. If you can do your own conveyancing yourself, however, you aren't breaking any law.

Some *conveyancing firms* have been successfully prosecuted for breaking the law — but others go on operating. If you use one, you may find them cheaper than a solicitor, but you may not get quite as strong safeguards as if you'd had a solicitor to do the conveyancing. Solicitors, for example, must have professional indemnity insurance, which will pay out if they are sued for negligence. And they have to keep money held on behalf of their clients (like deposits) in special accounts separate from their main business accounts — so the money isn't lost if they go bankrupt. Nor can they run off with it.

Reckon on paying a solicitor between £250 and £350 if you're buying a home, and around another £200 or so if you're selling too. These figures include the building society's solicitor's fees (▷ below). Conveyancing firms may be £50 to £100 cheaper.

What's involved in conveyancing

(The details given here apply to England and Wales. For Scotland and N. Ireland ▷ right.)

When you find a home you want to buy, you make an offer for it subject to *contract and survey*. Neither buyer nor seller is legally committed to going through with the deal at this stage — the seller can choose to sell to someone who makes a better offer and the buyer can change his mind.

Before exchanging contracts make sure that you want (and have the money) to buy the home. In particular you need to be happy with:
● the mortgage offer you have received
● the inquiries you or your solicitor make about the property — for example, that there are no doubts about the boundaries of the garden, that there are no plans to build a motorway past your front door, that the owner of the home isn't under any obligation to the council to pay for roads to be made up
● the results of your private survey
● that you have sold your current home (if you've got one to sell).

Exchange of contracts to completion
When you exchange contracts you have to pay a deposit (normally to the seller's solicitor and usually 10 per cent of the price of the home). You won't get this deposit back if you pull out after exchanging contracts — indeed, if you pull out after this stage the seller can also sue for costs (less your deposit) he incurs as a result.

After exchanging contracts, the legal work consists mainly of checking on the seller's ownership of the home, and drawing up the documents which will prove the buyer's ownership of the home, making sure that no-one else has made any claims on the property (eg that the seller's wife who is not the joint owner hasn't registered an interest because it is the matrimonial home), making sure that the building society is happy with the way the legal work has been done and so on.

On completion day, the buyer pays the seller a banker's draft for the money owing (which would include the balance of the purchase price plus, for example, any money that the seller has paid in rates bills for the period after completion). The seller gives the buyer the original documents which prove his ownership of the property, the signed document which transfers ownership to the buyer and proof that any mortgage has been paid off (or a solicitor's undertaking that it will be within a stated period). The buyer is then free to move in.

Building society's solicitor's fee

You have to pay a fee to the solicitor who draws up the mortgage deed. If you yourself are using a solicitor, he will normally be able to act for the building society as well — in which case he will include his fee in the amount he charges you. Assume at least £35 (plus VAT) for a low mortgage (around £5,000, say) and double that for a large one (around £25,000). If you aren't using a solicitor to do your conveyancing, these fees will be approximately 60 per cent higher.

Land registry fees

The land registry is a government department responsible for keeping a register of all properties (in England and Wales) which have registered titles. If the property (or more correctly, the land on which it stands) is *registered* at the Land Registry, the government virtually guarantees that the person whose name is on the register is the owner — and a copy of the relevant part of the entry at the Land Registry may be seen with the draft contract the seller sends to the buyer.

Property is registered the first time it changes hands after the area it is in has become a registration area, and the buyer of the home has to pay the fee for registering the transfer of ownership.

If the home is already registered the fee (June 80) was:
● for homes costing up to £20,000: £2.50 for each £1,000 (or part of £1,000)
● for homes costing more than £20,000: £50 plus £2.40 for each extra £1,000 (or part of £1,000).

If the home is being registered for the first time the fee (June 80) was:
● for homes costing up to £10,000: £1.70 for each £1,000 (or part of £1,000)
● for homes costing more than £10,000: £17 plus £1.50 for each extra £1,000 (or part of £1,000).

Scotland

In Scotland there has been a long-standing tradition for solicitors to sell property (for which they charge a maximum commission of 1½ per cent excluding advertising costs).

Advertisements for homes in Scotland may not include the price of the property (but they do usually include the rateable value), and some say offers over so many £££. So you have to rely on local knowledge to know whether you will be able to afford the home, although, if you ask, the seller will probably give you some idea of how much he is expecting.

Offers are usually made by the 'sealed bid system'. The seller states that all offers should be made for a home by a particular *closing* date when one of the offers may be accepted. The buyer can withdraw or change his offer up to the closing date.

The offer has to be made in writing in the correct form so that it could be used as evidence in court (this is also true of the acceptance of any offer).

Once the offer is accepted, both the buyer and seller are committed to going through with the deal. So the buyer has to be sure that he will be able to go through with the deal *before* he makes an offer.

If the buyer needs a mortgage, he should arrange for his lender's valuer to visit the property before the offer is made. He should also arrange for any structural or specialist damp, rot or woodworm surveys that are needed.

The work involved once the offer has been accepted is largely similar to that done between exchange of contracts and completion in England and Wales.

● Solicitor's fees
Solicitors in Scotland
have a recommended
scale of fees but these
are normally the
maximum any solicitor
can charge for
conveyancing. And in
practice, the solicitor
may well charge less.

Buying or selling

Cost of home	Solicitor's maximum fee (VAT extra)
£15,000	£200
£20,000	£250
£30,000	£350

Northern Ireland
Here, the main
difference is that the
contract between buyer
and seller becomes
binding once both
sides have signed it
(which normally
happens about a
week after the verbal
offer by the buyer).

If the buyer hasn't a
mortgage, the contract
should have the
qualification that it is
subject to the buyer
getting the mortgage
he needs.

When the contract is
signed and accepted
the buyer pays a
deposit – normally
about 10 per cent of
the purchase price –
normally to the seller's
solicitor.

Stamp duty

This is a tax that, under current rules, the buyer of a home costing over £20,000 has to pay. It is based on the price of the home (▷ Fig. 5.5).

But you don't have to pay stamp duty on money you pay for fixtures and fittings that come with the home. So you may be able to reduce your stamp duty bill by knocking the value of these off the price of the home. This can be especially worthwhile if the price is just above a point where the tax rate goes up. For example, if the price of the home was £31,000, there'd be £465 to pay in stamp duty. But if the price included £1,000-worth of carpets, curtains, and so on, the buyer could agree (*before* the contract is made) to pay for these separately – and pay a reduced price of £30,000 for the home. Stamp duty would then come to only £300 – a saving of £165.

Figure 5.5   Stamp duty

Cost of home	Stamp duty
£20,000 or less	Nil
£20,001 to £25,000	$\frac{1}{2}$% of price
£25,001 to £30,000	1% of price
£30,001 to £35,000	1$\frac{1}{2}$% of price
£35,001 or more	2% of price

Estate agent's fees

You only have to pay these if you're selling – and if you are, it's worth trying to sell privately before you engage an agent. An agent is likely to charge between 1$\frac{1}{2}$ and 2 per cent of the home's selling price, plus VAT – ie between £300 and £500 (plus VAT) if the home sells for £20,000. Charges may vary within your area, so it's worth shopping around.

Note that if you decide to sell privately, you must do some research to find out what price to ask. Find out how much similar homes in your area have been sold for – eg by calling in at local estate agents.

Survey fees

There are three main types of survey:
● building society (or other lender's) valuation
● private structural survey
● specialist survey (of dry rot, damp, electrical system, for example).

Building society (or other lender's) valuation

Lenders normally obtain a report on the value of any property they grant a mortgage loan on – and building societies have to do this by law.

The person applying for the mortgage normally pays for this valuation – but, since the report is commissioned by the lender, the potential borrower has no right to see the report.

There is a standard scale of fees for building society valuations (related to the price of the property – ▷ Fig. 5.6). But you may well end up paying for more than one building society valuation because a purchase falls through.

Figure 5.6   Cost of a building society valuation

Price of property	Cost of valuation (*VAT extra – 15% when we went to press*)
Less than £15,000	£5 plus £1 for each £500 (or part of £500) by which price exceeds £2,000
£15,000 to £30,000	£31 plus £1 for each £1,000 (or part of £1,000) by which price exceeds £15,000
£30,000 to £40,000	£46 plus £1 for each £2,000 (or part of £2,000) by which price exceeds £30,000
Over £40,000	No set scale

It's important to recognize the limitations of a building society valuation. The aim of it is to make sure that the property is adequate security for the loan – so that, for example, if the borrower refuses to make the mortgage payments, the society can be sure of getting enough to pay off the loan by selling the home. The valuer is not responsible to you, the buyer, for pointing out any major defects such as dry rot, woodworm or a faulty roof – and an offer of a mortgage from the building society is no guarantee that such defects don't exist. A society may, however, tell you of a defect which its valuer reported, and hold back part of the loan until you've put the defect right.

Private structural survey

This is the type of survey you commission yourself if you want to find out if the property you are intending to buy is in good condition and reasonably good value for money.

● What does the survey include?

It should include an examination of, and full report on, the whole of the property, inside and out – including, for example, the roof, ceilings, walls, floors, doors, windows and outbuildings. The surveyor will probably comment briefly on the electrical system, plumbing and heating – but won't normally do a full examination of these unless you ask him (and pay extra).

If the surveyor notices there's something wrong which he's not expert on (eg woodworm, beetle, dry rot, poor plumbing), he will probably recommend that you have a specialist survey to find out just how serious the problem is.

If you have noticed anything about the property that you're worried about, mention it to the surveyor so he can put your mind at rest, or confirm your fears. And it may be useful to chat to him after he has done the survey, instead of relying just on his written report.

The report may not automatically include a valuation of the property – but you should get one if you ask (and, perhaps, pay extra).

A surveyor has a duty to carry out his structural survey *with reasonable care and skill*. This means that if you find the surveyor hasn't pointed out a defect he should have told you about, you can sue him for negligence and claim damages. But proving negligence can be difficult. Few cases are clear cut; and you'll have to find a new surveyor to testify against the negligent one.

● Cost

Some surveyors base their fees on the price of the home you want to buy, others on the numbers of rooms, others on the time they spend on inspecting the home – and charges vary quite widely (between £90 and £180, say, for a 3-bedroomed house).

You can ask for a partial survey, which may be cheaper (but make sure you know what you are getting for your money). This may be useful if, for example, you want to check up on just one or two things and are confident that the house is otherwise in good shape.

Some surveyors also charge less if you agree not to have a written report, just a verbal one. A drawback with this is that you'll have no written evidence (other than

your notes) of what the surveyor said, if you later discover that he failed to report a serious fault.

And you may be able to save money by asking the building society valuer to do a structural survey for you at the same time as doing his valuation for the society.

Specialist survey

Your surveyor may advise (or the lender insist on) special surveys if he suspects the presence of woodworm, rot, or faulty wiring, say. Get several surveys from specialist firms – their estimates of the extent of the problem may differ widely.

Insurance

There are two kinds for you to worry about.

Insurance of the property

The lender will be breathing down your neck about this as soon as you accept an offer of a mortgage, because the home you're buying needs to be insured by the time you exchange contracts. A building society may insist on arranging the insurance itself. Most societies encourage borrowers to use one of a small range of insurance companies – but they are obliged to offer you a choice of at least three insurance companies. If you don't like any of the three offered, you can suggest a different company, if it gives equivalent cover.

Make sure you insure for enough (▷ p. 86) and keep the valuation up to date – most easily done by taking out an index-linked policy. Your building society may also keep you up to date by telling you what you must insure for. Cost varies with the cost of rebuilding your home. Assume around £1.50 a year for each £1,000 of cover (more if your home is of unusual construction). More details on pp. 84–9.

House contents insurance

You need this by the time you start to move your belongings in (unless your existing policy covers you automatically). More details on pp. 90–96.

Repairs and Redecoration

Some points to watch out for are on p. 68.

Incidentals

These include:
● expenses of arranging bridging finance (▷ p. 75)
● removal expenses – the cost usually depends on the distance of the move and the work the firm has to do (which depends, for

example, whether you've a fourth-floor flat or a bungalow, whether you want the firm to pack for you). Most removal firms will send round an estimator to see the work involved and then give you a written quote. It's sensible to get estimates from two or three firms
● possibly, the premium on an indemnity policy (▷ p. 80)
● costs of deals that fall through – survey fees, valuation fees, etc.

**Checklist to estimate
moving costs**

Make sure that any VAT is included in estimates
you get (eg from solicitor, removal firm)

Selling	£
Estate agent's fee (1)	
Solicitor's fee (1)	
Buying	£
Solicitor's fee (including fee for acting for lender – eg building society) (1)	
Lender's valuation fee	
Own surveyor's fee (1)	
Land registry fee	
Stamp duty	
Cost of necessary repairs, decoration, new carpets, curtains, installing telephone, etc (1)	
Cost of looking for home – eg petrol, fares, time off work	
Other costs	£
Removal firm's charge (1)	
Allowance for surveys, solicitor's fee, etc on deals which fall through	
Total	£

1. Cost to some extent at
your discretion – ie in
most cases could choose
to do it yourself.

Example
Victor and Valerie Watson have decided to sell their mansion flat and buy a modern house on Property Street. They arrange the sale of their flat for £17,000 (using an estate agent), and are spending £24,950 on their new terraced home. Below we show how their expenses mount up.

They have really been quite lucky. They have not had to carry out major structural repairs to their new house, and the redecoration can for the moment be confined to the hall and the living room. They managed to buy the carpet in one bedroom cheaply along with the house. Nevertheless, Victor and Valerie need to raise about £2,300 to complete their move (as well as finding a deposit of about £6,200 before they can buy their new home). Small wonder that many home-owners, faced with such expenses, think first about extending their existing property rather than moving.

On buying		On selling	
Solicitor's fees, building society's solicitor's fees	£320	Estate agents' fees	£430
Stamp duty	£125	Solicitor's fees	£200
Land registry	£62		
Building society's valuation fee	£47		
Independent surveyor's fee	£100		
Removal expenses	£70		
Extra house buildings insurance	£10		
Extra contents insurance	£5		
Redecoration	£250		
New carpets and curtains	£690		
Total	£1,679	Total	£630

Victor and Valerie bought their existing flat 3 years ago for £12,000, putting down a deposit of £2,000; and they have since paid off capital of £500. So they have £7,500 cash from the sale of their present home; and they have savings of £400 to go into the kitty too. They still need to borrow from the bank but they hope to be able to get rid of the debt, despite their higher mortgage commitments, within a year. They moved partly with the idea of starting a family: but since they need Valerie's income, that will have to be postponed for a while.

Special problems

Can't get a mortgage?
Possibly the problem is that your income is too low, or too erratic (▷ p. 66). If, however, it's simply that money is tight, or that you haven't been saving with a society for long enough, two courses are open to you:
● try another source of loans – your employer (if you have not already tried this), your local authority, or an insurance company
● go to a mortgage broker.

Most mortgage brokers are insurance brokers too, and you want to treat their services with a certain amount of care. You might find you end up with an endowment mortgage which doesn't really suit your needs – if you have to take an endowment policy, go for a lower-cost type (▷ p. 72). Alternatively, you'll have to pay a fee for getting the mortgage (2 per cent, say)

A broker might ask you for a deposit before he agrees to try to get a mortgage for you. If he doesn't fix you up with a loan – or if you don't take up the loan within six months – you're entitled to all except £1 of your deposit back.

Note that some people have lost deposits when fly-by-night brokers have gone bankrupt. So before you hand over a deposit (or a survey fee made out to the broker rather than a building society) make sure that the broker is reputable – check with your bank, for example.

Can't get a big enough loan?
Ask the lenders who are offering you too little whether they will advance more on the strength of an *indemnity policy*. If they agree, they apply to an insurance company for cover (indemnity) against any loss which may result from giving a higher-than-normal loan. This will cost the borrower a once-and-for-all premium (probably in the

region of 4 per cent of the extra amount you borrow), but it's likely to work out much cheaper, in the long run, than taking out top-up policies, or applying to a broker (unless you've decided to take out an endowment policy anyway).

Seller asks a higher price at a late stage

In England and Wales (although not in Scotland) buyer and seller are not committed to the agreement until contracts are exchanged. If the seller demands a higher price ahead of the exchange of contracts, you must:
● pay it

or

● withdraw, and start all over again.

If you threaten to withdraw, it's possible that the seller will change his mind about raising the price. He may be less likely to do so if there are other buyers interested in the property already.

Your survey is unfavourable

Nearly all surveys are unfavourable. What you have to work out is how unfavourable yours is.

If the surveyor says that the property is basically structurally sound, that means that it's safe enough to buy, however much he may deplore the cracked ceilings or the poor paintwork.

If he starts talking about rot, rising damp, the necessity for extensive repointing, major repairs to the roof, replumbing and the like, you ought to weigh up carefully the cost of repairs. You may be able to get the seller to agree a lower price with the survey under your belt.

If your surveyor starts talking about the heavy expenditure required to bring the property up to an adequate standard, it may be time to consider pulling out – unless you can get a low enough price to leave you the money to make major repairs. Whatever you've sunk in the attempt to buy already, it may be dwarfed by the amount to come if you go ahead.

You are buying and selling simultaneously

Ideally, you want to synchronize both operations, but it may not turn out that way. The person who's selling to you is probably buying from someone else at the same time, and his seller is someone else's buyer too – the chain may stretch a long way, and when one link snaps (a mortgage offer doesn't come up to scratch, say) a lot of sales may collapse or be delayed. There's nothing

much you can do about this, except be aware of the possibility.

Aim to exchange both sets of contracts on the same day: you don't want to find yourself committed to selling your own house with no certainty of buying another, or vice versa.

It's sensible, too, to let the bank manager know what you are doing, just in case you have to call on him for a bridging loan (▷ p. 75).

Improving your home

Faced with the expense and stress of moving home, you may find yourself looking favourably on the alternative of improving it instead. On these two pages we talk about financing improvements, whether they'll work out as a good investment, and what you should watch out for if you go ahead.

Finding the money

Unless you've saved enough to cover the cost of the work to be done, you'll have to try for either a *grant* or a *loan*.

Grants

● What you may get a grant for

Your local authority has the discretion to make certain grants to help you improve your home. They can make *improvement grants* for a wide range of improvements or repairs to a house or to help convert a large house into flats.

You may be able to get an improvement grant for any of these common improvements or repairs:

● putting in a damp-proof course
● installing electric power points, or rewiring if the present wiring is unsafe
● repointing
● making the front door water-tight
● taking out a fireplace or chimney breast.

There are many other alterations which may be eligible for grants too (ask at your council offices for details).

Local authorities also have discretion to make *repair grants* for basic repairs to pre-1919 homes and to homes in certain areas which the council feels need special attention, and *special grants*, for putting 'standard amenities' (eg a lavatory, bath, kitchen sink, hot and cold running water) into houses shared by more than one family – but these grants aren't available in Scotland or N. Ireland.

Councils vary in what they'll give discretionary grants for – so check early on what your council's attitude is.

Councils also make statutory grants (ie they have to give you the grant if you meet certain conditions) called *intermediate grants*, for putting 'standard amenities' (▷ above) into a home which is without them, and for repairs to bring such a home up to a fit state of repair.

● Conditions for getting a grant

Conditions vary with the different grants – but generally you must certify that you live in and own (or rent out) the home, and that you'll go on doing so for a certain number of years. Tenants can, in certain circumstances, also apply for grants. The home must come up to a certain standard after the work has been done, and you mustn't start work without getting your grant application approved. For improvement grants and, in some cases, repair grants, the rateable value of your home must be below a certain limit.

● How much?

The size of grant depends on the estimated cost of the work. In most cases you get 50 per cent of the estimated cost, but for homes shared by more than one family, you may get 75 per cent (higher limits may apply in cases of hardship, or for privately rented homes). There are upper limits on the estimated cost on which each grant is worked out (eg £2,000 for an intermediate grant, £5,000 for improvements or repairs to a home with an improvement grant, £2,000 for a repair grant).

● Other grants

You may also be able to get:

● a grant to insulate your loft and lag water tanks and pipes – the grant is $\frac{2}{3}$ of the cost of the work (90 per cent if you're a needy pensioner), up to a limit of £50.
● a grant towards installing standard amenities if the existing ones are inaccessible to someone elderly or disabled in the household
● a grant towards the cost of repairs to a building of architectural or historic interest.

For all grants, remember you shouldn't start work until the grant has been approved – and that can take some months.

● Further information

Department of Environment leaflet *Your guide to house renovation grants* (available at Citizens' Advice Bureaux, consumer advice centres or council offices).

Loans

A grant would take you part of the way to financing your improvements. But you may still need to borrow money too.

Read chapter 19 on Borrowing to see which type of loan would suit you best. You'll find details of how loans from various sources work on pp. 210–214.

If your employer gives cheap loans, this may well be the cheapest form of borrowing for you. Failing that (if you're buying your home on a mortgage), you could ask if your building society will consider adding to your loan.

Borrowing from an insurance company (if you have policy with a cash-in value) may also be cheap. And all the High-Street banks now offer home improvement loans.

Note that you'll qualify for tax relief on

The conditions that apply for grants were under review when this book went to press – and the intention was to relax them somewhat so that more people could apply for grants. In particular, it looked as if repair grants might be more readily available, and that higher grants might be paid in particularly high-cost areas. The estimated cost on which improvement grants are based, may go up too. Check with your local authority for the latest rules.

Where any alteration is concerned, don't forget the possible effect it may have on what you pay in rates each year. You can get an idea of the kind of improvement which is likely to raise your valuation by turning to Fig. 7.2, p. 100.

the interest you pay on the loan, provided broadly that your total borrowing to buy or improve your home doesn't come to more than £25,000 (▷ p. 223). This could reduce the cost of the loan quite a lot.

Is it worth it?
There are two ways you might get back the cost of the work you've done. The first is through lower running costs for your home (eg if you put in draughtproofing, central heating, roof insulation); the other is through improving its resale value. If the work you have in mind doesn't do either, the only return you're likely to get for your money is intangible (the pleasure of sitting out on your new patio, say, or of soaking in your sunken bath).

Cutting running costs
Cutting down on heat lost through your home's doors, windows, roof and walls will cut your fuel bills. Draughtproofing round door and window frames (which is relatively cheap to do) could pay for itself in less than a year. Putting a 100 mm thick layer of glass fibre blanket in the loft could give you a better return on the money you've spent (compared with putting it in a building society, say) after 3 years, and cavity wall insulation after 4 to 9 years. Double-glazing, on the other hand, takes much longer to pay off – what you save in fuel bills isn't likely to match the return you would have got in a building society in less than 10 years.

You might cut running costs by installing a shower (provided you actually use it rather than the bath), but again, it'll take a long time to pay off unless you heat water by an expensive method.

Improving resale value
If your home has a poor heating system, putting in central heating should boost its resale value. Even if central heating doesn't get you a higher price, it should speed up finding a buyer for your home.

Other improvements may or may not be worthwhile from the resale point of view – a lot depends on the kind of home and the area it's in. Putting a second bathroom or extra bedroom in a 4-bedroomed detached house in a pricey road may be a good investment. Doing the same for a 3-bedroomed semi in a less pricey area is less likely to be.

It may be worth going through a few estate agents' lists to see whether or not the presence of, say, an extra bedroom or bath-room or garage seems to make a difference to the price asked for a house (but this won't tell what prices sellers are actually getting).

What you want to avoid – if you can't improve your home's resale value – is definitely lowering it. It's not impossible to do this, unfortunately. Filling the garden of your small semi with a swimming pool may well knock a fair bit off the price you'll get for it. And having structural work done so badly that the fabric of the home is damaged certainly will. So take care when choosing your improvement and your builder.

Things to watch out for
● check with your local council that the work you're having done meets all the building regulations which are relevant, and whether you need planning permission
● if you have a mortgage, check that the lender doesn't object to the work planned
● get estimates from a number of firms (at least 3 or 4) – and find out how long their prices are likely to stand for
● if you can, check with your bank manager on the financial standing of the builder (if he's local), and ask the builder to give you names of previous customers for you to check back with
● get in writing a date when the work will start and finish.
● don't expect an original estimate of the cost to be spot on. An estimate is just that: a guess at how much you'll have to pay. A quote is different: a price you've been quoted is what you should get charged (unless provision has been made for some costs to vary after the quote).
And when the time comes to settle up:
● check carefully that the work has been carried out to your satisfaction.

6 Insuring your home

Each year, hundreds of millions of £££ worth of damage is done to homes by fire, theft, flood and other misfortunes. In 1978, in England and Wales alone, there were over 100,000 fires involving property, and nearly 200,000 home burglaries.

As a protection against perils like these, every home should be covered by insurance for the buildings (▷ pp. 84–9), and insurance for the contents (▷ pp. 90–96).

Buildings insurance
This is generally the responsibility of the person who owns, or is buying, the property. Most policies cover loss or damage caused by the disasters or misfortunes (known as perils) that are specifically listed in the policy. The most important of these are fire, theft, storm and flood – ▷ Fig. 6.1 opposite for full details.

The cover you get
Each company's policy is worded slightly differently, but most policies cover damage to the following:
- the house – ie the foundations, walls, floors, ceilings, roof, doors and windows
- the garage, greenhouse, tool-shed and outbuildings
- paths, drives, gates, fences, walls and swimming pools
- plumbing, fixed central heating and sanitary fittings (wash-basins and lavatories)
- things normally left behind after a move – eg fitted kitchen units, bathroom cabinets, loft insulation, decorations.

As Fig. 6.1 shows, not all bits of the home are covered for all the perils listed – fences and gates, for instance, aren't normally covered for flood or storm damage.

If your home is damaged by one of the perils listed in the policy, you can usually claim certain expenses – such as architects' and surveyors' fees and the cost of removing debris and shoring up the building. If you normally let your home, you can also claim for the rent you lose while it is being repaired. And many policies cover the cost of alternative accommodation (over and above normal household costs) you might incur if you and your family have to move out while the repairs are being made. The most that can be claimed for loss of rent and alternative accommodation is normally 10 per cent of the amount insured for.

Buildings policies also cover certain damage – eg broken wash-basins, broken glass in windows and doors, and damage to underground gas pipes – no matter how it was caused (but not deliberate damage).

The cover you don't get
It's your responsibility to keep the buildings in good repair, so buildings insurance doesn't cover, for example, the garage door coming off its hinges because you haven't repaired it properly. You aren't covered, either, for damage due to normal wear and tear, or damage caused by things like dry rot and woodworm.

Many policies don't give full cover if you leave your home unfurnished for long periods (more than 30 days, say).

The cover for architects' and surveyors' fees is usually limited to the published scale of charges of the Royal Institute of British Architects and the Royal Institution of Chartered Surveyors. These scales, however, are only guidelines and the charges could be higher. If you had to pay more, the policy would not cover the difference.

The following *landslip* or *subsidence damage* is generally not covered:
- damage to paths, drives, gates, fences, walls and swimming pools, unless the house or outbuildings suffer at the same time
- normal settlement or shrinkage
- erosion of the land by sea or river.

Subsidence is what happens when the foundations of a building move downwards because of, say, the ground shrinking or expanding due to changes in the weather.

Note that damage caused by *heave* (where the ground expands – eg by taking up moisture – and causes the foundations to move upwards) is increasingly being covered.

Some policies – called *all-risks* policies – cover your home against loss or damage by any cause. For details ▷ p. 86.

Figure 6.1   Typical house buildings policy

Note This diagram does not include extra cover given by all-risks policy
▷ p. 86.

Covered	Not covered
	Normal wear and tear, war, rebellion and similar risks, radioactive contamination
Standard perils	
1 Aircraft and things dropped from them	Sonic booms
2 Storm (but you may have to pay the first £15)	Damage to fences and gates. Frost damage
3 Lightning	
4 Riots, strikes, labour and political disturbances and (though you might have to pay the first £15) malicious persons	In N. Ireland. Elsewhere if house unfurnished more than 30 days in a row or damaged by war, rebellion, revolution
5 Breaking or falling TV or radio aerials	The aerials themselves (unless damaged by one of the other perils covered)
6 Fire, explosion	
7 Water escaping from tanks, pipes, plumbed-in washing machines etc (but you may have to pay the first £15)	If house left unfurnished for more than 30 consecutive days
8 Theft and damage caused by thieves	If home unfurnished more than 30 days in a row
9 Subsidence, landslip, often heave (but excess of £250 or 3% of cost of rebuilding home from scratch maximum excess £500)	Normal settlement or shrinkage. Damage to paths, drives, gates, fences, walls, swimming pools, unless house or outbuildings damaged too
10 Oil leaking from central heating system	
11 Impact by road or rail vehicles, cattle, horses (but if vehicle or animal owned by, or under control of, you or your family, you may have to pay the first £15)	
12 Earthquake	
13 Flood (but you may have to pay the first £15)	Damage to fences and gates. Frost damage
14 Reasonable architects' and surveyors' fees	Cost of preparing a claim
15 Cost of removing debris, demolishing or shoring up building, and meeting any statutory or local authority requirements	
16 Cost of alternative accommodation, or loss of rent, while home being repaired (up to maximum) 10% of amount insured	
17 Accidental damage to underground gas, water, oil, drain or sewer pipes and underground cables for electricity or telephone	
18 Accidental breakage of glass in window, doors, etc, and of sanitary fittings	When house left unfurnished
Property owner's legal liability (eg if you let out the home and have responsibility for its upkeep and someone is injured because you've neglected repairs)	Occupier's liability — ▷ Fig. 6.3 Cover for property owner's liability restricted to £250,000 (with some companies £500,000) plus legal costs, for each claim

Excesses

With most policies, you have to pay the first £10 or £15 of some types of claim – for example, for damage caused by:

- storm
- flood
- escaping water
- malicious persons
- and with some policies, a vehicle or animal owned by, or under the control of, you or a member of your family.

Most policies also have a large excess on damage caused by:

- subsidence or landslip.

This is commonly £250 or 3 per cent of the total cost of rebuilding your home if it were destroyed, with a maximum of £500. Note that it is *not* 3 per cent of the amount of any claim. And some policies don't put a maximum on the excess. For these policies, if for example the total cost of completely rebuilding your home would be £30,000, the excess would be £900 – and if you had £3,000 of subsidence damage, the insurance would pay out only £2,100 – ie £3,000 – £900.

With many of the policies, it is possible to delete (get rid of) the storm, flood, escaping water and malicious persons excesses by paying an extra premium – perhaps £3 or £4 a year. You can't usually do this to the subsidence or landslip excess, however.

Types of policy

There are two main types of policy: indemnity and new-for-old.

Indemnity policy

With this type of policy, the insurance company pays out enough to restore the home to the condition it was in just before the damage.

So if, for example, a room which you last decorated some time ago is damaged by fire, the insurance company won't pay the full cost of redecorating it, because the old decorations will be replaced by new. A deduction will be made for wear and tear. In principle, if the decorations were, say, a quarter way through their expected life, the insurance company would deduct a quarter of the cost of replacing them when settling a claim.

If it's the *structure* (eg the walls or roof) of the house which is damaged, the insurance company may, in practice, pay the full cost of rebuilding or repair – provided you have kept the house in good repair. If you haven't, you could be asked to pay part of the cost.

New-for-old policy

With this type of policy, provided you have kept the house in good repair, you can claim the full cost of repairing or rebuilding and the company will make no deduction for wear and tear.

How much to insure for

Buildings must be insured for their *full value* – ie for the full cost of rebuilding both home and outbuildings if they were completely destroyed.

The home's market value (the amount you could sell it for) is *not* the same as the amount you should insure for. The cost of of rebuilding a home could be much higher than its market value.

Guidelines on building costs

Some companies issue guidelines about building costs. And the British Insurance Association (BIA) issues a leaflet giving a range of building costs for different types of homes in various regions of the UK. Free copy from BIA, Aldermary House, Queen St, London EC4N 1TU. You can use this leaflet (or the company's guidelines) to help you decide what to insure for.

If you have no other guidelines to follow, the method outlined opposite should help you work out roughly how much you should insure for to cover the cost of rebuilding your home.

The BIA leaflet gives a rough guide to the cost of rebuilding your home if it's of a fairly standard kind. If, however, any of the following applies, the cost is likely to be higher:

- access to it is difficult (eg there's no road suitable for a lorry leading to it)
- the home is isolated – so that a builder would have a long way to travel to get there
- it is built of expensive materials (eg Cotswold stone) or materials which aren't in common use any longer. But if you're willing (and the local authority will allow you) to rebuild with cheaper materials, you could ask the insurance company to let you insure for the cost of rebuilding with these materials
- it has a lot of expensive features (eg double glazing, a luxurious bathroom or kitchen)
- it's of historic or architectural interest
- there are local authority building regulations or byelaws which would make the house especially expensive to rebuild.

All-risks cover

The normal types of buildings policy cover you for damage to your home from most causes, *except* for damage caused accidentally – for example, by you putting your foot through the bedroom ceiling when you are busy insulating your loft.

All-risks policies cover all such accidental damage to the home. There is a catch, however – you usually have to pay the first £10 or £15 of some or all types of claim, and some of the policies have drawbacks in the cover they offer (eg no cover for alternative accommodation).

All-risks policies usually work on a new-for-old basis and cost a bit more than the company's normal new-for-old policy.

Example

Jenny Johnson works out roughly how much to insure her 2-bedroomed semi-detached house for:

Floor area of house and garage (square feet)	1100
Rebuilding cost (roughly £26 a square foot)	£28,600
Add on around 15% for architect's fees	£32,900
Add on allowance for inflation (say, 30%)	£42,800

Jenny should insure for £42,800 if she goes for an ordinary policy, £32,900 if she gets a policy that's index-linked.

Inflation

Whatever it would cost to rebuild a house now, it would almost certainly cost more to rebuild it in a year's time. Between March 79 and March 80, for example, building costs rose by around 20 per cent (▷ Fig. 6.2 overleaf, which shows the rise in house rebuilding costs over the past 5 years).

The simplest way to cope with this problem is to go for an index-linked policy. With most index-linked policies the cover goes up automatically each month in line with an index of building costs – usually the Housing Cost Index prepared by the Royal Institution of Chartered Surveyors for the magazine *Building* (the one used in Fig. 6.2). This index measures changes in the basic costs – ie raw materials, labour – of building an average 3-bedroomed semi-detached house.

Making your own estimate

Step 1
Find out the size of your home. To do this, measure the area of each floor (taking the outside measurements if possible). Add on the area of any garage or outbuildings which you haven't counted as part of the ground floor of your home.

Step 2
Multiply the answer to Step 1 by building costs per square metre (or square foot) in your area. For guidance on these, see opposite. Building costs can vary considerably from area to area and for different types of home – in March 80, building costs based on the BIA leaflet ranged from around £21 to £38 a square foot (around £225 to £410 a square metre) depending on the area and the size and age of the property. If your home is not covered by the guidelines, you could get an idea of the cost that might apply in your case by phoning a few builders and surveyors in your area.

Step 3
Add on another 15 per cent or so. This is to allow for architects' and surveyors' fees (which would probably arise if any major rebuilding work was needed) and debris removal and shoring up your home (in the event of a major disaster).

Step 4
If the policy is not index-linked, add on an allowance for inflation (▷ above).

Professional valuations
The guidelines on p. 86 give a rough idea of how much to insure a fairly standard home for. A professional insurance valuation may help to give you a more accurate idea (especially if you have an unusual home).

To find a qualified valuer in your area, contact:
● The Information Centre, Royal Institution of Chartered Surveyors, 12 Great George Street, Parliament Square, London SW1P 3AD. (01–222 7000)
● The Assistant Secretary, Incorporated Society of Valuers and Auctioneers, 3 Cadogan Gate, London SW1X 0AS. (01-235 2282)

The two associations have the same scale of fees for insurance valuations: 0.25% for the first £5,000 home is valued at; then 0.15% between £5,000 and £50,000; then 0.1% between £50,000 and £200,000. No guideline for valuations over £200,000. You pay VAT (15 per cent in mid-80) as well. There's a minimum fee: £10 in mid-80.

Members of these associations don't have to stick to this scale – so ask for an estimate first.

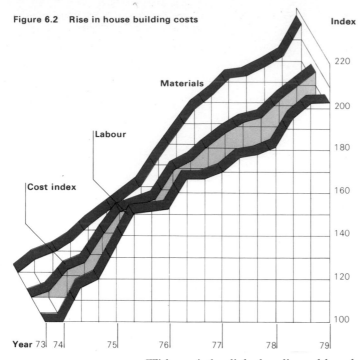

Figure 6.2   Rise in house building costs

Index

220
200
180
160
140
120
100

Materials

Labour

Cost index

Year 73 74   75   76   77   78   79

With an index-linked policy, although the insurance cover changes each month in line with building costs, the premium goes up only once a year when you renew the policy.

The alternative to an index-linked policy is to insure for a higher amount. Ideally, you should add 2-years'-worth of inflation to the current cost of rebuilding your home. This will protect you against the possibility of your home being destroyed towards the end of the 12 months you insured for and the rebuilding being a long-drawn-out affair. If you were insuring in 1980 you should have added on, say, 30 per cent. Check on inflation over the past year to see how much to add on.

Some companies now issue *only* index-linked policies. With those that give a choice, the cost of each £1,000-worth of cover is the same for a company's index-linked policy as for its ordinary policy. An index-linked policy works out cheaper, however, because you need to insure for a lower amount.

What if you're under-insured?

If a home is insured for less than its *full value*, most insurance companies' policies allow them to refuse to pay anything at all when the claim is made. The companies are likely, in practice, to meet some or all of the claim, depending on the extent to which the home was under-insured. They might, for

example, apply the principle of *average* (▷ below). But they would never pay more than the amount insured for, so being under-insured could leave you hundreds, or even thousands, of £££ out of pocket.

Lloyd's, and a few insurance companies, have an *average* clause written into their policies. This says that any claim will be scaled down by the degree of under-insurance – so if you insure your home for only half the amount it should be insured for, the company will pay you only half the cost of any repairs of rebuilding covered by the policy.

How average works

Mark Millet's home is damaged by fire and he makes a claim for £4,000 to cover the cost of the repairs. But he had insured his home for only £15,000 (close to its market value) when he should have insured it for £20,000. Applying the principle of average, the insurance company pays out only ¾ of the cost of repairs ie, £3,000. Mark has to find the other £1,000 out of his own pocket.

Over-insured?

There's no point in over-insuring. The company won't pay out more than the actual cost of rebuilding your home, if it is totally destroyed – even if you've insured for more.

Cost

For each £1,000 of insurance, the rate in 1980 was about £1.50 a year for an indemnity or new-for-old policy, around £1.80 for an all-risks policy. With all types of policy you'll have to pay extra to have the excesses deleted (▷ p. 86).

To take out £30,000 worth of insurance for instance, with the excesses deleted as far as possible, the cost might be in the region of £50 a year for an indemnity or new-for-old policy, or around £60 a year for an all-risks policy.

What boosts the cost?

The cost of insurance may be substantially higher (and some insurance companies may refuse to insure the home at all) if:
● the home has a thatched roof – premium might be between £5 and £10 for each £1,000 of insurance (ie between £150 and £300 a year for £30,000 of insurance)
● the home is built of wood or anything that burns easily – premium might be between £2 and £10 for each £1,000 of insurance, depending on how much of the home is built of wood.

If the home is in an area prone to flooding, the company may charge extra, or it may refuse to give you cover for flood damage, or it may impose a large excess ($\triangleright$ p. 86) on flood claims. Most companies don't have a general rule, but consider each case individually.

Some companies are reluctant to insure the homes of people in certain occupations – like professional entertainers, sports personalities, people in the night-club or gambling business.

If any of these points apply, it's worth getting quotations from several different insurance companies.

Choosing a policy

Policies vary not only in their cost, but also in the cover they offer. Some policies offer more than normal cover – eg smaller-than-normal excess for subsidence or landslip, or cover for theft when the home is left unfurnished for long periods. Some offer less-than-normal cover – eg no cover for accidental breakage of windows or sanitary fittings, no cover for theft unless a break-in is involved, or higher-than-normal excesses on many types of claim. A few companies offer reduced cover (eg fire cover only) at a reduced cost. And policies issued by Lloyd's can often be modified to suit individual circumstances.

So to choose a policy, you will have to consider not just the cost but the cover wanted. Check on a number of policies (*Money Which?* June 78 has details of many).

Company safety

Turn to p. 141 for details of the protection offered to insurance policyholders.

Claiming

You claim on a buildings policy in much the same way as you would on a contents policy. Details for both are on p. 96.

Problems

Homes occupied for only part of the year

Insurance companies sometimes impose restrictions on homes (like holiday cottages) that are lived in for only part of the year.

In general, if a home is left unfurnished, it isn't normally covered for broken glass or sanitary fittings. If it's left unfurnished for more than 30 days, it isn't normally covered for damage caused by thieves and malicious persons, and by escaping water. If it's left furnished but unoccupied for long periods, some policies require that the gas, electricity and water be turned off at the mains, the water system drained (if possible), and arrangements made for someone to inspect the home regularly – say, once a week.

If you're worried about squatters moving into your home while you're away on holiday or on business, it may be wise to take out a policy to protect yourself. One issued by Lloyd's costs about £10. But you can't get this cover for second homes.

Mortgages

When a house is bought with a mortgage from a building society, the society normally insists on arranging the buildings insurance. Building societies must offer their borrowers a choice of at least three insurance companies. If the borrower doesn't like any of those offered, he can suggest another, provided that it offers equivalent cover to those suggested by the building society. Most of the large societies now prefer their borrowers to take out index-linked cover.

Moving home

Homes should be insured from the time contracts are exchanged (in Scotland, from the time the offer has been accepted by the seller). Don't wait until completion date (the date at which the home becomes yours). If the house burns down after contracts have been exchanged, the buyer still has to pay the seller the price agreed.

It's prudent, however, for the seller to keep his house insured right up to completion date, in case, for example, the buyer flees the country, or dies before completion.

This means that for a short period, you may be insuring two houses. It shouldn't cost much extra.

Renting

Tenants don't normally need house buildings insurance, even if they are responsible, for instance, for repairing broken windows, wash-basins and toilets. This is because the necessary cover should be included in their house contents policy.

It may be wise, however, for tenants to check that their landlord has sufficient house buildings insurance cover. If not, they are the people who will end up living in a hovel if the home is badly damaged and the landlord can't afford to repair it.

Is the NHBC scheme enough?

The National House Building Council is a body whose aims are to improve the standard of new homes and safeguard home-buyers. It operates a type of insurance scheme under which it undertakes to put right certain defects which appear in the first 10 years of a home's life.

Ordinary house buildings insurance is needed, even under an NHBC scheme. The NHBC scheme covers, in the main, shoddy building; it does not cover damage by fire or flood, for example.

Contents insurance

The cover you get
Most types of house contents policy cover the contents of the home against loss or damage caused by the perils listed in the policy. For a full list of the standard perils covered by most policies ▷ Fig. 6.3.

Policies usually cover loss of, or damage to, the things you, and the members of your family who live with you, normally keep in the home, garage or outbuildings. So they cover loss of, or damage to:
- household effects – things like televisions, hi-fi, cookers, carpets, sheets, saucepans, furniture (but not fitted furniture which would normally be left behind after a move – this is covered under a buildings policy)
- personal effects – things like clothes, watches, pens, wallets
- valuables, personal money.

Things usually kept in the garden – like swings, benches, garden gnomes – are often not covered, but television and radio aerials, even if on the roof, generally count as part of the contents.

Most policies also cover things for which you are responsible (like rented televisions) and belongings of domestic staff (au pairs, nannies and the like) – though of course the value of these things must be taken into account when deciding how much to insure for. (If you have domestic staff, their money may not be covered.)

Valuables
Most companies want to know if the total value of certain belongings (listed in the policy) exceeds a certain amount (commonly a third of the amount insured for). Most companies count things made of gold, silver or other precious metals, jewellery, and furs as valuables for this purpose. Some also count pictures, curios, other works of art, and stamp, coin and medal collections.

Nearly all companies set another limit for the value of any single valuable article – usually 5 per cent of the amount insured for (but with a few companies 10 per cent and, with some, a limit of, say, £100).

The majority of companies use the wider definition of valuables (that is, including pictures, curios, etc) for the individual valuable limit. A few companies also count some or all of antiques, cameras, binoculars, watches and porcelain as valuables for this purpose. And some companies want to know about any article other than furniture, pianos, televisions, radios, fridges and other household electrical equipment which exceeds the single article limit.

If your valuables exceed either the valuables limit or the single article limit, you should let your insurance company know. It may want to charge a higher premium to cover them and it may ask for safes, special locks, and so on to be put in.

Note of warning: if you don't tell the insurance company that valuables exceed one of its limits, the company may pay out no more than that limit if some or all of those valuables are stolen. If it is the total valuables limit that has been broken, the company may scale the claim down, as in a case of under-insurance (▷ p. 94).

Money
Money means personal cash and postage stamps (and, with some companies, postal orders and travel tickets). Most policies set a limit on the amount of money they will cover – commonly £50 or £100. Often money is not covered against theft unless there is a break-in.

Things like share certificates, deeds, bonds, luncheon vouchers, and so on, are *not* money and are not covered by most policies. The policies that do give some cover usually restrict it to the cost of replacing the certificates, documents or whatever – with a limit of, say, £250.

Televisions, radios, etc.
Some policies cover accidental damage to a television – caused perhaps by a child tripping up and knocking it over – as well as damage caused by the standard perils. A few companies extend this to include accidental damage to things like radios, record players, and so on. Portable sets are sometimes excluded from cover. No insurance company will pay out if the television just breaks down, or for damage caused by someone fiddling around with the set.

Broken glass
Mirrors and glass that is part of furniture (eg a glass-topped table) are covered for breakage, no matter how they get broken – even through carelessness. But glass in framed pictures is not normally covered for accidental breakage. Glass in doors and windows is covered under a buildings policy, not a contents one.

Life cover
If you or your wife (or husband) are killed at home by fire or thieves, most companies will pay out life cover of £1,000 or 50 per

Some policies – called all-risks policies – cover the contents of your home against loss or damage by *any* cause. For details ▷ p. 92.

**Figure 6.3
Typical house contents
policy**

Note This diagram does
not include extra cover
given by all-risks
policy
▷ p. 92.

Covered	Not covered
Loss or damage to the belongings that you, and members of your family who live with you, keep in your home, garage or outbuildings, caused by the standard perils – eg theft, fire, flood. For full list ▷ p. 85.	Contents don't include: cars, car accessories while in the car, animals, boats, caravans, or any money over £50 No cover for perils not listed in your policy, nor for normal wear and tear, war, rebellion, revolution, sonic boom, radioactive contamination

Covered	Not covered
1 Personal possessions of servants (if they live in)	But their money may not be covered
	2 No single valuable (for what this means ▷ p. 90) is covered for more than 5% of amount insured for, unless you inform the insurance company of its value. Company must also be told if *total* value of valuables is more than $\frac{1}{3}$ of amount you're insured for
3 Accidental breakage of mirrors or glass in furniture. Accidental damage to TVs – including damage through your own carelessness	Glass in framed pictures. No cover if TV tube fails, or if you're fiddling around with the works
	4 Things normally kept in the garden – eg garden bench, gnomes
	5 Theft of money often covered only if there's a break-in – and only up to £50 Nothing covered against theft (unless there's a break-in) if home is let or part-let, or not self-contained
6 Tenants' liability – if you are a tenant, contents policy covers you against most types of damage to buildings – except fire damage – if maintenance of buildings is your responsibility	But cover restricted to 10% of amount you're insured for. You may have to pay first £15 for some kinds of damage – eg by storm or escaping water
	7 Lost or mislaid things – eg a valuable ring down the drain
8 Employer's liability – ie compensation you may have to pay for injury to domestic staff – eg if daily help trips over loose stair carpet and falls downstairs	
9 Personal liability – ie compensation you may have to pay if you or your family cause injury to others, or damage to their property	Cover for personal liability and occupier's liability restricted to £250,000 (with some companies £500,000) plus legal costs, for each claim
10 Occupier's liability – ie compensation you may have to pay if, for example, your hanging basket falls on the postman	
11 Cost of alternative accommodation (or loss of rent) while home being repaired	But cover restricted to 10% of amount you're insured for
Things temporarily moved from your home (including your clothing, etc) are covered against the standard perils while in most buildings (including your office, place where you're staying, and the cleaners, say). Also covered in a bank or safe deposit	But cover restricted to 15% of amount you're insured for

cent of the sum insured for, whichever is less – so long as the death happens not more than 3 months after the event.

Things away from home
Nearly all the policies give some cover for belongings when they are not in the home – so long as they are still in the UK, Channel Islands, Isle of Man or Republic of Ireland. Most companies restrict the cover to 15 per cent of the amount insured for.

In general, your belongings are covered for all the standard perils so long as they are in a building (including the laundry, cleaners and so on, but not a furniture depository, exhibition room or saleroom). They are covered against theft only if a break-in is involved. In hotels, places of work or someone else's home, belongings are covered for walk-in thieves too (except for theft of money).

Empty houses
Most companies restrict the cover they give (or charge extra) for a home that is left empty for long periods (probably no cover for theft, malicious people, escaping water and leakage of oil). Some companies insist that gas, electricity and water are switched off at the mains, that the water system is drained (if possible), valuables put into safe keeping, and that someone checks the home every week.

Legal liability to other people or other property
For occupier's, tenant's, employer's and personal liability, ▷ Fig. 6.3. For more about personal liability, ▷ also p. 97.

Excesses
A few companies make you pay the first £10 or £15 of any claim for damage by malicious people, or by impact from vehicles or animals belonging to you or your family. Tenants may have to pay part of a claim for some types of damage to the buildings. The sum you have to pay out of your own pocket is known as an *excess*.

All-risks policies (▷ right) normally have an excess of between £5 and £25 on each claim (apart from occupier's or personal liability claims).

Excesses on a house contents policy can't usually be deleted.

Types of policy
There are three main types of policy: indemnity, new-for-old, and what we call in this book *hybrid policies* – a mixture of indemnity and new-for-old.

Indemnity policy
With this type of policy, the amount the insurance company pays out to settle a claim should leave you no worse off – and no better off – than you were immediately before the loss or damage took place. So if, for example, you're claiming for the theft of a 5-year-old television set, the insurance company will deduct a certain amount for wear and tear. How much is deducted depends mainly on the age of the set, how long it could have been expected to last from new, and the condition it was in at the time it was stolen. If the set was in average condition for its age, and a quarter of the way through its expected life, the insurance company would pay out three-quarters of the cost of a new set because the set had three-quarters of its useful life to go.

So an indemnity policy could leave you out of pocket if you have to replace partly worn-out belongings with new ones.

If you claim for something that is new (or as good as new – which could apply to things like mirrors) the company should pay the full cost of replacement. With antiques, which go up in value rather than down, wear and tear is largely irrelevant – you are entitled to the amount you would have to pay out to replace them with similar ones.

New-for-old policy
With this type of policy, the insurance company agrees to pay out enough to replace anything stolen, destroyed or damaged beyond repair with a *new* replacement. For things which are not beyond repair, the company will pay out the cost of repairing them to the state they were in before the damage. (But the indemnity method still applies to household linen and clothes.)

So a new-for-old policy covers the full cost of buying brand new replacements for, say, 7-year-old curtains destroyed by fire, or an elderly record player that is stolen.

To qualify for the full replacement cost, the amount insured must be kept up to the full amount it would cost to replace *all* the contents of the home with new things (apart from household linen and clothes where wear and tear must be taken into account).

A few policies give new-for-old cover only for things up to a certain age – eg 2, 3 or 5 years. Older things get indemnity cover.

All-risks cover
Some policies give wider-than-normal cover (in return for a higher premium). Instead of covering your contents against the perils named in your policy, they cover them against *all* perils *except* those named in your policy. So you get normal cover *plus*, for example, cover for accidental damage and, with most policies, wider-than-normal cover while your contents are away from home. These all-risks policies would, for example, cover the loss of a diamond out of a ring or damage to your carpet if you accidentally spilt wine on it.

The single article, money and valuable limits (▷ p. 90) still apply. So an all-risks policy may not be such a good deal as it seems at first sight. To cover any extra valuables fully, a higher premium may be necessary. It is possible to buy separate insurance to cover specified items only (rather than *all* the contents) on an all-risks basis.

All-risks policies do not normally cover you for mechanical or electrical breakdown and often not for breakage of china or other fragile things. And it isn't normally possible to get all-risks cover if the home is lent or let.

Hybrid policy

With this type of policy, furniture, carpets, televisions, radios, record players, stereo equipment, and household electrical appliances get new-for-old cover. With the rest of the contents, indemnity cover applies. With nearly all hybrid policies, the televisions, stereos and so on must be no older than a certain age limit to qualify for new-for-old cover – eg 2, 3 or 5 years.

How much should you insure for?

Most companies ask for a declaration that the contents are insured for their *full value*. This is the amount it would cost to replace them with brand-new ones – less an allowance for wear and tear for those things which get indemnity rather than new-for-old cover.

This means that the amount of insurance you need is least for an indemnity policy, most for a new-for-old and in between for a hybrid policy. How much difference there is in the amount of cover depends on how old the contents are and how long they could be expected to last.

The checklist on p. 94, and details below, should help you decide how much to insure for. Note that the checklist is *not* comprehensive.

Cost of new replacements

Column 1 overleaf is for what it would cost to replace all your contents with new ones. Visit a few shops (or phone them) to check on prices – it's often surprising how much articles have increased in price. For things not on sale any more – like old-fashioned sideboards – look for things which seem to be their modern equivalents. For articles like antiques which go up rather than down in value, search for similar items.

Any of the contents that you are going to insure separately (like a valuable camera) should not be entered on the checklist.

Allowing for wear and tear

Column 2 is for amounts that have to be deducted for wear and tear for things that get indemnity cover. For things that get new-for-old cover, don't enter anything in column 2.

Some things – eg very solidly-built furniture – may have a very long expected total life, so that the deduction for wear and tear might be quite small. But things like televisions, radios, record players and domestic appliances are normally considered to have an expected total life of only 10 years or so.

For articles like antiques, which should rise in value over time, don't enter anything in column 2.

Remember that even with new-for-old or hybrid policies, some of your contents will get indemnity cover rather than new-for-old cover – so some deductions will have to be made. How much depends on what the thing is, how much longer it can be expected to last and its age. The example below for a carpet gives the general principle:

Current age	5 years
Estimated future life (taking condition into account)	10 years
So expected total life	15 years
Current shop price of equivalent carpet	£400

so deduction for wear and tear:
$$=\frac{\text{Current age}}{\text{Expected total life}} \times \frac{\text{Current}}{\text{shop price}}$$
$$=\tfrac{5}{15} \times £400 = £133.33$$

...the answer

If you add up the amounts in column 2 and deduct them from the total of the amounts entered in column 1, you'll get an answer that's getting close to the amount the contents should be insured for.

It's wise to add on something – say 5 per cent or so – to allow for things you'll buy during the year, and things you've forgotten. You may also need to make an allowance for inflation (▷ below). Add these amounts on and you'll end up with the total your contents should be insured for.

Inflation

Because of inflation, the cost of replacing your contents with new ones will rise. So the cover you need with a new-for-old policy will go up during the year. One way of coping with this problem is to go for an *index-linked* policy. With most index-linked policies, the cover goes up automatically each month (or sometimes each quarter) in line with an index of the cost of belongings – with a few insurance companies, the *Retail Price Index*, but with most, the *Durable Household Goods* section of that index (both are published each month in the Department of Employment Gazette).

Although the insurance cover rises each month, the premium goes up only once a

Professional valuations
If you are insuring valuable things, like furs and jewellery, it may be sensible to get them professionally valued. It would be fairly expensive to get everything in your home valued, so choose only those things whose value is uncertain.

The associations mentioned on p. 87 will advise on qualified valuers in your area – but tell them what sort of contents you want valued. An insurance company may also suggest a valuer.

The associations mentioned have the same standard rates. In mid-80 these rates were: £1.05 for each £100 they value the contents at (with a minimum fee of £10). VAT (at 15 per cent in mid-80) is added to the fee. Members of the association don't have to stick to the standard charge, so ask for an estimate first.

Antique dealers and jewellers also do valuations – their charges vary, but reckon on around 1 per cent of the valuation.

Checklist: How much to insure for

	Column 1 Cost to replace contents with new ones	Column 2 Less Wear and tear (▷p.93)
The items in blue get new-for-old cover under a hybrid policy		
Living rooms, Dining room	£	£
Curtains, blinds, rugs. Carpets, furniture (sideboards, tables, chairs, piano, bookcase etc) China and glassware, drink, pictures. Ornaments, lamps. Televisions, radios, Hi-fi. Records, tapes, books, musical instruments.		
Kitchen		
Curtain, blinds, mats. Carpets, cooker, fridge, freezer, washing-machine, mixer etc, free-standing kitchen cupboards. Cutlery, crockery, saucepans, linen, utensils etc. Food and drink.		
Hall, Cupboards, Landing, Stairs		
Curtains, blinds, rugs. Carpets. Clothing, linen. Hallstand, telephone table. Tools, cleaning equipment. Vacuum cleaner Toys, photographic equipment etc.		
Bedrooms		
Curtains, blinds, rugs. Carpets, furniture (beds, wardrobes, dressing tables, bookshelves, chest of drawers etc). Bed linen, clothing. Pictures, ornaments, lamps, jewellery, valuables, cameras, binoculars. Televisions, radios, Hi-fi. Records, tapes, sports equipment, toys, books.		
Bathroom, Toilet		
Curtains, blinds, mats. Carpets, bathroom cabinets (and their contents). Linen (towels, sheets etc), scales, mirrors.		
Loft, Attic		
Suitcases and contents. Things being stored etc.		
Garage, Shed, Outbuildings		
Lawn mower, tools, bicycle, ladders. Do-it-yourself equipment etc.		
Totals		£
Subtract total of column 2 from column 1		
Add allowance for things to be bought during year (say 5%)		
Add allowance for inflation, if necessary		
Amount of insurance you need		£

year. It is normally based on the amount of cover at the time the policy is renewed.

If you take out a new-for-old policy which is not index-linked, it would be prudent to insure for a higher amount, allowing for a year's worth of inflation. (This way, if your contents are lost or damaged at the end of the year, you're unlikely to be under-insured.)

With new-for-old policies which have an age limit, hybrid policies and indemnity policies, the problem is less clear cut – because although the cost of replacing the contents is increasing during the year, so too is the amount which should be deducted for wear and tear. If the company offers index-linking, however, it might be as well to take up the offer. It will involve no extra payment during the year – and if, at renewal, the cover seems too high, you can ask the company to reduce it.

Whatever the policy, you should review your cover at regular intervals – preferably once a year. And let the insurance company know if you buy anything which exceeds the 5 per cent allowed for new things.

What happens if you're under-insured?

Lloyd's and some insurance companies have an *average clause* written into their policies which they apply in cases of under-insurance. (For what happens if this clause is applied, ▷ p. 88.) Some of the other companies have a clause in their new-for-old and hybrid policies which says that in cases of under-insurance claims will be settled on an indemnity basis (▷ p. 92).

The remaining companies' policies don't mention what happens if you are under-insured. They could refuse to pay anything at all – but in practice they are likely to pay the full amount of any claim (if the amount of under-insurance was small), or apply the principle of average, or if the cover is new-for-old, settle the claim on an indemnity basis.

If you're over-insured

You can't look forward to a bonanza from an insurance company if you've got more cover than you should have. The most a company will pay out for your contents is the cost of replacement *less* wear and tear if applicable. So if you've insured your contents for £10,000 but needed only £8,000 cover, the company won't hand over the extra £2,000 even if your contents are a complete write-off.

Cost

For an indemnity or hybrid policy, the minimum charge (and you may have to pay more – ▷ below) is around £2 to £3 for each £1,000 of cover. With a new-for-old policy, the charge is likely to be £2.50 to £3.50 for each £1,000 of cover.

All-risks policies are rather more expensive than the normal type of policy. Most companies charge at least £6 for each £1,000 of cover (and some companies charge more – £10 for each £1,000 of cover, say – for all valuables).

Most policies have a minimum premium – usually between £5 and £10 (but may be £20 or more, particularly with some of the all-risks policies).

When comparing costs don't forget that the amount of insurance cover you need varies with the type of policy you go for. You need most cover with a new-for-old policy, least with an indemnity policy and in-between with a hybrid policy.

Higher rates will probably apply (and some insurance companies will restrict the cover they will give, or refuse to insure altogether) if you, your home, or contents count as extra risky. This may happen, for example, if:
● your home is in London, Glasgow, Liverpool, or certain other large cities
● your home has a thatched roof, or is built of wood or anything that burns easily
● your home is in an area which has a history of flooding
● you are a professional entertainer, in the gambling business, a night-club owner, a sportsman, market trader or student. You should tell the insurance company if a member of your family who lives in the same home is likely to be counted as extra-risky
● you have a lot of antiques, valuable jewellery, expensive equipment, and so on
● your home is lived in only occasionally – eg a weekend cottage
● your home is part of business premises – eg a flat over a shop
● you have a bad track record for claims (more than 2 or 3 claims a year, say).

Choosing a policy

When choosing a policy, you have to balance cost against cover. First decide whether you want the standard sort of cover (against the perils named in the policy) or the more expensive all-risks cover (ageinst a wider range of misfortunes, including accidental damage – ▷ p. 92). Then decide on the type of policy – new-for-old,

indemnity, or hybrid. New-for-old policies are the most expensive – they tend to cost more for each £1,000 of cover, and it's necessary to insure for a higher amount than with hybrid and indemnity policies. This type of policy, however, is least likely to leave you out of pocket if you have to make a claim.

Some new-for-old policies have an age limit for new-for-old cover; things older than this get indemnity cover. Avoid policies like this if you want full new-for-old cover.

There are also some important differences in the cover the different policies offer. Some give more-than-normal cover (eg cover for things in the garden, cover for accidental damage to radios, record players and the like, cover when moving home, cover for your belongings when on holiday).

Some give less-than-normal cover (eg no cover for personal liability, no cover for accidental damage to televisions, no cover for things away from home, no cover for accidental breakage of glass).

So to choose a policy, you'll have to weigh the cost against the cover you get. Check on a number of policies (for details of many, see *Money Which?* September 78 and 79).

Company safety

Turn to p. 141 for details of the protection given to insurance policyholders.

Claiming

How to claim

Contact your insurance company (or broker, if you are insured with Lloyd's) as soon as possible after the loss or damage, giving the policy number, and brief details of what happened. If there's been a theft, tell the police.

The insurance company will then send you a claim form which must be filled in and returned, usually within 30 days of the damage.

With a claim of around £100 or more, the insurance company may send someone along to assess the damage, to consider whether the property has been insured for the right amount, and to discuss the claim.

If the company's offer appears to be less than reasonable, it's worth contacting them again, and outlining why it seems so. If you can't reach an agreement you could try contacting the following for advice:

● if you're insured with Lloyd's:
The Manager, Advisory Division, Advisory and Legislation Dept, Lloyd's, Lime St, London EC3M 7HA

● if you're insured with a company:
The Consumer Information Dept, The British Insurance Association, Aldermary House, Queen St, London EC4N 1TU.

Claiming on buildings insurance?

To fill in the claim form the company sends you, you'll need to get an estimate of the cost of repairs. But you shouldn't generally begin the repairs until the company has approved your claim. However, if emer-

gency repairs are needed to prevent further damage (repairs to the roof, say to prevent the inner structure of the house being damaged) tell the company what the position is and go ahead with repairs at once.

Claiming on contents insurance?

If you're claiming for something that's been damaged but can be repaired, claim the cost of repairs (unless this comes to more than the company would pay had the thing been damaged beyond repair). You'll need to send the company an estimate of the cost of repairs.

If you're claiming for something that's been damaged beyond repair or stolen, your claim should cover what it will cost you to replace it, less anything to be had for salvage, and less an allowance for wear and tear, if indemnity cover applies (▷ p. 92). If you have receipts or valuation certificates, it may speed things up if you send them to the company.

Be wary when you make a claim – some companies' claim forms are difficult to find your way through and some may be confusing. For example, some claim forms don't include a space for the current shop price of the article you're claiming for. You may end up deducting the allowance for wear and tear from the price you *originally* paid for the article, instead of from the current shop price. With claim forms like this, add another column, headed 'Current shop price' (as shown in Fig. 6.4) and make clear to the company that you are using this figure as the basis for your claim.

Full description of property lost or damaged	Where purchased (name, address)	Date purchased	Price paid	Allowance for wear and tear, depreciation, salvage	Net claim
20 inch colour television (model: Ferguson 3722)	Will Worthing 194 Bozley Street Twickenham Middlesex	1976	£200 / Current Shop Price £300	£120	£180

I've inserted a new column – current shop price – and based my claim on that.
Since the TV is 4 years old, has an expected total life of 10 years and no salvage value (it was stolen) the allowance I've made for wear and tear is $\frac{4}{10} \times 300 = £120$

Figure 6.4
Amending a misleading claim form

Personal liability insurance

What it is

This type of insurance covers you for compensation you have to pay if, through negligence, you or a member of your family are responsible for damaging someone else's property, or for killing or injuring someone – eg by poking them in the eye with your umbrella, or carelessly throwing away a lighted cigarette which causes a fire. Some policies cover you for damages you are awarded because of someone else's negligence, and which you are unable to collect (eg because they can't afford to pay up).

Note that accidents while driving your car are covered under your car insurance policy. And accidents caused through the ownership (or occupation) of your home are covered by your house buildings (or contents) policies – ▷ pp. 85 and 91.

How much cover to go for

Until the past couple of years, you probably wouldn't have been left out of pocket, no matter what disaster you caused, if you had £100,000 worth of personal liability cover. But recently things have changed. Awards in the courts to people injured by another person's negligence have been very high – over £200,000 in some cases of severe injury. So to be on the safe side you should go for £250,000 worth of cover at the least – £500,000 would be a safer level to aim for.

To give some indication of the kind of figure that might be awarded nowadays for personal injuries, look at Fig. 6.5 right.

Figure 6.5 Adjusted amounts of awards for injuries (1)

	£
Quadriplega	161,300
Very severe brain damage	204,800
Blindness	64,200
Loss of finger	10,200
Dog bite	120
Indignity and injured feelings	780

1. Amounts don't include special damages (cost of care to date, loss of earnings to date, etc – which could be substantial) only general damages which cover pain and suffering, loss of earnings, future expenses, pension rights. Amounts adjusted to take account of inflation up to March 80.

The sums quoted are adjusted to take into account inflation in the period between the award and March 80.

Awards for fatal injuries may also be substantial – it wouldn't be impossible for an award above £125,000 to be made for the death of a man with a young family to support. Even damage to property could set you back several thousands of £££ (as in the example below). So if your personal liability cover is below £250,000 you should revise it right away.

How you buy it

Personal liability insurance is usually included in your house contents policy. Check whether your policy gives this cover (and also how much cover you get – some policies give £500,000 of cover, but many policies give £250,000, a few give only £100,000). If personal liability cover is not included in your house contents policy, you may have to take out an extension to your policy or take out an entirely separate policy (see *Money Which?* June 79 for companies which offer this kind of policy).

What it costs

No separate charge if it's included in your house contents policy. If you want to add personal liability insurance as an extension to an existing contents insurance policy, there will be a small charge – probably less than £1 a year. Bought separately, it's more expensive – it could cost up to £10 a year (June 79 prices). But that's still a small price to pay to avoid the possibility of having to foot an enormous bill for damage to people and property.

Deirdre, deep in thought about her O-levels, walks out into the street without looking, causes a Rolls-Royce to swerve and pile through the front window of an antique shop. The bill for damages to the Rolls, the window and the antiques comes to £12,000.

7 Rates

Most of the taxes you pay – such as income tax, capital gains tax and capital transfer tax – go straight to central government. Rates are the exception: they are a tax levied by and paid to your local authority.

The money from rates goes towards paying for local services of various kinds – eg education, council housing, police force, and street cleaning. It also goes towards the council's administrative costs.

Rates are levied on all kinds of property, commercial and private. Normally the occupier of the home is the one who has to pay the rates – but he or she must have control over the home rather than simply the right to use it. This means that an owner-occupier is certainly liable for rates, a tenant usually is, but a lodger usually isn't.

Some people with low incomes who are liable for rates can get help – called a *rate rebate* – towards paying them. Tenants as well as owner-occupiers can qualify for this help, even if their landlord pays the rates bill directly. If you think you might qualify for a rate rebate (details on p. 231) it's well worth applying for one.

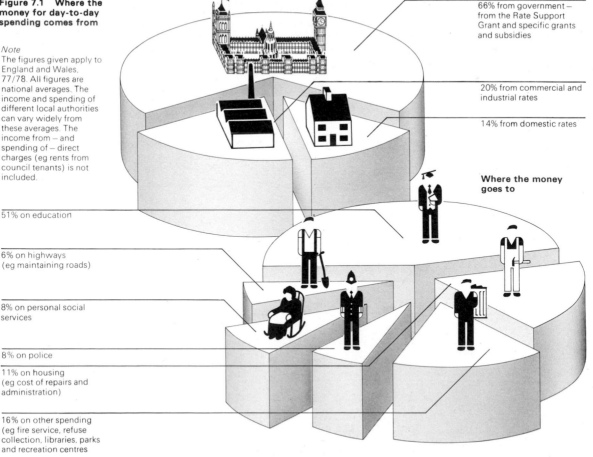

Figure 7.1 Where the money for day-to-day spending comes from

Note
The figures given apply to England and Wales, 77/78. All figures are national averages. The income and spending of different local authorities can vary widely from these averages. The income from – and spending of – direct charges (eg rents from council tenants) is not included.

66% from government – from the Rate Support Grant and specific grants and subsidies

20% from commercial and industrial rates

14% from domestic rates

Where the money goes to

51% on education

6% on highways (eg maintaining roads)

8% on personal social services

8% on police

11% on housing (eg cost of repairs and administration)

16% on other spending (eg fire service, refuse collection, libraries, parks and recreation centres

What determines your rates bill

What you pay in rates depends on two factors:
- the rateable value of your home
- the rate in the £ which your council decides to levy in a particular year.

The rateable value is calculated from the gross value of the home (▷ p. 100 for how this is done), and the rate in the £ depends on the council's assessment of how much money it needs to raise through rates.

As Fig. 7.1 shows, only around 14 per cent of the money local government spends from day to day comes from domestic rates – the major part comes in one way or another from central government.

Besides showing where local authority revenue comes from, Fig. 7.1 shows how it tends to get spent. Between them, education and housing account for around 60 per cent of total spending (although the proportions will vary to some degree from region to region and year to year).

When you pay

Most rates bills are payable half-yearly, commonly in April and October, but domestic ratepayers have the legal right to choose to pay their bill in instalments. The number of instalments each year is commonly 10 – but some councils collect the money in 11 or 12. To find out more about this, write to your council at the address on your rates demand note.

Paying in instalments is usually less painful than facing a big bill for rates twice a year. Even if you have the cash available to pay the bill in two bites, it would make sense to invest the money (somewhere safe like a building society account or a National Savings Bank investment account) and pay out smaller sums through the year.

What happens if you can't (or won't) pay

By law you should pay your rates within 7 days of the beginning of the half-year for which they are due (ie by 7 April for the half-year beginning 1 April) or within 7 days of the delivery of the demand note, if it arrives later than the beginning of the half-year (so if it arrived on 10 April you should pay by 17 April). But in practice the local authority will allow you some weeks or months to pay before it takes any action.

If you can pay part, but not all, of your rates, offer to do so and to make up the full amount later. A realistic offer like this may stop the council taking further action against you to get the money. If there seems

no hope that you will be able to pay at all, the council can waive payment altogether – but it is most unwise to count on them doing this.

If you fail to pay your rates, the council can, as a last resort, ask the magistrates' court for a distress warrant. This means they can sell your furniture and other belongings to meet your rates bill and the legal costs of proceeding against you.

If this doesn't produce enough money, and you still refuse to pay, the magistrates can send you to prison for up to 90 days. Alternatively, the council can take steps to have you declared bankrupt.

Empty homes

Since 1966 local authorities have been able after a certain period of time to charge rates on empty (ie unfurnished and unoccupied) homes, and in most cases they will eventually do this.

For the first 3 months the home is empty (6 months if the home is newly built or has not been used as a home before) no rates are payable. After that, you may have to pay between half and full rates for the property, and pay at the (higher) commercial rate. And if you buy a house that has been empty for 3 months or more already, you are liable for rates as soon as you become owner.

Garages

If your garage is entirely separate from your home (as it would be if you lived in a block of flats and had a garage elsewhere) you'll get a separate rates bill for it. You can't pay this bill in instalments or get a rate rebate for it, and rates are charged at the higher commercial rate.

Water and sewerage rates (England and Wales)
Since 1974, these have been payable to a *regional water authority* or *water company* (although they may still be collected by the council).

Regional water authorities charge either a rate in the £ multiplied by the home's rateable value, or a fixed (or standing) charge of £5 or so a year for each service on top of a lower rate in the £.

Regional water

authorities cannot make a sewerage charge to those without mains drainage.

There is no system of rebates to be claimed against water and sewerage rates. If you have difficulty in paying a water bill, it's worth asking the water authority whether you can pay your bills by instalments.

Rates in Scotland
Gross values (called gross annual values) are worked out in much the same way as in England and Wales. The last revaluation year was 1978.

Properties with gross values over £100 have a statutory deduction of £20 plus one-sixth of the amount by which the gross annual value exceeds £100. The rules are more complicated for homes with a gross annual value of less than £100 – so check with your local valuation department if you have a query concerning one.

Water and sewerage rates are included in the general rate demand. For appeals in Scotland ▷ p. 103.

The disabled
The gross values of the homes, garages, car ports etc, of disabled people are assessed in just the same way as for everyone else. But the disabled can get a special rebate to lower their rates bill.

To get this rebate, the applicant (or the member of household for whom they are applying) must be able to show – eg by means of a medical certificate – that he or she is disabled, or must be registered as disabled.

The special feature for which the rebate is claimed must be essential or of major importance to the well-being of the disabled person – like a ground-floor bedroom or an extra bathroom or lavatory for the disabled person to use, a garage for an invalid car, or extra space to house, say, a kidney machine.

For more details, get leaflet *Rate relief for disabled persons* from your local council (you apply to them *not* the valuation officer).

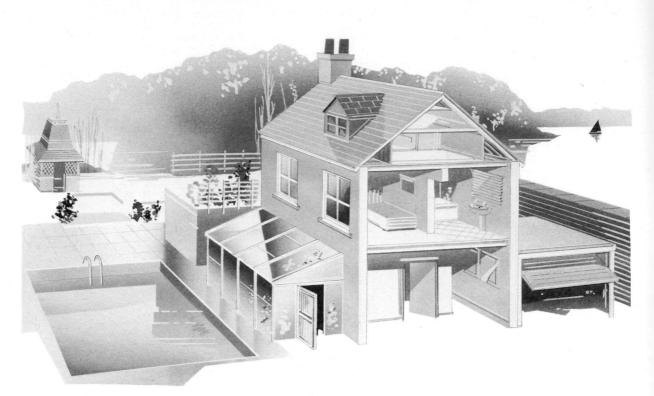

How your rates are worked out

Gross value

A property's gross value is meant to represent the yearly rent a typical tenant would be prepared to pay to rent it unfurnished, assuming the landlord paid for repairs and buildings insurance and the tenant paid the rates. The gross value is supposed to be based on an 'open market' rent: in other words, it should assume that any laws restricting what the landlord can charge as rent don't apply. Since few properties are let on these terms, calculating gross values can be difficult.

The people responsible for arriving at the valuation are *valuation officers*, employed by the Inland Revenue (*not* by local authorities).

By law, all gross values should be updated every 5 years, but postponements have meant that revaluations are made less frequently than this. The last one was in 1973, but the next one (planned for 1982) has been postponed again.

● How gross values are worked out.
The valuation officer's aim is to see that similar homes have similar gross values.

To work out gross values, the valuation officer studies the information on the *rent returns* – the questionnaires sent out to all occupiers in the year or so before a revaluation. Then he divides all the property in his area into categories (containing homes of similar size, age, and situation) and may reach a formula for a basic rent per square metre for each category.

He makes allowances for a home's particular advantages or disadvantages. There is no firm rule about how much every factor affects gross value. See Figs. 7.2 and 7.3 for the kind of thing he takes into account. Note that general state of repair does not affect the valuation.

● Improvements
If you improve your home between general revaluations – by adding a couple of rooms over the garage, for example – the property could be revalued. If so, the valuation officer will work out the new gross value according to what he thinks the rent would have been in the year or so before the start of the last revaluation year (April 73). He tries to ensure that these new gross values are comparable with existing ones.

In England and Wales provided the im-

Figure 7.2
These may raise your home's gross value

Extensions to home, eg extra bedroom, extra WC, kitchen extension

Garage or car port

Loft conversion

Central heating, full or partial

Conservatory, roof garden, swimming pool, tennis court

Built-in furniture, double glazing

Close to shops, station, parks, schools

Exceptional view

Sometimes: greenhouse, shed, outhouse

For improvements made to the home after the last revaluation ▷ left

provement would not raise the gross value by more than £30, your gross value won't change until the next general revaluation (unless you make further improvements which would bring the total increase in gross value to over £30). But the same improvement may affect gross value by different amounts, depending on the area you live in. In London, adding a car port might take you over the £30 limit; in a rural area, with lower gross values, even a large alteration, like a new bathroom or kitchen extension, might not raise gross values by more than £30. One important concession is that the installation of central heating after March 74 won't lead to the valuation officer proposing a change in your gross value until the next revaluation year, no matter how much it raises your home's gross value.

Rateable value

Rateable value is always less than gross value. The difference between them is what is known as the *statutory deduction*: this is meant to represent the annual cost of repairs and insurance for the property. For low gross values, the deduction may be as much as 45 per cent of gross value; for high values, it may be as little as about 20 per cent. See Fig. 7.4 for details.

Rateable and gross values of all properties (as well as descriptions of the properties – eg house or flat) are listed in the *valuation list*, which you can see at your town hall or council office.

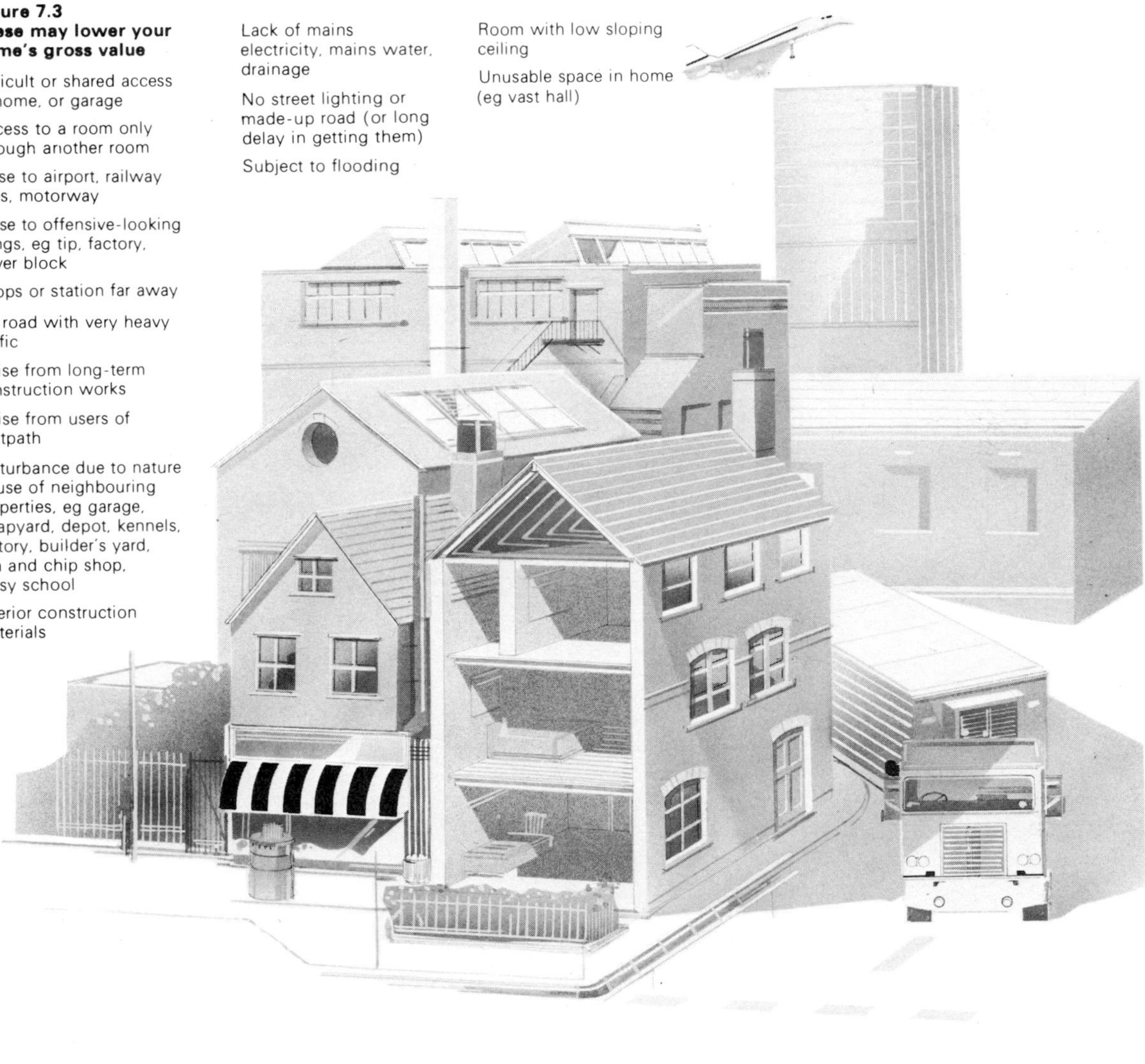

Figure 7.3
These may lower your home's gross value

Difficult or shared access to home, or garage

Access to a room only through another room

Close to airport, railway lines, motorway

Close to offensive-looking things, eg tip, factory, tower block

Shops or station far away

On road with very heavy traffic

Noise from long-term construction works

Noise from users of footpath

Disturbance due to nature of use of neighbouring properties, eg garage, scrapyard, depot, kennels, factory, builder's yard, fish and chip shop, noisy school

Inferior construction materials

Lack of mains electricity, mains water, drainage

No street lighting or made-up road (or long delay in getting them)

Subject to flooding

Room with low sloping ceiling

Unusable space in home (eg vast hall)

The rate in the £

Each year, the local council fixes on the number of pence you must pay for each pound of your home's rateable value. This is called the *rate-in-the-£* or *rate poundage*. The rate-in-the-£ is different for different types of property (lowest for homes).

Example

Rateable value	£306
Rate-in-the-£	85p
So rates for year	
306 × 85p =	£260.10

For information on appeals procedure in Scotland ▷ opposite.

Think your rates are too high?

You have no chance at all of getting your own personal rates bill reduced simply because you happen to disapprove of your council's spending policies. If you withhold your rates as a protest, the council can eventually sue you for them. Your best bet would be to join (or form) a ratepayers' association and try to put pressure on your council to change its policies.

Nor will you be let off your rates simply because you feel you can't afford to pay them. But you may well be able to get a rate rebate (▷ p. 231).

If you feel you are paying too much in rates because your gross value is too high, you could try appealing for a lower valuation. The Route Map (▷ p. 104) takes you through the appeals procedure step by step. But remember: even if you do win your appeal, the reduction in gross value is likely to be small – it's more likely to be £10 to £30 than £50 or £100.

Arguing for a lower valuation

The commonest ground for a reduction in a home's gross value is a change or decline in its surroundings since the last revaluation – the re-routing of heavy traffic so that it passes your home, for example, or the opening of a noisy pub across the street. Check back to Fig. 7.3. on p. 101 to see if some change in your home's surroundings may have reduced its gross value.

If nothing like this has happened, you'll

Fig. 7.4 Gross values and equivalent rateable values for England and Wales

Gross value	Rateable value	Gross value	Rateable value	Gross value	Rateable value	Gross value	Rateable value
£25	£14	£325	£245	£625	£492	£925	£742
£50	£27	£350	£266	£650	£513	£950	£763
£75	£43	£375	£286	£675	£534	£975	£784
£100	£60	£400	£306	£700	£555	£1,000	£805
£125	£78	£425	£326	£725	£576	£1,025	£826
£150	£98	£450	£347	£750	£597	£1,050	£847
£175	£119	£475	£367	£775	£617	£1,075	£867
£200	£140	£500	£388	£800	£638	£1,100	£888
£225	£161	£525	£409	£825	£659	£1,200	£972
£250	£182	£550	£430	£850	£680	£1,300	£1,055
£275	£202	£575	£451	£875	£701	£1,400	£1,138
£300	£223	£600	£472	£900	£722	£1,500	£1,222

How to work out values not in the table

Gross value:	What you subtract to arrive at rateable value
Up to £65:	45 per cent of gross value
£66 to £128:	£29 and $\frac{3}{10}$ of amount by which gross value exceeds £65
£129 to £330:	£48 and $\frac{1}{6}$ of amount by which gross value exceeds £128; but most you subtract is £80
£331 to £430:	£80 and $\frac{1}{5}$ of amount by which gross value exceeds £330
Over £430:	£100 and $\frac{1}{6}$ of amount by which gross value exceeds £430

Note: If answer included pennies, ignore 50p or fewer – but if over 50p, round up to £ above.

have to check whether there are homes comparable to yours which have lower gross values. If so, you may have a case, and it's worth following the Route Map.

You may find that the valuation officer agrees with you early on about lowering the home's gross value. If he doesn't, and you want to pursue your proposal for a lower valuation, you'll have to argue your case in the Valuation Court eventually.

The Valuation Court

This is a local court, open to the public and independent of the valuation officer. Hearings are comparatively informal. The chairman and members of the court are unpaid, but they have the help of a paid clerk of the court on legal points. The court can't award costs.

It may help you to sort out your arguments if you go along to hear some other cases at your local Valuation Court. The clerk of the court, or someone at your town hall, should be able to tell you when the hearings are. Remember that you'll want to listen in to *domestic* appeals – not commercial ones, which deal with offices and property.

Before the hearing

Ask the valuation officer what evidence he is going to bring forward: gross values of other homes or rent returns ($\triangleright$ p. 100). If he's going to use gross values, ask which homes are being used and check if they are comparable to yours – ie in size, type of area, advantages and disadvantages. Then scout round to find homes whose gross values will support your case for a reduction in the gross value of your home. This is what you need to find:

Home you're looking for	Valuation you hope to find
Closely comparable to yours – eg in size, type of area, advantages and disadvantages	Lower than yours
Much like yours, but with extra advantages	Same as yours, or lower
Much like yours, but larger	Same as yours, or lower
Much like yours, but smaller	Very much lower than yours

If the valuation officer is going to use rent returns, he has to give you 14 days' notice, send you addresses of the properties he has chosen, and allow you to see the rent returns. You can then choose an equal number of homes and ask to see *their* rent returns. Choose homes similar to your own – same type of area, size, etc – and (since you're trying to find out about *rent* levels) try to find homes which have been let for some years. Note that you can't use rent returns unless the valuation officer decides to – and you're at a considerable disadvantage, because you can't check through all the rent returns to find ones which back up your case.

Procedure at the court

The clerk of the court will write to tell you when your case is to be heard. You can bring witnesses to support your case, and you can be legally represented if you wish (although you can't get legal aid for this purpose).

You and your witnesses can be questioned by the objector to the proposal (usually the valuation officer) and by the members of the court. The local authority can also be represented, and can ask you questions. Then the valuation officer will give his reasons for objecting, and he can be questioned by you and by the members of the court. Finally, you can reply to his arguments.

The court then comes to a decision – sometimes on the spot, sometimes not. The court's decision will be confirmed to you in writing, and you can ask for the reasons for the decision. If you win a reduction, it may be worth applying to your council to have the reduction backdated (although this happens in exceptional cases only – eg your valuation includes a garage and you haven't got one).

Presenting your case

Remember that the court is interested in how an imaginary, typical tenant (who they may call a *hypothetical tenant*) would be affected by the particular advantages or disadvantages of your home. So it's no good basing your case on the fact, for example, that you are particularly sensitive to traffic noise (if that's the thing you are complaining about).

Here are some practical points:
● prepare your case thoroughly and present it as clearly and concisely as you can
● type out any lists of comparisons or other factual evidence, and hand out copies in court. You may need as many as 6 copies of each document
● bring with you any plans, photographs or sketches which support your case.

Appeals in Scotland
The basic procedure for appealing is the same in Scotland as in England, but at present it's only in a revaluation year that you can appeal because you think your home's gross annual value is unfairly high.

At other times you can appeal only if:
● your home is new or has been substantially altered
● your home's surroundings have changed
● a court decision on another home applies to yours too.

You can always appeal if the assessor (Scottish for valuation officer) wants to change your home's gross annual value.

If you can't agree with the assessor, your case will be heard by a Valuation Appeal Committee (Scottish for Valuation Court). Further appeals go to the Lands Valuation Appeal Court in Edinburgh – which usually doesn't award expenses (Scottish for costs).

How to appeal for a lower valuation

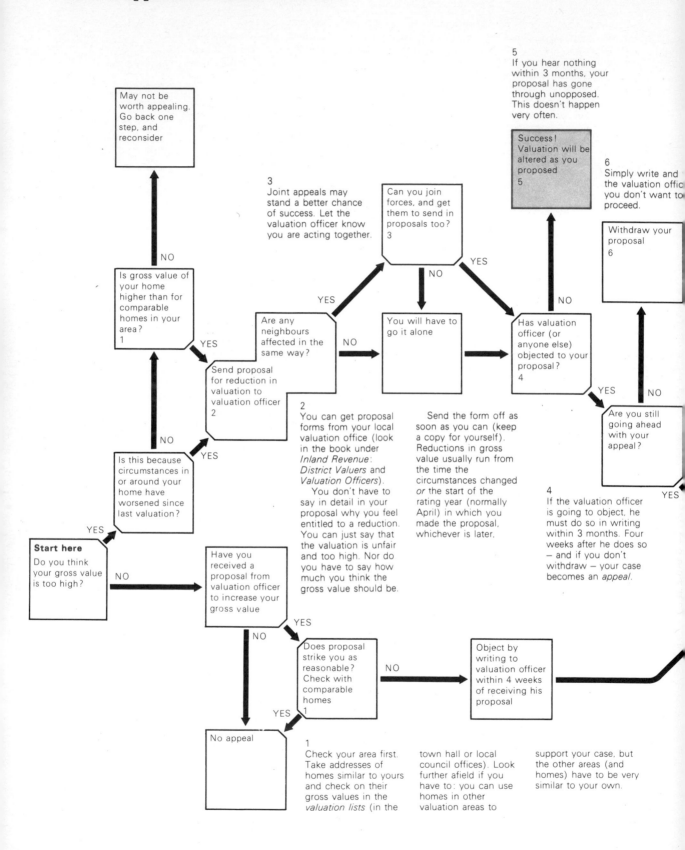

5
If you hear nothing within 3 months, your proposal has gone through unopposed. This doesn't happen very often.

Success! Valuation will be altered as you proposed
5

6
Simply write and the valuation offic you don't want to proceed.

May not be worth appealing. Go back one step, and reconsider

Withdraw your proposal
6

3
Joint appeals may stand a better chance of success. Let the valuation officer know you are acting together.

Can you join forces, and get them to send in proposals too?
3

NO

YES

Is gross value of your home higher than for comparable homes in your area?
1

NO

YES

Are any neighbours affected in the same way?

YES

NO

You will have to go it alone

Has valuation officer (or anyone else) objected to your proposal?
4

NO

Send proposal for reduction in valuation to valuation officer
2

YES

YES

Are you still going ahead with your appeal?

YES

NO

Is this because circumstances in or around your home have worsened since last valuation?

YES

2
You can get proposal forms from your local valuation office (look in the book under *Inland Revenue: District Valuers* and *Valuation Officers*).

You don't have to say in detail in your proposal why you feel entitled to a reduction. You can just say that the valuation is unfair and too high. Nor do you have to say how much you think the gross value should be.

Send the form off as soon as you can (keep a copy for yourself). Reductions in gross value usually run from the time the circumstances changed *or* the start of the rating year (normally April) in which you made the proposal, whichever is later.

4
If the valuation officer is going to object, he must do so in writing within 3 months. Four weeks after he does so — and if you don't withdraw — your case becomes an *appeal*.

Start here
Do you think your gross value is too high?

NO

Have you received a proposal from valuation officer to increase your gross value

NO

YES

Does proposal strike you as reasonable? Check with comparable homes
1

NO

Object by writing to valuation officer within 4 weeks of receiving his proposal

YES

No appeal

1
Check your area first. Take addresses of homes similar to yours and check on their gross values in the *valuation lists* (in the town hall or local council offices). Look further afield if you have to: you can use homes in other valuation areas to support your case, but the other areas (and homes) have to be very similar to your own.

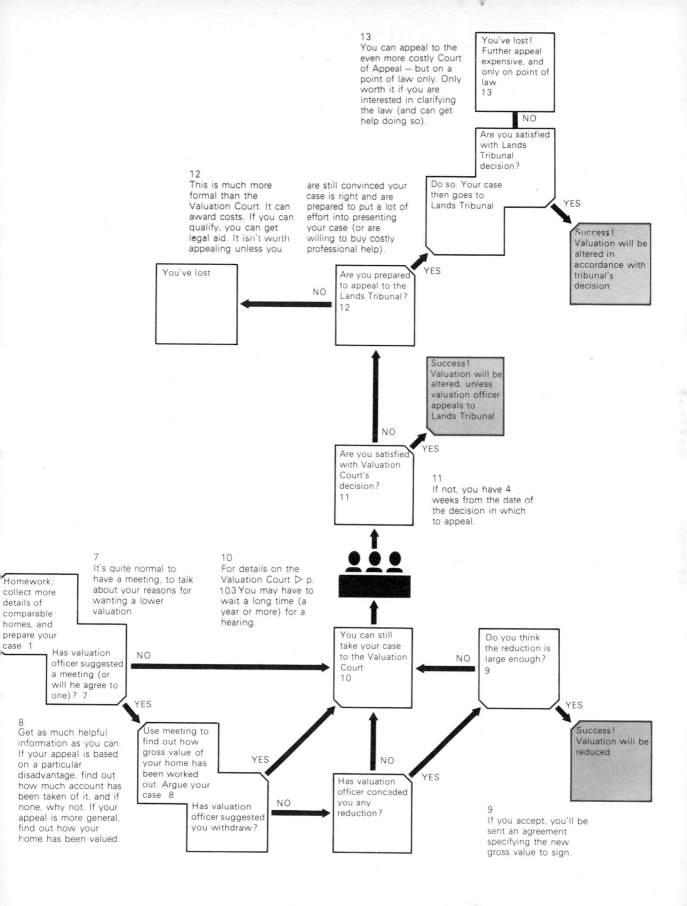

13
You can appeal to the even more costly Court of Appeal – but on a point of law only. Only worth it if you are interested in clarifying the law (and can get help doing so).

You've lost! Further appeal expensive, and only on point of law
13

Are you satisfied with Lands Tribunal decision?

NO

Do so. Your case then goes to Lands Tribunal

YES

Success!
Valuation will be altered in accordance with tribunal's decision

12
This is much more formal than the Valuation Court. It can award costs. If you can qualify, you can get legal aid. It isn't worth appealing unless you are still convinced your case is right and are prepared to put a lot of effort into presenting your case (or are willing to buy costly professional help).

You've lost

NO

Are you prepared to appeal to the Lands Tribunal?
12

YES

Success!
Valuation will be altered, unless valuation officer appeals to Lands Tribunal

YES

Are you satisfied with Valuation Court's decision?
11

NO

11
If not, you have 4 weeks from the date of the decision in which to appeal.

7
It's quite normal to have a meeting, to talk about your reasons for wanting a lower valuation.

10
For details on the Valuation Court ▷ p. 103 You may have to wait a long time (a year or more) for a hearing.

Homework: collect more details of comparable homes, and prepare your case 1

Has valuation officer suggested a meeting (or will he agree to one)? 7

NO

You can still take your case to the Valuation Court
10

NO

Do you think the reduction is large enough?
9

YES

YES

8
Get as much helpful information as you can. If your appeal is based on a particular disadvantage, find out how much account has been taken of it, and if none, why not. If your appeal is more general, find out how your home has been valued.

Use meeting to find out how gross value of your home has been worked out. Argue your case 8

YES

Has valuation officer suggested you withdraw?

NO

Has valuation officer conceded you any reduction?

NO

YES

Success!
Valuation will be reduced

9
If you accept, you'll be sent an agreement specifying the new gross value to sign.

8 On holiday

A holiday horror story can be amusing, but you'd probably rather not end up telling one yourself. You can improve your chances of enjoying a carefree holiday by doing two things well before departure date:
● think about money – how you are going to take it, spend it, and look after it
● think about insurance – what kind you are going to need while you're away.

This chapter deals with money questions first. For insurance ▷ p. 109.

How to take your holiday money

There's no ideal way to take your holiday money. Cash is cheap but risky. Other methods will cost you maybe a couple of pounds for every hundred £££ worth of foreign money you end up with. Convenience and safety, rather than cost, are probably the most important factors to consider.

A combination of two or more of the following should meet your needs:
● cash (either £££ or foreign money)
● travellers' cheques
● credit card
● Eurocheque scheme
● open credit.

See opposite and p. 108 for details of these.

Where to change your holiday money

Banks, bureaux de change, many hotels and camp sites, and some big stores have money changing facilities. You may get a better rate of exchange in a bank or bureau de change than a shop or hotel. Banks abroad often keep different hours from those in the UK – and they tend to have more bank holidays. Check on this with your travel agent, or tourist office before you set off.

In countries with strict currency regulations (like Poland and Egypt) you may be approached by people offering a better rate of exchange for cash than you would get at a bank. Changing money like this (on the blackmarket) is illegal in most countries. You could go to prison if you are caught.

Limits on what you can spend abroad

There are now no limits on how much money you can take abroad – whether on holiday or for investment.

Looking after your money

Don't keep all your money (travellers' cheques, cash, etc) in the same place. Then, even if you lose your handbag or wallet, you won't find yourself penniless. If you are taking travellers' cheques, you'll normally be given a list of their serial numbers by whoever issues them. If you're not given one, make one yourself and keep the list separately from the cheques themselves. Make a note of which cheques you've cashed – if the cheques are lost or stolen, the list of serial numbers will help you claim a refund.

At a hotel or camp site, you could try asking if you can keep your money in their safe.

Cash

● British money
Make sure you take some British money with you. You will need it on your return — eg for train fares. You can take any amount.

● Foreign money
It's sensible to get some foreign money before you leave — especially small denomination notes for bus fares, etc. You can get it through banks and some travel agents. Government rules on holding foreign currency were abolished in October 79.

Order your foreign money at least a week in advance. If you wait to change money until you arrive at a port, airport, or border post you may get a poor rate of exchange, and find yourself at the back of a long queue as well. Many countries restrict the amount of their currency you can take into or out of the country — check with your bank.

● Insurance
Make sure you are covered against theft or loss of money. Most policies don't cover the first £5 of each claim, and there is usually an upper limit (ranges from £50 to £500 — but is often around £150). You normally have to wait until you get home for the insurance company to pay out.

● Left-over foreign cash
You can change foreign notes back into £££ at banks, main post offices and some travel agents. You may also be able to change foreign coins (but at a poor rate of exchange).

Travellers' cheques

● How they work
You buy them before you go on holiday. They are available in units of £2, £5, £10, £20 and £50, and you can choose any combination of these units. You should be asked to sign each cheque when you buy it.

The cheques can be changed back into money at a bank or bureau de change, and you may also be able to cash them at your hotel or camp site. You can use them to pay bills at many hotels, restaurants, and shops as well.

To cash a cheque, countersign it in the presence of the cashier. He will accept it if the two signatures on it match. Abroad, you'll need your passport as identification.

If you intend to travel outside western Europe, check — before you buy — that the brand you intend to take will be easy to cash in the countries you are visiting.

● Where you buy them
Buy at any branch of the High-Street banks, the TSB, Cook's, American Express, or a main post office. You don't have to be a regular customer of the organization you buy from.

Post offices and small branches of the TSB need a week's notice to get travellers'

cheques. You may also need to give a week's notice to get travellers' cheques in a foreign currency (▷ right) from any source.

● What they cost to buy
You pay around 1 per cent of their total sterling value. If you buy foreign currency travellers' cheques you also pay a charge for changing £££ into foreign currency.

● What they cost to cash
They usually cost nothing to cash in the country of the currency they are made out in — eg sterling cheques in the UK, or dollar cheques in the US.

When you cash them into a different currency, you pay the local charge for changing money — eg if you cash a sterling cheque in Italy you pay for changing £££ into lire. The charge may be included in the exchange rate. In some countries (Belgium, for example) you may have to pay an extra charge for cashing a sterling or dollar travellers' cheque — find out from your travel agent or bank beforehand.

● If you lose them
As long as you signed the cheques when you bought them, and had not countersigned them, you get a full refund. You may have to wait until you get back to the UK to get

it. Having the serial numbers of the lost cheques should speed up getting your refund.

Report the loss at once to the cheque company — by telegraph or telephone, if there's no convenient local branch to call at.

● Foreign currency cheques
The main advantages of these are that they may be easier to cash than sterling cheques in some parts of the world — eg US dollar cheques in South America — and you will not have problems changing money abroad in a sterling crisis.

Government rules on holding foreign currency were abolished in October 79.

You can try to get cheques in the currency of the country you are going to. But you may be given cheques of a foreign local bank, and if you take these you may have trouble cashing them except at branches of that particular bank.

It may be more convenient to take a well known brand of cheque in a 'strong' foreign currency — such as the German mark. But this is a relatively dear way to take your holiday money because you pay twice for changing it: once into the strong currency and again into the local currency.

Credit card

● Using it in the UK
Many organizations accept credit cards in payment for package tours and tickets.

You can buy travellers' cheques and foreign money with Barclaycard or Access at banks displaying their signs, and at Cook's. They charge as if you'd borrowed cash with your credit card.

● Using it abroad
You can use a credit card abroad in much the same way as in the UK. For an expensive purchase (costing more than £300, say) the credit card company may want to see the receipt you get at the customs when you bring it back into the UK.

Access, Barclaycard, Diners Club, and American Express are all fairly widely accepted in many countries.

Access is accepted wherever you see the Eurocard or Master Charge symbols (shown on the back of the card). For Barclaycard, look for the blue, white, and gold Visa symbol.

● What it costs
The bill you sign is made out in local currency, and is converted into £££ when the credit card company gets it. It could take a long time for the bills to reach the credit card company — sometimes up to 6 months or so — so you might get a long period of interest-free credit. If the exchange rate changes during that time, you may end up paying more (or less) than you expected.

Eurocheque scheme

● How it works
If you have a High-Street bank current account and cheque card, you can cash a cheque at any bank which belongs to the Eurocheque scheme. You write a cheque for the £££ you want, and show your cheque card (customers of Barclays need to get a special Eurocheque encashment card from their bank — their Barclaycard alone is no longer enough). Abroad, you get paid in local currency.

Most countries in Europe and round the Mediterranean have banks in this scheme.

You can't use the scheme for cheques to settle bills in shops, hotels, etc.

● How much you can get
You have to keep within the current limits on this scheme. In 1980 you could draw up to £50 a day in the UK, and abroad you could cash 2 cheques a day, each up to £50.

● How to find a bank in the scheme
Look for the blue and red Eurocheque symbol illustrated above (though it's worth checking in any bank, if you can't find one showing the symbol).

● What it costs
Your bank will make its usual charge for handling each cheque. Foreign banks vary widely in the amount they charge for each cheque. It may be worth shopping around.

One advantage of this scheme is that you don't have to pay for your holiday money until the cheques reach your bank — which may take up to 3 weeks or so.

Open credit

● How it works
You arrange to cash cheques at a bank in the town you are going to. You can do this if you have a current account with any High-Street bank.

● What it costs
Costs vary widely from bank to bank. If you can make the arrangement for less than 1 per cent (£1 for each £100 you can draw) this could work out cheaper than travellers' cheques — it depends how much you get charged for cashing each cheque. Unfortunately there's no way of finding this out beforehand.

● Other places you can cash cheques abroad
You may be able to cash cheques at some banks in British colonies (or ex-colonies) — Hong Kong and the West Indies, for example. Get details from your bank.

If you have an American Express card you can — in an emergency — cash cheques at American Express offices. There is a limit to the amount you can cash — in 1980, £500 within a 21 day period.

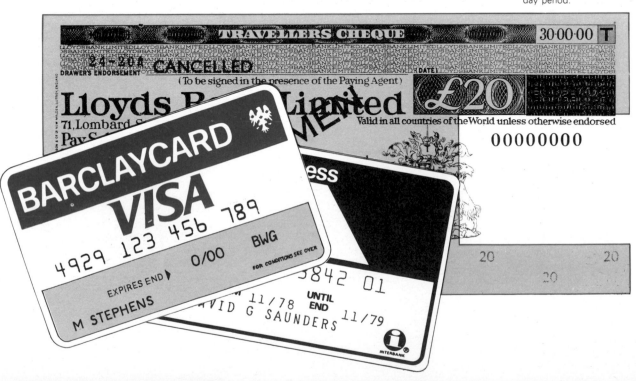

Holiday insurance

There are two kinds of holiday insurance. *Package holiday insurance* gives you fixed amounts of cover for a standard range of mishaps or disasters – like illness, cancellation, and stolen luggage. You can get this kind of insurance whether you are holidaying independently or on a package. *Selective holiday insurance* lets you choose (within reason) the amounts and types of cover you want.

Since package holiday insurance is likely to suit most people holidaying abroad, and works out cheaper than the same cover bought with a selective policy, this chapter concentrates on package-type insurance. On p. 110 we give a summary of the cover you'd get with a typical package policy.

How to buy it

● Going on holiday independently

You can buy insurance direct from an insurance company, or through a broker or travel agent. Almost all companies will give you a copy of the full policy wording if you ask for it. It's worth getting this *before* you buy the insurance.

To apply, you fill in a proposal form. Read it carefully before signing: you may be signing a declaration that, for example, the people you are going on holiday with are in good health. If this turns out to be untrue, the company can refuse to pay up when you make a claim.

You are under an obligation to tell the insurance company about any facts which they would reasonably want to take into account. You have to disclose these *material facts* whether you are specifically asked to or not – if you don't, the company could again refuse to pay up. Facts about your own health are obviously material, but so are facts about the health of people whose illness might affect your holiday plans.

● Going on a package holiday

Tour operators nearly always offer you insurance. You may have to buy it from them, but it's generally optional. The insurance policy may be slightly different from the company's normal one if you buy this way.

The holiday brochure normally gives a summary of the cover and tells you the name of the insurance company. You don't normally see the full policy wording until you have bought the insurance, and you may not even see it then unless you ask to do so or call at the tour operator's office to see the master policy.

To apply, you normally don't have to fill in a proposal form; you just say you want the insurance when you book the holiday. You still have to declare any material facts which might affect the insurance. And when you book and say you want the insurance, you automatically accept the terms of the policy.

● What it costs

For a package policy bought through a tour operator, the price per person is £5 to £7 for a fortnight's holiday in Spain or Italy, for example. The same kind of package policy if you are travelling independently would cost only a little more. Check on the cover you get (particularly the amount of medical cover) before going for the cheapest.

What can go wrong?

The main thing that can go wrong is to find yourself in some predicament not covered by your policy. So it's very important to check *before you take out the policy* what you are and are not covered for. Here are a few examples of what a policy may *not* cover.

● Pre-existing illness

Unless you've told the company about any recurring illness you had before you applied for insurance, you may not be covered – even if your policy does not specifically exclude claims arising from pre-existing illness. This is because this would count as a material fact (▷ left) which you should have told the company about.

● Illness or injury due to drink, drugs, pregnancy, attempted suicides, etc. Companies vary in what they exclude – read your policy carefully.

● Illness not reported immediately

This applies before you go on holiday as well as while you are away. If an illness or accident happens which may force you to cancel your holiday, play safe by letting the company know at once: if you wait and see, you may not be covered if you finally have to cancel.

● Special risks

If you take a holiday which involves special risks – like mountaineering or skiing – get a policy which covers you for that activity. If you are offered one which does not, either ask to have it altered (which may cost extra) or go elsewhere.

● Lost money not reported to police within 24 hours

● First £x of any claim

You may have to pay the first £5, say, of each claim – and the very young (under age 5 or so) and those over 70 or 75 may have to pay more than the normal amount of each claim.

Package holiday insurance

What a typical policy might offer	What you need

Medical expenses: £1,500 to £5,000
This covers such things as doctors' bills, hospital bills, ambulance charges, emergency dental treatment. It also covers extra hotel and travelling expenses brought about by your illness or injury — both for yourself and, if essential on medical grounds, for a companion.

This is the most important part of the package. Hospital bills abroad can be very heavy, and, in addition, there may be extra hotel and travelling expenses (for example, if you have to fly back on a stretcher).
Even if you can get free or reduced-cost medical treatment in the EEC and some other countries (▷ p. 111) there are still the extra costs that could be incurred getting home.
It seems sensible to get the full amount of medical insurance you might need: in Europe and North Africa, at least £2,000 for each person (for holidays in North America very much more).

Note for those who have medical bills insurance (▷ p. 146): you are advised to get holiday insurance as well, because your medical bills insurance may well not cover you fully for treatment abroad — and doesn't cover you at all for such things as extra hotel and travelling expenses.

Cancellation and curtailment: £200 to £400
This covers you for what you forfeit if you cancel the holiday, in quite a wide range of situations — eg because of your own illness or injury, or that of someone you were going on holiday with, or that of a close relative or close business colleague. May also cover you if you cancel because you are called for jury service or as a witness, or if you lose your job shortly before the holiday. Also covers you if you have to cut the holiday short, for the same sorts of reasons.

This is probably the next most important part of the package. The cover here should match what you stand to lose if you cancel the holiday or cut it short. Cover of £250 or so may just be enough, but you might need more for lengthy or long-distance holidays.

Delays: up to £60
Some policies pay compensation if you are delayed eg at the airport because of strike or industrial action (a few cover all delays). Most pay up an amount (£20, say) per 24 hour delay up to the maximum of the policy (commonly £60, sometimes £30). Some cover delays at both ends of the journey; others just the UK end.

The money you get may soften the blow of sitting at the airport rather than on the beach. Check the policy conditions carefully — they vary widely.

Luggage and belongings: £400 to £500
Not more than, say, £100 for any one thing

Check that this will be enough to cover what you are taking with you. If, for example, you have a valuable camera or expensive clothes, it will not be. If you are in the habit of carrying valuable things around with you, you probably need an all-risks policy — which covers you in the UK, and usually for up to 30 days a year abroad.

Money: up to £100
'Money' includes things like travel tickets and petrol coupons.

This ought to be enough. But if you decide to take more than this in cash you may need more cover.

Personal liability: up to £100,000 or £250,000
This covers your legal liability if, through negligence, you injure people or damage property (▷ p. 97). There are situations where you are not covered, eg when driving a car or power boat.

You need this kind of insurance throughout the year — not simply on holiday — and £100,000 may not be enough (▷ p. 97). Personal liability insurance may well be included in your house contents policy (if you have one), but it does not always apply abroad — read your policy to find out.

Personal accident
This commonly provides a payment of £2,000 on death, loss of an eye or limb, or permanent total disablement; for other injuries, it pays out a weekly amount for up to two years — if you are off work as a result of the injuries.

Do not attach much — or any — importance to this part of the policy. If you need insurance for death or injuries, you need it throughout the year — not simply on holiday. Moreover, assuming you do need it, you would certainly need very much more insurance than any of these holiday policies provides.

What happens if you fall ill abroad

In general, you have to arrange treatment and pay the bills. You claim from the insurance company when you get home. You shouldn't have many problems in getting the hospital to wait for payment if you can show evidence (like the policy document) that you will be able to pay. But don't rely on this for the USA.

If you need more money, you could telephone your bank (if you have one) and explain. Or you could try contacting your insurance broker.

Tour operators' representatives normally help you arrange treatment, and some tour operators may even settle bills – which could be one advantage of taking the insurance offered by a tour operator.

Free or reduced-cost medical treatment

If you fall ill in a country with which the UK has a reciprocal health agreement, you are entitled to free or reduced-cost medical treatment. To find out about this, ask your local social security office for leaflet SA28/30 (*Medical treatment during visits abroad*). Another leaflet SA36 (*How to get treatment in the other EEC countries*) tells you how to go about this in the EEC. Take the leaflet on holiday with you.

If you are holidaying in the EEC, you usually have to have form E111 with you. You'll get an application form for form E111 in leaflet SA28/30. Ask your social security office for this at least a month before you go.

Insurance checklist

● don't waste time shopping around for the cheapest policy; concentrate on getting a policy which suits you. If you're going on a package holiday, it is generally convenient to buy the policy offered by the tour operator – but, again, check that it suits you

● read the full policy document before committing yourself

● if you might possibly become pregnant, or if your holiday plans depend on the health of an elderly relative, or if you're buying insurance for small children or the elderly – make sure the policy is suitable

● buy at least £2,000 of medical insurance (and think about taking out more for holidays in North America)

● check that the policy provides you with the amounts of insurance you need for cancellation, money, luggage and other belongings, and – if your house contents policy doesn't already provide it – personal liability (▷ p. 97)

● take a copy of the policy document on holiday with you. You'll need to refer to it if anything goes wrong – and may need to reassure a hospital or doctor that you can afford the fees

● if you're going to an EEC country, take the right leaflet and form with you (▷ left)

● carry out your part of the bargain – eg by giving all the information which the insurance company needs to have when you apply for a policy, and by acting as the policy tells you if something goes wrong. You can then demand – from a position of strength – that the company carries out its part of the bargain.

9 Owning a car

Owning a car has many financial implications but its convenience far outweighs, in many people's minds, its running costs. When considering the pros and cons of this particular purchase, it's important to consider both factors.

If you *do* have a car, it tends to affect your lifestyle quite appreciably. You use it for Sunday picnics in the country or visits to friends, for example – activities that you might not contemplate without your own transport. If you gave up running a car, you'd probably have to change more than just the way you get about – to some extent, you'd have to change the way you spend your free time too.

For much the same reason, it's almost impossible to predict, if you *don't* have a car at present, how much you'd use it if you did. You can't just work it out from how much you use public (or hired) transport at the moment.

If you reckon you'd use a car mainly for occasional, planned, fairly lengthy trips, it may be that hiring rather than buying would save you money. Figure 9.1 gives an idea of the relative costs of hiring versus buying. The table assumes that if you decided to buy a car, you'd get a new one. If you bought a secondhand car, you'd find that the costs of ownership were appreciably lower (mainly because of lower depreciation – ▷ p. 113).

You can see, from the table, that it's only at relatively low mileages that hiring works out cheaper. And if you are considering hiring, remember to add on what public transport will cost you over the year for the trips you use it for. This way you'll get a *total transport bill* to compare with the costs for the likely mileage you'd do if you owned a car.

Figure 9.1   Cost of owning versus hiring (1)

Miles covered (2)	Escort 1300		Cortina 1600		Granada 2800	
	Owning	Hiring	Owning	Hiring	Owning	Hiring
3,000 (say, 2 weeks' holiday plus 20 days)	£1,115	£740	£1,300	£975	£2,045	£1,700
5,000 (say, 2 weeks' holiday plus 40 days)	£1,240	£1,220	£1,440	£1,605	£2,220	£2,795
7,000 (say, 2 weeks' holiday plus 60 days)	£1,365	£1,700	£1,585	£2,235	£2,400	£3,895

1. Based on hire charges, running costs, etc in April 80, and assuming petrol costs £1.50 a gallon.

2. Assuming you do 1,000 miles in the 2 weeks' holiday, and 100 miles on each of the other days you use the car.

What does a car cost to run?

Whether you're thinking of becoming a car owner, changing a car, or just checking on current car expenditure, it's well worth getting an idea of what a car costs to run.

The costs fall into two categories: fixed costs (insurance, tax, depreciation, loss of interest on the money you've put into the car) which are, in the main, unaffected by how much you use the car; and variable costs (petrol, oil, spares, repairs) that, in the main, go up with use.

Figure 9.2 gives an indication (for mid-80) of the likely running costs for 7 different cars, assuming you do about 12,000 miles a year and the car is just out of its guarantee period (new cars would have lower repair bills, but substantially higher depreciation). 12,000 miles a year is fairly representative of the mileage covered in the first few years of a car's life. Owners of older cars, however, tend to do lower mileage than this.

Even for the cheapest car to run, the costs were more than £1,300 a year (about 11½p a mile), and to run a Jaguar XJ5.3 the costs were over £5,500 (about 46p a mile). Whatever car you're running, you're taking on a fairly heavy annual cost.

Petrol

How much you use of this depends both on the size and make of your car, and on the conditions you drive in. Driving in town traffic tends to use up more petrol than driving the same distance on the open road (though, of course, it depends on how fast you're driving, how often you stop and start, and so on). It's worth bearing this in mind when you read advertisements which quote the government's test figures of so many miles per gallon, for the car they are selling. The government figures give petrol consumption at a constant speed of 56 mph (and sometimes at 75 mph too) and for a mix of conditions meant to represent town driving – commonly called the *urban figure.*

Oil

Unless you have a car that uses more oil than it ought to because something is wrong with it, this should not add up to much – £10 a year at the most.

Spares, repairs and servicing

The cost of servicing, spares, repairs and so on will vary considerably, according to the car's make, how old it is, and how lucky you are. A new car's guarantee helps in the first year – but you'll still have to spend something on servicing.

Costs tend to mount over the years – reaching their highest, on average, when a car is about 5 to 7 years old (they may then be well over twice the amount they were in the first year of a car's life). As cars get older than this they tend to be used less, and perhaps people get less fussy about repairing them. Figure 9.2 gives an idea of servicing and repair costs for a range of cars just outside their guarantee periods. Don't take these average figures too literally – just bear in mind that you'll be lucky if you have a car that *doesn't* develop faults of varying seriousness, at least once a year.

Even if you're handy enough to do the car repairs yourself, you will still have to pay for spares – and they can be expensive.

Insurance

What you have to pay for this depends mainly on your car's size and performance, the area it is kept in, and the driving record and ages of the drivers (▷ p. 118 for more details).

Road tax

Unless the government decides to scrap road tax in favour of higher taxes on petrol, road tax is a fixed cost, whatever the car. Buy a year's worth at once if possible: in 1980, it cost £60 compared with £66 at the 4-monthly rate.

Depreciation

The trickiest factor to take into account when doing your calculations is depreciation – the difference between what you paid out for your car in the first place and what you could sell it for now. It's important to allow for this cost in your calculations, even though you won't know exactly how much your car has depreciated until you come to sell it. You can get a rough idea of the depreciation on your car by looking up the prices of cars in one of the guides mentioned on p. 116.

One of the reasons why depreciation is difficult to work out is inflation. Just as inflation affects the price of new cars from year to year, it affects what you can get when you sell yours. Figure 9.2 gives an indication of the depreciation in a year for a range of cars, assuming they're in their second year, and that car prices increase over the year at 10 per cent.

But these £££ figures don't take into account the loss in buying power of the money over the year. Very roughly, in *real* terms, a car loses 25 per cent of its value in the first year; after that (again, in *real* terms) it loses around 15 per cent of its current value each year. So a £4,000 new car might, in terms of buying power, cost its owner £1,000 in depreciation in the first year – bringing its value down to £3,000. In its second year, it might cost its owner around 15 per cent of £3,000 (ie £450) – and so on for subsequent years.

This distinction between the depreciation cost in £££ and depreciation cost in buying power is particularly important if you're thinking of replacing your car – you'll have to allow not just for the drop in value of your old car, but also for the increase in price of the new one.

When you actually want to trade your car in, you may find it is worth less (has depreciated faster) than you thought; dealers will quote one price if they are buying a second-hand car from you, and a higher price if *you* are buying a second-hand car from *them*. There is usually at least a 10 per cent difference between the buying and selling prices. This could make selling your car privately (as opposed to selling to a dealer) something worth considering – you should, in theory, be able to get something between the dealer's buying and selling prices.

Other factors which affect the rate at which your car falls in value are:
● the make and model – if it has a good reputation (especially for reliability and durability) it will depreciate more slowly
● changes in the model – modifications in

the design usually speed up depreciation, and if the model is actually discontinued, it has an even worse effect on resale values
● country of manufacture – foreign cars may depreciate faster than British ones
● how well the car has been looked after – the better its condition, the less it will have depreciated.

What this all adds up to is that although you can count on the gap between the current value of your car and what it would cost to buy a newer one widening over time, there is no sure-fire way to predict exactly how fast it will depreciate. But, in general terms, the longer you keep a car, the less you will lose out in strict financial terms through depreciation.

Loss of interest

If you chose not to buy a car, you could invest the money and earn interest on it instead. Figure 9.2 shows the interest lost if, instead of having the car, you'd invested the money at 10½ per cent.

Total annual cost of owning a car

Figure 9.2 sums up what it might cost you to run a car (April 80 prices). When using this table, don't forget the effect of inflation on running costs – you may have to pay more for items than the table indicates.

Figure 9.2   What a car might cost to run

Annual costs (1)	Mini 1000	VW Polo 1100	Ford Escort 1300	Ford Cortina 1600	Vauxhall Cavalier 2000	Ford Granada 2800	Jaguar XJ 5.3
Petrol	£475	£515	£580	£645	£645	£820	£1,285
Servicing and repairs	£200	£125	£170	£215	£185	£245	£520
Annual variable costs	**£675**	**£640**	**£750**	**£860**	**£830**	**£1,065**	**£1,805**
Insurance	£95	£160	£110	£130	£160	£220	£265
Road tax	£60	£60	£60	£60	£60	£60	£60
Depreciation	£360	£360	£485	£565	£605	£1,050	£2,300
Loss of interest	£200	£290	£275	£330	£335	£445	£1,090
Annual fixed costs	**£715**	**£870**	**£930**	**£1,085**	**£1,160**	**£1,775**	**£3,390**
Total annual cost	**£1,390**	**£1,510**	**£1,680**	**£1,945**	**£1,990**	**£2,840**	**£5,520**
Cost per mile	**11½p**	**12½p**	**14p**	**16p**	**16½p**	**23½p**	**46p**

1. Based on prices and costs, for a year from April 80, for a car just out of its guarantee period. Assumes petrol costs £1.50 a gallon and that you could have got 10½ per cent return on your money, if you'd invested it, rather than buying the car.

Buying a car

Whether you buy a car new or second-hand (▷ below), before you decide to buy a particular car, think about:

● reliability – has it a good reputation?

● repairs – ask a garage or two if they are likely to be more expensive than average

● spares – can you get them easily, and are they more or less pricey than average?

● petrol consumption – look the car up in a motoring magazine to check this.

Each October, *Motoring Which?* publishes a car-buying guide which should be useful for checking up on all these points.

New versus second-hand

New cars have some obvious plus points:

● if things go wrong with your car in its first year, you shouldn't have to pay for repairs (when the car is under warranty) – and there should be fewer maintenance problems than with a second-hand car

● you needn't have doubts about how it has been driven or looked after by its previous owner

● you may get a better price for your old car if you are trading it in against a new model.

The drawback to buying new, of course, is the one mentioned on p. 114:

● depreciation is greatest in the first year of a car's life.

By buying second-hand instead of new you'll avoid the first hefty slice of depreciation. Provided you don't mind missing out on a new car's gloss and extra reliability, you can get a lot more for your money buying second-hand. In 1980, for example, for the price of a brand new Ford Fiesta, you could have bought a 2-year-old Renault 16TL or a 5-year-old Jaguar XJ 4.2.

British or foreign?

Times change and cars change with them, but some makes of car (all of them foreign) have, in surveys done by *Motoring Which?* over a number of years, been consistently above average for reliability. The surveys picked out BMW, Colt, Datsun, Honda, Mazda, Mercedes-Benz, Toyota, Volvo and VW-Audi as being better than average. Buying one of those makes meant it was likely you would get fewer faults and breakdowns.

Some makes – mostly British – on the other hand, did worse than average: Chrysler (now Talbot), Fiat, Reliant, recent Rovers, and older Vauxhalls. It makes sense to get as up-to-date information as possible before you decide on one make.

Beware the hidden extras
The prices quoted in advertisements for a new car sometimes don't include extras like number plates and delivery charges – which may cost you £100 or more – items sometimes called 'preparation' (pre-delivery inspection, petrol, anti-freeze, etc), and 'optional' extras (like a heated rear windscreen) which you have to take to avoid waiting a long time for a model without them. So find out what the price you have been quoted includes.

The cost of spares and servicing tends to be lower for British than foreign cars – but if you have to pay for them more often (because the car is less reliable) then it might still be cheaper, so far as repairs are concerned, to have a more reliable model with more expensive spares.

Size

If you want a big car to move a lot of your things fairly often, you may find an estate car or hatchback (ie a car with a back loading door) more convenient than a saloon. But these types of car score over a saloon mainly for carrying large, bulky things – extra luggage may well fit into a saloon's boot and back seat. Other reasons for considering a big car are that you have a large family or travel often with more than one or two passengers. Some people also think that large cars tend to be safer than small ones, but size is obviously not the only factor that makes a car safe.

Generally, the bigger the car, the higher the price – and the higher the running costs too – so it's worth thinking carefully about whether or not the extra space is worth the extra the car will cost to run.

Petrol consumption

How much petrol a car uses up has an obvious effect on what it will cost you to run – a car that does 35 miles to the gallon may save you, over 12,000 miles, around 60 gallons of petrol compared with a car that does only 30 mpg. The higher petrol prices go, the more the extra gallons are going to cost you.

The heavier your present car is on petrol, the more even a small improvement in miles to the gallon would save you in £££. For example, if you drive about 12,000 miles a year, a car that does 15 mpg rather than 12 mpg might save you £6 or so a week in petrol. At the economy end of the range, say at 35 mpg, you're going to have to go up to about 40 mpg to save £1 a week.

The conditions you drive in will affect how many miles you get to the gallon for any particular car. Some cars are relatively less economical at a constant speed of 70 mph (for motorway driving, say) than they are in heavy traffic. Make the best estimate you can of the conditions and speed at which you will be doing most of your driving before deciding which of the three government mpg figures usually quoted (constant speed at 56 mph, at 75 mph, or in mixed conditions) is most relevant to you.

Buying second-hand

At current prices, more and more people simply can't afford to buy a new car even if they'd prefer to. Some guidelines are given here for those entering the traditionally shady world of second-hand car deals.

What price to pay

There are two ways to try to establish what is a fair price for the sort of car you want. You can go through the monthly guides (eg *Motorists' Guide, Parker's New, Used and Trade Car Prices, What Car?*) for systematic information on prices. Or you can look at ads in local papers, motoring magazines, *Exchange & Mart*, visit dealers (and perhaps go to car auctions) to find out what prices are actually being asked – and taken.

The best strategy is perhaps to use one of the guides to establish how much you ought to pay for the particular car, year and condition. Then use this to check likely prices in ads and so on – and, where necessary, use it as a basis for haggling.

For example, dealers' asking prices tend to be higher than the maximum prices in the guides. But a cash offer of, say, £100 below the asking price may bring the price to within the range of the guide prices.

Where to buy

● Buying from a dealer

This is likely to be the most expensive option. And you can still end up with a car that brings you nothing but trouble (▷ right for your legal rights). Many dealers give some sort of guarantee – either exclusive to the particular dealer, or organized by manufacturers for their franchised dealers. Names like Leyland Gauntlet, Ford A1 and so on generally cover makes other than the ones named. The guarantee (which can't take away your legal rights) is generally for at least 3 months or 3,000 miles, whichever you reach first. Check the small print, and try to negotiate with the dealer for terms better than the minimum ones offered by the basic guarantee – eg that labour costs as well as spare parts are covered, that the guarantee lasts for 6 rather than 3 months.

● Buying privately (through an ad, say)

This may be cheaper – but there is no guarantee attached. Do what you can to establish that the seller is the real owner – check the log book – and that the car is roadworthy (▷ right). Find out when the next MOT is due, and check the car's condition particularly carefully if it will have to take its MOT soon after you buy – the seller may be unloading the car because he's pretty sure it would fail the next test anyhow.

● Buying at an auction

This may give you the cheapest price of all, but you will not get much chance to examine the car beforehand. You will be bidding against dealers, and you will have to think fast. If you end up with a heap of trouble, you have no guarantee to fall back on, either. If you are interested, see the yellow pages of the phone book for where to find a car auction.

How to buy

Wherever you go to buy, it is a good idea to have technical advice. If you have no friend who can provide this, you can pay for advice.

The AA, the RAC and several other organizations have inspection services – costing around £20 in mid-80. If you are contemplating paying that much for advice, it makes sense to look a car over carefully yourself before calling in the experts. And even an inspection isn't likely to show up everything that's wrong.

As a general rule:

● don't try to inspect the car when it's dark, or raining

● don't wear your best clothes – it's important to grovel around underneath the car

● persuade a friend to come along, if only as a witness.

Cash or loan?

Once you decide to buy, you may have the choice of paying cash for the car or borrowing to buy it instead. See chapter 19 for some help with making the choice – and, if you go for borrowing, which loan to get.

If you pay in cash for your car, you lose only the interest you could have got by investing the money instead – in a building society, say. And you may be able to get a large enough discount by paying cash to make up for the interest you forgo.

If you borrow the money, you will have to pay the interest on the loan as well as losing the interest you would have got by investing regularly in a building society.

Be wary of schemes which offer 'free HP'. A year's interest-free loan, or a 2-year low interest loan may be a worse buy than getting a cash discount (even if you have to borrow money from the bank to get it) – shop around to see how cheaply you could buy the car for cash elsewhere, and find out if you could get a bank loan to raise that amount. If you're offered a discount if you buy on HP, use the Route Map on p. 208 to check whether the offer is worth taking.

Legal rights

If you buy from a *garage*, you get the same protection from the Sale of Goods Act 1980 as with any retail sale:

● the car must fit the seller's description. If an independent inspection reveals that it didn't have a 'new clutch', say, you can claim compensation. So take notes of any claims the garage makes.

● the car has to be of merchantable quality and fit for the purpose it was sold for. This means major faults (like complete engine failure), or a series of minor faults, which show up within a fairly short time (3 to 4 weeks, say) should mean you can claim money back – unless the fault was something you ought to have noticed when you bought.

Unless the garage makes clear to you that the car needs repair before you drive it, then the dealer is legally responsible for making sure that the car can meet the Motor Vehicles (Construction and Use) Regulations. Any car that meets these regulations should be able to get through the MOT test – so if you get the car tested immediately and it fails, you've a strong case for having the garage put the faults right at their expense. If you buy *privately*, you don't even get the protection of the Sale of Goods Act or the Supply of Goods Act. Unless you have proof that the seller lied about the car, you get no compensation.

If a car you buy turns out to belong to a finance company (because the seller was buying it on HP), the company can't reclaim it from you – they can only claim against the seller, with whom their contract was.

In insurance parlance, the third party is the person who's claiming against you. You are the first party and your insurance company the second party.

Car insurance

The rest of this chapter concentrates on car insurance: what types you can get (▷ below) what it can cost you (▷ pp. 118–20) how to get it (▷ p. 121) and how to claim (▷ p. 123).

Types of cover

Car insurance is compulsory, but you have some choice about what sort of insurance to get. The four types are listed below (details of costs are in Fig. 9.5): each one includes the cover in the previous one, and then some additional cover.

● Road Traffic Act cover

This is the cheapest and most basic type of insurance that satisfies the law. It covers you only for claims made as a result of causing death or injury to someone else (including your passengers) in an accident on a public road. It doesn't cover damage to other people's cars, property or other belongings (eg houses, prams); damage to your own car and belongings; theft of your car; or accidents off the public road (eg in your drive, on a camp-site).

● Third party cover

This gives the cover above *plus* cover for damage to other people's cars and property; accidents on private property as well as public roads; damage or injury caused by your passengers to other people or their property (eg opening the car door onto someone else's paintwork, or a cyclist's kneecap).

● Third party, fire and theft cover

As well as giving third party cover, this also covers damage to your car by fire, explosion, theft, or attempted theft – as well as loss by theft. (It usually includes cover for a fitted car radio or tape player (up to, say, £40), though not for things like rings, clothing, etc, loose in the car.)

● Comprehensive cover

This gives third party, fire and theft cover *plus* cover for: damage to your car and for its contents (eg clothing, car radio or tape player, personal belongings – but only up to a limit of, say, £50); your medical expenses if you are injured while driving your car (again up to perhaps £50); death or disablement (up to perhaps £1,000 for death, £500 for losing a limb). You are covered for repairs to your car if it is damaged in an accident, even if the accident was your fault.

Which kind of policy to go for

It's risky to choose a Road Traffic Act policy, because it doesn't cover you for damage you do to other people's property. Many insurance companies would be reluctant to let you have it. The extra cost of a third party, fire and theft (TPFT) policy over a third party policy – perhaps 10 or 15 per cent extra – is usually small enough to make the TPFT cover worthwhile.

So your choice really lies between a TPFT policy and a comprehensive policy.

Comprehensive cover normally costs about twice as much as Third Party Fire and Theft (▷ p. 118). In theory, it should be cheaper – over a long period – to pay for your own accident repairs. This is because only about three-quarters of the premiums you pay are paid out in claims. But in practice, whether paying the extra is worthwhile depends on the value of your car. If your car is valuable (worth £1,000 or more, say) you're likely to think it's worth paying the extra rather than running the risk of having to pay up to £1,000 out of your own pocket to repair, or replace, your car after an accident. But if your car is worth only £100 you'd clearly be throwing money down the drain if you paid more than £100 extra for comprehensive insurance (because the company wouldn't pay out more than £100 for repairing your car).

Note that if you are buying your car on HP, you'll have no choice – the finance company will normally insist that you buy a comprehensive policy.

How much it costs

The charge for an insurance policy is called the *premium*. Working out the premiums for car insurance is complicated. Insurance companies will take into account the records of the people who will be driving the car, their ages, the use to which the car is going to be put, whether the car is kept in a garage at night – and any other special circumstances that they feel increase the risks they take in covering you.

The basic factors (but not necessarily the most crucial ones) are:
● the make, model and condition of car you want to insure
● the area you're going to be keeping it in.

The car

Most companies sort cars into one of seven or so groups. The faster, the bigger, the more expensive to repair – the higher the group, and the higher the premium. Figure 9.3 gives some examples of how this works (use it together with Fig. 9.5).

Obviously there are some cars that go beyond even the seventh group – there's no Rolls-Royce included, for example.

The area

Because a car is more likely to have an accident in busy streets than in deserted ones, companies divide the country into a number of areas – often as many as seven – which very broadly reflect traffic density (for examples ▷ Fig. 9.4).

The basic premium

The combination of seven car insurance areas with seven car insurance groups means that each type of policy offers a wide range of basic premiums. Figure 9.5 (p. 120) shows typical premiums in Dec. 79 for the two types of policy most likely to be of interest – third party, fire and theft, and comprehensive. Figures for Group 7 cars have not been included – these tend to be worked out on an individual basis.

What you actually have to pay

The car and area aren't the only factors which push premiums up or down. Individual factors, such as who is going to be driving the car can have an even greater effect on the price. And most companies give discounts too (▷ p. 120).

There may be more to pay for drivers who are under 25, those who have a physical condition (like angina) that might make them an extra high risk, those with a bad record of accidents, those who haven't been driving long, those with convictions for motoring offences and those who've previously been turned down for insurance. People in what the insurance company considers particularly 'high-risk' jobs may have to pay higher premiums too – this commonly applies to students, publicans, bookies, and professional sportsmen among others. If you are considered an exceptionally high risk for whatever reason, you may find it extremely difficult to get cover at all.

On the other hand, you may get offered lower premiums if only you (and your wife or husband) are going to drive the car, or if you have what the insurance company considers a 'safe' job, like being a civil servant or a teacher. Your premium may also be lower if you buy through your union or employer.

Figure 9.3 Examples of car insurance groups

Group 1	Group 3	Group 4	Group 5	Group 6
Citroen 2CV	Austin Allegro 1500	Austin Allegro 1750HL	Alfasud ti 1300	Citroen CX 2000
Citroen Dyane	Citroen GS Club	Datsun Sunny	Audi 80	Citroen CX 2400
Fiat 126	Datsun Cherry L	Honda Civic	Ford Cortina 2300	Fiat 132
Ford Fiesta 950L	Fiat 128	Mazda Hatchback 1300	Ford Escort 1600	Ford Granada 2800
Mini 850, 1000	Fiat Strada 65	Maxi 1750HLS	Ford Granada 2300	Lancia Beta 1300
Renault 4	Ford Cortina 1600	Peugeot 305	Honda Accord	Renault 30
Talbot Sunbeam 1.0	Ford Fiesta 1100L	Princess 2000	Opel Rekord	Rover 2300
	Ford Fiesta 1300S	Renault 14	Peugeot 504GL	Saab 99GL
Group 2	Lada	Renault 18TL	Talbot Avenger GLS	Triumph Dolomite Sprint
Austin Allegro 1300	Mini 1275 GT	Talbot Alpine GL	Vauxhall Carlton	Triumph TR7
Fiat 127 900	Morris Marina 1.7	Triumph 2000	Volkswagen Passat	Volvo 244GL
Ford Cortina 1300	Peugeot 104GL	Triumph Dolomite 1850	Volvo 244DL/343	
Ford Escort 1300	Renault 5TL	Vauxhall Cavalier 2000		**Group 7**
Maxi 1500	Renault 12TL	Vauxhall VX 2300		Audi 100LS
Morris Marina 1.3	Renault 16TL	Volkswagen Golf 1100		BMW 520
Renault 6TL	Simca 1100LE			Jaguar XJ 5.3
Talbot Avenger 1300	Talbot Avenger 1600			Lancia Gamma
Vauxhall Chevette L	Talbot Hunter			Mercedes-Benz 230
Vauxhall Viva 1300	Toyota Starlet			Opel Senator
Volkswagen Beetle	Triumph Dolomite 1500			Volvo 265 Estate
	Volkswagen Polo L			Volkswagen Scirocco

Figure 9.4
Car insurance areas

Terry Thomson owns a
Ford Cortina 1600 (a
Group 3 car). Depending
on which part of the
country he lives in, his
basic premium for
comprehensive car
insurance would range
from £202 to £329 a year.

For more examples of car
insurance areas ▷ right.

Area 1
Scottish Islands
Isle of Man
Isle of Wight
Rural parts of:
Devon
Cornwall
Somerset
Rural counties like:
Wiltshire
Lincolnshire
Salop

Area 2
Most of Wales
Much of Scotland
Semi-rural counties like:
Avon
Hampshire
Hereford
Worcester
Norfolk
N. Yorkshire

Area 3
Middle-sized towns like:
Luton
York
Averagely populated
counties like:
Oxfordshire
Northumberland
Non-industrial parts of
W. Midlands

Area 4
More populated counties
like:
Greater London
(except postal area)
Greater Manchester
(except inner area)
Lancashire
(industrial parts)
North Merseyside
Towns like:
Birmingham and
surroundings
Blackpool
Cardiff
Edinburgh

Area 5
Liverpool
Inner Manchester
Outer Glasgow

Area 6
Outer London
(postal area)
Central Glasgow

Area 7
Inner London
(postal area)
Northern Ireland

Inverness
£232

Paisley £305

Motherwell
£279

Northern Ireland
£329

Isle of Man
£202

Liverpool
£279

Scarborough
£220

Norwich
£220

Leicester
£232

Finchley
£305

Cardiff
£253

Chelsea
£329

Croydon
£253

Bodmin
£202

Poole £220

Isle of Wight
£202

Figure 9.5   Examples of basic premiums

In black: Comprehensive policy
In blue: Third party, fire and theft policy

Areas	Groups													
	1		**2**		**3**		**4**		**5**		**6**		**7**	
	£	£	£	£	£	£	£	£	£	£	£	£	£	£
1	144	74	167	84	202	98	243	117	282	133	334	154	404	182
2	158	81	182	91	220	108	265	127	309	144	365	167	441	199
3	167	86	191	95	232	114	279	135	324	153	384	178	464	209
4	183	93	210	105	253	124	305	146	357	167	420	193	508	229
5	201	102	231	116	279	137	334	159	390	183	460	212	557	251
6	219	112	252	125	305	151	366	176	427	201	503	231	611	275
7	235	120	272	136	329	161	395	189	461	216	545	251	659	296

Discounts

Car insurance will cost you less than the basic premium if you can get a discount. The no-claims discount – which increases with every consecutive year you don't make a claim – is the most valuable.

Other discounts which may be offered are:

● an introductory discount – up to 20 per cent, to people who haven't had car insurance recently and are considered good risks

● a quantity discount – up to around 10 per cent off for those insuring 2 or more cars at one time

● a restricted cover discount – up to around 10 per cent off if you agree, say, that only you (or your husband or wife) will drive

● a voluntary excess discount – up to 10 or 20 per cent if you agree to pay the first part (£25 or £50, say) of any claim for damage to your own car.

Whatever discounts are being offered, it's still worth shopping around to see if you could get a better deal elsewhere.

● More than one discount?

If you get more than one kind of reduction in premium, you work the discounts out consecutively (rather than simply adding them together).

For example, if your basic premium were £100 and you had 60 per cent no-claims discount, 10 per cent discount for voluntary excess, and 10 per cent discount for being the only driver, you would work your actual premium out as follows:

	£
Basic premium	100.00
minus 60 per cent, leaves:	40.00
minus 10 per cent, leaves:	36.00
minus 10 per cent, leaves:	32.40

No-claims discount (NCD)

This means that you get a reduction to your premium for every year that goes by without making a claim against your insurance. There are various systems for working out the reductions, but a common version goes like this:

No claim	Discount
1 year	30%
2 years	40%
3 years	50%
4 years	60%

The penalty for making a claim is to go back two steps (for example, from 50 per cent to 30 per cent). More than one claim in a year takes you right back down to no discount. You then have to work your way back up the ladder again, one step for each claim-free year.

Protected discount

Some companies offer a special policy which costs the same whether you make a claim or not – there's no NCD to lose.

You generally have to be considered a 'good risk' to get accepted by the company. So you may not be able to get a protected discount policy if:

● you have a recent conviction (within the past 3 or 4 years, say) for a motoring offence (not counting a parking or, maybe, speeding offence)

or

● you have made a claim against your insurance within the past few years (3 or 4, say).

With these types of policy you generally have to pay the first £25 to £50 of practically all damage claims. They can work out cheaper to buy than a straight policy with NCD. So it's worth seeing if you can find a company to quote for this sort of cover for you.

Getting insurance

With getting on for a hundred car insurance policies to choose from, you're likely to get quite a range of premiums quoted to you. Some of them offer special services and features – eg premiums by instalment, or cover for car hire and new car replacement for cars up to one year old.

Given the number of factors to consider, it's worth shopping around for the insurance package that suits you best.

To establish a range of prices for the cover you want, you can either contact companies yourself direct, or get a broker or agent to do it. (They get their fees from the company, so you won't have to pay directly for their advice.) It may help to find a broker who will get you a quote through *Moquote*, *Quickquote* or *Quotel*. These are schemes which enable brokers to find out, without doing a lot of tedious work, what a number of companies would charge you.

Company safety

Insurance companies have been known to go bust in the past. If this happened to you while you had a claim in the pipeline, you would be protected under the Policyholders Protection Act (▷ p. 141). Claims against you for causing death or injury would be paid in full. And so would 90 per cent of the cost of repairing cars and other property (including the cost of repairing your own car if you've got a comprehensive policy).

If you're injured in an accident by someone who is not insured (and who can't pay your compensation out of his own pocket) the Motor Insurers' Bureau will come to the rescue. The Bureau pays compensation to people injured by drivers who can't be traced or who aren't insured. It pays compensation only for personal injury and death – not for damage to cars or other property.

Taking out insurance

Filling in the proposal form

It is essential to fill this in correctly. All answers to the questions on this form are the basis for the *contract* between you and the insurance company. As with all insurance agreements, it is based on the principle of *utmost good faith*.

This means the insurance company accepts that everything you say on the proposal form is true, and that you haven't withheld any information – whether asked for or not – which might be relevant to your application (eg that your 92-year-old grandma drives your car quite often). If

you've not told the whole truth, the insurance company can refuse to pay up.

If your circumstances change after you've filled in the proposal form

You have to tell the company. The cost of your insurance is based on details you put on your proposal form – so, for example, changing your job or the area in which you live may affect your premium.

Obviously it's hard to remember which facts you were asked to give when you filled in the proposal form – it makes sense to keep a copy.

Other documents

There are two other important documents.
● a certificate of insurance – which you get each year after paying your premium. This is evidence that you have at least the minimum insurance required by law. It must be produced when you tax your car, or if a policeman asks to see it
● a cover note or temporary certificate of insurance. Cover notes are commonly issued for a month at a time while your application for insurance, or a change of cover, is being considered.

Read the policy carefully

Unless you take the trouble to read all the details of your policy, you may get a nasty surprise when you put a claim in. Did you know that:
● most policies give third party cover – to the policy holder but no-one else (not even a wife or husband) – to drive other people's cars (with their permission)
● many policies cover other people to drive your car (with your permission). But some policies cover only *specifically named* drivers
● although many policies have *open certificates* (which give cover for any car you own) you must tell the company about any extra cars you buy, and let them know if you change your car – or you will probably get only Road Traffic Act cover for them
● if your car is not roadworthy – eg its tyres are substandard – the company may refuse a claim
● you need to extend your policy cover if you want to drive abroad. If you don't, you may end up with the bare legal minimum which applies in the country you're going to or even with no cover
● it's *your* responsibility to renew the policy every year (though most companies send out reminders). Check that you are getting the right no-claims discount (particularly if you change companies).

Summary of what to
do if you have an
accident
● STOP
● get names of
witnesses, and the
registration numbers of
other vehicles at the
scene of the accident
● get details of the
other driver involved:
name, address,
insurance company, car
number
● make notes of how
the accident happened
and draw a sketch
map.

Accidents

You aren't likely to have this book beside
you to refer to if you have a car accident.
And in the heat of even a minor incident you
may not be thinking clearly.

It's a good idea to fix basic procedure
firmly in your mind now, and hope you'll
do the right thing automatically if you have
to. Details below, summary on the left.

At the scene of the accident

1. You must stay at the scene of the accident
for a reasonable time if any person or animal
has been hurt, or any vehicle apart from
your own has been damaged.

2. As soon as possible, write down names,
addresses, and phone numbers of as many
witnesses as possible. If you let them
wander off, you may never see them again.
At least get registration numbers at the
scene; you can trace names later (write to
Vehicle Licensing Centre in Swansea –
£2 a go). Even if you think it was your
fault, still get witnesses – you may be wrong,
for they may have seen the other driver do
something silly.

3. Write down the time (and date) of the
accident.

4. Talk to the other driver: get his name,
address, telephone number, registration
number, and insurance company. If the
other driver is not the owner, get the
owner's details as well. (You have the right
to insist on all of these except the insurance
company – you can insist on even that if
there is an injury.) Do not discuss whose
fault the accident was and do not (even if
you feel you caused the whole thing) offer
to pay for the damage yourself at this stage.
If you do, you are admitting liability and in-
validating your insurance, and the damages
may turn out to be more than expected. The
golden rule is DO NOT ADMIT
LIABILITY.

5. If you think the other driver has committed an offence, call the police. They
don't have to come if there is no injury, but
if they do their notes may be useful to you,
especially if the other driver is successfully
prosecuted.

6. With or without police help, take notes
at the scene of the accident. You can refer
to them in court if necessary (but may not
be allowed to refer to notes made later). The
notes, with a sketch map (and a photograph,
if possible) should cover the following
points:
● any injury to people, or damage to
vehicles and other property
● the state of the traffic (eg heavy, fast-
moving)
● weather conditions
● road surface conditions (eg greasy, dry),
approximate road speeds, and direction of
travel, of everybody concerned
● positions of cars immediately before and
after the accident; and distances they were
from each other, from road junctions, and
from the side of the road
● lengths of skid marks
● names, widths and gradients of roads
● positions of any witnesses
● any traffic signs or markings
● any obstructions to the view of the traffic
(eg sharp bend, brick wall, hedge or parked
vehicle)
● any signals which were being made by
you, or anyone else

Accident map and notes

On Sunday 27
June 1980 I was
driving towards Sissing
on the B231 from
Dish, at about 45 mph.
At 1.30 pm, as I was
about to negotiate a
sharp right-hand bend,
a young man walked
out of the drive of a
small cottage on my
left, carrying a large,
rectangular, flat case. I
braked and swerved to
avoid him. Seeing my
approach, the man
turned, lost his footing,
and as he fell he
seemed to throw his
case into the air in
panic.

The case hit the
bonnet of my car and
burst open, throwing
pieces of paper into the
air. A number of these
stuck to my wind-
screen, totally
obstructing my field of
vision. Before my car
came to a halt, I was
aware of a loud crash
involving the front
nearside of my car.

When I got out I
realized that my car
and a Minibus carrying
13 children and a
young woman driver
had collided. Nobody
was hurt, but both
vehicles had sustained
damage involving bent
bodywork.

Nobody on the
Minibus (registration
number ZYX 3232B)
would admit to seeing
anything of the
incident prior to the
collision.

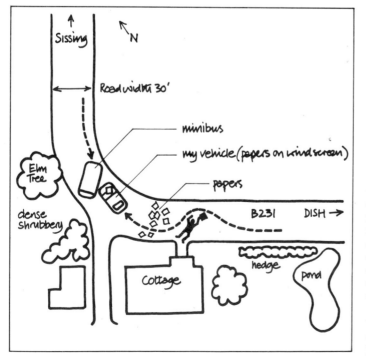

- points of the compass
- what other people said
- what you said (hopefully nothing that might suggest you admit liability).

7. If the police ask you for a statement, remember you do not have to give it – and it may be better not to, as you could be in a state of shock and may incriminate yourself. If you do make a statement, make sure *you* word it, write it, and check it; sign it just below where it finishes, and keep a copy.

8. Report the accident to your insurance company. They will send you an accident report form.

Should you claim?

Whether you decide to claim from your own insurance company or not, you *must* fill in the accident report form and return it. Be completely truthful, but make it clear whether or not you are claiming.

Deciding about claiming is worth careful thought. The crucial sum is whether the effect on your no-claims discount (NCD) is worth it. First work out what you can claim from your insurance company (taking into account repair costs, what someone else may be claiming off you, and anything your policy demands that you have to pay yourself). To establish the loss in NCD, you need to know how your company's scheme operates, and then work out how much extra you would have to pay out over the years to get back the NCD you lose if you make the claim.

Figure 9.6 shows what you might lose (under the system of NCD given on p. 120) as a result of making one claim. If your company has a different system, follow the method used in the table to find out how much *you* would lose. If you would end up losing more than you would gain, it's better not to claim but to pay for the damage yourself. The table shows that what you lose depends on how much discount you start with. If your basic premium is £100, making a claim would cost you at least £30 in lost discount if you have 60 per cent NCD. (In practice it is likely to cost you more than £30 because your basic premium is likely to go up each year.)

So if, for example, you work out you can claim £20 from the insurance company, but that it would cost you at least £30 in lost NCD, you would be better off paying for the repairs yourself.

(Of course, your sums will be out if you have any more accidents or if premium rates rise.)

If the accident is not your fault...

Your NCD may still be affected. Most companies have agreed with each other that if any of the cars they insure comprehensively is involved in an accident, each company will pay for the damage done to the car it provides insurance for. This is known as a *knock-for-knock* agreement.

The idea is to save the time and money involved in arguing about who is to blame and whose insurance company should therefore pay for the damages done. But if your insurance company pays for repairing your car you could lose part or all of your NCD unless you can convince your company that you were not at all to blame for the accident, and can tell them who the other driver was.

How to claim

If you are going to make a claim on your policy, make sure you read it carefully to see what the company requires of you.

For example, you may be allowed to get work started on your car right away, provided it comes to a total of less than £100, say – and provided you send the insurance company the repairer's estimate right away. If your policy doesn't allow you to do this (or if the repair bill comes to more than £100) you may have to send the estimate in first, to be approved before work starts.

The insurance company may suggest a payment for 'betterment'. For example, if a dented bumper was ruined in an accident, the company may suggest you pay part of the cost of replacement.

If the cost of repair is higher than the car's value, the insurance company may decide to *write it off*. This means that you should get its market value (that is, the cost of buying a comparable replacement), unless it was insured for less. If you want to keep the written-off car, you get market value less scrap value.

If a third party is claiming for damage you have caused, simply send all the third party's letters on to your insurance company and ask it to deal direct with the third party. Never admit that you were to blame for an accident – otherwise your insurance company can refuse to pay up.

Claiming from a third party

If you are sure the other driver was responsible (better still, if he has admitted as much), you can write telling him that you are claiming, enclosing an estimate for repairs. Send the letter recorded delivery. You may also be claiming for personal injury, loss of pay, hiring a car, etc. Ask him to confirm that he will pay. Say your car is available for inspection if necessary.

If you hear positively from the third party or their insurance company, get the repairs done and send them the bill. If you don't get a satisfactory reply within 2 weeks, write again, threatening legal action.

If you don't hear (or don't get a reasonable offer, or they don't accept liability), you can take the case to the county court. The amount involved must be less than £2,000. See Consumers' Association's publication *How to sue in the County Court*. (For claims under £200 which don't involve injury to people, you can go to a small claims court.)

If you have a comprehensive policy, and you don't want to get involved in all this, you have the option of claiming from your own company – but if you do you may lose part or all of your NCD.

Third party claiming from you

Don't contemplate paying up out of your own pocket unless you are sure the accident was entirely your fault. If it was, you can look at Fig. 9.6 to decide whether to pass the whole thing on to the insurance company.

If you do decide to pay yourself, still don't admit liability – put *'without prejudice'* at the top of all your letters to the third party. Before you settle, you must make sure you get a written acceptance of your offer *'in full and final settlement'*.

Theft

If your car, or anything in it, has been stolen, tell the police and then your insurance company. The company may ask you not to fill in a claim form for a while, in case the car has been 'borrowed' for a joy ride, or a crime. (In any case, they will probably wait at least 6 weeks or so before they pay out.)

If the car isn't found, you should get back its market value at the time it was stolen. If the car is found after the insurance company has paid up, it becomes their property.

If it's recovered very quickly, still report that it was stolen to the insurance company – in case you find out later that there was some loss or damage for which you need to claim. Report it to the police as well – in case it was used in a crime.

Theft of your belongings from the car

Your car insurance may or may not cover you for things that get stolen from your car. There's usually a limit (£50, say) for what's paid out for stolen belongings. Check your policy for details. If claiming endangers your NCD, check to see if you can claim for them on some other insurance – your house contents insurance, for instance.

Figure 9.6   What the loss of your NCD might cost you The table assumes the commonest type of NCD system (▷ p. 120). If a different system applies, follow the method used in the table to arrive at the answers which apply in your case.

Discount at the moment (Year 1)	Per cent 60	Per cent 50	Per cent 40	Per cent 30	Per cent 0
Discount next year (Year 2) if you don't claim now	60	60	50	40	30
Discount in Year 2 if you do claim now	40	30	0	0	0
So discount lost in Year 2	20	30	50	40	30
Discount in Year 3 if you don't claim now	60	60	60	50	40
Discount in Year 3 if you do claim now	50	40	30	30	30
So discount lost in Year 3	10	20	30	20	10
Discount in Year 4 if you don't claim now	60	60	60	60	50
Discount in Year 4 if you do claim now	60	50	40	40	40
So discount lost in Year 4	0	10	20	20	10
Discount in Year 5 if you don't claim now	60	60	60	60	60
Discount in Year 5 if you do claim now	60	60	50	50	50
So discount lost in Year 5	0	0	10	10	10
So total discount lost	**30**	**60**	**110**	**90**	**60**

PART THREE

Your family

IO Marriage and tax

How income tax works
This chapter deals specifically with how marriage alters the way people are taxed. To understand it you need to know how income tax works in general.

You are liable for tax on income you get from earnings, pensions, investments, and so on, but you're unlikely to pay tax on the whole of your income. Almost everybody can claim some *allowances* (for example, personal allowance, allowance for supporting a needy relative). And you may be able to claim some *outgoings* (certain payments you have to make, such as mortgage interest). You pay tax on the rest of your income (known as your *taxable income*), at different rates depending on how much taxable income you have.

Tax on the first chunk of your taxable income is charged at the *basic rate*. *Higher rates* of tax are charged on successive slices of any further taxable income. You may have to pay an additional tax, called the *investment income surcharge*, if you have more than a certain amount of investment income.

Turn to chapter 20, p. 216, for more details about income tax, and to p. 196 for details about capital gains tax and marriage.

When a couple marry, their tax status changes. They are no longer treated as separate taxable individuals, with their own sets of allowances, outgoings, and tax bills. Husband and wife become a single unit for tax purposes.

Generally, only the husband is sent a Tax Return. On it he has to fill in details of both his own and his wife's income. He is ultimately responsible for paying the tax – on both his own and his wife's income. In practice, however, if the wife has a job, she normally pays tax under PAYE (▷ p. 10) on her earnings.

From the tax point of view, marriage has the following consequences:

First, the wife's income is treated as if it belongs to the husband.

Second, personal allowances change in three ways:

● the husband gets the married man's personal allowance instead of the (lower) single person's allowance

● the wife stops getting the single person's allowance. But if the wife works, the couple can claim the wife's earned income allowance (of whatever the wife earns – up to a maximum, which is the same as the single person's allowance). The husband can't claim wife's earned income allowance if his wife doesn't have a job, or receives only investment income

● if the wife has a job, and the husband has no income, the couple can claim *both* the wife's earned income allowance *and* the married man's personal allowance to set against the wife's income.

Finally, after deducting allowances and outgoings from the combined income, the taxman treats the couple's taxable income in the same way as he would a single person's. The first chunk of their taxable income (£11,250 for the 80/81 tax year) is taxed at the basic rate. Anything over this level is taxed at higher rates.

How the rules about the way in which married couples are taxed affect *you* depends very much upon your personal circumstances.

Special rules apply in a number of cases:
● where the couple have chosen to have the wife's earnings taxed separately (▷ opposite).
● where the couple have asked for separate assessment (▷ p. 128).
● in the first year of marriage (▷ p. 128).

Both working?
Working couples will normally be better off after marriage, because instead of getting the single person's allowance, the husband can claim the higher married man's allowance, and the wife's single person's allowance is replaced by the wife's earned income allowance. How much better off the husband and wife may be varies from year to year, because the allowances change – but for the 80/81 tax year a married couple both working would have got between them up to an extra £770 of allowances.

Both high earners?
If both husband and wife have high earnings, they might end up paying more tax married than they would single. If their two incomes are treated as one for tax purposes, they could end up paying tax at higher rates on more of their joint income than they would if they were single. The couple may be able to avoid this position by choosing to have the wife's earnings taxed separately (▷ opposite).

Wife has investment income?

A wife's investment income always counts as her husband's when a couple's tax bill is worked out. So marriage can result in a larger tax bill if the wife has some investment income and, for example, doesn't work (or earns too little to get the full wife's earned income allowance). In this case, investment income which was tax-free before marriage may have tax charged on it after marriage.

Marriage may also mean a heavier tax bill if the wife's investment income, when added to her husband's, has tax charged on it at a higher rate than before (eg higher rather than basic rate) or becomes liable to investment income surcharge.

There's nothing you can do about this situation (except separate). A couple can't choose to have the wife's investment income taxed separately.

Husband or wife has to stay at home?

If one of you has to stay at home – to look after children, say – it works out to your advantage taxwise if the wife can go out to work, rather than the husband. This is because the couple can have both the wife's earned income allowance and the married man's allowance (as well as any other allowances and outgoings they are entitled to) set against the wife's earnings.

Roy and Rita Rogers could each earn £4,000 if they worked. But one of them is going back to college. For the 80/81 tax year their tax bill would have looked like this (assuming they had no other allowances or outgoings to set against tax).

	Roy only working	Rita only working
Salary	£4,000	£4,000
Married man's allowance	£2,145	£2,145
Wife's earned income allowance		£1,375
Total allowances	£2,145	£3,520
Taxable income	£1,855	£480
Tax payable	£1,855 at 30%=£556.50	£480 at 30%=£144.00
Tax saving if Rita works instead of Roy		**£412.50**

Having the wife's earnings taxed separately

Couples with well-paid jobs may find they pay less tax if they choose to have the wife's earnings taxed separately – the *wife's earnings election*, as the Inland Revenue calls it.

Once you make this election, the wife's earnings will be taxed as her own, and her husband will no longer legally be responsible for paying the tax on them. But any investment income she has continues to count as her husband's.

Husband and wife will each get a single person's allowance (rather than the married man's allowance and the wife's earned income allowance). But a couple with high earned incomes may be able to offset this drop in allowances by having less of their combined income taxed at higher rates.

How high their income needs to be depends on what allowances they can claim and the level of each one's earnings. The minimum level will vary from year to year because of changes in tax rates and allowances. For example, in the 80/81 tax year, the combined income of husband and wife would have had to be £16,977 or over to make a claim worth considering. Nor will it pay you to make an election if you pay no higher rate tax on your combined income.

● How it works

Husband and wife each get the allowances to which they would be entitled as single people. If the wife supports a dependent relative, for example, she gets the allowance for that. The husband normally gets any child allowance. Neither husband nor wife can get additional personal allowances for children, or age allowance or housekeeper allowance.

Husband and wife each get the outgoings they are responsible for *and* pay for.

● How to apply

Get form 14 from any tax office. Both husband and wife have to sign it, and then it should be sent to the husband's tax office.

You can claim up to 6 months before the start of the tax year in which you want to be taxed separately, and up to 12 months after the end of it. Once made, the election will stand until you withdraw it.

● How to withdraw the election

Both husband and wife have to sign form 14·1 and send it to the husband's tax office, at any time up to 12 months after the end of the tax year for which they want to withdraw the election. Once the election is withdrawn you go on being taxed together until you again elect to have the wife's earnings taxed separately.

Note: The wife's earnings election does not mean that the wife will get her own Tax Return. Her income, both earned and investment, must be included on her husband's Tax Return. If husband and wife want separate Tax Returns, they have to apply for *separate assessment*.

Separate assessment

A claim for separate assessment is *not* a way of saving tax. It won't on its own make any difference to a couple's total tax bill: it just splits the bill differently, with the aim of making sure that each pays (and is legally responsible for paying) his or her own share. The couple are normally sent two Tax Returns each year – so that each can fill in details of their own income.

If they want to, a couple can have separate assessment as well as having the wife's earnings taxed separately. The result will be that, if the husband's taxable income includes investment income of his wife, the tax bill will be split between the two of them so that she pays her share.

● How to apply

Either husband or wife applies on form 11S, to the husband's tax office, in the 6 months before 6 July in the tax year for which they want to be separately assessed. Once you've applied, you will continue to be separately assessed until you tell your tax office to cancel the arrangement.

● How to cancel

The husband or wife gets form 11S–1, and sends it to the husband's tax office in the first 3 months of the tax year for which they want to cancel the arrangement.

Single-parent families

Single parents may be able to claim the additional personal allowance for children (▷ p. 221). This would effectively bring their single person's allowance up to the level of the married man's personal allowance. In the tax year of marriage, if the wife was entitled to additional personal allowance for children, she can continue to claim it for that year.

A married man can't get housekeeper allowance or additional personal allowance for children if he gets the married man's allowance – but he can choose to keep these allowances (and the single person's allowance) instead of claiming married man's allowance in the year of marriage. Whether or not doing so saves tax depends on how early on in the tax year the marriage is (and therefore how much married man's allowance he could claim).

Tax in the year you marry

In the tax year in which a couple get married, the wife's income is not combined with her husband's. The wife is taxed just as if she were single: she gets the full single person's allowance, she has her own Tax Return, and is responsible for paying tax on her own income (including her investment income). But if the couple happen to marry on the first day of the tax year (6 April) the rules for taxing their combined incomes apply at once – and the wife is treated as a married woman straight away.

The husband can claim the married man's allowance, but how much he gets depends on how early in the tax year he was married. If the wedding takes place between 6 April and 5 May, he gets the full allowance. After that, he loses $\frac{1}{12}$ of the difference between the married man's and the single person's allowance for every complete month after 6 April for which he stays single (▷ Fig. 10.1 for amounts of allowance for weddings in the 80/81 tax year).

The rules about tax in the first year of marriage clearly help those with high incomes, including large amounts of investment income. Because they will still pay tax as single people in the first year of married life, they will save both on higher rate tax and the investment income surcharge.

James Davis married Jill on 3 March 1981. That was 10 full months after the beginning of the 80/81 tax year (ie 6 April 80).

The married man's allowance for that tax year was £2,145
The single person's allowance was £1,375
So the difference was £770 and James loses $\frac{10}{12}$ of £770 from the married man's allowance, ie £641
His allowance for the year will be:

$$£2,145 - \tfrac{10}{12} \times £770$$
$$= £1,504$$

If he had put off marrying until 6 March, he would have lost another $\frac{1}{12}$ of £770 – ie £705 in all. He would have been allowed:

$$£2,145 - \tfrac{11}{12} \times £770$$
$$= £1,440$$

**Figure 10.1
Married man's allowance
in the 80/81 tax year**

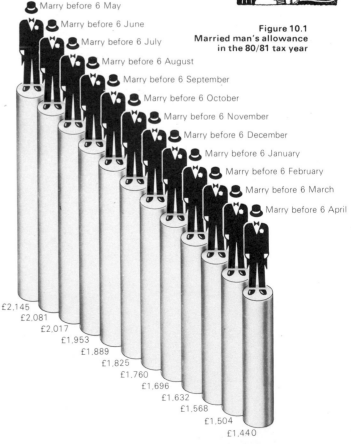

Marry before 6 May
Marry before 6 June
Marry before 6 July
Marry before 6 August
Marry before 6 September
Marry before 6 October
Marry before 6 November
Marry before 6 December
Marry before 6 January
Marry before 6 February
Marry before 6 March
Marry before 6 April

£2,145
£2,081
£2,017
£1,953
£1,889
£1,825
£1,760
£1,696
£1,632
£1,568
£1,504
£1,440

Tax on children's income

The child, not the parent, is liable for tax on the child's earnings – and on any investment income the child has which comes from gifts (or an inheritance) *from anyone other than the parents*. Grants and scholarships for education do not normally count as income. The child gets its own Tax Return, and can claim single person's allowance, and any other allowances for which he or she qualifies.

But if a child has investment income of more than £5 a year which comes from gifts *from the parents*, it's normally treated as the parents' income for tax purposes – and should be entered on the parents' Tax Return. Note that a 'child' as far as this rule is concerned is someone who is under 18 and unmarried at the end of the tax year.

If you get child allowance ($\triangleright$ p. 221) it may be affected by your child's income.

If you are a taxpayer and have a child or children aged 18 or older (or under 18 and married), you may be able to cut your tax bill by using a *covenant* ($\triangleright$ below) to make payments to them. The parent gets basic rate tax relief on the payments made under the covenant, and provided the child isn't liable for tax at basic or higher rates, he'll be able to claim tax back from the taxman.

Covenants

A deed of covenant is a legally binding agreement under which one person promises to make a series of payments to another. Covenant payments to an individual qualify for tax relief provided the following conditions are met:

● neither the person making the payments, nor his wife, may get any benefit from the money

● the covenant must not benefit the children of the person making them unless they are at least 18, or married

● the agreement must be for more than 6 years.

Note that different rules apply to covenants made to charities.

How a covenant works

Suppose you agree to pay a *gross* amount of £100 a year under a covenant – to your student son, say. You deduct tax from this gross amount at the basic rate (30 per cent for the 80/81 tax year) and hand over £70 (£100 – £30). Note that you deduct tax at the *basic rate* – even if you pay tax at higher rates. You're allowed to keep this £30 tax provided you pay tax at the basic or higher rates on at least as much of your income as the gross amount of your covenant payments.

If your son's income – including the £100 gross amount of the covenant – is low enough for him not to pay tax, he can claim £30 from the taxman. So at a cost to you of £70 a year, your son can get a total of £100. To claim tax from the taxman, your son should get form R185(AP) from you – get this form from the taxman.

If your son pays tax at the basic or higher rates, he can't claim any tax from the taxman – so there is no tax saving in using a covenant. But covenant payments received are not liable for higher rate tax or the investment income surcharge – so there is no extra tax to pay either.

If *you* pay no tax you'll have to hand back the £30 tax you've deducted.

Is it worth making a covenant?

If the parent can get tax relief on the payments he makes, there continues to be a tax advantage as long as the student child – or their husband or wife – pays no tax on his income (including the gross amount of the covenant payments). For the 80/81 tax year it would have been worthwhile for a parent to use a covenant to make the child's income up to £1,375 a year (the amount of the single person's allowance).

Does it affect the child's grant?

A child's income may affect his student grant. The rule is that if a child has after-tax income above a certain level (£310 for 80/81), his grant is reduced by £1 for every £1 of income over the limit. But the following do *not* count as income for this purpose:

● earnings from holiday jobs

● covenant payments from parents, unless the child is 'independent' (broadly, aged 25 or more, or had supported himself for at least 3 years before starting the course).

Does it affect your child allowance?

Child allowance is now paid only for certain overseas students and will disappear at the end of the 81/82 tax year ($\triangleright$ p. 221). But note that if your covenant payments are to a student son or daughter, the payments count as part of the child's income when you work out how much child allowance you can claim (check with the taxman for details).

Breaking up, widowed, unmarried

People who are widowed, divorced or separated (whether legally or not) are single people so far as tax is concerned. So are couples who choose to live together rather than get married.

A man or woman who comes into one of these categories and maintains a child may be able to claim *additional personal allowance for children* ($\triangleright$ p. 221). This would effectively bring his or her single person's allowance up to the level of the married man's personal allowance. If both parents claim the allowance, it will be divided between them in agreed proportions. If they cannot agree, special rules are used to divide the allowance between them.

Tax relief for mortgage interest on the family home is normally given to the person who owns the property *and* pays the interest. However, if you don't own the family home, but live in it and pay the interest, you can claim the tax relief. Contact your tax office to let them know about interest payments made. Where husband and wife each pay part of the interest, the relief is divided between them in proportion to what they pay.

The first year of separation or widowhood

In the tax year a woman becomes a widow (or separates from her husband), she is effectively treated as two different people by the taxman.

Before the date of the husband's death (or the date of their separation) the couple get the married man's allowance and wife's earned income allowance to set against their combined income in the normal way.

After that date, the woman gets a full single person's allowance to set against her income (both earned and investment) for the rest of the tax year. If she is a widow, for the tax year in which she is widowed she also gets the widow's bereavement allowance to set against this income. The amount of the allowance depends on when her husband died and is worked out in the same way as married man's allowance in the year of marriage ($\triangleright$ p. 128). So if the husband dies in the first month of the tax year, his widow gets the difference between the single person's and married man's allowances (ie £770 in the 80/81 tax year). For every month after the beginning of the tax year that he dies, her allowance is reduced by $\frac{1}{12}$ of £770.

A husband gets the full married man's allowance in the tax year he becomes separated or widowed – no matter how early in the year that happens. He can't get additional personal allowance for children or housekeeper allowance for that year. In the tax years that follow, a separated (not divorced) man continues to be entitled to the married man's personal allowance if he fully maintains his wife voluntarily ($\triangleright$ below). But he can't then get the additional personal allowance for children.

Note: If the couple have chosen to have the wife's earnings taxed separately, the single person's allowance they each get will remain unchanged in the tax year of their separation.

Alimony and maintenance

Certain payments you make to a former wife (or husband) may qualify for tax relief.

If you make payments

Payments to a divorced or separated wife or husband may be voluntary, or enforceable, or a combination of both. If you make voluntary payments, you can't get tax relief on them.

To qualify for tax relief, the payments must be made under a legally binding agreement, which usually takes the form of a court order or separation deed or other legally binding agreement. The procedure for making such payments (except small maintenance payments, $\triangleright$ opposite) is that you deduct tax at the basic rate and pay the net (after-tax) amount – so giving yourself tax relief. If you pay tax at higher rates or the investment income surcharge, you get extra tax relief – either by a change in your PAYE code or by claiming a rebate ($\triangleright$ p. 224). If you don't pay tax – or not as much as you have deducted – you normally have to hand over some or all of the tax deducted to the taxman.

Note that if the court order or separation deed includes payment of rates, heating bills, and so on, you should check with your tax inspector to see if you can get tax relief on these payments. If you can't get tax relief on them, don't deduct basic rate tax from them.

If you get payments

If you get voluntary payments, you have no further tax to pay on them.

If you get enforceable payments, they are taxable. Since 6 April 78 they have not been liable to the investment income surcharge however. Basic rate tax will have already been deducted – except for small maintenance payments ($\triangleright$ opposite). If you pay tax at higher rates, you will have to pay extra tax. If you do not pay tax – or are not liable for as much tax as has been deducted – you can claim tax back from the taxman. To do this, complete a repayment claim form and send it to the taxman together with a form R185 giving details of the tax deducted (get it from the person making the payments). The first time you claim tax back, you have to provide a copy of the legally binding agreement. If you need the repayment of tax more often than once a year, the tax office will normally arrange for regular repayments to be made.

With payments under the court order or separation deed for rates, heating bills, and so on, check with the tax inspector whether they count as income and whether you'll have to enter them on your Tax Return.

Small maintenance payments

These are payments made under a UK court order, the before-tax amounts of which aren't above a certain level. For the 80/81 tax year, the limits were £21 a week, or £91 a month, for each person, except for children under the age of 21 in which case the limit was £12 a week, £52 a month.

● If you make payments

If you make such payments, the whole amount must be paid without deducting any tax, but you will get tax relief (at your top rate of tax, including the investment income surcharge, if you pay it) either by a change in your PAYE code or by claiming a rebate.

● If you get payments

If you get small maintenance payments, you will have to pay tax on the gross (before-tax) amount if your taxable income is sufficiently high. The payments aren't liable for the investment income surcharge. The tax will be collected through the PAYE system if you are working (▷ p. 10) or you will be sent a tax bill, in which case you pay the tax in one lump sum.

Maintenance payments and children

Where payments are stated to be payable *to* the former wife *for* the maintenance of the children, they are treated as the wife's income and not the children's. They will be included in her Tax Return and taxed at her top rate of tax.

On the other hand, if they are payable *to* the children direct, they are taxed as the child's income. The child will be able to claim the single person's allowance. So there could be tax savings.

A word of warning about payments to a child who is under 18 and unmarried. To qualify for tax relief, and to count as the child's income, the maintenance payments must be made direct to the child under a court order. If the payments are made under a separation deed, for tax purposes they remain the income of the parent making the payment.

Stella and Simon Stubbs divorced in March 80. Simon pays £20 a week under a court order towards the maintenance of their 2 children, Tom and Tessa. These payments count as small maintenance payments, so Simon pays the whole amount over and claims tax relief from the taxman. If the court order makes Simon pay the money to Stella, it is taxed as her income, and she will pay basic rate tax on it, since her allowances are taken up by her earnings. Simon will hand over, in a year, £1,040 – but after paying tax all Stella will get is £728.

If the court order makes Simon pay the same amount in total to Tom and to Tessa direct (ie £520 a year to each) there will be no income tax to pay (because each of the children can claim the single person's allowance), and the family will be £312 better off. Simon is careful to make quite clear what should happen to the money – it's to go towards meeting the fees of their private day school.

The saving would have been even greater if Stella were liable to tax at higher rates.

II Insuring your life

There are two kinds of life insurance (known technically as *life assurance*). The first gives *protection* only: you buy it with the sole aim of protecting your dependants from suffering financially as a result of your death. The second kind – *investment-type* life insurance – is a form of long-term saving, combined with some protection for your dependants. For a given premium, it provides very much less life cover than protection-only insurance.

This chapter is concerned with protection-only life assurance. For life insurance as part of your investment strategy ▷ Route Maps on pp. 188 and 190.

Do you need life insurance?

If anyone depends on you financially, the answer is probably yes. Your family would almost certainly take a severe drop in its standard of living if they had to get by on State benefits alone (▷ pp. 135–6).

If you have no dependants at the moment, it may still be worth considering taking out life insurance (if you plan to have children later on, say): the older you get, the more expensive it will be to take out (although, of course, it depends on how long you pay for which works out more expensive in the long run). And if you leave it until

Figure 11.1 The main causes of death

Age range		20-24	25-34	35-44	45-54	55-64	65-74
Men Chief causes of death (in order of importance)	1	!	!	♥	♥	♥	♥
	2	🦀	🦀	🦀	🦀	🦀	🦀
	3	🎈	♥	!	!	🎈	🎈
Out of 10,000 in each age range, number dying during one year		10	9	20	68	190	490

Age range		20-24	25-34	35-44	45-54	55-64	65-74
Women Chief causes of death (in order of importance)	1	!	🦀	🦀	🦀	🦀	♥
	2	🦀	!	♥	♥	♥	🦀
	3	🎈	♥	!	🎈	🎈	🎈
Out of 10,000 in each age range, number dying during one year		4	6	14	42	98	253

Key

!	Accidents, (including car crashes) and suicide
♥	Heart attacks, strokes and other blood-system diseases
🦀	Cancer
🎈	Pneumonia, bronchitis, flu, common cold, and other respiratory diseases

your health is poor, the cost of life insurance is even higher.

Don't assume that just because you're young and healthy you've no need for life insurance. As Fig. 11.1 shows, the major cause of death in the under 35 age group is accident.

What do you need to protect your dependants against?

● Death of a breadwinner

The death of any member of the family who brings in income can have financial consequences for the others. If both parents earn, the family needs protection against the death of either parent. The same applies if the income from a pension, an annuity or a trust will stop when a member of the family dies.

● Death of the home-minder

It is possible to depend financially on someone without getting money from them. A person who looks after the home and children full-time provides unpaid labour which would be extremely expensive to replace.

Unless the breadwinner remarries or can rely on relatives and friends to help out regularly, he (or she) will have to pay someone to take on the job of caring for the home and children until they can do without.

● Death of both parents

This major disaster may have simpler consequences than the death of just one parent. Unless the oldest child is old enough – and determined enough – there is no question of trying to keep on the family home. Even so, parents who are not content to leave their children to the care of charity or the local authority need to see that the children will get a large enough sum to pay for their living expenses (possibly private education too) until they can fend for themselves.

● Death of someone who supports an adult

If you have to provide just for your children, at least you can be fairly sure when they'll stop being dependent. But an adult dependant (an elderly aunt, or a crippled husband, for example) may go on needing your financial help until they themselves die. Insuring your life may be one way to give this help – though if you're elderly yourself, it's unlikely to be the cheapest way.

How much cover?

The amount of cover you need depends on:
● the income your dependants are likely to need to meet their living expenses
● the length of time they are likely to go on needing your support.

Mike Scott (30) and Maggie (26) have 2 children, aged 4 and 1. Mike earns £6,000 (plus some overtime – say around £600) a year. The mortgage outstanding on their house is around £12,000, but they have no other debts. At present they have no life insurance on either of their lives.

If Mike died now, Maggie could face years of depending on State benefits before the children were old enough for her to return to work. She would be very hard pressed indeed to manage.

If Maggie died, Mike would be in a bad way too. His job involves some overtime, and he would have to find someone to live in to care for the children – it could cost him at least £35 a week in pay until the children are old enough to be left on their own.

Of course, in time either Mike or Maggie might re-marry but it would be disagreeable to be virtually forced into remarriage by poverty.

Paula Gregor lives in a rented flat and has 3 children, aged 6, 4 and 2, whom she supports on her own – her husband walked out last year. If she were to die now, her parents are prepared to look after the children. But with only their pensions to live off they would not find it easy to do so (even taking State benefits into account). And if Paula's father were to die before the children were grown-up, Paula's mother would certainly not be able to cope: the children would have to go into care.

Tom Turner, aged 50, pays £400 a month towards his mother's bills in a private residential home. All the income she has is a slim pension (adequate 20 years ago) from her late husband's job, and her State pension.

If Tom died now, she would simply have to move out – a nasty prospect for a woman in her seventies – and depend on supplementary benefit (▷ p. 229) to make ends meet. She may have 20 years or more of life ahead of her (her own mother lived to 103). If Tom does nothing to provide for her, those last years may be grim.

The longer you expect them to have to rely on your financial support, the more essential it is to make a generous estimate of the size of income they will need. For one thing, as your children grow older their expenses will rise – clothes, food and telephone bills all cost more for a teenager than a toddler. For another, inflation will cut the purchasing power of their income year by year. Unless they are going to be financially independent soon, you need to compensate for the effect of inflation on the income you provide for them.

What would your dependants need?

They will probably need:
- income – to live off
- a lump sum – to pay off debts, perhaps, and to provide for emergencies, inflation, old age, and capital transfer tax (CTT).

The size of both the income and the lump sum needed depend on the standard of living your family is used to, and your view of their future needs. The two kinds of cover are interrelated, too: if you provide a large enough lump sum for your family to be able to pay off the outstanding mortgage, then they won't need such a high income to survive on. Alternatively, they could invest the lump sum to give extra income.

You can expect some living expenses to fall after you die: the family will be smaller, and there should be less to spend on food, clothing and travel. Other costs may be unaffected: the house still has to be heated, rates paid, the roof repaired. And other costs may rise – notably baby-sitting or childminding expenses if your widow or widower goes out to work.

If you keep some kind of record of where your money goes at the moment (▷ ch. 14), it should be easy enough to work out what income your family would need to cover their day-to-day expenses. See p. 139 for the ways you could provide this for them.

How big a lump sum is needed is a less straightforward calculation. If the breadwinner dies, then the husband or wife left behind may well want a large lump sum – to invest for income or to pay off the mortgage and cut running costs. On the other hand, a person who was able to go on in a well-paid job might prefer to keep on the mortgage. If so, he (or she) could get by with a smaller lump sum (but would maybe want more income, to cover childminding costs). That kind of decision is entirely a personal one, and you have to sort out your preferences yourself.

The same is really true for the size of lump sum you want to leave for your wife or husband to invest for their old age. He (or she) may qualify for their own pension anyway. But if it seems possible that they would have only a State pension to look forward to (maybe even a reduced one, if their contribution record is poor) then it may be particularly important to provide a lump sum which can be invested to give them more income in their old age. Work out roughly how much *more* they will need than the pension they can count on – and insure

to give them a capital sum of, say, 10 times that amount at least.

Any other outstanding debts – bank personal loans (if you don't get life insurance cover for them automatically, ▷ p. 210) or HP commitments, for example – should also be added on to the lump sum needed should you die. Allow a reasonable sum to cover funeral expenses – at least £400, say (but may need adjusting because of inflation). And don't forget about the impact of CTT on what you leave your dependants. Insure for a large enough sum to let them pay any tax they have to, and still have enough to live off.

Tax

Income tax
Ideally, your calculations should allow for any income tax your dependants would have to pay. But if the income your widow and children will get is not very great, they won't have to pay much tax – so you can conveniently forget about income tax. On the other hand, if tax could make a big difference to the income, you ought to work out how much income they would need before tax, to end up with the right amount of money after tax to live on. Note that there is no income tax on income from a family income benefit policy (▷ p. 140).

Note also, that in the first year of widowhood, a widow gets widow's bereavement allowance (▷ p. 130), which could reduce the amount of tax for that year.

Capital transfer tax
If leaving things other than to your wife (or husband), you will have to take into account any capital transfer tax payable on your death (▷ p. 168) You should also take out life insurance policies in a way which keeps this tax to a minimum (▷ p. 172).

Capital gains tax
There is no capital gains tax to pay on your death.

Tax subsidy on life insurance premiums
Most regular premium policies – eg endowment policy, mortgage protection policy – qualify for a subsidy from the taxman (at 17½ per cent in the 80/81 tax year; 15 per cent for 81/82). There's no subsidy, however, for a single premium policy (eg single premium property bond). And no subsidy on premiums above certain limits (in the 80/81 tax year, those in excess of £1,500 a year, or ⅙ of your 'total income' – ▷ p. 216 – if this is greater (up to ⅙ of *joint* 'total income' for married couples, if this is greater than £1,500).

Since April 79, you haven't had to claim the subsidy on the premiums: the insurance company automatically gives you the amount you're entitled to. With most policies, your premiums are reduced to give this subsidy. But with some *home service* policies (where the premiums are collected by someone who calls at your home) the premiums aren't reduced; instead the benefits you're entitled to under the policy are increased.

Under these new rules, you can get the subsidy even if you don't pay tax.

What your dependants would get

Your dependants may get financial help after your death from various sources: from the State, your employer, your investments, or relatives, for example. We discuss these kinds of help on pp. 135–7.

The difference between what your dependants can count on from all sources, and what they're likely to need is the gap your insurance should aim to fill. On p. 138 we give a detailed example of how one couple works out their life insurance needs.

Help from the State

Death grant
● Who qualifies?
Virtually everyone. It's normally paid to the executor or administrator of the dead person's estate or to the person who pays for the funeral.
● How much?
Depends on the age of the person who died. The most payable in November 80 was £30, tax-free.
● How to claim
Fill in the back of the special death certificate issued by the Registrar of Deaths (address in the phone book under *Registration of Births, Deaths and Marriages*) and send it to your local social security office to get claim form BD1. Claim within 6 months of the death.
● Further information
NI 49 *Death grant* (available from local social security offices).

Widow's benefits

Widow's allowance
● Who gets it?
A widow aged under 60 when her husband dies (or over 60 if husband was not drawing State pension) provided her husband had paid enough NI contributions. But a widow doesn't get it if she remarries or lives with a man as his wife.
● How long for?
Paid for first 26 weeks of widowhood.
● How much?
In November 80 it was £38 a week, plus *widow's earnings-related addition* (up to £17.67 a week at that time but ▷ left) if the husband had paid enough full Class 1 contributions in the relevant tax year (▷ p. 235). An extra amount (£7.50 a week in November 80) may be paid for each child the widow supports. Widow's allowance (and any earnings-related addition) is taxable, but ▷ *widow's bereavement allowance*

on p. 130. Extras for dependent children are not taxable.
● How to claim
Same procedure as for death grant, but ask for form BW1. Claim within 3 months of the death.
● Further information
NP 35 *Your benefit as a widow for the first 26 weeks*
NI 155A *How your earnings-related benefit is worked out*
(Available from social security offices.)

Widowed mother's allowance
● Who qualifies?
A widow with a child under 19 living at home, provided her husband paid enough NI contributions. A widow expecting a baby by her husband also qualifies. But a widow does not get the allowance if she remarries or lives with a man as his wife.
● How long for?
Paid from the time widow's allowance ends until the children no longer meet the conditions (under 19 and living at home).
● How much?
Up to £27.15 a week in November 80, less if the husband had an incomplete contribution record. If a man dies on or after 6 April 79, his widow may get an additional pension based on his earnings since 6 April 78 (maximum in November 80, £3.45 – will go up again April 81). An extra amount (£7.50 a week in November 80) may be paid for each child the widow supports. This allowance (and any additional pension) is taxable. Extras for dependent children are not taxable.
● How to claim
It should start automatically when widow's allowance stops. If not, ask at your local social security office.
● Further information
NP 36 *Your benefit as a widow after the first 26 weeks* (available from social security offices).

Widow's pension
● Who qualifies?
A widow aged 40 or over when her husband died, who is not entitled to widowed mother's allowance – provided her husband paid enough NI contributions. Widows whose widowed mother's allowance has ended also qualify. But a widow can't get this pension if she remarries or lives with a man as his wife.
● How long for?
Continues until widow reaches retirement age, when she can choose between going on

With most benefits, the amounts paid change each year (normally in November, but sometimes in April). When we say that 'in November 80 the amount paid was ... we are giving the rates that apply for the year starting in November 1980 – ie until November 1981.

● Changes on the way The Government has proposed to abolish earnings-related addition paid with widow's allowance (and probably that paid with industrial death benefit) from January 82. As a first step, it is proposed that the amount of the addition should be reduced from January 81.

claiming widow's pension or claiming a retirement pension.

● How much?

Depends on wife's age when her husband dies (or age she stops getting widowed mother's allowance). In November 80 it ranged from a minimum of £8.15 a week, for a widow aged 40, to a maximum of £27.15 a week if she is aged 50 or over (less if her husband had a poor contribution record). An additional earnings-related pension may be payable, as for widowed mother's allowance). In November 80 it ranged from a minimum of £8.15 a week,

● How to claim

It should start automatically when widow's allowance (or widowed mother's allowance) stops. If not, contact your local social security office.

● Further information

NP 36 *Your benefit as a widow after the first 26 weeks* (available from social security offices).

Industrial death benefits

● Who qualifies?

A widow of an employee who dies as a result of an accident at work, or certain diseases caught at work (called *prescribed industrial diseases*). Other dependants of the employee – including children and the person who looks after them (if not the widow) may also qualify for some benefit.

The widow can't get the benefit for herself, though she can still get allowances for her children, if she remarries or lives with a man as his wife. On remarriage, the widow gets a lump sum equal to one year's pension.

● How much?

A flat rate (£38.00 in November 80) plus a *widow's earnings-related addition* (▷ Widow's allowance, above) is payable for the first 26 weeks. Then a lower flat rate (£27.70 a week in November 80) with no addition is payable. Young widows (ie under 50 at husband's death) without children, or widows under 40 when the children no longer count as dependent get less (£8.15 a week in November 80). What the other dependants get, depends on their circumstances. Industrial death benefit for widows (and addition) is taxable – but ▷ *widow's bereavement allowance* on p. 130. Benefit paid for children is not taxable.

● How to claim

For widows claiming, same procedure as for death grant, but ask for form BW1. Claim for dependants on form B1 200, available from social security offices. You must claim within 3 months of the death.

● Further information

NI 10 *Industrial death benefits*
NI 2 *Prescribed industrial diseases*
Both leaflets are available from social security offices.

Other help

If your children are left without either parent, the person who looks after them can claim *guardian's allowance* (▷ p. 156) as well, of course, as *child benefit* (▷ p.155).

And if your dependants couldn't manage on the benefits listed here, they could try claiming *supplementary benefit* (▷ p. 229).

Example

Here is what Maggie Scott would have got from the State if Mike had died at the end of 1980, leaving her with 2 young children to bring up:

	£ a week
For the first 26 weeks after Mike died:	
Widow's allowance	38
Widow's earnings-related addition (1)	11.67
Child benefit (£4.75 a child)	9.50
Child addition to allowance £7.50 a child)	15.00
Income each week	74.17
After 26 weeks her widow's allowance would stop and she would get:	
Widowed mother's allowance *plus* additional pension (2)	30.35
Child benefit (£4.75 a child)	9.50
Child additions (£7.50 a child)	15.00
Income each week	54.85

1. Allowing for the reduction in earnings-related addition proposed for January 81.
2. Based on Mike's NI contributions from April 78, until his death at the end of 1980.

Six months after Mike's death, Maggie would find herself very hard-up indeed if she had to rely on the State benefits alone – although she could apply for supplementary benefit (▷ p. 229) to help make ends meet.

Help from your employer

Many employers offer some life insurance cover as part of the firm's pension scheme (or separate from it) – but some don't, so check up before you rely on financial help from this source. And the level of insurance cover varies too – both where widows' pensions are concerned and in the size of the lump sum payable. The amounts also depend on when you die.

Death before retirement

● Lump sum

This is usually related to your yearly pay at the time of your death (and therefore has some protection against inflation built into it). It might be between 4 times and twice your yearly pay. Most pension schemes are set up so that there will be no capital transfer tax to pay on the lump sum.

● Income

Most schemes provide a pension for your widow – usually a proportion of the pension you would have been entitled to if you had reached retirement age. The proportion paid is often $\frac{1}{2}$ (more rarely $\frac{2}{3}$) of what you would have got – but some schemes could offer a lower proportion. If your own pension has inflation proofing, your widow's pension normally does too. With a few schemes you have to pay higher contributions into the pension scheme if you want your widow to get a pension.

Your other dependants, including children, may get some pension too – usually a proportion of the widow's pension.

● Refund of contributions

Most schemes refund your contributions if you die before retirement, possibly with interest as well. With a few schemes this is *all* the scheme does for your dependants, but many refund contributions *as well* as providing some of the benefits mentioned.

Death after retirement

● Lump sum

There probably won't be any lump sum payable if you die after you retire. But your full pension may be guaranteed for a certain number of years after you retire (5 years, say). If you die within the 5 year period, the balance of 5 years' pension will normally be paid in a lump sum to your widow, widower, or personal representative.

● Income

Most schemes provide a widow's pension. You may have the option to decide when you retire whether to take a lower pension yourself to make sure that your widow (or other dependants) would get a pension if you die first. The widow's pension will normally be $\frac{1}{2}$ the pension you were getting (more rarely, $\frac{2}{3}$ your pension). With some schemes, you may have a number of options to choose from. If your own pension has inflation-proofing, your widow's pension normally does too.

Warning

Even if your firm offers very good life insurance cover, it could be a mistake to rely on it exclusively:

● you may change jobs later in life and find it hard and expensive to take out life cover then, when you will be older and possibly in poor health

● you may want to retire early, or be forced to do so because of poor health – your life insurance cover would end when you stopped work, and again, at that age and in poor health, you would almost certainly find it hard and expensive to get new cover.

Help from your investments

When you add up what your dependants will have to support them, don't forget any investments – National Savings Certificates, building society savings, shares, etc – that you have already. Even if you don't get much income from them at the moment, you might be able to rearrange them to produce more income if need be ($\triangleright$ Route Map on p. 190 for some suggestions).

It might also be possible to use some of the money from the investments to cut down your family's running expenses: by putting in better insulation, for example, or buying a washing machine instead of sending clothes out to be laundered.

Help from life insurance policies

Don't forget to take into account in your calculations any life insurance you've already taken out. For example, if you are buying your own home on a mortgage, you may have taken out a *mortgage protection policy* ($\triangleright$ p. 140) to clear your mortgage if you should die before the repayment period is up. But don't forget there'll still be rates and so on to pay.

And you may have taken out life insurance in the past as an investment, rather than for the cover it gives. If you have an *investment-type life insurance policy*, you will probably find that the cover it offers is small, but include it nonetheless.

Example

Mike and Maggie work out what each would need if the other died.

If Mike died, this is what Maggie thinks she and the children (aged 4 and 1) would need:

	Lump sum £	Yearly income £
Maggie would need:		
Outstanding mortgage (1)	12,000	
Lump sum for Maggie's old age (2) (1,600×10)	16,000	
Extra lump sum for funeral	400	
Income to live off (3)		£3,800
Total Maggie would need	£28,400	£3,800
Maggie would get:		
From the State (4)	30	2,852
From Mike's firm (5)	18,000	
Investment income (6)		40
Value of investments (6)	400	
Total Maggie would get	£18,430	£2,892

Gap for insurance to fill: about £10,000 lump sum, plus £900 a year income.

1. Maggie would definitely want to pay off the mortgage if Mike died.
2. When Maggie retires, she'd have to rely mainly on the State pension (£27.15 a week at present), the income from her investments (£40 a year at present) and on any pension she could earn for herself later on. They feel she'd need at least an extra £1,600 a year in today's money. So they aim (▷ p. 134) for a lump sum of
$$10 \times £1,600 = £16,000.$$
3. Without the mortgage, and allowing for having one less person in the family, they work out that Maggie would need around £3,800 a year as income.
4. See p. 136 for how they work out how much Maggie would get from the State after the first 6 months of being a widow.
5. They would pay 3 times his basic salary (£6,000) but don't pay a widow's pension.
6. They have an emergency reserve of about £400 in a building society account.

If Maggie died, Mike thinks he'd need (in addition to what he'd earn):

	Lump sum £	Yearly income £
Drop in Mike's earnings (1)		600
Income to cover child care (2)		1,820
Lump sum for funeral	400	
Total Mike would need	400	2,420

1. Mike would go on working, but might do less overtime so that he could be with the children more. He'll need income to make up for a possible drop in his earnings (around 10 per cent, Mike feels), at least initially.
2. Mike might have to pay £35 a week (taking NI employers' contributions into account) even for an untrained person to live in and look after the children. He'll go on needing the help for 10 years, at a guess. He doesn't need to allow for the child-minder's living expenses: what she adds to the household bills will balance more or less the absence of his wife's share of the expenses.

They decide that Mike would need £2,420 a year to cope if Maggie were to die now. They round that up and decide they need £2,500 of cover a year. They decide not to bother to get insurance to cover Maggie's funeral expenses – because of the minimum premium they would have to pay.

What about inflation?

The sums Maggie and Mike have done to work out how much Maggie would need if Mike should die have some provision for inflation built into them:
● the lump sum his firm would pay is linked to Mike's salary (which would rise over time)
● State benefits are currently index-linked, so should rise as fast as inflation
● the outstanding debt on their mortgage will fall as time goes by – so more of the amount they've allowed for paying it off can go towards providing for Maggie's old age.

But they realize that they'll want to protect the income they need against the effects of inflation.

What about tax? Maggie and Mike realize there'll be no tax to pay on income from a family income benefit policy ▷ p. 140 but they decide to treat this as a bonus, and ignore it in their calculations.

The cover they get

They check opposite on which policies would suit them best.

They buy index-linked family income policies ($\triangleright$ p. 140) to cover both Mike's income needs if Maggie should die and Maggie's if Mike should die. This won't give complete inflation proofing (the policies are only index-linked until the person insured dies), but unless the rate of inflation rises dramatically, either should be able to manage on the income even in 10 years' time. They get a policy lasting for 20 years on Mike's life – to cover the whole period of the children's education. They get a policy lasting 10 years on Maggie's life – to cover the time until the younger child is at secondary school.

They buy a 20-year term insurance policy on Mike's life for £10,000 to cover the lump sum they need.

And the cost?

For the index-linked family income benefit policy on Maggie's life: £34
For the index-linked family income benefit policy on Mike's life: £20
For the lump-sum term insurance: £26
So they pay about £80 a year for cover.

How to get the cover you need

Lump sum

The cheapest way of ensuring that your dependants get a fixed lump sum if you die is to buy lump-sum *term insurance* ($\triangleright$ Fig. 11.2). For somewhat extra per month, you could buy *convertible term insurance*, which gives you the chance to change to *investment-type* insurance later on or, with some policies, to take out more protection-type insurance too, even if your health gets worse.

If all other lump sum needs are covered in other ways (eg by employer's scheme) and all that's left is the mortgage debt, then buy *decreasing term insurance* ($\triangleright$ p. 140).

Income

One way of giving your dependants an income is simply to increase the lump sum you insure for, so that they would be able to live off the interest. But they would have to pay tax on their investment income – possibly including the investment income surcharge ($\triangleright$ p. 194). They might also have to pay for professional help with their investments, and ups and downs in rates of interest might be unnerving to contemplate.

Figure 11.2 Examples of cost for life insurance of £20,000

Type of insurance (policies except whole life are for 20-year term)	yearly premiums (1) might be:	
	man aged 28	man aged 43
Protection only		
level term	£27.40	£118.90
decreasing term (2)	£21.70	£81.30
convertible term	£30.90	£135.40
family income benefit (3)	£13.50	£42.90
index-linked family income benefit (4)	£9.70	£25.70
Investment-type		
non-profit endowment	£511.80	£555.30
with-profits endowment (6)	£862.10	£911.60
non-profit whole life (5)	£134.30	£275.10
with-profits whole life (7)(5)	£362.30	£564.60

(1) Allows for tax subsidy – $\triangleright$ p. 134.
(2) Cover starts at £20,000; decreases over term.
(3) Cost is for policy which would pay out £1,000 a year from time of death (ie £20,000 in all if man died immediately after taking policy out).
(4) Cost is for policy where cover is increased in line with retail price index until policy holder dies. Income rises at 10% a year after death. Cost is for policy paying £350 in first year (£20,000 in all if man died immediately after taking policy out).
(5) With some policies may stop paying premiums before death (eg at age of 65).

(6) Cover increases during term of policy by addition of bonuses. At end of 20 years, policy might pay out £20,000 plus £25,500 in bonuses. May also be a 'terminal' bonus on top of this.
(7) Cover increases during term of policy by addition of bonuses. If our 28-year-old man died at age 75, policy might pay out £20,000 plus £125,900 in bonuses; if our 43-year-old man died at age 76, policy might pay out £20,000 plus £56,600 in bonuses.

The alternative is to go for a type of term insurance called a *family income benefit* policy. These guarantee to pay out a certain income each year – starting from the time you die and continuing for the rest of the period of the policy. Your family wouldn't have to pay tax on the income paid out.

Most policies pay out a fixed amount in income each year, set at the time you take out the policy. With some companies you can ask to have income which increases by a fixed percentage each year – between 3 and 10 per cent, say. And the Legal & General policy is *index-linked* up to the death of the person insured in return for a premium that also goes up each year in step with inflation. After the death of the person insured, the income goes up by 10 per cent each year. Other companies may produce similar policies – so it's worth shopping around (or getting an insurance broker to do so for you). None of the policies gives index-linked benefits *after* the death of the person insured – take that into account when you are working out how much your family may need, if they would have to rely on the income from the policy for more than a few years.

How to buy life insurance: Words of warning
Brokers and other people who sell life insurance normally earn their living from the commissions they get from selling policies. And, in general, the higher your premiums, the more commission they get. So it pays them to persuade you to pay more than necessary to buy the life cover you need – by persuading you to go for investment-type life insurance as well as (or instead of) protection-only insurance. See Fig. 11.2 for an idea of how the premiums work out in practice for the different types of insurance.

Before you go to a broker for advice on which company's policy to choose, sort out for yourself which type of policy you want: protection, or an investment. And work out how much cover you need, and for how long. Doing this *before*

you take out a policy should improve your chances of ending up with one that suits *your* needs – not the seller's.

Choosing a broker
If you don't already know of a good broker, you could ask your friends whether they could recommend one. Or you could ask a professional adviser (eg a solicitor or accountant) – though they might try to sell you a policy themselves if they are agents for a particular insurance company. It would be as well to go for a broker who has adequate professional indemnity insurance – £250,000 or more, say.

All insurance brokers will eventually have to be registered with the Insurance Brokers Registration Council (a body set up by the government to oversee brokers). To be registered, a broker will have to meet certain requirements and will have to comply with a

Code of Conduct drawn up by the Council. This code lays down how a broker should act towards his client – eg in providing information on request about different types of insurance, their costs, and the commission the broker gets on them. The Council will have a complaints system for people dissatisfied with a broker.

In addition, there are a number of professional bodies to which brokers can belong – eg the British Brokers' Association, the Corporation of Mortgage and Finance Brokers, the Life Insurance Association, and the Institute of Insurance Consultants. If you felt hard done by after using a broker who belonged to one of these organizations, you could try taking your complaint to them too.

Types of life insurance
The cheapest way to buy protection for your dependants is through protection-only life insurance. That's what we give details of on this page. For details of investment-type life insurance ▷ pp. 198–203.

The types of insurance policy described here pay out only if you die within an agreed period (the term of the policy).

Level term insurance
● How it works
The amount the policy would pay out stays the same throughout the term of the policy.
● What if you stop paying? You stop having life cover, and you get nothing back for the premiums paid.

Verdict
This is a cheap and simple way to buy cover. If you expect to need more cover in the future, consider increasing term insurance, an insurability option, renewable or convertible term insurance too (▷ below).

Decreasing term insurance (eg mortgage protection policy)
● How it works
The amount the policy would pay out goes down over the term of the policy. For the same premium you get much more insurance in the early years than with level term insurance – but very much less in later years. This kind of policy is often linked with a repayment mortgage on a house or flat, so that it covers the outstanding debt for the term of the loan.
● What if you stop paying? Same as for level term insurance.

Verdict
Cheap way to make sure that if you die your family have the option of paying off the mortgage – but note that with large changes in interest rates on mortgages (and corresponding

changes in the lengths of loans) you may find yourself not fully covered.

Convertible term insurance
● How it works
During its term, you can choose to replace this type of policy with another one, normally an investment-type policy, but sometimes another term insurance policy (giving you cover for longer, or for a higher amount). The advantage of convertible term insurance is that the company will accept you for the new policy whatever your health and charge the same as for someone your age in good health.

If you die before switching, the policy pays out the lump sum you insured for. If you die after switching, what is paid out depends on the type of policy you switched to.
● What if you stop paying?
If you stop paying before you switch, you get nothing (just as for level term insurance, above). If you stop paying after you switch, what happens depends whether you go for more protection or for an investment.

Verdict
Good for people who want to keep their options open – either to switch to investment-type insurance later on, or to take out more term insurance (for a longer period or a higher amount) without worrying about their health.

Renewable term insurance

● How it works
This is a fairly short-term policy (commonly 5 to 10 years) where at the end of the period you can buy the same again. With some of these policies, you can increase the amount of cover you have at the renewal date or (occasionally) during the term of the policy. The premiums you pay for the new policy aren't affected by your state of health.
● What if you stop paying?
Same as for level term, above.

Verdict
Suitable for people who aren't quite sure of their insurance needs and want to keep their options open. But remember to keep your eye on the rate of inflation if your policy doesn't allow for you to increase the sum insured at renewal.

Increasing term insurance

● How it works
The amount paid out on your death increases over the period of the policy. The rate of increase is fixed when you take out the policy — eg 10 per cent a year. Watch out for low rates of increase. If you want your cover to keep pace with inflation ask for the highest rate of increase the company will give you.
● What if you stop paying? Same as for level term insurance.

Verdict
Offers the chance of providing your dependants with a lump sum whose buying-power won't fall too far behind inflation.

Family income benefit

● How it works
This kind of policy pays a tax-free income instead of a lump sum, starting from the time you die and continuing until the term of the policy comes to an end. You can choose a policy where the income paid out stays the same each year, or one which rises each year. None pays out an income guaranteed to keep pace with inflation, however. Your dependants may be able to choose to have a lump sum instead of part (or all) of the income.
● What if you stop paying?
Same as for level term, above.

Verdict
Cheap way to ensure your dependants get an income in the event of your death — but allow for the effects of inflation when you work out how much cover you need.

Insurability option

● How it works
This allows you to increase the lump sum or income for which you're insured. How often you can increase your cover and by how much, varies widely from policy to policy. Options sometimes arise at any time before a fixed date, sometimes on specified dates (every 3 years, say). The premiums you pay for the new amount of cover won't be affected by your state of health.
● What if you stop paying? Same as for level term insurance.

Verdict
Suitable for people who aren't quite sure of how much cover they need, but reckon they'll need more in the future.

Other kinds of life insurance

For details of the following ▷ entries on pp. 198–203
● endowment insurance
● unit-linked insurance
● single-premium bonds
● life insurance linked to building societies

Company safety

Insurance companies are closely supervised by the Department of Trade. The Secretary of State for Trade can intervene in the affairs of an insurance company if he thinks it's getting into difficulties. He can, for example, prevent it taking on any new business. Friendly societies (which issue some of the types of policy covered in this book) are supervised in much the same way — but by the Chief Registrar of Friendly Societies (the head of a different government department).

Insurance companies but not friendly societies, are covered by the Policyholders Protection Act. If your company fails, the Policyholders Protection Board — set up by the government to administer the Act — has to take certain steps to protect your interests. The rules that apply depend on whether your insurance policy counts as a *short-term* policy or a *long-term* one. (Note that Lloyd's is not an insurance company, but has its own fund from which policy holders would be compensated if one of the Lloyd's underwriters went bankrupt.)

Short-term policies
This covers insurance of the type where the company renews your policy each year, giving you, in effect, a new policy. It covers things like house buildings and contents insurance, car insurance, medical bills insurance.

For these policies, the Act guarantees you'd be paid at least 90 per cent of what you were entitled to for any claim you had in the pipeline at the time your insurance company went bust.

There might be a delay before you were paid your money — and you might have to find up to 10 per cent of any claim yourself. Even if you didn't have a claim in the pipeline, you might lose what was left of your year's premium. And it's up to *you* to insure with another company immediately.

Long-term insurance
This covers insurance of the type where a new policy is not issued each year (eg life insurance, sick pay insurance).

For these policies, if your company fails, the Policyholders Protection Board has to try and get another company to take over your policy. In this case, provided you carry on paying any premiums due, the Act guarantees that, in the end, you'll get at least 90 per cent of the amounts guaranteed at the time your company went bust — unless the Board considers these amounts to be 'excessive'. If the benefits are considered excessive you are guaranteed a smaller proportion of them.

If the policy you have when your insurance company goes bust is a with-profits endowment one (where bonuses are added which depend on the company's investment performance), there's no guarantee under the Act for future bonuses. So you get no guarantee of what bonuses the new insurance company which takes over your policy will add.

If you have unit-linked life insurance (where the performance of your bond, savings plan, or whatever depends on the performance of a fund of investments), it's important to realize that *you do not own the investments*. If the insurance company were to go bust, you would have no special rights over other policyholders. For these types of policies, if your company goes bust, the Act guarantees you'll get back at least 90 per cent of what you were *owed* when the company failed. But this amount will not necessarily be the value of your units or bond at the time. And if your policy has other benefits, such as a guaranteed cash-in value, which are considered excessive, you may get back less than 90 per cent of what you were owed.

Verdict
The Policyholders Protection Act gives policyholders quite a lot of financial protection. But you aren't protected from the worry and stress resulting from your insurance company failing, there could be a long delay before your money comes through, and, with investment-type life insurance, you could lose out fairly substantially from a financial point of view.

So it still makes sense to be cautious when choosing a company. You could ask a professional adviser (eg accountant, solicitor) or an insurance broker about the financial standing of a particular company before insuring with it.

12 Insuring your health

Not everyone cares to weigh their own chances of falling ill, still less how well they could manage if they were off work through illness for a lengthy period. But only the very lucky get through their working lives without a spell of sickness – and the unlucky may have spells off sick of 6 months or more at a time.

Figure 12.1 shows the proportion of men in various age groups who were off sick on a particular day, and had been for more than 6 months before that (in blue), or for more than 2 years (in black). You can see how dramatically the proportion of men off sick increased with age. While about 6 in 1,000 of the men in the 30 to 39 age group were off sick for more than 6 months, the proportion rose to 47 in every 1,000 men aged 55 to 59.

Stopping work because of illness or accident can mean real hardship – particularly for a family with growing children. Employers may carry on paying employees who are off sick for a while, but most don't do so for more than a few months. And the benefits paid to the sick by the State (▷ p. 17), while providing a safety-net for those with no other financial cover, don't go far.

But there is a form of insurance which pays out a regular income if you are prevented from working through illness. In the first part of this chapter we look at *sick pay insurance*, what it costs and what it covers.

Sickness can mean a spell in hospital as well as off work. Treatment under the NHS need not cost you a penny. But if you feel strongly enough about the advantages of private medical treatment you may feel it's worth taking out a different kind of insurance to cover medical bills. Details of *medical bills insurance* begin on p. 146.

We also look at three other types of insurance which – although apparently attractive – offer much less cover (▷ p. 144).

Sick pay insurance
How it works
Sick pay insurance will pay out a regular income if you are off sick for longer than an agreed period – typically 3, 6 or 12 months. This income is paid out until you are fit enough to go back to work, or until you reach the age specified in the policy (usually 65 for men and 60 for women, unless you choose an earlier age).

Most policies are worded so that the insurance company will pay up if, through illness or injury, you become unable to follow your own occupation and are not following any other. But some companies word their policies more restrictively – so that, for example, they can stop paying out if you become fit enough to follow another *reasonable* occupation.

Sick pay insurance will also pay out if, when you are able to work again, you have to change occupations entirely and take a drop in earnings (for example, if you have to stop being a computer programmer and become a lift attendant). But fewer companies issue policies which pay out anything after you return to your old occupation – even if you earn less because of the illness.

Insurance companies call sick pay insurance *permanent health insurance*, because once they have agreed to insure you and received their first premium, they can't put up their price to you (unless you increase your cover) or refuse to continue your policy. They *can* put up the premium or refuse to continue the policy if any of the policy conditions is broken – if you change to a job which the company considers more risky, say. But provided the policy conditions are not broken, the insurance company must continue the policy no matter how poor your health has become.

Do you need it?
There are two questions you should ask yourself when deciding whether to take out sick pay insurance.

Is what you would get from the State enough to support you if you were ill for a long time?

Most people are currently entitled to *sickness benefit* if they are off sick for more than 3 days, and, after 28 weeks, *invalidity benefit* ($\triangleright$ pp. 17–18). If your job is not especially well paid, you might find that what you'd get from these benefits could be enough to live on – especially if topped up by supplementary benefit ($\triangleright$ p. 229).

Is what you would get from your employer and the State enough to support you if you were ill?

Most white-collar workers who are off sick are likely to continue to get some or all of their normal salary for some time ($\triangleright$ p. 20). In addition, some employers provide sick pay insurance as a fringe benefit – so that sick employees continue to get a proportion of pay from the time their sick pay entitlement runs out until retirement age. You may not need to take out more cover than your employer provides. But if any sick pay your employer provides runs out after 6 months or a year, then it could make sense to take out sick pay insurance to pay out income thereafter.

If you work for an employer but aren't covered by a sick pay insurance scheme, try asking your employer to introduce one. You don't normally have to pay tax on the premiums your employer pays for you – and the cover usually rises automatically in line with your salary.

If you don't work for an employer at all (eg if you're self-employed or a housewife) you obviously can't expect any help from this source in time of illness.

The only help you can count on if you're self-employed and become unable to work through illness is what you'd get from the State – but you won't get the earnings-related amounts which currently top up the basic benefits for employees. Without some form of sick pay insurance, you could be much worse off if illness struck. Note that from January 82, when earnings-related supplement will have been abolished ($\triangleright$ p. 19), employed people will be in much the same predicament.

What sick pay insurance doesn't cover
Most insurance companies limit the cover offered by their policies if the person insured travels outside a specified geographical area (eg the UK, the EEC, Western Europe) for a lengthy period – more than 13 weeks in a year, say. And insurance companies frequently exclude illness or injury due to pregnancy, childbirth, self-inflicted injury, alchohol, criminal acts, drugs not prescribed by a doctor, war and civil commotion. Claims arising from dangerous pastimes may also be excluded: for example, private flying, mountaineering, motor-racing – and even winter sports, like skiing.

Figure 12.1   Off work through illness

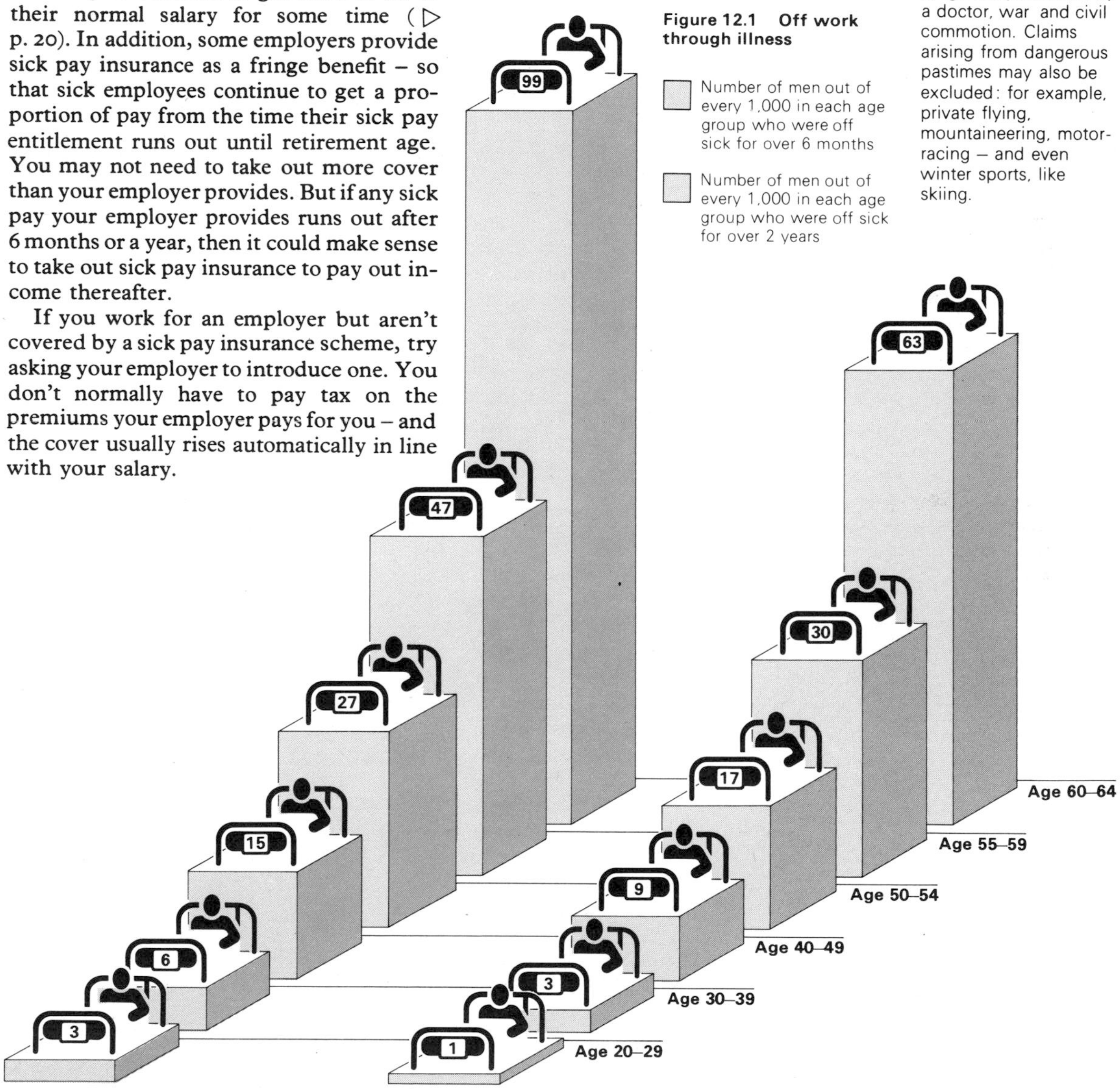

☐ Number of men out of every 1,000 in each age group who were off sick for over 6 months

☐ Number of men out of every 1,000 in each age group who were off sick for over 2 years

99

63

47

30

27

17

15

9

6

3

3

1

Age 20–29

Age 30–39

Age 40–49

Age 50–54

Age 55–59

Age 60–64

If you're a housewife, and don't go out to work, you may have to shop around for a company prepared to cover you – many won't. A regular income, particularly if you have young children, might be invaluable to help you cope with the extra expenses (home help, childminders) you'd have if you fell ill. There's normally a limit to the amount of cover for housewives who don't go out to work – usually between £20 and £50 a week.

How much to insure for

All companies put limits on the income they'll pay out if you claim. The idea is to make sure that no-one is better off staying away from work.

The most common rule is that the income paid out by the policy, *plus* some (or all) of the benefits you get from the State, mustn't come to more than three-quarters of your average earnings over the previous 12 months. Money from your employer is often taken into account too. Some companies set lower limits for people earning more than a certain amount (£10,000 or £15,000, say). And some companies put cash limits on the actual amount they will pay out – £300 a week or more, say.

Note that the companies differ in which State benefits they take into account – eg some take account of *all* benefits, others just the single person's invalidity pension (▷ p. 18). This can have a drastic effect on the cover you can get.

What *you* need to insure for depends on your circumstances. You might feel that you can face a fairly large drop in pay, if you are single with relatively few financial commitments; but if you support a young family and are paying off a large mortgage, you might want the most cover you can get. There's no point in insuring for more money than the company will pay out, however, so check what limits they set and what deductions they make for State benefits.

Inflation

Rising prices can eat away the buying power of the cover you get from sick pay insurance. A prudent person who took out a policy in 1970 paying an income of £12 a week might have felt that this was reasonable cover – £12 was around half the average earnings at the time. Yet after the inflation experienced in the 70s, £12 a week today would seem a very small amount.

It is simple enough to increase the amount of cover from time to time by taking out extra policies – if your health stays good. But if your health deteriorates, the insurance company may well refuse to let you buy additional cover, or may charge much higher premiums.

Some companies provide variations on the standard type of policy which go some way towards coping with inflation. The variations fall into four main categories:
● you have the option to increase your cover at regular intervals no matter how poor your health becomes. Whenever you take up the option, your premium goes up to take account of the increased cover. With many companies, you can arrange for the income from the policy to increase while you're claiming
● your cover increases automatically in return for automatically increasing premiums – whether or not you're claiming
● your cover increases automatically in return for a fixed premium – whether or not you're claiming
● the income paid out by the policy increases automatically while you're claiming. But you get no increase in cover (and no option to increase your cover) when you aren't claiming.

Unfortunately, because of the relatively low rates of increase allowed by most of the companies, very few policies can come anywhere near coping with present-day inflation rates. In Fig. 12.2 we show how income going up by 3 per cent a year or by 7½ per cent a year would lose its buying power over the years if inflation were running at 10 per cent (a low rather than a high figure for the present day). You'd be even worse off, of course, with income that didn't rise at all.

The ideal policy would
● increase cover *before* you claim in line with inflation
● increase income *after* you claim in line with inflation.

Sadly, no company comes up to this ideal. But at the time we went to press one company, Permanent (and its parent company, Medical Sickness), offered policies which allowed for some index-linking – you can increase your cover each year (except while you're claiming) in line with the Retail Price Index – with a maximum amount of cover of 3 times the original level. While the policy is paying out, the income rises automatically at 7 per cent simple a year (ie 7 per cent of the *original* income is added each year).

Other companies may follow suit, or even improve on these policies – so if this is what you want, shop around.

Tax
Income from sick pay insurance is treated by the taxman as *investment income* – ▷ p. 194 for how much investment income you can have before paying a surcharge on it. But, in practice, the income is not taxed until it has been paid for a complete tax year. So if you start getting income from a policy in June 80, say, all payments made up to April 82 should be tax-free.

Three other ways of insuring your health

Hospital cash insurance
This type of insurance pays a fixed amount of cash (commonly £4 or £5) for each day spent in hospital – although certain illnesses, such as mental illness, may be excluded. But it's no substitute for medical bills insurance because it's unlikely to pay out enough to cover private hospital bills. And as it only pays out while you are in hospital (which is likely to be a relatively short time – ▷ Fig. 12.3) it won't cover you for loss of earnings in the way that sick pay insurance does if you're off sick at home.

Hospital contributory schemes
This type of scheme – usually subscribed to by people working for a particular firm – pays out a fixed amount of cash (commonly between £3 and £6) for each day spent in hospital. Small sums may also be paid out (for example, £3 or £6) to help pay for glasses and false teeth. And there may be other benefits (eg a free stay in a convalescent home for up to a fortnight, maternity benefit, and help with the cost of a home help). Again, it's no substitute for medical bills insurance or sick pay insurance.

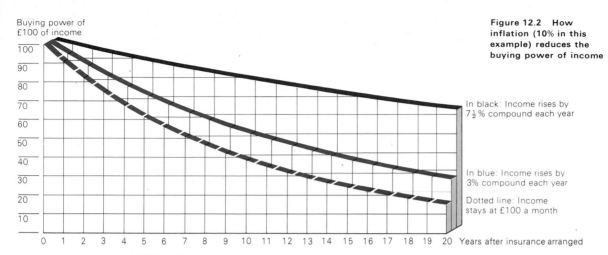

Buying power of
£100 of income

Figure 12.2 How
inflation (10% in this
example) reduces the
buying power of income

In black: Income rises by
7½ % compound each year

In blue: Income rises by
3% compound each year

Dotted line: Income
stays at £100 a month

Years after insurance arranged

Accident insurance
This type of insurance
pays out fixed amounts
of cash if the person
insured is injured,
disabled or killed as a
result of an accident –
for example, £1,000 for
the loss of an arm or
leg, £2,000 on death. It
normally pays a fixed
income (eg £20 a
week for up to 2 years)
if the person covered is
unable to work
because of the injury.
The policy may also
pay a somewhat lower
income, if the injury is
not completely
disabling. Unlike sick
pay insurance, when
the policy is renewed
each year, the company
has the option to
refuse to renew.
    Instead of buying
accident insurance, you
might do better to get
term life insurance (to
pay out on death) and
sick pay insurance (to
pay out if you're
disabled).
    Note that accident
insurance might give
cover for some
dangerous activities (eg
mountaineering, hang-
gliding) which might
be hard to cover with
term insurance and sick
pay insurance.

What it costs

The premium you pay depends on a
number of factors. Some of them you can't
do much about:

● your age – the older you are, the more it
costs to buy cover

● your sex – women pay up to 50 per cent
more than a man for cover ending at the
same age. In practice, the difference may
not be as much, because women tend to go
for policies ending at 60 rather than 65

● your state of health when you take out the
policy – if you're considered to be a poor
risk, you'll have to pay more. You normally
have to give details of your medical history
when you apply – and there could be a
medical examination if you are over 50 or
so, in poor health, or taking out more than
a certain amount of cover (eg more than
about £50 a week)

● your job when you take out the policy –
some occupations (eg roadmender, factory
worker, actor) are considered more risky
than others (eg office worker, accountant,
dentist).

But some of the factors that affect what
you pay *are* within your control:

● age you want cover to stop – cover for
men can normally go up to age 65 (or until
retirement, if earlier). Some companies
won't cover women beyond the age of 60.
If you want your cover to end, say, 5 or 10
years before normal retirement age, your
premiums will be lower – perhaps 25 per
cent lower for a 29-year-old man if he
wanted his cover to end at age 60

● type of policy – in general, the cheapest
type of policy is the standard one which
pays out a fixed income and doesn't allow
you to increase your cover. Buying any of
the variations which help cope with inflation normally means higher premiums

● waiting period – this is the gap between
you stopping work and the company starting to pay you an income. With most companies you can choose waiting periods of 3
months, 6 months or 12 months. The longer
the waiting period, the lower the premium.
A policy with a 6-month waiting period
might cost only half as much as one with
a 1-month waiting period

● when you pay the premiums – if you pay
quarterly or monthly it will cost you more
than if you pay yearly.

A policy which pays out £250 flat a
month after 6 months off sick could cost
from around £27 a year or more for a man
aged 29 (assuming the cover lasts to age 65).
For a woman, the cost might be from
around £31 a year or more (assuming the
cover lasts to age 60). If the amount of cover
provided by the policy goes up automatically each year, the premiums will normally
be higher than this, eg £44 and £49 respectively for Permanent's index-linked policy.
The premiums will be much higher if the
cover goes up without any increases in
premium.

Choosing a policy

Many of the large life insurance companies
(and some small ones) offer sick pay insurance – so it makes sense to shop around.
But don't just go for the lowest premium
for the cover you want: check the following
points first.

● Does the policy cover the sort of things
which are likely to happen to you?
If, for example, you frequently travel
abroad, or you enjoy sports which some
companies consider dangerous (eg mountaineering), you must read the small print
in the policy before taking it out, to avoid
being left high and dry when you claim.

● Will the policy meet your requirements if inflation continues at current rates – or worse?

If you are close to retirement age and likely to get a good pension when you retire, a policy which offers a flat-rate income if you fall ill might be quite adequate. But if you are looking for protection for the next 30 years, for example, you should clearly go for a policy which stands a chance of coping with inflation.

● Is the company still likely to be here to pay out an income if you fall ill in 20 years' time?

Under the Policyholders Protection Act, you should not be too badly off if your company goes bust (▷ p. 141). But, if your company goes broke just when you need to claim on your policy, you could be subjected to a lot of stress and worry at a time when you are least able to cope with it – and there could be a delay before you get the money owing to you. So it makes sense to be cautious when choosing a company. If you're at all worried about the standing of the company which looks like a best buy for you, try to get advice from more than one source. People you could try for advice include:

● your accountant
● your bank manager
● an insurance broker recommended by your bank manager.

How to claim on a sick pay policy

Make sure you read your policy carefully to find out what to do if you have to claim. In general, the company has to be notified of any illness well before the end of the waiting period – with a 6-month waiting period, for example, the company might want to be notified when you have been off for 3 months.

It is worth claiming even if you think the company may refuse to pay out – eg if you have broken one of the policy conditions, or your illness is excluded by the policy wording. At worst, the company will turn down your claim – but some often pay out even when, strictly speaking, they don't have to.

Medical bills insurance

Paying for private medical treatment

Most medical treatment is free under the NHS. So, in theory, the cost of treatment shouldn't leave anyone seriously out of pocket. But some people prefer to be treated privately in order to have some element of choice in their treatment – of hospitals, of rooms, of specialists. More important, many people want to avoid the delay involved in waiting for certain operations under the NHS (▷ Fig. 12.3). For key executives and self-employed businessmen, for example, choosing private medical treatment is no idle luxury – it may be a financial necessity.

Private medical treatment doesn't come cheap – even a fairly common operation like having varicose veins removed could cost several hundred £££ and other treatment would cost you more (▷ Fig. 12.4 on p. 148). So it's worth thinking carefully about the factors that some people feel make it worthwhile to go for private health care.

Speed

Patients who need non-urgent operations often face a long wait for NHS treatment (▷ Fig. 12.3). In some areas, waiting times may be longer still. This kind of medical treatment can generally be arranged much faster privately.

However, with urgent operations (eg a cancerous growth, where delay could lead to death) going private has no such clear advantage – NHS treatment is almost invariably arranged without delay (if there's no operation, waiting times are fairly short too).

Convenience

With NHS treatment (unless you can face losing your place in the queue) you have to take an appointment when it's offered, however inconvenient. If you pay for treatment, you can time it to suit your other plans.

Privacy

Most NHS patients end up in wards with large numbers of beds (unless they're infectious or very ill). Private patients generally can get a room to themselves, in which they can have visitors, for example, much more freely than those in open wards.

NHS patients may be able to get a bed in a single room by paying extra (£3 a day in May 80). But these amenity beds are not always available.

Figure 12.3 Average waiting times for admission to an NHS hospital and average length of stay there for treatment under NHS (1)

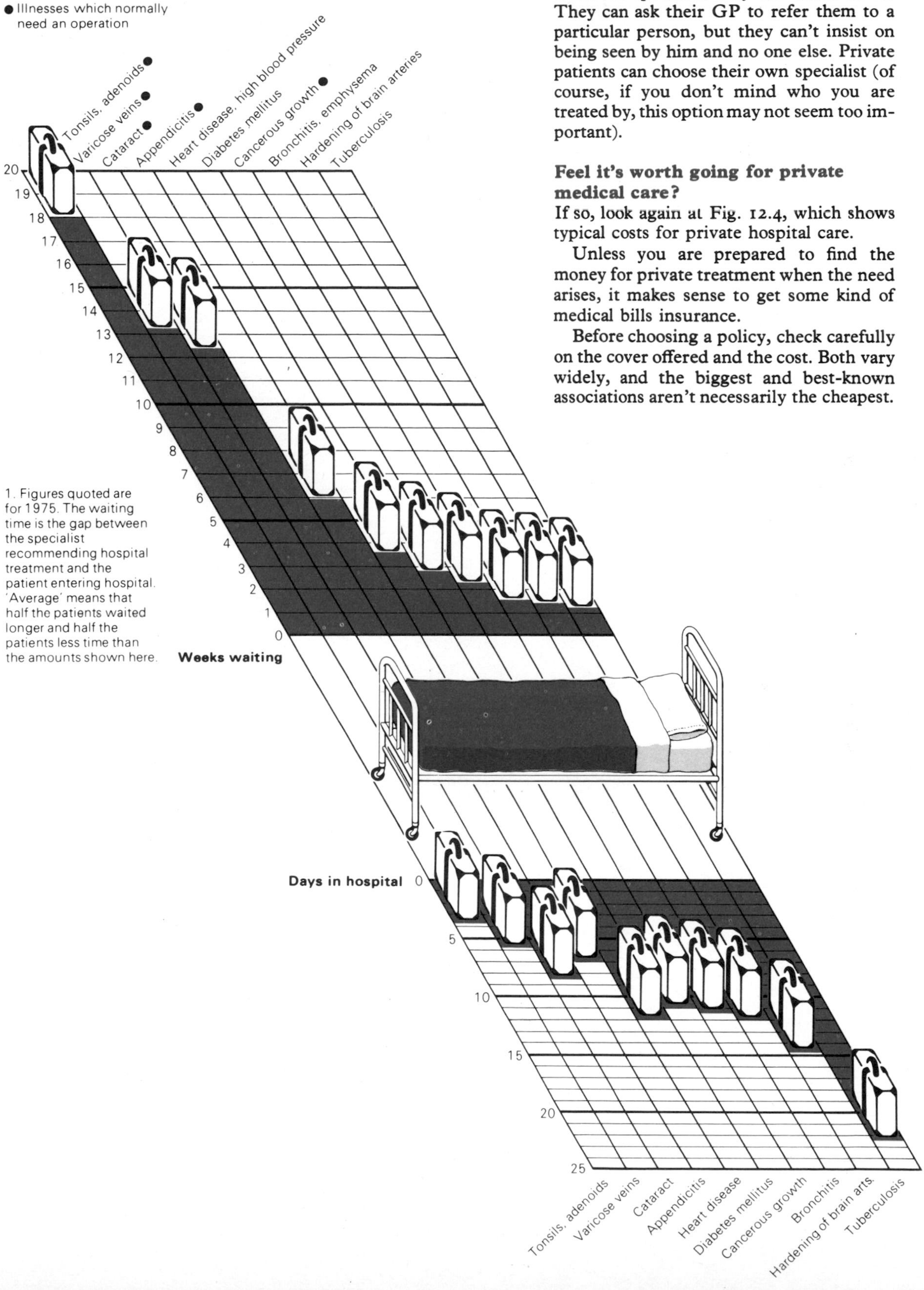

● Illnesses which normally need an operation

Tonsils, adenoids ●
Varicose veins ●
Cataract ●
Appendicitis ●
Heart disease, high blood pressure
Diabetes mellitus
Cancerous growth ●
Bronchitis, emphysema
Hardening of brain arteries
Tuberculosis

20 19 18 17 16 15 14 13 12 11 10 9 8 7 6 5 4 3 2 1 0

Weeks waiting

1. Figures quoted are for 1975. The waiting time is the gap between the specialist recommending hospital treatment and the patient entering hospital. 'Average' means that half the patients waited longer and half the patients less time than the amounts shown here.

Days in hospital 0

5

10

15

20

25

Tonsils, adenoids
Varicose veins
Cataract
Appendicitis
Heart disease
Diabetes mellitus
Cancerous growth
Bronchitis
Hardening of brain arts.
Tuberculosis

Choice

NHS patients usually have to be treated by whatever specialist they are allocated to. They can ask their GP to refer them to a particular person, but they can't insist on being seen by him and no one else. Private patients can choose their own specialist (of course, if you don't mind who you are treated by, this option may not seem too important).

Feel it's worth going for private medical care?

If so, look again at Fig. 12.4, which shows typical costs for private hospital care.

Unless you are prepared to find the money for private treatment when the need arises, it makes sense to get some kind of medical bills insurance.

Before choosing a policy, check carefully on the cover offered and the cost. Both vary widely, and the biggest and best-known associations aren't necessarily the cheapest.

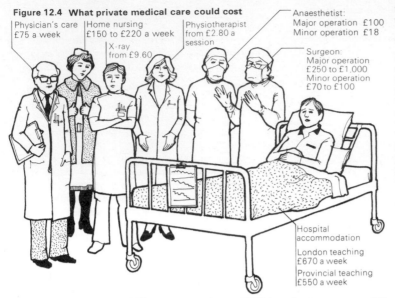

Figure 12.4 What private medical care could cost

Physician's care £75 a week

Home nursing £150 to £220 a week

X-ray from £9.60

Physiotherapist from £2.80 a session

Anaesthetist: Major operation £100 Minor operation £18

Surgeon: Major operation £250 to £1,000 Minor operation £70 to £100

Hospital accommodation
London teaching £670 a week
Provincial teaching £550 a week

What you might have to pay for treatment

Ailment	London hospital	Provincial hospital
Appendicitis	£840	£720
Cancerous growth	£1,400	£1,200
Cataract	£1,000	£830
Tonsil extraction	£540	£470
Varicose veins	£650	£550
Bronchitis	£1,150	£940
High blood pressure, heart disease	£1,160	£960
Stroke	£1,520	£1,260
Diabetes	£1,050	£860
Tuberculosis	£2,240	£1,850
Arthritis	£1,920	£1,580
Hernia	£880	£750

The cover the policies give

These policies cover the cost of:
● seeing a specialist, if your GP thinks this is necessary
● hospital treatment recommended by the specialist (including costs of hospital accommodation, operations, X-rays, etc).

There are two basic ways the policies may arrange this cover.

The most common arrangement is for the policy to give cover up to a set limit for each part of your medical bills – eg up to £320 each week for hospital accommodation and nursing fees, and separate cover up to a set limit for major operations (say, £250 for each one), out-patient treatment (say, £100 a year – which may not be enough), and so on. Less commonly, the policy may just set a yearly limit on what it will pay out – eg £20,000.

How much cover you need

Before you can decide how much cover to take out, you have to decide what sort of hospital you would want to be treated in. Costs vary widely from one kind of hospital to another. London NHS teaching hospitals are the most expensive (leaving aside one or two private hospitals); provincial nursing homes the cheapest. Figure 12.4 gives an indication of what treatment for some illnesses would have cost carried out privately in September 79, and the cost of accommodation in different types of hospital. It is a good idea to check on costs yourself by ringing round to the hospitals you feel you might want to be treated in before making up your mind what cover to take out.

The cover you don't get

The things you are *not* covered for vary from policy to policy, but the most common exclusions are those below.

Long or recurrent illnesses

With chronic conditions – like senility, multiple sclerosis, and so on – your medical bills may be paid initially, while you need specialist care. But payment may be stopped after a period (13 weeks, say) when specialist care is no longer likely to affect your condition. The policy may also rule out cover for costs associated with the recurrence of an illness you have had in the past (unless the company agreed to cover you for the illness when you took out the policy).

Normal pregnancy and childbirth

Complications arising from pregnancy, and from abortions recommended by your GP, *are* usually covered – but some associations will only give this cover if you have been insured with them for at least a year.

Illness in the first 3 months after taking out insurance

Cover normally doesn't begin until 3 months after you have joined the association. But if you belong to a group scheme (▷ opposite) this rule may not apply to you.

Routine treatment

Routine treatment which can be carried out by your GP is not usually covered. Neither are routine sight testing, dental treatment, or treatment by a chiropodist. Some associations will pay out for dental operations, however.

Non-recognized treatment
Acupuncture, treatment by an osteopath, or other treatment outside 'recognized' medical fields, is not generally covered (but it may be if the person carrying out the treatment is a qualified doctor). Stays in a health hydro or a nature clinic won't be covered either.

Cosmetic surgery
Unless the surgery is medically necessary – as it may be after severe burns, for instance – you won't normally be covered.

Not sure if you're covered?
If you're in any doubt about whether or not your policy covers a particular treatment, it's sensible to check with the insurers before going ahead.

Getting insured
You can apply for insurance for yourself, and your immediate family (wife, husband, children). Most associations won't take on new members who are 65 or over, and some have a lower cut-off age.

At the time you apply, you have to fill in a form giving the medical history of all the people who will be covered. You (or any of them) may have to take a medical examination before being accepted (you have to pay for this yourself).

You insure for only a year at a time, but most schemes guarantee to allow you to renew each year even if your health gets worse in the meantime. The same cover may not be available when you want to renew, however, because companies have the right to change schemes they offer (and the price of cover).

What it costs
What you pay will depend on
● number in the family being insured
● amount of cover
● what discounts you can get ($\triangleright$ below). The costs vary widely – as the examples on the right show. So it's very well worth checking what is available, and what discounts you might get, before signing on with any association.

Here are some examples of the kind of discount you might find:
● some employers offer private health insurance as a 'perk' to employees and their

families (you'll have to pay tax on the amount your employer pays out on your behalf, though). Other employers run schemes which the employees pay for, but which offer discounts of around a third compared with individual insurance
● group schemes (of at least 5 people) can work out cheaper – you can start one up yourself. You can get discounts of up to a third by doing this – but one of you will have to do the paper work
● with some companies, buying on Access or Barclaycard

In addition to the discount, payment through a group may mean:
● you get covered immediately, rather than at the end of the 3-month qualifying period ($\triangleright$ opposite)
● if the group is a big one (50 plus), you may get better terms than you would on your own, if your medical history has been poor. Most insurers reckon that spreading the risks over a sizeable group reduces the impact of one individual's poor record.

Steven and Frances Shaw are both in their late twenties and have 2 young children, aged 5 and 3. They want to be sure they'll get quick treatment for non-urgent conditions, so they plan to take out medical bills insurance. Steven can either join a scheme on his own, or go through a newly formed group at his office. They live in Leicester, and decide that they want cover for a provincial non-teaching hospital. For the whole family, the cost quoted in mid-1980 by five of the companies providing insurance ranged between £138 and £215 for a year's cover (between £92 and £160, with the group discount).

Joy Bellini has recently had some experience of the NHS, when she went into hospital for a hysterectomy. Though she had no grumbles about the quality of the medical care, she hated being in an open ward; so she and her husband Rick have decided to take out private health insurance for the first time. She is 54, and he is 59 – and apart from her recent operation both of them are in good health. They live in London, so they ask five associations for quotations for a year's cover for care in both a London teaching, and a London non-teaching hospital. In mid-1980, the answers they received for a London

teaching hospital ranged from about £200 a year to about £300 a year. For a London non-teaching hospital, one of the quotes was the same, the rest were between about £40 and £60 cheaper.

13 The cost of children

Not many parents would argue with the statement that children are expensive. They consume increasing amounts of food, need new clothing at frequent intervals and push up the household bills for heating, lighting and, later on, the telephone. But perhaps more important in these days of two-earner households, they can mean a large drop in family income.

This chapter looks at the costs involved in having children – and at the help offered by the State (▷ below and pp. 155–8). It begins with the loss of earnings for the time when the wife stops work.

Stopping work
For most families, the loss of the wife's earnings will be a major blow to the family budget. Women on average still earn less than men, but a typical working couple can expect a drop in before-tax income of around 40 per cent if the wife stops work.

The three main things which balance this drop in income are *maternity allowance* paid by the State, *maternity pay* paid by employer, and, perhaps most important of all, the rules which may give a mother the *right to return to work* after time off to have a baby. On this and the next two pages, we look at these forms of help.

Maternity allowance
This currently has two parts: a flat-rate allowance and an earnings-related supplement.
● Who qualifies?
A woman having a baby, who has paid enough full Class 1 or Class 2 NI contributions can get the *flat-rate allowance*. You may get an *earnings-related supplement* on top, if you qualify for the full flat-rate benefit and have paid enough in Class 1 contributions in the relevant tax year (▷ p. 235 for rules about contributions).
● When does it start?
The basic allowance starts in the 11th week before the baby is due (provided the mother

stops work then). The supplement normally starts 2 weeks later.
● How long for?
Maximum of 18 weeks for flat-rate allowance (2 weeks less for earnings-related supplement). But if you do not stop work until after the 11th week before the baby is due, or if you go back to work sooner than 7 weeks afterwards, you can't draw the basic allowance or the supplement while working.
● How much?
The flat-rate allowance in November 80 was £20.65 a week – less if the woman's NI contribution record is incomplete. The basic allowance might be increased for dependent children (▷ p. 227) and, in certain circumstances, for an adult dependant (▷ p. 228).

The earnings-related supplement was a maximum of £17.67 a week in January 80 – a woman would have had to have earnings from employment of £6,000 or more in the 78/79 tax year to get this. Earnings-related supplement is to be reduced in January 81, and abolished in January 82.

Both parts of maternity allowance are currently tax-free – though there are plans to tax the flat-rate benefit from April 82.
● How to claim
Claim as soon as possible after the 14th week before the expected date of birth, even if you haven't stopped work. If you claim after the 11th week before the baby is due, the claim can't normally be backdated. Claim on form BM4, available from maternity or child health clinics or social security offices. Take or send it to your local social security office with form MAT B1 (Certificate of Expected Confinement) which you get from your doctor or midwife.

● Further information
NI 17A *Maternity benefits* (from maternity or child health clinics and social security offices).
NI 155A *How your earnings-related benefit is worked out* (from social security offices).

With most benefits, the amounts paid change each year (normally in November, but sometimes in April). When we say that 'in November 80 the amount paid was ...' we are giving the rates that apply for the year starting in November 1980 – ie until November 1981.

150

Action plan for maternity rights

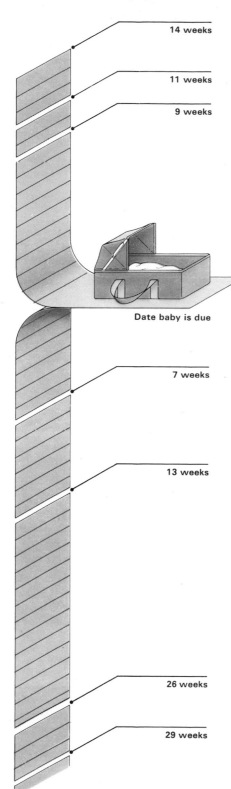

14 weeks

11 weeks

9 weeks

Date baby is due

7 weeks

13 weeks

26 weeks

29 weeks

Action plan

● 14 weeks before baby is due
Claim maternity allowance (▷ p. 150) and maternity grant (▷ p. 155)

Think about when you want to stop work – if you qualify for maternity leave, you are entitled to stop work 11 weeks before the baby is due, if you give 3 weeks' written notice now. If you intend to return to your job, let your employer know in writing 3 weeks before you leave to have the baby (and give date baby is due).

● 11 weeks before baby is due
Maternity allowance is payable if you qualify – you'll lose benefit if you claim after this week.

Earliest date you can start maternity leave if claiming maternity pay and the right to return to work.

● 9 weeks before baby is due
Earnings-related supplement part of maternity allowance can start now.

● 7 weeks after baby is due
Maternity allowance ends. Your employer can from now on ask you to confirm your intention to return to work under maternity leave rules. *You must reply within 14 days.*

● 3 months after baby is born
Last day to claim maternity grant – ▷ p. 155 (except in exceptional circumstances)

● 26 weeks after baby is born
Last date to let your employer know that you intend to return to work under minimum maternity leave provisions.

● 29 weeks after baby is born
Back to work if you want to go back to your old job under maternity leave provisions (unless you're ill, in which case you get 4 weeks' grace).

Maternity pay (paid by your employer)

● Who qualifies?
A woman who normally works for an employer 8 hours or more a week – provided that she works up to at least the 11th week before the baby is due, and has worked continuously for her employer for at least the previous 2 years (5 years if she works between 8 and 16 hours a week).

● When does it start?
Any time after the 11th week before the baby is due, depending on when you stop work.

● How long for?
For the first 6 weeks after you stop work. Note that some employers may pay more than this legal minimum.

● How much?
The minimum is $\frac{9}{10}$ of the woman's weekly pay *less* the weekly amount of the flat-rate part of maternity allowance (whether or not you get this allowance). But some employers pay more than this. Maternity pay is taxed as normal earnings. A woman getting full maternity allowance (ie flat-rate *plus* earnings-related supplement) would end up getting roughly full pay for 6 weeks.

● How to claim
Give your employer at least 3 weeks' notice of when you want to stop work (this is a legal requirement). He can ask you to give this information in writing and to produce your Certificate of Expected Confinement.

● What about paternity pay?
Still a rarity – no legal right to it.

Keeping your job open

A pregnant woman who normally works 8 hours or more a week for an employer is protected by law from being dismissed simply because she is pregnant. But she has to have worked continuously for that employer for a certain length of time to get this protection – 6 months if she works 16 or more hours a week, 5 years if she works between 8 and 16 hours a week. If a woman is dismissed in these circumstances, she can complain of unfair dismissal to an industrial tribunal.

Note that (even if she satisfies the conditions about length of service) dismissing her may be held to be fair if being pregnant makes it impossible for her to do her job properly, or if it would be against the law for a pregnant woman to do the job. But even in this situation, the employer is supposed to look for suitable alternative work to offer her. If there is none, and the woman is dismissed more than 11 weeks before the

Not going back to work?
Even if you feel sure you won't want to go back to work after having your child, it could make sense to keep your job open under the maternity leave provisions. If you decide to stick to your decision not to go back to work, you can tell your employer when you are quite sure, and before the time comes to return. But if a few weeks at home convinces you that you don't want to be a full-time housewife, you won't have burnt your boats.
Note that a period off work to bring up children need not mean that you lose out on pensions and benefits which depend on your NI contribution record (▷ p. 236).

baby is due, she still has the right to return to work after the baby is born, and the right to maternity pay, provided that she would have worked continuously for her employer for 2 years if she had been able to work up to the 11th week before the baby was due.

Maternity leave

A woman who normally works 8 hours or more a week for an employer can take a little over 6 months off work in maternity leave. But she has to have worked continuously for her employer for a minimum time to get this right: 2 years if she works 16 hours or more a week, 5 years if she works between 8 and 16 hours a week.

To get this leave she must:

● stay at work until 11 weeks before the baby is due

● give at least 3 weeks' notice of when she intends to stop work

● tell her employer in writing at least 3 weeks before leaving to have the baby that she intends to return to work and the expected date of confinement. He must then hold her job (or where this is not 'reasonably practical' a suitable alternative) open for her. The employer can ask for confirmation of the mother's intention to return to work not earlier than 7 weeks after the expected date of confinement – she must reply within 2 weeks.

She can return to work at any time up to 29 weeks after the baby is born. She must give her employer at least 21 days' notice in writing of when she is coming back. She can delay going back to work for up to 4 weeks after she was supposed to if she is ill. And if there's an interruption to work (like an industrial dispute) when she's supposed to go back, she can delay her return until the interruption is over.

When she comes back to work after maternity leave, she should have the same pay, holidays and other conditions as if she had not stopped work. Her pension and seniority rights carry on from where they were when she stopped work – the period of absence will not count towards them (unless the employer offers this as a part of her contract of service). Some employers offer more than the legal minimum in maternity leave – check with your employer about this.

Warning: the Government has proposed removing the right to maternity leave for women working for small businesses (those with 5 or less workers). Ask your local jobcentre or employment office for details of

changes, which were not finalized at the time of going to press.

● Further information
Employment rights for the expectant mother (published by the Department of Employment, and available from jobcentres, employment offices and unemployment benefit offices).

How much does having children cost?

What children would cost *you* depends on your own circumstances. But for an average couple, with average earnings, having a child could cost more than £32,000 over 18 years. Having 2 children could cost £48,500. See the example on p. 154 for how we arrive at these figures.

It's most unlikely that, if you hope to have children, you'll be put off by the figures we give. Starting a family inevitably means a change of lifestyle: less to spend on going out, new clothes and so on, more to spend on the family. If you want children, you are likely to be prepared for this change and to find the cost easier to bear than it looks at first sight.

Loss of wife's earnings

For most people, the loss of the wife's earnings is one of the most important costs of having children – on average, a working woman earns around £3,500 a year (1979 figures).

Of course, if the wife chooses to go back to work soon after having a baby – as she may be legally entitled to (▷ p. 151) – the loss of earnings can be kept to a minimum. But someone will have to look after the child while she is at work, certainly until the child starts school. A helpful friend, neighbour or relative can come in very handy here, but if you can't produce one of these, you'll have to pay for child care. A childminder might cost you £14 to £18 a week, a crèche £35 or more a week, a nanny living in £55 or more.

A mother who doesn't go back to work soon after having a baby can lose more than her earnings. She can lose seniority, entitlement to holidays or fringe benefits, pension rights and so on – as well as ending up with less pay when she does go back, through missed promotion, experience, and so on.

One plus point which arises from stopping work: a mother at home may be saving money which she had to spend while working – for example, fares to work, working clothes, more expensive lunches.

The figure shows what a family spends on children of different ages out of each £ of income they take home. As the child grows up, the number of pence in the £ spent on him or her rises — to 26p for a child in the 16–17 age group.

Our figures are based on families with incomes between ⅔ and twice the national average — families with very low incomes are likely to spend a higher proportion of their incomes on supporting their children. And families with above-average incomes might well wish to spend more on their children — sending them to private school, or training them in more expensive sports like skiing or flying.

On average, about 18p of each £ spent by a family with one child goes on supporting the child up to the age of 18. For a family with 2 children the figure rises to 28p of each £. So on average, a family earning £6,000 a year, and spending the whole of its take-home pay of £4,700 or so, will spend £850 a year on supporting 1 child £1,300 on 2.

What parents spend on their children

It isn't at all easy in practice to put a figure on what it costs to support a child, because so much depends on individual circumstances. For example, it'll cost less if the mother is able and willing to make clothes and toys herself, or to grow some food in the garden. A working mum may have to spend more, because she'll be buying more items rather than making them.

Even if we assume that families buy all their necessities in shops, the problem still exists. For example, different families have different eating patterns, and different expectations about how closely their children's diet is going to match their own. What one parent regards as necessary expenditure may seem ludicrously low to some people, and needlessly extravagant to others.

So, rather than set out a guide to what you might spend, we have shown in Fig. 13.1 what people *on average* spend out of each £ of income on their children — and we have ignored the problem of whether they could spend less or more if they had to.

One point to bear in mind is that costs are not spread evenly over the years. They are likely to be particularly heavy around the time the first child is born, for example. Buying the layette, let alone hardware like a pram, cot and so on, could set you back as much as £250 — unless you can beg or borrow some of the necessities from others.

The cost of education

Education is, of course, available from the State at no direct cost to the parents — although (in 1979) it cost taxpayers around £325 a year for each primary schoolchild, £450 for each secondary schoolchild (£800 for secondary school children over 16). However, the indirect costs of education can soon mount up: you'll probably have to pay out for school uniform, school meals, fares, and extra-curricular activities too.

If you send your child (or children) to a private school, the cost is of course, much higher. Typical fees for the year beginning September 80 were:

Preparatory school (boarding)	£2,300
Public school (boarding)	£3,000
Public school (day-fees)	£1,000–£1,250

A child going to boarding school is, in addition, likely to need several spare sets of clothing and sports kit — all of which add to the expense.

More and more children go on after leaving school to further and higher education. If yours do this, you are unlikely to have to pay their fees for most courses, but you may have to make a large contribution towards their maintenance.

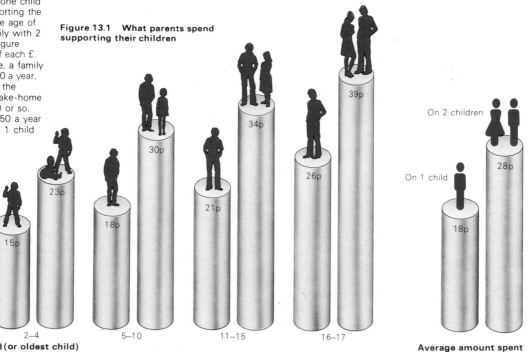

Figure 13.1 What parents spend supporting their children

8p — 0–1
15p — 2–4
23p
18p — 5–10
30p
21p — 11–15
34p
26p — 16–17
39p

On 1 child — 18p
On 2 children — 28p

Age of child (or oldest child)

Average amount spent

Example of what children cost

Derek and Susan Field are a couple with around average incomes. Derek earns £6,000 and Susan around £4,000 a year.

We'll assume that Susan would stop work if she had a child, until the child had gone to school – so that the Fields would lose her take-home pay for that time (around £2,800 a year, after deduction of tax, NI contributions and fares to and from work). They would be left with Derek's take-home pay of around £4,700.

What they'd actually spend on a child while Susan was off work would be relatively small – perhaps £375 or so a year in the child's first 2 years, rising to £700 or so a year as the child approached school age.

What one child could cost the Fields (1)

	£
Loss of Susan's take-home pay for 5 years(2)	14,000
What the Fields might spend on one child(3)	23,000
Total cost	37,000
less State cash contribution(4)	5,000
Net cost of bringing up one child	32,000

What two children could cost the Fields (1)

	£
Loss of Susan's income for 7 years(5)	19,600
What the Fields might spend on 2 children(3)	38,400
Total cost	58,000
less State cash contribution(6)	9,500
Net cost of bringing up 2 children	£48,500

Adding this cost to the loss of Susan's earnings gives an averge cost of around £3,500 a year for the first few years. What the Fields would get in child benefit (around £250 a year in November 80) would go only some of the way towards meeting this cost.

Once the child had gone to school, they might (if they were lucky) get Susan's £2,800 take-home pay back again – but more of their income would go on the child. Below we give an idea of how much bringing up one child to the age of 18 would cost the Fields. It also shows how much it would cost if the Fields decided to have 2 children, 2 years apart.

1. In practice, children would cost the Fields much more in £££ – because of inflation. These figures give you an idea of the cost, in terms of today's buying power.

2. Assuming Susan goes back to work at her old rate of pay when the child starts school.

3. Based on figures in Fig. 13.1 assuming the Fields spend all their after-tax income (£4,700 while Susan is not at work, £7,500 after she goes back to work).

4. November 80 figures: maternity grant of £25, *plus* child benefit at £4.75 a week (£247 a year for 18 years), *plus* maternity allowance of £20.65 a week for 18 weeks, *plus* earnings-related supplement of £6.50 a week for 16 weeks (allowing for decrease in January 81).

5. Assuming second child born 2 years after first child, and that Susan goes back to work at her old rate of pay when her second child starts school.

6. November 80 figures. The total for 2 children is slightly less than twice the total for one child (see footnote 4) because we have assumed Susan would not qualify for maternity allowance for the second child.

Easing the burden

Working couples who hope to start a family later on can ease the financial strain of losing the wife's earnings by planning ahead. For example, consider saving the wife's income while she is still working, so that you can get used to living on the husband's earnings. The money you save can be used to reduce your commitments (for example, HP or other debts), or to meet the initial expenses of having the child (pram, cot, etc).

If you're buying your home with a mortgage, you could ask the building society to let you make higher-than-normal repayments in the early years of the mortgage – this is known as a *high-start mortgage*. When you decide to start a family, the mortgage repayments can be reduced so that you can cope on your reduced income.

And if having children means moving to a larger house, it could make sense to get the move over before they are born. Buying a house is a big enough drain on your resources at the best of times – it could prove overwhelming if you have to do it soon after the wife stops earning.

Once the wife has to stop work, make sure you claim all the allowances and social security benefits you can. And if private education is part of your plans, consider a school fees plan ($\triangleright$ p. 159) to help you spread the cost over several years.

Further help from the State

On p. 150, we gave details of maternity allowance. Here we give details of the other social security benefits for parents and children. You may also find material in chapter 21 (on claiming benefits, appealing against decisions and so on) of use to you.

The rates for all the State benefits normally rise each year – usually in November. We give the latest rates available. When we say 'in November 80, the rate was ...' we mean the rate that applied for the year starting in November 80 – ie ending in November 81. For up-to-date rates of benefits, get the DHSS leaflet NI 196 *Social security benefit rates* (from social security offices).

Maternity grant

● Who qualifies?
A woman having a baby. Government proposals would mean that in 1982 no NI contributions would be needed to qualify. Most potential parents meet the current contribution conditions.
● How much?
£25, tax-free. If you have twins, triplets, etc, you get a grant for each child who lives more than 12 hours (although if all died, one grant would still be paid).
● How to claim
Claim on form BM4 which you can get from social security offices and maternity or child health clinics. Take it or send it to your local social security office, with form MAT B1 (Certificate of Expected Confinement) which you get from your doctor or midwife. If you are entitled to get maternity allowance ($\triangleright$ p. 150), you can claim both benefits together – ie between the 14th and 11th weeks before the baby is due. If you aren't entitled to maternity allowance you can claim maternity grant any time between the 14th week *before* the baby is due and 3 months *after* it is born.
● Further information
NI 17A *Maternity benefits* (available from maternity or child health clinics and social security offices).

Child benefit

● Who qualifies?
Almost anyone who is responsible for a child under the age of 16 (or under 19 and still at school or college full-time).
● How much?
In November 80, the rate of child benefit was £4.75 a week (tax-free) for each child who qualified (extra for some one-parent families – $\triangleright$ Child benefit increase, p. 157).

But a child over 16 and under 19 does not qualify for child benefit purposes if:
● on an advanced course of education (broadly, above A-level standard) *or*
● sponsored by an employer or the Manpower Services Commission on a full-time education course *or*
● getting non-contributory invalidity pension ($\triangleright$ p. 233).
● How to claim
The person responsible for the child must claim on form CH2 and index slip CH3, both available from social security offices. If the child lives with both parents, the mother should normally claim, sending back the completed claim form, index slip CH3 and the child's birth or adoption certificate. It may take a while for the decision on the benefit to come through.
● Further information
CH1 *Child benefit*
CH5 *Child benefit for people entering Britain*
CH7 *Child benefit for children aged 16 and over*
(All available from social security offices.)

Family income supplement
● Who qualifies?
A family with at least one child under the age of 16 (or over 16 and still at school), if the *total family income* falls below a certain level. But to qualify, the head of the family (the man in the case of a couple) must be in full-time work. Full-time work is defined as working 30 hours or more a week (24 hours or more a week for single parents and others bringing up children on their own).

The level of *total family income* (broadly, the before-tax income of husband and wife, not counting child benefit and certain other social security benefits) to qualify depends on the number of children in the family. For example, in November 80, the supplement was payable if total family income fell below £67 a week for a family with one child. Income level to qualify goes up by £7 for each additional child.
● How long for?
Normally a year at a time – and the amount doesn't normally change even if your circumstances do. So don't claim just before you expect your income to drop sharply for a long while – wait for the fall in income and *then* claim.
● How much?
The amount of family income supplement payable is half the difference between the total family income and the level at which the family qualifies for the supplement. For example, if the family has 2 children and a total family income of £50 a week, they could have got family income supplement of £12 a week in November 80 – ie half the difference between £50 and the £74 level at which the family qualified for the supplement. There is a maximum amount you can get, which depends on the number of children you have. In November 80, the maximum with one child was £17 (maximum goes up by £1.50 for each additional child). The supplement is tax-free.

A family getting family income supplement is automatically entitled to the welfare benefits mentioned on the right.
● How to claim
The claim form is in leaflet FIS 1 (▷ below). If you think you are eligible, claim by sending the form and the other documents it asks for to the address given in the leaflet. Don't delay claiming if you haven't got the relevant documents – claims can't be back-dated, but documents can be sent in after a claim is made.
● Further information
FIS 1 *Family income supplement* (available from post offices and social security offices).

Child increases
With certain social security benefits, extra amounts called *child increases* may be payable for each child for whom child benefit is paid. There are two rates of child increase:
● short-term rate – payable with benefits which only last for a few months or so – eg sickness benefit, unemployment benefit and maternity allowance.
● long-term rate – payable with benefits which can last many years – eg invalidity pension, widow's benefit, retirement pension.

But note that a married woman living with her husband can get a child increase only if her husband cannot support himself because of a physical or mental disability.

The rates of child increase were £1.25 a week (short-term) and £7.50 (long-term) in November 80. They are payable in addition to child benefit and are tax-free.

Welfare benefits
Children under 16 qualify for free NHS prescriptions, dental treatment and glasses; children over 16 and still at school can get free NHS dental treatment and glasses. For free prescriptions, simply fill in the back of the prescription; for free dental treatment and glasses, tell the dentist or optician – he will give you a form to sign.

Families on supplementary benefit or family income supplement can get daily milk and vitamins for all children under school age – as can a family whose income is low (▷ p. 230 for what counts as low). For details of other people who can claim these benefits ▷ p. 231.

Guardian's allowance
● Who qualifies?
Anyone who takes an orphan child into the family, provided he or she gets child benefit for the child. Normally both the child's parents must be dead, but in some circumstances the allowance may be paid where only one parent is dead – for example, if the surviving parent is in prison on a long sentence, or has disappeared. Note that you don't have to be the legal guardian of the child to claim.

One of the child's parents must have been born in the UK, or been present in the UK for a total of at least 52 weeks in any period of 2 years after the age of 16, or meet certain other requirements.
● How much?
In November 80, the rate of guardian's allowance was £7.50 a week (tax-free) for each child taken into the family (paid in addition to child benefit).
● How to claim
Claim on form BG1, available from local social security offices, within 3 months of taking in the orphan child – if you claim later than this, the allowance will normally only be back-dated 3 months.

● Further information
NI 14 *Guardian's allowance* (available from social security offices).

Extra help for one-parent families
One-parent families may be able to claim the two benefits listed in the next two columns, and a widow may be able to get widow's benefit too (▷ p. 135). A lone parent can normally claim supplementary benefit (▷ p. 229) without having to be available for work.

Child benefit increase
● Who qualifies?
A lone parent (widowed, divorced, separated or single) provided he or she is not living with someone as husband or wife. Also anyone other than a parent who has sole care of a child (eg a lone grandparent).

As this is an *increase* in child benefit, you must be entitled to child benefit in the first place for at least one child who lives with you.

Child benefit increase is not payable if you are getting the following:
● guardian's allowance (▷ opposite)
● industrial death benefit for a child (▷ p. 136)
● child's special allowance (▷ right)
● a child increase at the higher, long-term rate (▷ opposite) — for example with widow's benefit or retirement pension.

Child increases (▷ opposite) paid for the first or only child with benefits such as sickness, invalidity or unemployment benefit, will be reduced by the amount of child benefit increase that is payable.
● How much?
In November 80, £3 a week extra (tax-free). Only one child benefit increase is payable, however many children you support.
● How to claim
Claim on form in leaflet CH11 (▷ below). If you are single, widowed, divorced, or legally separated, claim immediately; if you have recently separated from your husband or wife, you can claim 12 weeks after the separation — the increase is paid after 13 weeks of separation.

● Further information CH11 *Child benefit increase for one-parent families* (available from social security offices).

Child's special allowance
● Who qualifies?
A divorced woman whose ex-husband is dead, if she has a child for whom she is entitled to get child benefit. But she must have been entitled to child benefit for the child when her ex-husband died, or if the child is her ex-husband's child, *he* must have been entitled to the child benefit when he died. The ex-husband must have contributed (or been liable to contribute) at least 25p a week in maintenance for the child, and have paid enough NI contributions. No allowance is payable if the woman remarries or for any period during which she lives with a man as his wife.
● How much?
The rate of child's special allowance was £7.50 a week in November 80 (paid in addition to child benefit). The allowance is tax-free.
● How to claim
Claim on form CS1, available from social security offices, within 3 months of your ex-husband's death. You have to produce your marriage certificate, evidence of your divorce or annulment, and details of how your ex-husband contributed towards the child's support. But don't delay your claim if these documents are not available — if you claim more than 3 months after your ex-husband's death, the allowance can't normally be back-dated more than 3 months.

● Further information NI 93 *Child's special allowance* (available from social security offices).

State help with the cost of education

Free school meals
● Who qualifies?
Children at school (but not private school) in families getting supplementary benefit (▷ p. 229) or family income supplement (▷ opposite) qualify. Local education authorities also have discretionary powers to provide free school meals for children of families with below-average incomes — but with present cut-backs in public spending they may not use these powers.
● How to claim
Get a claim form from your education office or the educational welfare officer — show your supplementary benefit or family income supplement order book as evidence that you qualify.

Fares to school
● Who qualifies?
Children of compulsory school age (ie between 5 and 16) who attend their nearest school and who live more than a certain distance from it. A child under 8 years of age must live more than 2 miles away.
● How to claim
Claim from your local education office (address in phone book under name of county council, metropolitan district council or London borough). Note that help with the cost of travel to school may be available for children who don't qualify under the above rules, at the discretion of the local education office (▷ p. 158).

Student grants

● Who qualifies?

Anyone who is accepted on a full-time or sandwich course in the UK and who has lived in the UK for the previous 3 years is normally entitled to a grant from their local education authority (in Scotland, from Scottish Education Department) if the course is a *designated course*. Broadly, a designated course is one which leads to a first degree (eg BA, BSc), an initial teacher training qualification, or certain other qualifications.

● How much?

The grant is in two parts:

● the tuition fees for the course – normally paid direct to the college or university

● a maintenance grant to cover living costs (eg rent, food, clothing and books) – normally paid direct to the student. The amount depends mainly on where the student lives during term-time, and a means test.

To work out the amount of maintenance grant payable, the local authority works out what *basic maintenance grant* the student is entitled to. The amounts which applied for 80/81 ranged from £1,695 for a student living in London lodgings, to £1,125 for someone living at home.

The local education authority can add on an *additional maintenance grant* in certain circumstances – for example, if the student supports a husband, wife, or children, or if the course involves a longer period of study in college than the normal 30 weeks in the year.

The maintenance grant may be reduced (but not normally below £385 a year) to take account of the student's *resources*, which include:

● the parents' income if the student *does not* count as independent (▷ below)

● the income of the student's husband or wife if the student *does* count as independent

● the income of the student, whether or not the student counts as independent.

In general, students count as independent if, before the start of the academic year, they are aged 25 or over, or have supported themselves for at least 3 years.

● When to claim

Apply as early as possible – even if you have only been provisionally accepted on the course. If you apply later than the January before the course starts, the first grant cheque may come through after you start the course.

● How to claim

Contact your local education authority (look in the phone book under the name of your county council, metropolitan district council, or London borough) and ask for an application form. You'll have to supply details of your income. In Scotland, apply direct to Scottish Education Department (▷ address below).

Note that even if you're not entitled to a *mandatory grant* (the type described above), you might be able to get a *discretionary grant* from your local education authority. The amounts payable (and the conditions for getting one) vary widely – ask your local education authority for details.

● Further information

Grants to students – a brief guide available from the Department of Education and Science, Room 1/27 Elizabeth House, York Road, London SE1 7PH.

In Scotland, try *Guide to students' allowances*, available from Scottish Education Department, Haymarket House, Clifton Terrace, Edinburgh EH12 5DT.

Local authority help
We've looked at the help with the cost of education provided by the State on a national basis – normally administered by local education authorities throughout the country. However as well as these nationally available forms of help, local education authorities have discretion to offer, for example:

● School uniform and clothing grants
These are for families with low incomes (the level to qualify is decided by the local authority). The help, which can take the form of cash, vouchers or articles of clothing, can cover compulsory uniform, sports clothing and shoes.

● Help with fares to school
Children who live too close to school to get the help mentioned on p. 157 may still be able to get help with the cost of travelling to and from school, especially if they go to a school which is not the nearest to where they live.
live

● Educational maintenance allowance
This is an allowance for families keeping a child on at school after 16, whose incomes are low (the level to qualify is decided by the local authority).

Note that these are all *discretionary benefits* – and your local education authority might exercise its discretion by not providing them. Ask at the education office for details (address in phone book under name of county council, metropolitan district council, or London borough).

School fees policies

Parents who decide to send their offspring to a private school face substantial bills ($\triangleright$ p. 153). Even relatively well-heeled families will find the prospect of paying out £6,000 a year or more to send 2 children to a boarding public school somewhat daunting. But with a little planning, the burden can be spread.

Various insurance companies and brokers specialize in arranging schemes to provide money for school fees at the time it is needed, normally through investment-type life insurance policies and annuities. These schemes are not some form of magic – they are merely a way of investing money now (either in a lump sum or by regular payments) to make a set of payments some time in the future. You could put together your own package of policies, but the beauty of these schemes is that someone else sorts out the timing of investments and payouts, and copes with the tax implications.

A point to bear in mind is that school fees schemes don't *guarantee* to pay your child's school fees regardless – they merely pay out sums of money at various intervals. It's up to you to sort out how much you think you'll need when the child starts at private school, with some allowance for rises in fees before that date.

Broadly, school fees schemes fall into two groups (though, of course, you can go for a mixture):
● capital schemes – for people with a lump sum to invest
● income schemes – for people who want to save money on a regular basis.

Capital schemes

With most of these schemes, the minimum investment is around £1,000 – but if you have a just-born child, you would need to think about investing a lump sum of £20,000 or more to fully pay for private boarding education (assuming fees went up from current levels at 10 per cent a year). With many private schools, you can pay your lump sum directly to the school as a *composition fee*, with much the same outcome.

With some capital schemes, the money is held in trust for the child – and there can be tax advantages in this. If the parents are prepared to forgo the right to cash in the scheme, using a trust avoids a capital transfer tax (CTT) bill if the parent who gives the money dies ($\triangleright$ p. 168 for details about CTT). With certain trust schemes involving annuities, there is no income tax to pay on the money paid out. With other schemes (whether in trust or not), you may be liable for some income tax on the money paid out by the scheme. If parents set up the scheme, there will be no CTT to pay either when it is set up or when fees are paid. If anyone else sets up the scheme, there may be some CTT to pay.

Income schemes

These schemes typically involve a series of investment-type life insurance policies, ending year by year as the fees become due. If you were hoping to provide private boarding education for a just-born child (assuming fees went up from current levels at 10 per cent a year), you would have to think about investing around £2,500 in the first year, rising to £4,000 in the year in which the child starts school and falling back to around £500 in the last year of the child's education.

These income schemes are normally arranged so that there's no income tax due on the money they pay out. There's generally no CTT to pay on the payments made into the scheme, whether parents or other people make them. And if the insurance policies are held in trust for the child, there's no CTT to pay if the person paying the premiums dies.

Where to go for school fees schemes

Your bank or a reputable insurance broker should be able to help you – or put you in touch with an insurance company or broker specializing in school fees schemes. But get quotes from more than one source – different schemes suit different people, and you could save money by shopping around.

Left it too late?

If you haven't planned ahead, or the fees are more than you had anticipated, all may not be lost:
● you might be able to get a bank loan (using, as security, investments you do not want to cash, or your home if your mortgage is small)
● you might be able to get a loan from an insurance company if you have an investment-type life insurance policy with a cash-in value ($\triangleright$ p. 212)
● you might be able to borrow from a bank under a special scheme where you take out an investment-type life insurance policy to pay off the loan.

If all else fails, contact the school – there may be a charity or trust fund which could help out.

14 Managing your money

This chapter is about how to:
- keep track of where your money goes
- try to forecast your future cash needs, so that you can plan your spending wisely.

The chances are that – to some extent – you do both these things already. You may feel you have a fair idea of where the money goes each month or week without keeping a written record of day-to-day spending. And even if you don't draw up a budget on paper, you can still have at the back of your mind a pretty clear idea of what bills are due when, and how easy they are going to be to meet.

The point of writing your records or budgets down is simply to make it easier for you to keep tabs on them. Remembering what you spent yesterday may be easy – but casting your mind back a week or a month is a different matter. The same goes for the assumptions you make when working out your budget – it will be much easier to see how various demands on your purse dovetail (or clash) if you have all the details down on paper before you. On p. 167 there's a checklist of key information to keep handy when you're getting to grips with routine or emergency financial transactions.

Your income
Budgeting depends on forecasting what money is going to come in, as well as what will go out. So you need to form a clear idea both of how much money you should be getting in over the year and of when you can expect to get it.

The largest item will probably be the amount of wages or salary that you (and your wife or husband) have left after deducting tax, NI contributions and contributions to pension schemes.

If your job pays guaranteed overtime, include that – as well as any commission, bonuses or freelance earnings that you are reasonably sure of getting. But don't forget to take into account the effect of tax and other deductions on these earnings too. (For details of how to interpret your pay-slip ▷ p. 11.) If you know you'll be getting a pay increase during the year, then include it – but be realistic about the amount, and remember to take the usual deductions into account.

After taking your earnings into account, add on any other income you get – eg from State benefits, pensions, interest on investments and so forth. Again, don't forget to deduct any tax you have to pay on these sources of income. If the amount you will get is uncertain, make a conservative guess as to its size – that way you shouldn't get too great a shock if your income from that source falls.

Self-employed?
It may be more difficult for you to estimate your likely income if you're self-employed. Both the size and the timing of your income may be uncertain, and you may just have to make a conservative guess, if you don't feel your earnings in the past year are a good guide to the future.

What you spend
It doesn't make sense to get down to planning future spending before you have some idea of how you spend money right now. The past may be a poor guide to the future, but it's better than none.

Broadly speaking, your spending will fall into three main categories:
- day-to-day spending – the money you spend on things you buy often (like food, newspapers, petrol and household goods, for example)
- regular lump sums – the bills which turn up regularly and at predictable intervals (like the mortgage, the rates, car tax, and the fuel bills)
- irregular lump sums – money spent on things like buying a refrigerator, paying for holidays, and getting the car repaired.

Checking on what you spend
Use the checklist on p. 162 as a starting point for what you spend your money on.

The easiest way to keep track of day-to-day spending is to write it down in a notebook small enough to carry around with you. You should keep this kind of record for 6–8 weeks – don't choose a time when your spending pattern is going to be quite exceptional, like the build-up to Christmas or the time you buy all the children's clothes for the year. And if anyone besides you spends the household money, get them to keep a record of what they spend too.

Regular lump sum spending often leaves a record (counterfoils in your cheque book, entries on your bank statement, old bills, and so on). So keeping track of it shouldn't be difficult.

Irregular lump sums tend to be the hardest items to account for, because they don't follow any firm patterns. The checklist on p. 162 may give you some ideas of what you may have been spending (or may have to spend) in this way. And if you keep a file of receipts, you'll be able to use it to help gauge the kind of sum you're likely to have to fork out in the future.

What about emergency spending?

Some bills are likely to take you by surprise, however carefully you plan ahead. Maybe your car blows a gasket, or a freak storm blows a dozen tiles off your roof. To be able to stump up for repairs, you'll need to have set aside a fund to cover emergencies – around £400 should be enough, invested in some place where you'll be able to get at it immediately if need be (▷ Route Maps on pp. 188 and 190).

Drawing up your budget

To draw up your budget you will need the records of your spending (covering all the items in your list) and an estimate of your income for the year.

From your expenditure records and your old bills you should be able to estimate your spending for the year. You will need to know how your expenditure varies from month to month – your gas bills, for example, may be due in January, April, July, and October but the bills will vary, with April usually being the largest. As a result of working out your present spending, you may want to vary your expenditure – or cut some of it out altogether.

If you get paid monthly, you will probably find it easiest to budget on a monthly basis so that you can see:
● how much money comes in during the month
● how much goes out during the month.

The difference between what comes in, and what goes out will give you the amount you have to carry forward to the next month – ie the balance at the end of the month. And so on. On pages 164 and 165 you will find an example budget, done on a monthly basis.

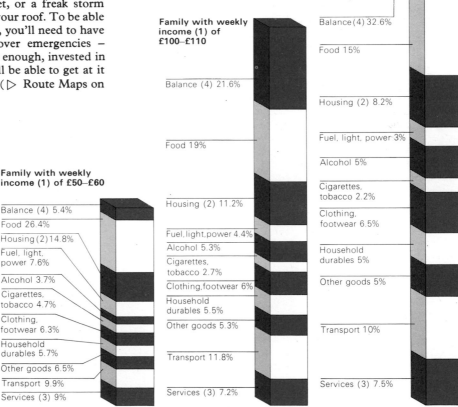

Figure 14.1 Average family spending in three income bands

1. Income before deducting tax, NI contributions, etc.
2. Includes interest on mortgage but not mortgage repayments.
3. Includes telephone, postage and miscellaneous.
4. Covers tax, NI, life insurance, savings, investments and mortgage repayments.

Family with weekly income (1) of £50–£60

Balance (4) 5.4%
Food 26.4%
Housing (2) 14.8%
Fuel, light, power 7.6%
Alcohol 3.7%
Cigarettes, tobacco 4.7%
Clothing, footwear 6.3%
Household durables 5.7%
Other goods 6.5%
Transport 9.9%
Services (3) 9%

Family with weekly income (1) of £100–£110

Balance (4) 21.6%
Food 19%
Housing (2) 11.2%
Fuel, light, power 4.4%
Alcohol 5.3%
Cigarettes, tobacco 2.7%
Clothing, footwear 6%
Household durables 5.5%
Other goods 5.3%
Transport 11.8%
Services (3) 7.2%

Family with weekly income (1) of £150–£200

Balance (4) 32.6%
Food 15%
Housing (2) 8.2%
Fuel, light, power 3%
Alcohol 5%
Cigarettes, tobacco 2.2%
Clothing, footwear 6.5%
Household durables 5%
Other goods 5%
Transport 10%
Services (3) 7.5%

Checklist for different types of spending

Day-to-day spending

Cleaning materials
Cosmetics
Cigarettes, matches, lighter fuel
Drink
Drinks and meals out
Dry cleaning, laundry, launderette
Entertainments (eg cinema, football)
Fares
Food
Gas and electricity slot meters
General household things (eg lavatory paper, cooking foil, light bulbs, batteries)
Hairdresser
Medicines, sticking plaster
Newspapers, magazines
Paraffin, candles, calor gas
Pet food
Petrol and oil for car
Films for camera, and developing charges
Pocket money for children
Soap, shampoo and chemists' goods
Stamps, telegrams
Stationery
Sweets, chocolate, ice cream, crisps,

Regular lump sum

AA/RAC subscription
Bank charges
Car servicing
Car tax and insurance
Christmas
Christmas clubs, holiday clubs and savings clubs
Coal, coke, firewood, charcoal
Covenant payments
Electricity
Gardener
Gas
Ground rent and service charges
HP and other credit payments
Help in the home, au pair
House buildings, contents, all risks insurance
Library subscriptions
Life insurance
Magazine subscriptions
Medical bills insurance
Maintenance and alimony
Mortgage
Oil for central heating
Overdraft interest
Payments to dependants
Personal pension scheme
Piano tuning
Presents
Private lessions (eg music, driving)
Rates (including water rates)
Regular savings
Regular servicing of household goods
Rent
School meals
School, nursery, college fees
Season tickets
Sick pay insurance
Subscriptions to clubs, associations, trade unions, charities
Telephone
Television licence
Television rental
Window cleaning

Irregular lump sum spending

Babysitter
Books
Car purchase
Car repairs
China, glass, cutlery, kitchenware
Clocks and watches
Clothes, shoes, shoe repairs
Dentist, doctor and other medical expenses
Domestic appliances (eg refrigerator, washing machine)
Furniture and furnishings
Garden and allotment (eg seeds, plants, fertilisers, tools)
Hobbies
Holidays
Home decoration, repairs, alterations
Household equipment and repairs
Jewellery
Luggage and leather goods
Motorcycle, moped, bicycle purchase
Musical instruments
Photographic equipment
Records, cassettes, tapes
Spectacles, binoculars
Sports equipment
Television, radio and stereo equipment
Tools, screws, nails

You can copy or adapt this. You will find it easiest to use a sheet of analysis paper obtainable at a stationers. It must be big enough to cover all the items on your list of income and spending and have a column for each month. If you fill in your budget sheet in pencil you should be able to alter the figures easily – you can complete the sheet in ink later. Our example budget runs from January to December but, of course, you can start at any time.

Coping with inflation

When you are drawing up your spending plans for the next year, you'll have to make some allowance for the way inflation will affect prices during that time. Unfortunately there is no straightforward or entirely satisfactory way of doing this. Not only is it hard to forecast inflation even a year ahead, but different items increase in price at different rates. Past rates of inflation are an unreliable guide to the future.

A step towards allowing for inflation is to adjust your spending estimate upwards by what you expect inflation to be. You could do this month by month, or say half-yearly. Your income is likely to rise during the year too – you should have allowed for any increases you know about.

When allowing for inflation, bear in mind that:
● some things will probably not increase in price – such as certain regular lump-sum spending, where you pay a fixed amount each month or year (eg life insurance premiums), or where price rises seem to be rare
● you may know about the amount of some changes in advance – eg a rise in school fees or union subscriptions. Allow for these in your budget
● you may be planning to spend more or less on some things anyway. Take this into account *before* you allow for inflation.

Alternatively, you could decide to ignore both price rises *and* pay rises – and hope that they more or less match. In this case you need to keep a particularly sharp eye on your budget – you may find, part-way through the year, that prices are shooting ahead of pay rises.

What *your* budget shows

Your budget should show you how easy or difficult it's going to be to make ends meet, month by month. If some periods look particularly grim, you can plan ahead for them now:
● by cutting down spending in the months ahead, to build up a greater balance

● by paying some bills in instalments (▷ p. 166), if this suits the way your income comes in
● by opening a bank budget account (▷ p. 166), to even out your regular commitments into equal monthly amounts
● by borrowing money
● by eating into your emergency fund (but only as a last resort).

With many items in your budget, there'll be *some* scope for cutting back spending. You could eat less meat, or less expensive cuts, wear extra sweaters instead of turning up the central heating, and so forth. But there may be some areas you feel strongly about *not* cutting back on (or where it would be very hard for you to do so). The Blakes have marked in blue the items they feel they could economize on, and you could do the same on your budget (your priorities will probably be different, of course).

If it looks as if even by cutting back as much as you can, you are still going to be pressed to make ends meet, you need to give careful thought to your long-term situation. If you are getting by on one income for the household, maybe your wife (or husband) could go out to work too, without raising your expenses too much. Or maybe you could move to a smaller house which would cost less to run. It may be worth looking into the cost of hiring rather than buying some items that you use infrequently – a hedge trimmer, say, or even a car, if yours spends most of its time in the garage.

In any case, make sure that you are claiming all the State benefits to which you may be entitled (▷ ch. 21).

Keeping up to date

If your circumstances change – eg you move house, have a new baby, or change jobs – you will need to draw up a new budget or, at least, modify the old one. But even if there's no change, you will need to keep your budget up to date. You may find your estimated inflation rate is wrong or that you have to meet a large unexpected bill for roof repairs, for example.

So review and update your budget regularly – every 6 months, say.

Rearranging your spending

If your spending consistently exceeds your income, you need to take some action to reduce it. But your problem may be more a pattern of uneven spending contrasting with a regular income. If you are in this position, it may help to take a look at ways of rearranging your spending ▷ p. 166.

		JAN	FEB	MARCH	APRIL	MAY		JUNE	JULY
	BALANCE	18.25	4.10	39.95	86.05	56.90		43.25	81.5
INCOME	Salary	496.60	496.60	496.60	496.60	496.60		526.60	526.
	Child Benefit	40.00	32.00	32.00	32.00	40.00		32.00	40.
	TOTAL	554.85	532.70	568.55	614.65	593.50		601.85	648.
SPENDING									
Regular lump sum spending									
	Mortgage	129.00	129.00	129.00	129.00	129.00		129.00	129
	Life Insurance	19.75	19.75	19.75	19.75	19.75		19.75	19.
	Rates	28.00	28.00			36.50		36.50	36
	Gas	75.00			85.00				55.
	Electricity	30.00			35.00				30
	Telephone		25.00			26.00			
	Water				20.00				
	House + contents insurance					70.00			
	Car insurance								
	Car Tax		22.00					22.00	
	TV Rental	10.20	10.20	10.20	10.20	10.20		10.20	10.2
	TV Licence								34.
	Playschool fees	6.00	6.00	6.00	6.00	6.00		6.00	6.
	School dinners	7.00	7.00	7.00	7.00	7.00		7.00	7.
	R.A.C. Subscription							12.00	
	Which? Subscription			4.75				4.75	
Day to day spending									
	Housekeeping ✳	120.00	120.00	120.00	120.00	120.00		130.00	130.
	Papers	6.40	6.40	6.40	6.40	6.40		6.40	6.4
	Petrol	20.00	20.00	20.00	20.00	20.00		22.00	22.
	Entertainment + sports	9.00	9.00	9.00	9.00	9.00		10.00	10.0
	Toys, books	3.00	3.00	3.00	3.00	3.00		9.50	3.4
	Haircuts ✳	5.00	5.00	5.00	5.00	5.00		5.50	5.5
	Meals at work ✳	25.00	25.00	25.00	25.00	25.00		27.00	20.2
	Stationery, Stamps	1.40	1.40	1.40	1.40	1.40		1.60	1.6
Irregular lump sums									
	Car Maintenance	10.00	10.00	10.00	10.00	10.00		11.00	11.0
	Repair/servicing equipment	6.00	6.00	6.00	6.00	6.00		6.60	6.6
	DIY + garden ✳	15.00	15.00	15.00	15.00	15.00		16.50	16.5
	Holidays								150.0
	Christmas								
	Clothes ✳	25.00	25.00	25.00	25.00	25.00		27.00	27.
	Dentist / Optician			60.00					
	TOTAL	550.75	492.75	482.50	557.75	550.25		520.30	737.
	BALANCE AT END OF MONTH	4.10	39.95	86.05	56.90	43.25		81.55	−89.

G	SEP	OCT	NOV	DEC
.60	-13.90	2.40	-19.50	34.60
.60	526.60	526.60	526.60	526.60
.00	32.00	40.00	32.00	38.00
.00	544.70	569.00	539.10	599.20
.00	129.00	129.00	129.00	129.00
.75	19.75	19.75	19.75	19.75
.50	36.50	36.50	36.50	36.50
		45.00		
		25.00		
.00				28.00
		20.00		
	55.00			
		22.00		
.20	10.20	10.20	10.20	10.20
	14.00	14.00	14.00	14.00
	4.75			4.75
.00	130.00	130.00	130.00	130.00
.40	6.40	6.40	6.40	6.40
.00	22.00	22.00	22.00	22.00
.00	10.00	10.00	10.00	10.00
.45	9.50	3.45	3.45	3.45
.50	5.50	5.50	5.50	5.50
.25	27.00	27.00	27.00	27.00
.75	1.60	1.60	1.60	1.60
.00	11.00	11.00	11.00	11.00
.60	6.60	6.60	6.60	6.60
.50	16.50	16.50	16.50	15.00
				115.00
.00	27.00	27.00	27.00	27.00
.90	542.30	588.50	504.50	594.75
.90	2.40	-19.50	34.60	4.45

Brian and Brenda Blake are in their thirties, with 2 children: Andrew, 7, and Paul, 4. They are buying their home on a mortgage. Brian currently earns about £500 a month (around £6,000 a year) after tax and deductions, and Brenda looks after the home and children. She gets child benefit each week for each child. They have around £40 a year interest from a building society ordinary share account (where they keep a fund for emergencies) — but they add this into their emergency reserve, and don't count it as part of their spending money.

Where their money goes
The Blakes pay their mortgage and life insurance premiums by monthly standing order. They spread their rates out in instalments over 10 months. They pay other bills as promptly as possible — how long they put off payment depends on the state of their finances.

Brenda has about £28 housekeeping a week (plus child benefit payments). The housekeeping covers their food, and general household items. Brenda has a small car which she uses to take the children to school and for shopping. Andrew goes to a local school and Paul goes to play group three mornings a week. In September, Paul will be 5, and he'll go to school too. Brian has a company car and pays only for the petrol for his private use of the car. In order to spread the bills for clothes for the family evenly throughout the year, the Blakes have a budget account with a large local store selling clothes and shoes. Brenda enjoys making some clothes for herself and the children.

Generally the Blakes

rent a self-catering chalet in Cornwall for their holidays, but this year they are spending 2 weeks camping in Scotland instead.

They spend quite a lot on decorating, do-it-yourself, and gardening.

Brian and Brenda try to get out together now and then. They generally arrange to babysit in return for any babysitting they need.

Apart from this, Brenda takes the children swimming every week at the local indoor pool and sometimes Brian and Brenda play squash at the local sports centre.

Brian and Brenda draw up their budget for a calendar year — ie from January to December. The budget we've shown is for 1980. They collected details of their spending by looking back at last year's bills and by keeping a record of their regular spending for some weeks.

The Blake's budget
Brian and Brenda had £18.25 left in their account at the end of the previous year — so they entered this as their *balance* at the start of the year. Brian expects to get a pay rise in June and he estimates that this will increase his take-home pay by £30 a month — so they include this expected increase in their budget and make corresponding adjustments. Jill's housekeeping goes up £10 a month, for example.

Then they estimated their spending on each item in their budget over the next 12 months and entered the figures in pencil so that they could be changed later.

They make a guess at how much the price of the things they pay for will rise over the year. They allow for paying around 10 per cent more for things

from July onwards.

They realize that some of the estimated figures will change over the year and, if they do, they will amend their budget. For example:
● the mortgage interest rate may change and this will affect their monthly payments. They've assumed that they will pay at their current rate of repayment — £129 a month — all year
● charges for gas, electricity and water may change. They allow for increases, but their guesses may turn out not to be accurate.

Unless they are sure when they will have to pay out their irregular lump sums, the Blakes prefer to build them into their budget at a level amount each month — they do this for car maintenance, repairs and servicing, clothes buying, for example. Since they know in which months they'll spend extra for holidays, children's birthdays (June and September) and Christmas, they budget for paying out the entire sums at the appropriate times.

They can see from their budget that they are likely to go into the red because of their holiday — they'll either have to cut back on some of their spending, or borrow. They could eat into their emergency fund (they have about £400 in a building society account at present) but only if they are sure they'll be able to build the fund up again pretty quickly.

They mark on their budget in blue the items which they feel they could economize on if need be. They'll resort to other economies only if they can't make their budget balance.

Paying by instalments

Most large regular bills can be paid by instalments.

● Rates

These can be paid by instalments, usually spread over 10 months. You should contact your local authority if you want to pay by instalments – the address is on the rates bill. Payments can be made by banker's order, by post to the local authority or across the counter at the council offices.

● Electricity and gas bills

There are a number of ways in which you can spread paying for your electricity and gas bills. But mostly they mean parting with your money *before* the bill is due. You may do better to save the money regularly yourself (in a building society account, say) and earn some interest on it, rather than make what amounts to an interest-free loan to the electricity or gas board.

Special payment schemes for gas and electricity bills include:

● regular budget payment schemes – an estimate is made of your annual bill for electricity or gas and you then pay in 12 monthly instalments through your bank

● savings stamps – these can be bought at your gas or electricity showroom. You can pay your bill with the appropriate stamps or with a combination of stamps and cash

● pay-as-you-go schemes – these let you make payments towards your quarterly bill whenever you wish. You decide how much you pay and when you pay it and the sums paid in will be deducted from your next bill. Payments can be made at any showroom or by post. Ask at your local showroom for an application form if you want to open an account.

Find out from your local electricity or gas showroom which methods of payment are available in your area.

● TV licence and telephone bill

You can buy television savings stamps at all post offices. You can pay for your TV licence with the stamps or a combination of stamps and cash. Telephone bill stamps work in just the same way for telephone bills. Note that, as with gas and electricity, you're really making an interest-free loan to the company when you use these stamps.

● Season tickets

There is no British Rail system for paying for season tickets in instalments – but you may be able to persuade your employer to give you a low-interest or no-interest loan to buy a quarterly or annual season ticket (which is substantially cheaper than a daily ticket). You can then pay off in monthly instalments.

Bank budget accounts

Most banks offer budget accounts. With a budget account, you add up all the bills you want to include in the scheme to get an estimate of the yearly total. Then the bank will have to agree your figures. You make out a monthly standing order for $\frac{1}{12}$ of the yearly amount (plus the charge the bank makes) and this is put into a special account. You then draw on this account to meet the bills you have included in the scheme. Sometimes the account will be overdrawn (and some banks then charge interest). Sometimes it will be in credit (banks are not keen on budget accounts permanently in the red). By the end of the year, the payments out should just about equal the payments in – you can make your own allowance for possible inflation if you want to. Each bank has its own policy for what it charges for a budget account, so find out how much it will cost before deciding to use this method.

Shop accounts

Many shops – especially department stores and clothes shops – run schemes which can help you spread paying for things over a number of months. With many, you use a special shop credit card. For more details ▷ p. 214.

There are three main types of shop account.

● Budget accounts

You agree to pay a certain minimum amount each month, but there's nothing to stop you paying more some months (to pay off what you owe, say). You're allowed to borrow up to some multiple of your agreed monthly payment (24 times it, say). You're charged interest on the amount you owe. The minimum payment is generally around £5, and there may be a set maximum.

● Monthly accounts

You buy things on credit. You get a monthly statement and have to pay off the full amount you owe each month. No interest is charged unless you break the rules and don't pay up on time.

● Option accounts

You buy things on credit. You get a monthly statement and can choose to pay off all your debt, or just part of it. You are charged interest on the amount that is outstanding.

Borrowing

It's only worth borrowing if you're sure you can afford to repay. For example, you can borrow to finance your spending on some large item like a washing machine by buying on hire purchase, by using a credit card, or by raising money through an overdraft or personal loan. A credit card can be a handy way of coping with a temporary problem – and it won't cost you anything in interest if you repay the debt within a month or so ($\triangleright$ p. 211). Otherwise, remember that you will have to pay interest charges as well as repaying the sum borrowed. We cover buying on credit in more detail in chapter 19.

Key information

Whenever you sit down to sort out your budget, you will find that you need quite a lot of information, which is probably scattered around in different places.

When you make up your budget you will include things like car and house insurance, mortgage repayments and so on. It will be easier to keep your budget up to date and to deal with any letters or problems if you keep a list of all the key information relevant to you and your family. Some of the things on the list may not involve weekly or regular payments but you may need to refer to them at some time – so keep all your information together.

You might find it convenient to keep bills (electricity, gas, telephone, rates, etc), in the same place, together with some of the numbers it is useful to know – like your National Insurance number, National Health number, passport number, and so on.

Information for your records

Building society
Name, address, telephone number
Amount of monthly repayment and
    date due
Savings account reference number
Amount of regular savings

Bank
Name, address
Current account number
Deposit account number
Standing orders
Cheque card number
Cash card number

Investments
Brief details of investment accounts,
    shares, etc

Post Office
Account number and address

Credit cards
Company address, telephone number
Credit card number

Insurance
Company name and address
Policy number and date
Amount of premium and date due
(keep these details for all your policies)

Loans
Details of HP, overdrafts, etc

Car
Car registration number
Driver's licence number
Road fund licence number and expiry
    date
MOT test certificate number and expiry
    date
Car key numbers
Car chassis and engine number

Tax
Tax office address
Tax reference number

Miscellaneous
TV licence – date and amount
National Insurance numbers
National Health Service numbers
Passport numbers

15 Passing your money on

You may not think of yourself as wealthy, but even if you have only fairly modest assets – your home, say, plus a few thousand £££ in the building society – you should sort out how you want them passed on. If you don't, you may find that, after tax has been paid to the Inland Revenue, your heirs get less than you bargained for.

How gifts are taxed

It used to be the case that, by giving your assets away at least 7 years before you died, you might escape estate duty altogether. This isn't so any more. Nowadays, if you make a gift to someone, as well as the *capital gains tax* (CGT) you may have to pay (▷ p. 195), you or the people to whom you make the gift may have to pay *capital transfer tax* (CTT) too. And the size of the CTT bill will be based, not simply on the money you leave when you die, but on the amount you have given away during your life as well. Figure 15.1 gives some examples of what CTT could mean to you and your family. This doesn't mean that you can't escape, or at least reduce, the effects of the tax. On the contrary, you can – if you take steps as soon as possible to put your affairs in order.

In order to reduce your CTT bill, you should aim to
● make gifts in ways which count as free of tax (▷ opposite)
● make gifts during your lifetime, when the rates of tax (▷ Fig. 15.2) are lower than those for gifts made on death

● cut down the number of times your money and other assets are passed on (and therefore the number of times they are taxable). For example, if you plan for your money to end up with your grandchildren in the long-run, leave it directly to them, rather than to their parents to pass on.

How capital transfer tax works

Capital transfer tax has replaced estate duty, but it goes beyond estate duty – because it applies to gifts made in your lifetime, as well as possessions left on your death. It's not only things like shares, unit trusts, money and jewellery that could be affected by capital transfer tax. *All* the things you own – your home, car, furniture and so on – can count as taxable gifts if you give them away. And when you die, you are considered to give away everything you own.

Certain gifts are tax-free (▷ opposite) – but any others count as taxable gifts. The taxman keeps a running total of all the taxable gifts you have made since 26 March 74.

You can clock up a certain amount of taxable gifts without paying tax. This amount changes from time to time – it was £50,000 at the time we went to press (until 26 October 77 the limit was £15,000; until 25 March 1980, it was £25,000). After you pass the limit, the amount of tax to be paid rises fairly steeply, not just with the size of the gift but with the total amount given already. So gifts given late in life may be much more

Figure 15.1 What CTT could mean to you and your family

If your taxable possessions add up to:	All given to your wife (or husband) during your life or on your death	All given to others (eg children) 3 or more years before your death – assuming they pay the tax out of what they get	All given to others (eg children) on your death – assuming the tax comes out of what you leave
£50,000	No tax	No tax	No tax
£75,000	No tax	£4,250 tax	£8,500 tax
£100,000	No tax	£9,500 tax	£19,000 tax

heavily taxed than those made earlier – even when the gifts made later are much smaller than the earlier ones.

Each person has only one running total – which covers both gifts made in life and those made on death. So when you die, any taxable possessions you leave (whether or not you have made a will) are added to your existing running total.

A husband and wife each have their own running total. This means they can each make £50,000 of taxable gifts, before they have to pay any CTT.

Because of the way CTT works, it is very important to keep track of how much you have given in the way of taxable gifts since 26 March 74 (when CTT was introduced) and how much tax you have paid.

Tax-free gifts

Some gifts are always free of tax, no matter when they are made. Others are free of tax only if you make them during your lifetime. And yet others qualify for freedom from tax only if the giver has died. These tax-free gifts *don't* count towards your running total of taxable gifts.

Gifts that are always tax-free
● gifts between husband and wife, including money or assets left under the terms of a will or when the giver dies intestate (▷ p. 177)
● gifts to charities and political parties – provided you make the gift at least a year before you die. For gifts made within a year of death, up to £200,000 can be given tax-free to a charity, and up to £100,000 to political parties
● gifts to certain national institutions – eg the National Trust, British Museum, and to certain museums, art galleries and libraries
● gifts to local authorities and universities
● gifts for the public benefit – eg gifts of outstanding scenic, scientific, historic or artistic merit. These gifts must have Treasury approval
● gifts of shares in a company into a trust set up for the benefit of employees of the company – provided that the trust will hold at least half the ordinary shares of the company.

Gifts tax-free if made during life
● gifts of up to £250 each to any number of different people in any one tax year
● wedding gifts: up to £5,000 tax free if the giver is a parent of the bride or groom; £2,500 if the giver is a grandparent or great-

grandparent; £1,000 if it's anyone else
● gifts made out of your income (but not by drawing from capital) which are part of your normal spending. For such gifts to be tax-free, you must be able to keep up your usual standard of living on what is left of your income
● gifts to support any of your or your wife's elderly (65 or over) or infirm relatives, or to support a widowed, separated or divorced mother or mother-in-law
● gifts to maintain an ex-wife or ex-husband, or to help pay for the maintenance of your or your wife's child (so long as the child is under 18, or in full-time education or training). In certain circumstances, helping maintain a child who isn't your own can also be tax-free, if he is not being looked after by his own parents
● up to £2,000 worth of gifts during the tax year which do not count as tax-free gifts for any other reason. A husband and wife between them can give up to £4,000 in one tax year. If you do not use up your full £2,000 allowance in one year, you can carry forward the unused part to the next tax year (but no further). So a husband and wife could give £8,000 between them over a 2-year period.

Gifts tax-free on death only
● lump sum payments from pension schemes (▷ p. 55) provided that the lump sum is payable not as a right but at the discretion of the pension fund trustees

Reasonable funeral expenses can be deducted from your estate before working out the capital transfer tax bill.

Warning: Capital gains tax and gifts
A gift made during your life normally counts as a disposal for the purposes of capital gains tax. So even though you have not benefited from any increase in value in what you've given, you may be taxed on the gain you are assumed to have made. Note that there's no CGT to pay on gifts left on your death. For details of CGT ▷ pp. 195–6.

How much tax?

The amount of tax due depends on whether the gift is made during your life (and for these gifts, whether the *giver* or the *getter* pays the tax) or made on your death.

Gifts made during your life

The key to mastering the capital transfer tax sums is to remember the taxman's golden rule: *tax is worked out on the amount by which the giver is worse off as a result of making the gift.*

If you, the *giver*, are to pay the tax, you will be worse off not only by the value of the gift you hand over, but also by the capital transfer tax you pay on it. So what you pay tax on is *more* than the value of whatever the getter receives.

This exaggerated value (the gift plus the tax) is the *grossed-up* value of the gift, and is added to your running total of taxable gifts and is taxed at the rates listed in column A of Fig. 15.2.

If the *getter* agrees to pay the tax, then you are worse off only by the value of the gift you hand over. So the getter pays tax on this amount, at the rates of tax listed in column A of Fig. 15.2. To get your new running total, you simply add what you hand over (*not* the grossed-up amount) to your old running total.

The giver should bear in mind that if the getter is to pay the tax, he or she could end up with a large tax bill unless arrangements are made for paying the tax. This could prove particularly inconvenient if the gift is something that is hard to cash in quickly, like a building or land.

If the giver is going to pay the tax and has extra expenses connected with giving the gift – transport or insurance costs, say – he can't deduct them from the value of the gift before working out the tax that's due. But if the person who receives the gift has such costs (and is the person who is going to pay the tax), then he or she *may* deduct these costs from the value of the gift before working out the tax that's due. So if you know there'll be heavy incidental expenses, there's a case for arranging for the getter rather than the giver to pay the CTT.

If you're making or planning to make gifts during your lifetime, there are some things worth doing:
● take full advantage of your chances to make tax-free gifts (▷ p. 169)
● keep track of your own running total of taxable gifts, to make it easier to work out what tax you will have to pay on a new gift
● let anyone you give a gift to know your running total, so that they can work out whether to take out life insurance on your life for the next 3 years (▷ below for why this may be necessary).

Gifts made on death

When anyone dies, they are assumed for the purposes of CTT to have given away all their assets. The value of their assets is added to their running total (including any tax paid by them so far). Tax is charged on the assets at the rates listed in column B of Fig. 15.2. This value is *not* grossed up (otherwise there could be too little money to pay the tax).

The value of assets left on death may be reduced by:
● income tax and capital gains tax liabilities still outstanding
● other debts
● reasonable funeral expenses.

Death within 3 years of making a taxable gift

If someone dies within 3 years of making a taxable gift, CTT will be charged at the higher rates which apply to gifts made on death.

The taxman recalculates the total tax due at these higher rates, and subtracts the tax already paid. The person who received the gift gets the bill for the difference.

If you get a gift on which you would have to pay a lot of CTT if the giver died within 3 years, it would be sensible to take out term insurance (▷ p. 140) on the giver's life to cover the possible debt.

Domicile
The rules set out left apply as long as you are not *domiciled* outside the UK. In the main you count as being domiciled in the UK if you
● have your permanent home in the UK
● intend to go on living in the UK permanently (or returning to it).

If you're domiciled abroad, normally only taxable gifts you make out of what you own *in the UK* get added to your running total for CTT – so you might end up with less CTT to pay than someone domiciled in the UK.

On the other hand, married couples only *one* of whom is domiciled in the UK could end up paying *more* CTT than the norm: only the first £50,000 of gifts made by the person domiciled in the UK to their husband or wife who is domiciled abroad will be free of tax (until 26 October 77, the limit was £15,000; until 25 March 80, the limit was £25,000).

If you have recently moved abroad, or are thinking of doing so, don't assume that selling everything you own here and moving away will automatically mean that you escape CTT.

It's by no means quick or easy to convince the taxman that you are domiciled abroad. Moreover, if by 9 December 74, the taxman was not convinced you had left the UK for good, then – even once he is convinced – there is a further 3-year wait before the CTT rules treat you as domiciled abroad. What is more, people domiciled in the UK who moved to the Isle of Man or Channel Islands after 10 December 74 will – for CTT – continue to be treated as domiciled in the UK, and so can't escape the tax.

Steven Sharp buys shares for £5,000 and gives them to his daughter a year later, by which time their market value is £7,500.

For CTT purposes, the value of the gift is taken to be £7,500 rather than £5,000. And Steven may be liable for CGT on the gain he's deemed to have made on the shares.

How gifts are valued

For the purposes of CTT, gifts are normally taken to have their open market value at the time of the transfer.

So it's no use trying to avoid CTT by selling at a token price, rather than giving away. You'll be charged CTT on the difference between the price you would want if you sold to a complete stranger, and the price you actually charged. The same rule applies if you lend money at less than the going rate or if you allow someone the use of a house and charge little or no rent. Here the value of the gift is the difference between the interest or rent you'd expect to have got from a complete stranger, and the amount you actually charge in each tax year.

How to assess your liability

If you look at Fig. 15.2, you can get some idea of what rate (or rates) of tax will be charged on a gift you're planning to make. But if the gift (combined with your current running total of taxable gifts) means that you'll be charged tax at a number of different rates, working out the grossed-up value of your gift ($\triangleright$ opposite) and therefore how much CTT you are liable for is extremely complicated. You may need help from an accountant or other professional adviser. Note that the *Money Which?* Tax-Saving Guide March 80 includes a Calculator for working out the tax due on gifts made before 26 March 80. Check the 1981 Tax-Saving Guide in March 81, for the new rules.

Figure 15.2 Rates of capital transfer tax

Tax on gifts made during your life, calculated on grossed-up value of gifts, and tax on possessions left on death

Running total of taxable gifts (including any tax paid by you so far)(1)	Total tax due for gifts made during life(2)	Total tax due on gifts made on death	On each £ over	Up to	Rate of tax for gifts made during life(2) **A**	Rate of tax for gifts on death **B**
Under £50,000	Nil	Nil	£0	£50,000	Nil	Nil
£50,000	Nil	Nil	£50,000	£60,000	15%	30%
£60,000	£1,500	£3,000	£60,000	£70,000	17½%	35%
£70,000	£3,250	£6,500	£70,000	£90,000	20%	40%
£90,000	£7,250	£14,500	£90,000	£110,000	22½%	45%
£110,000	£11,750	£23,500	£110,000	£130,000	27½%	50%
£130,000	£17,250	£33,500	£130,000	£160,000	35%	55%
£160,000	£27,750	£50,000	£160,000	£210,000	42½%	60%
£210,000	£49,000	£80,000	£210,000	£260,000	50%	60%
£260,000	£74,000	£110,000	£260,000	£310,000	55%	60%
£310,000	£101,500	£140,000	£310,000	£510,000	60%	60%
£510,000	£221,500	£260,000	£510,000	£1,010,000	65%	65%
£1,010,000	£546,500	£585,000	£1,010,000	£2,010,000	70%	70%
£2,010,000	£1,246,500	£1,285,000	£2,010,000		75%	75%

1. Including value of possessions left on death (but *not* any tax due on them), if tax on death is being worked out.
2. Provided gift is made at least 3 years before death; for gifts made within 3 years of death, use column B to work out tax due.

Gifts of life insurance policies,
If you take out policies on your life and arrange for the proceeds payable on your death to go directly to, say, your children, these proceeds are free of CTT.
The premiums you pay on such a policy count as gifts, but provided these premiums are paid out of your income (and without reducing your normal standard of living) there's no tax to pay on them.
Note that even if the premiums are too large to come out of your income and count as tax-free, there's still no tax to pay if you use your other tax-free gifts to pay the premiums (eg of £2,000 in each tax year – ▷ p. 169).
The most usual way of giving an insurance policy to your children is to have it worded to suit the provisions of the Married Women's Property Act 1882, the policy will then belong to your children, not to you.
Gifts of life insurance policies on your own life taken out after 26 March 74 won't be considered tax-free if you also have an annuity – unless you can satisfy the taxman that the policy and the annuity are unconnected (ie from different insurance companies, or on the same terms as if you had taken out the policy, or the annuity, on its own).
A wife can take out policies on her own life, and arrange for the proceeds to go to the children. If she can't pay the premiums herself, her husband can normally give her the money to do so (but to avoid tax, the husband shouldn't make taking out a policy a condition of the gift of the money for the premiums). The wife should keep the premiums within her tax-free gifts limit.

Gifts not taxed in the normal way
Certain gifts are taxed in a special way. If any of the following applies to you, contact the taxman for details.

Returned gifts
If you return a gift to the original giver (or the giver's widow or widower) or return a gift made from a trust, or disclaim something left to you in a will, it may not count as a gift to you at all.

Family businesses
If you transfer assets from a business which you have owned for at least 2 years, you or the person you give them to will have to pay CTT, but at a reduced rate – between 50 and 80 per cent of the normal rate, depending on the assets transferred.

Rapid succession
If you die within 4 years of receiving gifts on which CTT has been paid, CTT on your estate will be worked out at a reduced rate.

Farmland
If you transfer agricultural property you have owned as a working farmer for at least 2 years previously, you or the person you give it to will normally have to pay CTT at 50 per cent of the normal rate.

Woodlands
If you die leaving woodlands which you have owned for at least 5 years (or which were given to you or inherited) the value of the trees – but not of the land itself – may be disregarded when CTT is worked out.

Trust funds
For a general guide ▷ opposite. But seek professional advice if the sums are significant; and it's probably not worth setting up a trust if they aren't.

Property sold within a short time of death
If the dead person's personal representatives sell shares or unit trusts (within 1 year of the death) or houses or land (within 3 years) for less than they were worth on the date of death, they may be able to claim back some of the CTT paid.

War service
If, as a member of the armed services, you die on war service or its equivalent, there will be no CTT to pay on your estate.

Life interest
If your late husband or wife died before 13 November 74, leaving you a life interest in some possessions, estate duty rules will have applied at the first death, and there will normally be no CTT to pay on these possessions when you die.

How to cope with CTT
● give away what you can during your lifetime, rather than leaving it until you die, when the CTT rates are higher. But use your common sense – don't risk poverty in your old age just to thwart the taxman
● if your marriage is stable, split your assets equally between husband and wife
● provided that your husband or wife is left with enough to live on (taking inflation into account), leave your possessions to someone else rather than to each other. And remember that CTT strikes whenever a transfer is made – so it's best to give to beneficiaries as young as possible (to grandchildren or great-grandchildren rather than sons and daughters). You could always put the money in trust for them if you feel they're too young to have control over it themselves
● take full advantage of the £2,000 you can give away each year free of CTT. Remember that this is £2,000 for each person to give away, so husband and wife between them can give up to £4,000 in one tax year. Also remember that you can roll the tax-free sums forward one year but no further (so husband and wife can give up to £8,000 between them over the 2-year period)
● consider taking full advantage of the other tax-free ways of making gifts (▷ p. 169)
● if you get a large gift which is taxable, consider buying life insurance to cover the possible extra tax you'd have to pay if the giver died within 3 years
● if you're planning to leave large amounts to charities or political parties, do it during your lifetime (▷ p. 169). The gift will reduce the value of your remaining estate for CTT
● consider taking out life insurance policies in favour of your children (or other beneficiaries – ▷ left)
● keep your will up-to-date. Husband and wife should each make a separate will. If your current will was designed to save estate duty (which applied before 26 March 74), it probably *doesn't* save CTT. Check *now*, and change it if necessary.

When CTT is due

It's the giver's responsibility to tell the tax-man about any taxable gifts he makes. To do this, get form C5 from the Capital Taxes Office at the following addresses:
- England and Wales: Lynwood Road, Thames Ditton, Surrey KT7 0EB.
- Scotland: 16 Picardy Place, Edinburgh EH1 3NB.
- N. Ireland: Law Courts Building, Chichester Street, Belfast BT1 3NU.

If you're giving or receiving gifts which are liable to CTT, the safest course is for you to assume the tax will have to be paid 6 months from the end of the month in which the gift was made. This also applies to the tax due when someone dies. There are two exceptions to this rule:
- lifetime gifts made *after* 5 April but *before* 1 October of any year: tax payable on 30 April in the following year
- gifts of certain assets – whether made during life or on death: tax can be paid by instalments over 8 years. To qualify, the assets must be a business, or part of one, land and the buildings on it, shares in a company over which the giver had a controlling interest, or certain unquoted shares. The tax can be spread out over 8 yearly, or 16 half-yearly payments, the first being due when the lump-sum payment would have been. For lifetime gifts, it's only if the *getter* is paying the tax that paying by instalments will be allowed.

Someone paying by instalments on gifts of shares or a business (or part of one) won't have to pay interest on the amount outstanding (as long as the instalments are paid in time). With instalments of tax on the other types of gifts (and with late payments of lump sum tax), interest will be charged on the amount outstanding.

Trusts

What are trusts for?

If you want to reduce the amount of CTT that will eventually be paid on your assets, it makes sense to give them to beneficiaries as young as possible (ie to skip generations, where you can), and to do it as soon as possible. But you may be wary of giving them the money direct before they are old enough to look after it properly. If you're faced with this dilemma, a way out of the problem is to set up some kind of *trust*. Note that when you put money into a trust, it normally counts as a gift for CTT purposes. There's normally no CTT to pay when the money is handed over to the people who benefit

under the trust ($\triangleright$ p. 174 for details).

Under a trust, money can be controlled by adults (the *trustees*) for the benefit of the person or people it is held in trust for. You can be a trustee for a trust you have set up yourself, or you can appoint friends or family, or a professional (a solicitor or accountant, say) who will charge the trust for his services.

There are ways of setting up trusts without going through all the legal formalities discussed later on, and it is worth considering them first. Tailor-made trusts are much more expensive to set up. Even a fairly straightforward one might cost between £50 and £150 to set up – and there could be a charge each year from the trustees for running it (as much as £50 or more, say). So it's probably not worth setting up a trust unless you plan to give away a lot of money (£2,000 at the very least) and feel the cost of setting up and running the trust is worth it, or would be outweighed by tax savings.

Short-cut trusts
- Life insurance policies

Taking out a life insurance policy, so that the proceeds are payable to your children ($\triangleright$ p. 172) is a way of setting up a trust. If you die before the children reach 18, the money will be held in trust for them.

The premiums you pay count as gifts for CTT purposes (but may well come into one of the tax-free categories – $\triangleright$ p. 169). There is no CTT to pay on money paid out by the policy. And if the policy is handed over to the child after he reaches 18, any taxable gain on the policy is taxed as the child's income, not the parents. If the policy ends before it is handed over, however, the gain is taxed as the parents' income – though the trust pays any income tax due.
- Unit trusts

Some unit trust management companies run schemes which set up trusts if people want to invest for children. The investments are held in an *accumulation and maintenance trust* ($\triangleright$ p. 174).
- Investing on behalf of a child

Many investments (eg shares, premium bonds, building society accounts) can be held on behalf of a child, even if the child is too young to invest in his own name. Money invested in this way can be used only for the benefit of the child – and he can ask for it to be handed over to him at the age you specified when investing the money (18, if no age was specified). It can be handed over earlier if you agree.

More about trusts

There are several varieties of trust, and their taxation, in particular, varies widely. It's advisable to employ a solicitor experienced in trust work (local area offices of the Law Society should be able to put you in touch with suitable ones) to draw up the trust deed, which sets out details such as:

● who the trustees are
● who is entitled to benefit (may be one person or many)
● when income and capital are to be paid out
● ways in which trustees can invest the money.

Fixed trusts (often called *interest in possession* trusts)

● How they work
A particular person (or people) has the right to income from the trust (or the equivalent of income – eg the right to live in a rent-free home). The trustees have no choice but to hand over the income to the beneficiaries at the times stated in the trust deed.

● Income tax
Trust income is taxed at the basic rate (30 per cent for the 80/81 tax year). Income paid out by the trust comes with a tax credit of 30 per cent.

If the trust was set up by parents who are still alive for their child (or children) under the age of 18, the income paid out is taxed as if it were the parents', and they get the 30 per cent tax credit. If the parents are dead or the trust was set up by anyone other than parents (by the grandparents, say) it's taxed as the child's income.

If parent or child pays no tax, or less than has been deducted, he can claim tax back. But if he pays tax at more than the basic rate (including any investment income surcharge) he will have to pay extra tax.

● Capital gains tax (CGT)
When assets are first put into the trust, it counts as disposing of them, and there may be CGT to pay ($\triangleright$ p. 195). Their value is considered to be their market value at the time they are transferred into the trust.

Trusts set up after 6 June 78 pay CGT at 30 per cent on *all* gains (less allowable losses) they make.

If a beneficiary becomes entitled to some or all of the assets of the trust (eg when he reaches 18) this counts as the trust disposing of the assets and if there are gains, the trust has to pay CGT.

● Capital transfer tax (CTT)
With trusts set up after 26 March 74, the value of the money, property (or whatever) put into the trust counts as a gift at the time it is put in – and is taxed in the ordinary way. In the main, gifts into trusts count as tax-free if they would be tax-free when made to an individual.

Anyone who has the right to income or the equivalent of income (eg the right to live in a rent-free home) from the trust is considered to own the trust's capital – or part of the trust's capital, if the rights to the benefits are shared among several people. When a person's right to the trust's benefits comes to an end he is considered to be making a gift. For example, a widow may have the right to income from a trust set up by her late husband, which on her remarriage passes to their children, say. The widow is considered to make a gift at the time her right to the income ceases. The gift is valued at her share of the trust's capital at that time, and is added to her running total of taxable gifts and taxed in the normal way – *this tax is paid by the trust.*

When the trust finally comes to an end, and the capital is handed over to beneficiaries who at that time have the right to the income, there's no further CTT to pay.

Discretionary trusts

● How they work
Here it is left to the discretion of the trustees which of the possible beneficiaries should be paid income. They may also be free to decide which should get capital.

The trustees may be given power to accumulate income (not pay it out at all) until the trust ends. This type of trust is called an *accumulation trust*. An *accumulation and maintenance trust* is a type of accumulation trust from which income can be paid only for the maintenance, education or training of the beneficiaries.

● Income tax
The trust income is taxed at the basic rate (30 per cent for the 80/81 tax year) *plus* the rate for investment income surcharge (15 per cent for 80/81). So the total rate was 45 per cent for the 80/81 tax year. Income *paid out* by the trust comes with a tax credit for the tax already paid (ie for 45 per cent in the 80/81 tax year). See Fixed trusts (above) for who gets the tax credit and pays extra tax if it is due. The rules are the same.

Note that, with an *accumulation* trust set up for the benefit of children under 18, if the income is accumulated and not paid out until your children are 18 or over, there's no further tax to pay – but neither you nor your children can claim tax back if you pay tax at a lower rate than has been deducted (45 per cent for the 80/81 tax year).

● Capital gains tax (CGT)

The rules are the same as those for fixed trust (▷ opposite).

● Capital transfer tax (CTT)

Payments into a discretionary trust count as gifts in the same way as for fixed trusts (▷ opposite).

CTT once the trust has been set up depends on the type of discretionary trust.

Unless the discretionary trust is an accumulation and maintenance one (▷ below), when payments are made from the trust's capital, the trust is charged CTT. This tax is based on the running total of the person who first set up the trust immediately after he set it up – and is calculated in a special way.

But this kind of discretionary trust is charged CTT even if payments are not made out of the trust. CTT is automatically charged every 10 years on the value of everything in the trust. The amount charged is 30 per cent of the amount that would be charged if the entire trust fund were paid out on that date. No trust will have to start paying this 10-yearly tax until its first tenth anniversary after 31 March 82. These regular 10-yearly tax payments are allowed as credits – valid for 20 years – against any CTT charged on payments actually made from the trust.

Payments of capital from certain *accumulation and maintenance* trusts, by contrast, are free of CTT. And these trusts are also free of the 10-yearly tax bills. To qualify, a trust must be for the benefit of one or more people under the age of 25, who must get the capital in the trust (or at least a right to income, or use of the funds) on or before their 25th birthday. If any income is paid out from the trust before this, it must be used only for the maintenance, education or training of the beneficiaries.

If the trust was set up after 14 April 76, it will be free of CTT only if the children who benefit have a grandparent in common or the trust is less than 25 years old.

Warning

The impact of CTT on discretionary trusts apart from accumulation and maintenance trusts can be very tough indeed. So if you're planning to set up a discretionary trust for children or young people, make sure it is an accumulation and maintenance trust.

It isn't normally possible for the person setting up the trust to change their mind once the trust deed is signed. So think twice before you set one up. If largish sums of money are involved it's sensible to get professional advice before you go ahead.

Problems

● Stuck with a discretionary trust?

There are special rules to help trustees of discretionary trusts set up before 27 March 74 to reorganize their trusts without incurring massive capital transfer tax bills. But these rules end on 31 March 82 – so if they affect you, get advice now.

● Want the trust reorganized?

You could go to court to try to do this, but you're unlikely to succeed unless all the people who benefit from the trust agree with you.

● Dissatisfied with the trustees?

If you're a beneficiary of a trust and you think the trustees have been incompetent or even dishonest in carrying out their duties – for instance, if they have been selling assets to business associates at less than their market price – you can sue them for the restoration of what you think you have lost. You have to be 18 or over to do this – and you're likely to have a battle to win your case.

Scotland
It's difficult for a Scotsman or Scotswoman to disinherit their spouse or children, because they have, on his or her death, certain rights to the estate.

The widow (or widower) has the right to one half of her husband's (or wife's) moveable estate if there are no children, to one third if there are children.

Children have the right to one half of the moveable estate if the other parent is dead, to one third if the other parent survives. Moveable estate does not include things like land and houses (so these rules may sometimes be got round).

The rules about what happens when someone dies without leaving a valid will behind are different (and complicated) in Scotland. If you need expert advice, contact a solicitor.

Wills

You may find the thought of making a will unpleasant, but it will make things a great deal easier for your family and friends, in the event of your death, if you have made one.

A properly drawn-up will can also

● save tax
● cut out arguments

Most people use solicitors to draw up their wills. If you need extensive tax planning, have a business or a farm to leave, plan a complicated trust or want to cut your wife (or husband) or children out of your will, then it's sensible to go to a solicitor. But if your affairs are straightforward, and you are 18 or older, you could consider drawing up your own will. For details of how to go about this, see *Wills and Probate*, published by Consumers' Association. (Write to Consumers' Association, Caxton Hill, Hertford SG13 7LZ.)

The main thing to remember when drawing up a will is that clarity and precision are vital. What seems plain to you might seem much less so to the people who have to sort your intentions out. For example, if you write: 'I leave £500 to my brother and sister-in-law, David and Fiona Green', it's not at all clear whether you mean to give *each* of them £500, or to give £500 for them to share.

Choosing executors

The executors of your will are the people formally entitled to take on the legal side of managing the property you leave.

Strictly speaking, you need only one executor, but it's sensible to have two (or more) to share the burden of work. Check before you name them that they are prepared to do the job.

To try to improve the chances of choosing executors who'll outlive you, it may be as well to choose at least one who is reasonably young. Or instead you could choose an institution, like a bank, to act as your executor (a bank will certainly charge for the work, though, whereas a friend might not).

Appointing a guardian

A guardian has the right to determine questions relating to the home, education and marriage of children under the age of 18. It is sensible to appoint one (but not essential) if you have children under this age.

Don't forget about capital transfer tax (CTT)

Make sure you allow for CTT when you specify what you are going to leave to whom. If you don't, the residuary legatee (the person to whom you leave what's left of your estate after all your other bequests and legacies) may end up with very little.

You can't tell the beneficiaries what to do with the money

Once you have left something to someone in your will, it's theirs to leave to anyone else of their own choosing on their death. So there's no point specifying whom you would like them to leave it to. You could, however, leave the right to income to someone in your will (eg to your widow) with the provision that the capital goes to someone else on her death.

Revoke all previous wills

Say that you are revoking them even if this is the first will that you're making. It will save your friends and family hunting around. Destroy any previous wills.

Put the date on your will

Again, this is not essential, but it helps to make clear which will is the latest, if more than one turns up.

Sign the will

Do this within sight of 2 witnesses, who should then both sign the will too. Don't ask anyone who is to benefit by the will (or their wife or husband) to witness it, or they will lose their legacy.

Make it difficult for anyone to tamper with the will

Sign each page at the bottom, so that no-one can slip in any extra pages. Don't let there be any suggestion that something else was pinned onto the will. Don't leave the reverse side of the pages blank: write on them or cross them off and initial the crossing.

Don't make alterations to the text. If you want to change something, add a codicil (a supplement that alters some part of a will but leaves the rest intact) witnessed by 2 people, like the will itself.

Put your will in a safe place

You may decide to lodge your will at your bank. Or if you have a safe, this may be more convenient. Let your immediate relatives and your executors know where the will is, and if it's locked up, where the key is. It's useful to keep an up-to-date list of what you possess with your will, so that your executors can tell at a glance what's involved in winding up your estate. By keeping your affairs in an orderly fashion, you'll make their job much more straightforward.

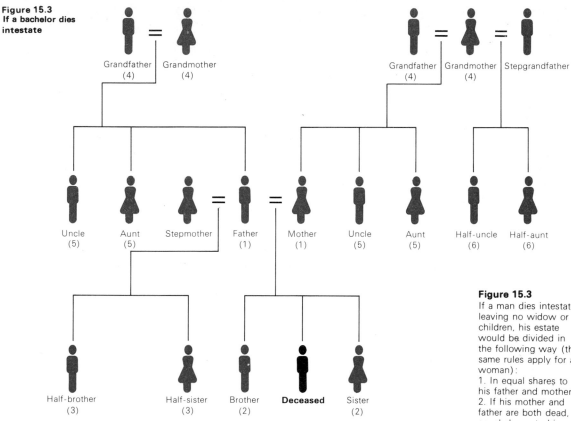

Figure 15.3
If a bachelor dies intestate

Grandfather (4) — Grandmother (4)

Grandfather (4) — Grandmother (4) — Stepgrandfather

Uncle (5) | Aunt (5) | Stepmother | Father (1) | Mother (1) | Uncle (5) | Aunt (5) | Half-uncle (6) | Half-aunt (6)

Half-brother (3) | Half-sister (3) | Brother (2) | **Deceased** | Sister (2)

Figure 15.3
If a man dies intestate, leaving no widow or children, his estate would be divided in the following way (the same rules apply for a woman):
1. In equal shares to his father and mother.
2. If his mother and father are both dead, in equal shares to his brothers and sisters (if a brother or sister is dead, their share is divided equally between any children they have).
3. If none are living, in equal shares to half-brothers or half-sisters (if a half-brother or half-sister is dead, their share is divided equally between any children they have).
4. If none are living, in equal shares to his grandparents.
5. If none are living, in equal shares to his uncles and aunts (if an uncle or aunt is dead, their share is divided equally between any children they have).
6. If none are living, in equal shares to half-uncles or half-aunts (if a half-uncle or half-aunt is dead, their share is divided equally between any children they have).
7. If none are living, the estate goes to the Crown.

What if you don't make a will?

The Administration of Estates Act lays down strict rules about what happens if you die without leaving a valid will (called *dying intestate*). The Act lays down who may benefit from the dead person's estate, and how it should be divided between them. If all the people who can benefit are dead, the estate goes to the Crown. The Treasury Solicitor (who administers such estates) may well distribute some or all of the estate amongst those who can show a strong moral claim – eg where a distant relative has looked after the dead person for many years.

We outline here the rules that apply in England and Wales when a person dies without leaving a will. Note that there is no provision under these rules for the estate of a divorced person to go to an ex-husband or ex-wife. And illegitimate or adopted children (but not stepchildren) count as full children for the purpose of inheritance.

Husband/wife still alive?

● If there are children
If you own *less than* £25,000 – everything goes to your widow (or widower).

If you own *more than* £25,000 – the widow (or widower) gets the personal effects (furniture, car, etc) and the first £25,000. Half of the rest goes to the children (adopted or illegitimate children included) to be divided equally between them, and the widow (or widower) gets a life interest in the other half – ie she gets the income produced by it for life. When she dies, the capital is divided equally among the children.

● If there are no children
The widow (or widower) gets the personal effects plus the first £55,000, plus half the rest. The parents of the dead partner get the other half of the rest.

No living husband/wife, but children?

The whole estate is divided equally between the children (legitimate, illegitimate, or adopted). The estate of an unmarried parent is treated the same way.

Unmarried, no children?

For details ▷ Fig. 15.3 above.

Problems

Fighting a will

You may be able to fight a will – for example, on one of the two grounds listed below. Get legal advice before you go ahead.

● **You are entitled to receive something under the will**

You have a good chance if you can show that the person who made the will (or failed to make it) was either supporting you or your father or mother, your husband or wife, your ex-husband or wife (not remarried), or your stepfather or stepmother. You would make a claim under the Inheritance (Provision for Family and Dependants) Act 1975.

● **Undue influence**

This means that the person making the will was greatly under the influence of one or more of the beneficiaries. This claim is often made when the person making the will is elderly and has left large amounts to their doctors, for example, or to the staff at their nursing home. Such a claim is unlikely to succeed if there are witnesses (preferably to the will) who can testify that the person who made the will was in their right mind at the time.

Changing a will

If all the beneficiaries agree that they want the will altered, this is possible up to 2 years after the person who made the will died (providing all the beneficiaries are aged 18 or over). This is called making a *deed of family arrangement*. Get professional advice before you go ahead.

When Agatha Andrews dies, her husband Peter can find no sign of a will. In addition to her personal effects, Agatha was worth some £110,000, most of the money tied up in property and shares.

Under the intestacy rules: Peter gets Agatha's personal effects (her car, her jewellery, some antique furniture). He also gets £25,000 (leaving £110,000 – £25,000 =£85,000 to be distributed).

Their daughter Mary (with whom Agatha was on rather bad terms), and Alice and Alan, the two children of their dead son Christopher, get half of £85,000 (ie £42,500) between them. Mary gets £21,250, and Alice and Alan get £10,625 apiece.

Peter gets a life interest in the remaining £42,500 (in fact, as he has a good income, he wouldn't have minded if this had gone straight to his grandchildren). On his death, the £42,500 will be split between Mary and the two children on the same basis as above.

Agatha always promised to leave her favourite niece Diana something. Under the intestacy rules Diana gets nothing. And, from a CTT point of view, Agatha would have done better to give her small gifts during the course of her life anyway.

The fact that Agatha didn't leave a will, means that her estate has not been divided as she would have wished. In addition, more CTT may have been paid than need be.

Agatha and Peter should have considered splitting the money between the two of them, to equalize the value of their assets for CTT. And passing Agatha's money directly on to a younger generation could reduce the amount of CTT payable in total (▷ below).

How Agatha and Peter could have saved tax We've worked out the amount of tax payable assuming that the current rules apply, and that there is no change in the value of the assets involved. Over time, both are likely to change, but the principles may well stay the same.

When Agatha dies, £25,000 plus a life interest in £42,500 goes to Peter. Neither of these amounts are liable for CTT since Agatha and Peter are husband and wife. The remaining £42,500 goes to Mary, Alan and Alice, and is liable for CTT – but below the level at which the tax begins to bite.

When Peter dies, he'll have £25,000 to pass on and his life interest in £42,500 (ie a total of £67,500). Assuming he's made no previous transfers:

Tax to pay on Peter's death is £5,625.

So the tax paid on what Agatha left will amount to £5,625.

But if they had split Agatha's belongings between them (so each had an estate of £55,000), and each left £55,000 direct to their daughter, or grandchildren, tax would have been payable as follows: On Agatha's death £1,500, and on Peter's death £1,500. Total tax is £3,000, so the total tax saved by splitting their assets would be £2,625.

Ian Hampton dies in a car crash, leaving no will. His estate adds up to £15,000. He was recently divorced from his wife Francesca, and was on the point of marrying Pauline, who has been living with him for the past year.

He has no previous children, and both his parents are dead.

He is on bad terms with his only brother, Stewart, but he is close friends with his cousin Margaret.

Under the intestacy rules:

● Francesca gets nothing but may be able to go to court to make a claim (▷ left)
● Pauline gets nothing – but she too may be able to make a claim in court (▷ left)
● Margaret gets nothing
● Stewart gets the lot.
However, if Pauline had been expecting Ian's baby at the date of his death:
● the baby when born gets the lot – apart from any claims allowed for Francesca or Pauline.

PART FOUR

Investing and borrowing

16 Investment strategy

The small-scale investor has a bewildering variety of choices open to him – a glance at the advertisements in any newspaper will confirm this. Choosing investments which suit your individual circumstances is no easy task. And deciding now on a particular set of investments isn't the end of the story. It's important to keep a close eye on your investments and to review them periodically. Changes in your circumstances, not to mention the effect of external factors (like inflation, political pressures throughout the world) could well mean that your choice of investments today would not be the best for you even a short time from now.

This chapter considers what you need to bear in mind when working out your investment strategy. In chapter 17, seven different people put their investment strategies into effect. Two Route Maps are included (one for lump sums and one for savings) to help you find which investments are right for you. Finally, chapter 18 gives details of the main investments open to small-scale investors and the main tax rules which affect them.

Investment priorities checklist

Your personal circumstances are bound to affect your choice of investments. But no matter what your situation is, some things are worth considering *before* you start thinking about investments in detail.

● Are your dependants protected against financial hardship if you die early?
If not, this should be your first priority. Read chapter 11 on insuring your life.
● Have you money put aside for emergencies?
Could you cope with an unexpected disaster (major car repairs or damage to your home, say)? If not, concentrate on building up an emergency fund in some place where you'll be able to withdraw it fast (within a week, say). See chapter 17 for investments to consider.
● Are you buying your own home?
Buying a home has proved a very good investment in the past (▷ p. 63). If you aren't buying a home (and don't already own one), pause for thought – and read chapter 5 – before you go for any other long-term investment.
● Are you making some provision for your retirement?
Don't assume that the State pension on its own will safeguard your standard of living. Try to work out – along the lines suggested in ch. 4 – how well off you'll be when you retire. If you're self-employed, or not covered by an occupational pension scheme, read about personal pension schemes (▷ p. 46) *before* you go for any other long-term investment.

Personal investment strategy checklist

Some investments only make sense for people of a certain age (annuities for the over-70s, say); others (eg school fees policies) are obviously only suited to those with children to educate. These are extreme cases of the ways in which your personal circumstances can shape your investment strategy – but there may be less dramatic repercussions too. Most people will be saving and investing for a number of purposes. Different investments may be suitable for each purpose – so most people ought to end up putting their money into a variety of investments. It's worth thinking about the points below, and reading the sections on keeping up with inflation (▷ p. 181) and on risk (▷ p. 182), before you decide on a particular investment.
● Age
If you are 50, for example, you are more likely to be concerned with saving up for retirement than with building up a deposit for your first home. Your children are likely to be off your hands too, and you may have more spare cash to save than you had in your thirties.
● Health
If you have a weak heart, for example, you may find it difficult to get the right kind or

amount of life insurance. You may have to protect your dependants by saving and investing instead. Investing through a life insurance policy is likely to be less worthwhile for you than for those in good health.

● Family
Apart from the possibility that you'll want to save for private education, you need to think about how your assets will be passed on when you die (▷ ch. 15). You may want to invest with an eye to building up a capital sum for your heirs to inherit.

● Expectations
If you expect your income to drop at some point (when you start a family, perhaps, or when you retire), you may want to build up savings to draw on when you're hard up. On the other hand, if you expect a big rise in salary (when you get an additional qualification, say, or finish training) you may feel you can run down your savings a bit since you expect to be better off later.

● Tax
Some investments are unsuitable for non-taxpayers, while others may be particularly good for higher rate taxpayers. For more details ▷ ch. 18.

● What you want from your investments
If you want to build up a fund for next year's holiday, you probably need to consider a different range of investments from someone saving up for retirement, or to pass on a capital sum to their heirs. Similarly, if you are looking for a fixed income from your investments, you will select different investments from someone prepared to accept an income that varies with general interest rates. For more details ▷ p. 183.

● How much can you invest?
If you have a lump sum to invest, some investments are open to you that small-scale savers can't consider. And other investments are open only to those who can save a regular sum each month. Still others are more flexible and can take your savings as and when they arise.

● How long can you invest for?
Think carefully before you commit yourself to saving a definite amount each month for a long time (25 years, say). All sorts of changes could happen over the period of the investment that might make it hard to continue, and most long-term savings plans penalize you if you cash in early.

Keeping up with inflation

With some investments the value of the capital you invest stays the same – but, of course, this doesn't allow for the effects of inflation. If you invest £1,000 now, spend the income from the investment and get your £1,000 back in 4 years' time, it will be worth only £680 or so in terms of today's buying power if inflation averages 10 per cent or so a year. And (with the same rate of inflation) if you got your money back in 20 years' time, it would be worth only £150 in terms of today's buying power.

Looked at another way, an inflation rate of 10 per cent means that you have to see the value of your investments rise by at least 10 per cent a year on average just for them to be worth the same to you in the future as they are now. That's a lot of running to have to do just to stay still.

There are only two investments which guarantee to keep pace with rising prices. Both of these are schemes run by the government and both are rather limited (▷ index-linked investments, p. 200).

The main alternative is to take the risk of losing some of your capital in the hope that you will make a high enough profit to compensate for the effect of inflation over the period you have been investing.

The value of property, shares and things bought as investments (such as stamps or antiques) should stand at least some chance of going up with prices in general. But there are drawbacks with these investments. If you do invest in these things, read the section on risk (▷ p. 182) for advice on how you can minimize the risks you're taking. And be prepared for the value of your investment to vary.

There's no guarantee, of course, that by taking risks you'll *get* a high rate of return on your investment. In Fig. 16.1 overleaf, we compare the rate of return you might have got over different periods of time from various 'safe' and 'high-risk' investments. As you can see, over some periods riskier investments like shares have done well. Over other periods, safer investments like building society term shares did better.

Of course, you may be prepared to put up with a drop in purchasing power in your investments because, for example, you're looking for a particularly 'safe' investment, or you want to be able to withdraw your money at short notice (for your emergency fund, for example).

Figure 16.1   After-tax returns on investments

Figures in blue are negative rates of return – ie you'd have made a loss over the period.	Yearly return (in%) for someone paying tax at (1)					
	30% basic rate			45% higher rate		
	over 10 years (to March 80)	March 72 to March 75	over 1 year (to March 80)	over 10 years (to March 80)	March 72 to March 75	over 1 year (to March 80)
British Government stocks (2)	7.0	−10.7 (7)	6.4	6.3	−12.1 (7)	5.0
Building society term shares	7.3	6.9 (7)	9.4	6.0	5.4 (7)	7.4
Property bond (3)	8.3	−5.0	12.1	7.4	−5.0	10.3
Shares (4)	9.0	−15.3	−3.0	8.2	−15.8	−3.7
House prices (5)	17.0	17.1	26.8	17.0	17.1	26.8
Rate of inflation (6)	13.5	14.1	19.8	13.5	14.1	19.8

1. All returns approximate.
2. Held to redemption. Allowing for buying and selling costs.
3. Longest running property bond. Allowing for buying and selling costs.
4. Based on *Financial Times* Actuaries All-Share Index – assuming income re-invested and allowing for buying and selling costs.
5. Based on Nationwide Building Society.
6. Retail Price Index.
7. April to April.

Risk

What kinds of risk are there?

One of the major risks you face is seeing the purchasing power of your investments drop over time as a result of inflation (▷ p. 181). This is a risk which applies to practically any investment. But with some investments (like shares, unit trusts or real assets, for example) you may run two other kinds of risk:

● Risk to capital

The value of what you've invested in shares, unit trusts, property and so on is likely to fluctuate. You may find that when you need to cash in your investment the value of, say, your shares or unit trusts is particularly low, and your investment will turn out to have been a poor one. Investments in real assets (eg antiques, jewellery, Persian carpets) are at risk in this way too – when you want to sell, you may not be able to find a buyer at a price which gives you a reasonable return. And the dealer's mark-up may be particularly high with this type of investment.

● Risk to income

The size of the interest (or dividend) you get may vary considerably, depending on the performance of the company, fund, investment or whatever. In the worst case, you might get no income from the investment at all.

What to do

Decide first what risk you are prepared to take with what proportion of your capital (if any). Accepting a degree of risk is, in the main, a price you have to pay to stand at least some chance of the value of the money you invest keeping up with inflation.

If you decide to go for a relatively high-risk investment (like shares or real assets), don't be tempted to withdraw your emergency fund from its safe home and put it at risk too. This should cut down the risk of having to sell your investments (because there's a hole in your roof) when prices are low.

If you know you'll need your money on a particular future date, be prepared to cash the investments beforehand (a few years in advance, if need be) ideally at a time when their value is high. If you wait until you need the money, you may find you have to cash your investments when prices are low.

As additional precautions, try to stagger investing over a long period (at least a year – preferably much longer), and to spread your money between different types of investment and different companies which issue each type. This reduces the risk of doing very badly with your investments. Bear in mind, though, that reducing your risk in this way also reduces your chances of doing extraordinarily well.

Spreading investments

How you do this depends on how much you invest – a relatively modest sum (say, less than £10,000), or a large one.

● Modest capital to invest?

It's still sensible to spread your capital among different types of investments – eg property bonds, managed bonds, unit trusts. You could put part of your money into real assets – but remember there will be insurance as well as dealing costs to meet if you do.

It's prudent to put your money into unit trusts or investment trusts rather than into the shares of individual companies. (To get a sufficiently wide spread of company shares, your buying and selling costs would form too high a proportion of your total outlay.) Even if you invest in unit or investment trusts, it would be wise to put your money into two or three different companies. And it may be sensible to choose some that invest abroad.

The kind of trust you choose should depend on what you hope to get out of it:
• if you're looking for income, go for trusts which pay high dividends, or for single premium investment bonds (eg managed bonds, property bonds) which have a withdrawal scheme – effectively giving you income (▷ p. 202). Don't forget that if you withdraw more through these schemes than the growth in the bond, you'll be eating into your capital.
• if you're looking for capital growth, a specialist fund (ie one which specializes in a particular industry or a particular overseas country, say) *may* achieve a better growth than a general fund. But it may also go down in value more quickly than a general fund (ie one that invests in the shares of a wide range of companies in different industries). If you invest in specialist funds you (or an adviser) should be prepared to take a particularly active interest in how things are going.
• A substantial amount of capital to invest? Again, spread your money around a number of different types of investment – eg property or managed bonds, shares, commodities, unit trusts, Krugerrands, things.

With this much money, you could buy shares directly. You should aim at investing in a number of different companies (ideally 10 or more), preferably in different industries, and possibly in different countries too. And it's sensible to invest a fair amount (not less than £700, say) in each of them. If you split your investment into smaller packages, the dealing costs may take a big chunk out of any gain you make. So you'd need *well* over £10,000 to invest directly in shares and a spread of other investments.

What do you want from your investments?

Most people want either income or capital gain from their investments – perhaps both.

To some extent, the line between wanting income and wanting capital growth is an artificial one. After all, you can always cash in some of your investments from time to time to give you income. And if you reinvest income from your investments the value of your capital should go up over time. For details ▷ right.

Looking for income right away?

You don't have to be hard up to be in this position. But if you are, you need to choose your investments rather differently from someone who just wants investment income to spend on extras.

Hard up?

Ask yourself first whether – quite apart from any extra investment income – you could make your life easier:
• could you take a job or an additional job – even a part-time unskilled job? Is there any scope for getting a better-paid job?
• are you entitled to more help from the State than you are claiming at the moment (▷ chapter 21)?
• could you cut your spending (▷ p. 163) or your tax bill (▷ chapter 20)?

Next, think about how long you're likely to go on needing extra income. If it's for more than a couple of years, you really can't afford to ignore the effect of inflation on the purchasing power of any income your investments produce. You'll need a rising income. To achieve this, you are likely to have to put some of your capital at risk (▷ Risk, opposite). It may be sensible to invest part of your money for capital growth, with a view to cashing part of it in on a regular basis to provide income (▷ right)

It's unwise to take risks with all your capital, in the hope that by doing so you will get a rising income: if your high-risk investments do poorly, you'll be in a worse position than you were to start out.

You have to make your own choice about how much of your capital to risk. Put the remainder in a place where the income from it will be safe – see the Route Map on p. 188 for suggestions.

If you don't anticipate having to rely on your extra investment income for longer than a year or two, you may well decide there is no point taking risks to get an income that will keep up with inflation.

Cashing in investments to give income
With certain lump sum investments (eg single premium bonds), it's possible to cash in part of the investment each year to give yourself an income – indeed, there are often special schemes where this is organized for you on a regular basis. But note that, for example, with single premium bonds or unit trusts which run a withdrawal scheme, because the value of your investment fluctuates, you may have to cash in a higher proportion of your investment from time to time – or else face a drop in your income.

With other investments (eg in shares, things, etc) there are no special schemes. And you may run into difficulties if you want to cash part of your investment to provide income: in the worst case, you might not be able to sell some of your investments at all – if dealing in your shares were suspended by the Stock Exchange, for example.

Building capital by reinvesting income
As the tax system stands at present, if you invest for income with a view to reinvesting it to build up capital, you may pay more tax than if you had got an equivalent rise in value through a straight capital gain. Rates of tax on investment income range from 30 to 75 per cent (figures for 80/81 tax year). The first £3,000 of capital gains each year are tax-free for most people – and above that the rate of capital gains tax is 30 per cent. So if you pay tax at higher rates or the investment income surcharge (▷ p. 194) it may be sensible to invest for capital gain rather than income.

Investing your emergency fund
When deciding on a home for this part of your capital, you want to look for three things:
• safety – no risk that when you cash in you'll get fewer £££ back than you put in
• instant accessibility – you don't usually get even 2 weeks' notice

of an emergency, so you want to be able to get the money back on the spot, or at most in a couple of days
• highest possible return – but you'll have to be prepared to take less than you'd get for an investment that tied your money up longer.

See the Route Maps on pp. 188 and 190 for some suggestions.

● Paying no tax?

If so, some investments may not give you such a good return as they do to taxpayers. We have marked these investments with ● in the Route Maps on p. 188 and 190 – but check that things have not changed since we went to press.

Comfortably off?

If you want your extra income for non-essentials, then you are in a better position to accept risks than those who are struggling to make ends meet. That does not mean, however, that you should think any the less carefully about *how much* of your capital you are going to put at risk than the hard-up.

● Higher rate taxpayer?

Some investments, where the return is tax-free, look more attractive the higher your rate of tax. These investments are marked ● in the Route Maps on pp. 188 and 190. Check in the Route Maps (and with current rates of return) that your investments are giving you as good a return as possible.

Looking for income later?

If you know you aren't going to want income from your investments for some years, then it may be sensible to invest now for capital growth and reinvest for maximum income when you actually need it.

Investing for capital growth

You may want capital growth to give you:
● income later
● more to pass on to your heirs
● a fund for some expensive luxury.

Capital growth to give you income later

If you're going to need your capital to give you an income later, you can't afford to risk all of it. But you do need to try to make up for the effects of inflation on its buying-power over the years between now and the time you plan to use it.

To a limited extent, people over retirement age can do this by investing the maximum (£1,200 in June 80) in National Savings Certificates (Retirement Issue). A married couple, with husband and wife both over retirement age, can each invest up to the maximum (so up to £2,400 in June 80). With this scheme, the value of what you've invested is adjusted each month in line with inflation (provided you've held the certificate for at least a year).

If you have capital left over, it makes sense to put some of your money into investments which may give a return high enough to make up for inflation.

To minimize the chances of all your risky investments doing a nose-dive at once, follow the guidelines on p. 182.

Capital growth for the benefit of your heirs

You may feel you can take risks with more of your capital for longer if your primary aim is to pass money on to your heirs.

What you need to be particularly aware of is the impact of CTT on what your heirs will get when you die. To minimize its effect, consider:

● giving away each year as much as is allowed without incurring any liability to CTT
● taking out life insurance with the proceeds going straight to your children
● leaving your possessions directly to the youngest generation (your grandchildren rather than your children) if you want the possessions to go to them eventually.

For fuller details of CTT ▷ ch. 15.

Capital growth to build up a fund for buying something

If you have a particular purchase in mind, and it looks like being some time before you have built up a large enough fund for buying it, watch out for inflation. As Fig. 16.1 shows, even by going for risky investments like shares, over the past 10 years, you probably would not have been able to get a big enough rise in the capital value of your investment to make up for the decline in the purchasing power of £££ over the same period.

If you are investing in order to buy something in the future, bear in mind that the value of some investments (eg shares, property, things) tends to fluctuate, so you may find that when you want to cash in your investment, the return is not very good. It makes sense to steer clear of these if the time when you are going to want to use the money is very close at hand.

If, on the other hand, you'll need the money in, say, 10 years' time, you could still go for investments which fluctuate in value – but be prepared to cash the investments *before* you need the money (preferably when they're doing particularly well). Don't be forced into cashing your investment when its value is depressed – eg by a slump in the share or property markets.

And before you decide to take extra risks with your capital, in the hope of getting a greater gain, consider borrowing money to buy now rather than waiting until you have built up a larger fund.

Rules to remember when investing for capital growth

- to cut risks, follow the advice on p. 182
- when you sell can be as important as when you buy
- take an active interest in events that may affect your investments
- if you reckon that prices of the things you've invested in (eg shares, property, antiques) are likely to fall, it may be worth moving into cash for a while
- if you reckon that interest rates are likely to fall, it may be worth putting your money into investments which offer fixed interest, but where the value of the capital can fluctuate (eg British government stocks).

If you feel unable to take these sorts of decisions yourself, ask someone else to advise you ($\triangleright$ below). But don't just hand the money over and forget it: learn about investments and take an active interest in what your adviser is doing.

Review your investments regularly

You can't assume that the best investments for you today will still be the best in a few months' time. For example, the rates of return offered by different investments will change. New types of investment may come on the market. Tax laws may change. And your circumstances may change too. So keep an eye on what's happening and change your investments when necessary.

Where to go for professional help

Various groups of people claim to give investment advice of one sort or another. For example:

- accountants
- bank managers
- bank investment departments
- insurance brokers
- investment consultants
- merchant banks
- solicitors
- stockbrokers.

But in a *Money Which?* survey of these groups of advisers in 1978, none of them stood out as being the ideal people to turn to for investment advice.

Bear in mind, too, that investment advice is likely to cost you money – either as a direct charge or hidden in the price you pay. Check what charges are going to be made (not just initial charges, but also any annual, possibly hidden, charges), and find out what you'll get in the way of advice for the money you pay. Some advisers may have a vested interest in a particular type of investment, and their advice may be coloured by commission they get paid. Again, check what *their* interest is in the investment they're suggesting for *you*.

If you want *general advice* on how to plan your investment strategy as a whole, you could try your bank, an accountant or a solicitor (or all three). If they're familiar with your finances already, this could be an advantage. Otherwise, try for someone who has helped people you know successfully (so far as you can tell) in the past.

For *specialist advice* (on one type of investment, like shares or investment-type life insurance) it's sensible to go to a specialist – a stockbroker or insurance broker, for example. Get advice from more than one specialist in each field you're interested in. And before you approach them, you need to have made up your mind whether you want the kind of investment they specialize in – don't expect them to give you the pros and cons objectively.

If you've got a lot to invest (£20,000 or more, say), you could ask a High-Street bank investment department, certain investment consultants, or a stockbroker to *manage your investments* for you (a merchant bank may do this if you're investing £100,000 or so). But again be particularly wary of being directed into the investments which the adviser specializes in. Unless you are following a personal recommendation from someone who has had dealings with the person or firm before, it is hard to choose one out of the many advisers in the business.

Whatever kind of help you want, and whoever you go to, make sure you've done as much homework as you can before you approach them. Bear in mind that the past performance of investments is generally little guide to the future. Use the information in our three investment chapters to construct your own investment strategy. No-one else will care quite as much about what happens to your money as you do yourself.

If you do decide to use an adviser, give him all the information about yourself that he will need to make sensible recommendations (like your age, state of health, family circumstances, income, prospects, pension arrangements, existing investments, life insurance, and how long you're prepared to tie up your money for).

17 Investment decisions

Choosing your investments

To help narrow down the choice of investments to those which would be most suitable for you, use the Route Maps on pp. 188 and 190. One is for lump sums, the other for savings (either on a regular basis or piecemeal).

Follow the Route Maps for each sum of money you want to invest – eg your emergency fund, money you're willing to see fluctuate in value, money you know you will be able to invest for 5 years, and so on. You'll end up with a different shortlist for each sum.

Next, turn to the table starting on p. 198 and look up details of the investments on each of your shortlists. The columns of the table are explained on p. 197.

Collect as much other information as you can on investments on the shortlist (the table tells you when the latest *Money Which?* report on each investment was published). Check in the newspapers for the up-to-date rates of return being offered by the investments you have in mind.

Armed with these facts, narrow down the investments on your shortlists to those which suit you best. Don't forget that work on your investments doesn't end there – you'll need to keep them under review to make sure that they continue to suit you.

To show you how this can be done, we follow the investment decisions of Roger and Rose Steele who want to find homes for both a lump sum and for their savings. Their strategy and decisions will be followed through from start to finish. The remaining six examples look at only one of the problems each family faces. Three families have to invest lump sums of varying sizes; with the other three, it's savings of various amounts which are presenting difficulties.

Of course, your own final choice out of the shortlist each family ends up with, might – because of your own particular preferences – have been different from that given in our examples.

Examples

Roger and Rose Steele have one child Alex. Roger earns around £7,000 at the local engineering works. They want to save for quite a few things – a holiday next year, and then a car, new furniture and so on. They don't want to lock their money away for too long. They've already got some money saved up in a building society ordinary share account and wonder whether that's the best place for it.

How Roger and Rose decide what to do with their money

They follow the investment priorities checklist on p. 180:
● both Roger and Rose have life insurance cover. They have policies which will pay out lump sums and a regular income if either dies
● at present they have £2,000 put aside in a building society ordinary share account. But they feel that £400 is as much as they need in an emergency fund
● Roger and Rose are buying their own home with a mortgage and don't intend to move in the next few years
● Roger is in his employer's pension scheme – which offers quite good benefits.

Roger and Rose would like to save something each month. So they've got to decide how to invest:
● their £400 emergency fund

- the additional £1,600 lump sum
- the money they manage to save.

They use the personal investment strategy checklist (▷ pp. 180–81) to help sort out their investment plan.

- age – Roger is 34 and Rose 28. Rose is hoping to go back to teaching when Alex, their 3-year-old, goes to school – but of course teaching posts are much sought after, so they're not going to rely on her getting one.
- health – both are in good health
- family – apart from Alex, there are no immediate dependants. They do feel that if any of the parents were widowed or became ill, they'd like to help out. At the moment, this prospect seems unlikely, but it means they don't feel like committing themselves to very long-term saving – which they might not be able to keep up if they do have to help out. They don't intend giving Alex a private education. If they did, they would consider saving in a school-fees scheme
- expectations – Rose would like to work again, and if she can't get a job teaching, would like to consider some sort of retraining. This might involve some expense – they don't really know.

There are no large inheritances coming their way – though eventually they will share in the proceeds from the sale of their parents' houses
- tax – Roger is a basic rate taxpayer, and any investment income won't put him into a higher tax bracket
- what they want from their investments – their main aims are: to pay for a holiday next year and later for a car and new furniture; to pay for any retraining that Rose may need in a couple of years or so; and to enable them to help out their parents should the need arise. They aren't looking for income from their investments
- how much they can invest – apart from the £2,000 in the building society, they reckon they can save about £40 a month – but most of this is earmarked for their holiday next year
- how long they can invest for – the Steeles have decided to keep £400 handy as an emergency fund. And they need £30 a month of their regular savings available for their planned holiday. The other lump sum of £1,600 and £10-a-month regular savings can be invested for somewhat longer. But long-term investment clearly doesn't suit their needs.

As long as most of their money is safe, they don't mind taking a risk with some of it. Like everyone else, they're worried about

inflation, but there's not much they can do about it – other than choose index-linked SAYE for their longer-term regular savings.

Once Roger and Rose have chosen their investments (▷ below), they'll keep an eye on what's happening and may move their money around from time to time.

How Roger and Rose choose their investments

Lump sum

First of all they try to sort out what to do with the £2,000 they have. They intend keeping £400 of this as an emergency fund and following the Route Map, they see there are three places they can put this money and get it out at short notice – a bank deposit account, building society ordinary shares, or an NSB ordinary account. They read about these – in the table on p. 198 and in the *Money Which?* reports mentioned there – and they check on the rates of return currently offered by these alternatives. They choose building society ordinary shares. They'll keep a close watch on rates of return in the future in case other investments offer a better return.

Now they follow the Route Map again to see what they could do with the £1,600. They arrive at the point on the Route Map where they're asked if they're looking for a shorter-term investment, and prepared to risk losing money for the chance of a capital gain on it. They don't want to endanger the whole amount but wouldn't mind putting half their spare lump sum (ie £800) at risk. They see that suitable investments include shares, unit trusts and single premium investment bonds. Turning to the table on p. 198 they see that they haven't got enough to make a sensible investment in shares and they decide to choose between single premium bonds and unit trusts – they feel they haven't enough to spread the money between the two. Roger believes that the prospects for commercial property are good – they decide to buy a property bond.

They now look for non-risky investments in the Route Map, and check the details of the shortlist they arrive at in the table. They also check on current rates of return. They don't want to commit their money for more than 2 years – and, in the end, decide to put their remaining £800 into 2-year building society term shares.

Regular saving

They follow the Route Map to see what to do with the £40 a month they reckon they'll

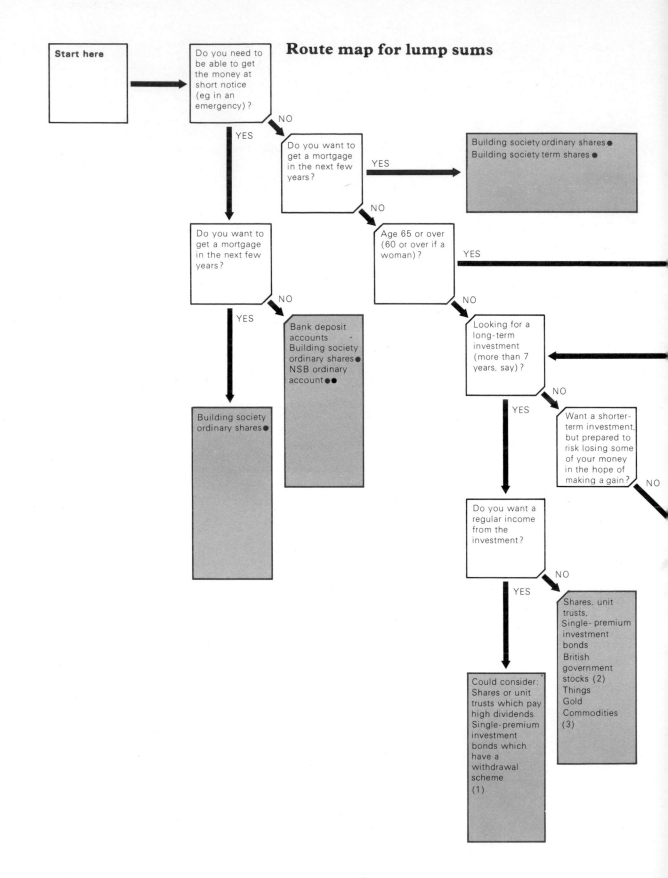

Route map for lump sums

Start here → Do you need to be able to get the money at short notice (eg in an emergency)?

— NO → Do you want to get a mortgage in the next few years?

— YES → Do you want to get a mortgage in the next few years?

(from "Do you need to ... short notice") YES branch:
Do you want to get a mortgage in the next few years?
- YES → Building society ordinary shares●
- NO → Bank deposit accounts / Building society ordinary shares● / NSB ordinary account●●

(from "Do you want to get a mortgage in the next few years?" — second box) YES:
Building society ordinary shares● / Building society term shares●

NO → Age 65 or over (60 or over if a woman)?
- YES →
- NO → Looking for a long-term investment (more than 7 years, say)?
  - YES → Do you want a regular income from the investment?
    - YES → Could consider: Shares or unit trusts which pay high dividends / Single-premium investment bonds which have a withdrawal scheme (1)
    - NO → Shares, unit trusts, Single-premium investment bonds / British government stocks (2) / Things / Gold / Commodities (3)
  - NO → Want a shorter-term investment, but prepared to risk losing some of your money in the hope of making a gain?
    - NO →

188

1. If you're a non-taxpayer, could also consider British government stocks. finance company deposits, income bonds, local authority investments, NSB investment account – but ▷Inflation, p. 181.
2. Worth considering if you want a shorter-term investment but are prepared to take a risk. Stock prices could be expected to rise if interest rates in general fall, and vice versa.
3. If you're a non-taxpayer, looking for a long-term investment, could also consider British government stocks, finance company deposits, growth bonds, local authority investments, NSB investment account – but ▷Inflation, p. 181.

● Non-taxpayers can normally get a higher return elsewhere.

● May be particularly worth considering if you pay tax at higher rates or the investment income surcharge.

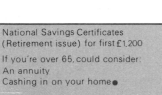

National Savings Certificates (Retirement issue) for first £1,200

If you're over 65, could consider:
An annuity
Cashing in on your home●

Anything left?

YES

Investing for at least 1 year?

NO

Bank deposit. accounts
Building society ordinary shares ●
Finance company deposits
NSB investment account
NSB ordinary account●●

YES

If you want regular income:
British govt stocks. Building soc term shares● Finance co deposits, Income Bonds, Local authority investments. NSB investment account, NSB ordinary account●●

If you're not bothered about a regular income, could also consider:
Growth bonds
National Savings Certificates (19th issue)●

be able to save. They come to the question – Prepared to save a regular amount for five years or so? – and decide they can commit the £10 month they won't need for their holiday for this period. They choose to put it all in index-linked SAYE, but decide to split the money into two lots of £5 a month – so that if they can't keep up all their saving they'll still get index-linking on the half they can keep up. For their other £30 a month they end up with a shortlist of six investments. After looking at the table and checking on current interest rates, they see that building society subscription shares offer them the best return and the opportunity to withdraw their money at short notice without losing out.

Summary

They're going to invest £400 in building society ordinary shares, £800 in a property bond and £800 in building society term shares. They're going to save £30 a month in building society subscription shares and £10 a month in index-linked SAYE.

Paul and Sheila Plantin, in their mid-40s, are well off. They expect to pay tax on the top slice of their income at 45 per cent. But with 3 children still living at home (aged 12, 14 and 16) there seems less for luxuries than they'd hoped for.

Sheila has just inherited £23,000 following the settlement of her parents' estate. They want to invest £20,000 for their retirement and don't mind taking a bit of a risk. They'd like to get a regular income from this part of their investment, but are worried about extra income tax they might have to pay. The rest of the money they'll invest relatively safely (they're willing to tie this money up for 5 years or so at a pinch).

First they follow the Route Map for their long-term investment until they come to the question about whether they want a regular

Route map for savings

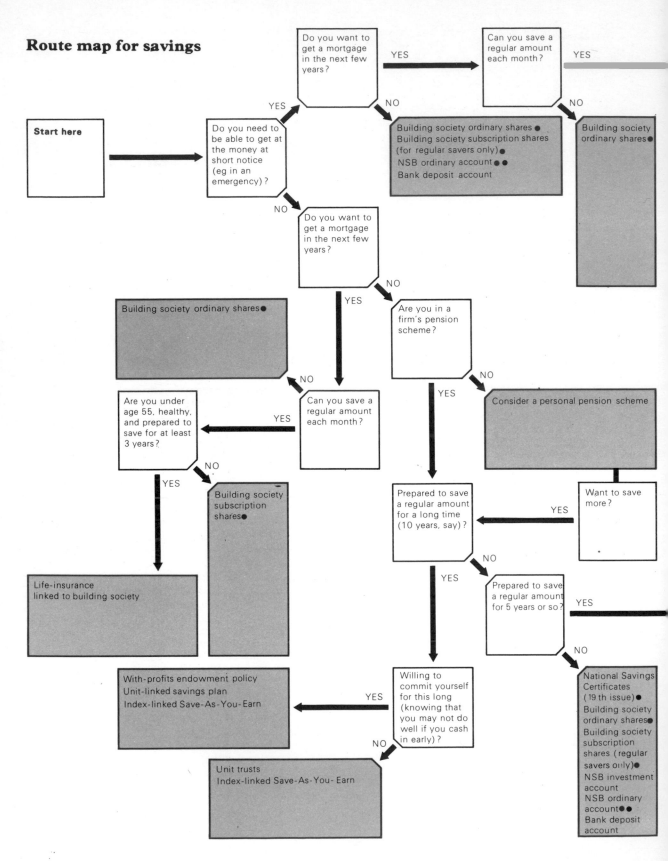

Building society
subscription
shares ●

● Non-taxpayers can
normally get a higher
return elsewhere.

● May be particularly
worth considering if
you pay tax at higher
rates or the investment
income surcharge.

Life insurance
linked to
building society
Index-linked
Save-As-You-
Earn

income – they see they can choose between shares, unit trusts and single premium investment bonds. These are all investments which, hopefully, will rise in value in the long-term. They discover that if they invest in single premium bonds, they can withdraw up to 5 per cent of their investment each year for 20 years without paying tax. In 20 years' time, they'll have retired and are unlikely to be paying higher rates of tax, or the investment income surcharge – so may avoid paying any extra tax on this investment. They plan not to withdraw the full 5 per cent each year – to leave themselves with a sizeable chunk of their investment when they retire. They decide to invest £10,000 split equally between a managed bond and a property bond.

They decide to invest £10,000 in unit trusts – they go for those that aim for capital growth rather than income. They plan to cash in some of their units each year, but to make sure that they don't make net capital gains above the £3,000 limit free of capital gains tax – ▷ p. 195.

They turn again to the Route Map for their safe investment – they've got £3,000 to invest. They bear in mind that they should have a careful look at investments with a ● next to them. This means that the investment may be particularly worth considering if you pay tax at higher rates or the investment income surcharge.

They see that the return on National Savings Certificates (19th issue) is tax-free and fixed at the time they buy the certificates – but that they have to keep their money invested for 5 years to get the best return. They check on interest rates and find that the certificates offer the 50 per cent taxpayer a relatively good after-tax return. While checking on the rates of return, they see that index-linked SAYE and life insurance linked to building societies would also give them a good after-tax return, but they're both for regular savings. They decide to split their safe investment, putting £1,500 into National Savings Certificates and the remaining £1,500 into a building society ordinary share account. They'll withdraw £10 a month from this account, and invest it in life insurance linked to building societies.

Mike and Sue English, in their late 20s, with one baby and another due soon, live off Mike's income of £3,300 a year. They pay no tax – and feel they've got little cash left over at the end of each month, what with food, rates, mortgage payments and so on. Mike is worried because they have no savings or life insurance.

For someone in Mike's position, with dependants, life insurance should come before any attempt to save money. If he died, Sue would have to rely on social security to make ends meet. And if Sue were to die, Mike would have a hard time looking after the baby and going to work. They turn to p. 133 in chapter 11 to work out how much life insurance they need.

Once they've sorted out their life insurance, the next thing to think about is an emergency fund. They follow the Route Map on p. 190. They see that building society ordinary shares and NSB ordinary accounts each have ● beside them, indicating that non-taxpayers can normally get a higher return with other investments. That leaves bank deposit accounts. They check up on rates of interest and find that a bank deposit account currently offers a non-taxpayer a higher rate of return. So they plump for that for any bits and pieces they can put aside.

Once they've built up a large enough emergency fund, they'll go through the Route Map again and look for a somewhat longer-term investment for their additional savings. And, at mid-80 rates of interest, they'd end up choosing a NSB investment account – which isn't suitable for their emergency funds because they have to give a month's notice to withdraw money.

They'll keep an eye on what happens to rates of return in the future – in particular they'll keep an eye out for building society ordinary shares offering a higher rate of return than bank deposit accounts (which does happen from time to time).

Miss Simmons, 72, has lived alone since her mother died last year. She lives on her pension and wonders what to do with the £4,500 she has to invest – which is at present in a bank deposit account. She's alarmed at the way inflation has made inroads into the buying power of the interest she gets. She'd like to get a bit of extra income to allow her a few more treats.

She realizes that she can leave some of her money in the bank deposit account to act as an emergency fund – but she reckons she won't need more than £300 for this. Thinking about it, though, she decides to leave twice this amount in her account – so that she can draw on it for extra income.

She follows the Route Map for lump sums until she comes to the question – Are you 65 or over if a man (60 or over if a woman)? She sees that the recommended investment for her is National Savings Certificates (Retirement Issue).

Next she turns to the table. She sees that this investment does not pay out a regular income, but she could cash certificates to get an income. She also notices that the value of what she invests will go up in line with the Retail Price Index (though not if she cashes the certificates before a year is up). This index-linking seems a big plus to Miss Simmons. So she decides to put the maximum £1,200 into these and, after the first year, to cash bits of her investment if necessary if she feels particularly hard-pressed.

Since she's over 65, she decides to put the remaining £2,700 into an annuity. She realizes that the income from this won't be protected against inflation. She decides to give more thought to moving to a smaller house, and investing any money from the sale to give her more income.

Marianne Fortune, 21, has just inherited £3,000 from her grandmother. She's single, lives with her parents and has a large enough emergency fund. She reckons that some time in the future she'll want to buy a home, and decides to put £2,000 towards this. She decides to try to turn the remaining £1,000 into something bigger – so she's prepared to take risks with it.

Unlike most of our other example investors Marianne isn't going to be cautious and spread this £1,000 among several different investments. She follows the Route Map for lump sums, and sees she should invest the £2,000 earmarked to go towards buying a home in a building society. She sees from chapter 5, that she should check up on building society lending policies before she invests, and preferably split her money between two (or more) building societies. Since she already has her eye on the type of flat she'd like, she sorts out from a number of building societies, the ones that seem most favourable. She decides it'll be at least a couple of years before she buys the home, so invests in 2-year term shares.

She goes back to the Route Map, to see how she should invest the £1,000 she's going to gamble with. She's looking for a shorter-term investment but prepared to take a risk. She looks up the shortlisted investments in the table and checks the latest *Money Which?* report on them. She toys with investing her money in shares of just one company (a very risky strategy) or a commodity fund – but balks at the last minute. She decides instead to put the £1,000 towards improving the 18th-century glass collection she started a couple of years ago.

Anne Stevens is a basic rate taxpayer. She wants to go to Australia to see her daughter and her grandchildren. She finds out that the cheapest return fare is about £400. She can afford to save about £7 a month – and she's worried about how inflation will affect the air fare over the 5 years or so she reckons she'll have to save for.

She follows the Route Map until she comes to the question: Prepared to save a regular amount for five years or so? She sees she can choose between life insurance linked to building societies and index-linked SAYE. Looking at the table, she finds that index-linked SAYE guarantees to increase the value of her savings in line with the Retail Price Index – and decides to plump for this.

Anne realizes that, sadly, though the value of her savings will keep pace with inflation, she's likely to have to save for much longer than 5 years to build up enough money to pay the air fare. This is because the amount of her index-linked savings will start off at a much lower amount than the air fare – ie £7 in the first month, £14 in the second month, and so on. So whereas she'll benefit from index-linking only on the amount already saved, inflation is likely to affect the whole of the £400 air fare from the start.

To try and make the saving period as short as possible, Anne decides that, whenever she has spare money she'll try to put it in something like building society ordinary shares – a suitable home for small, irregular sums of money. She also decides to approach her bank manager to see whether, once she's saved for 5 years or more, she could get a loan.

Bob Mason, self-employed, earning around £7,000 a year, and his wife, Cathy, are in their mid-40s. Their 3 children have all left home and Cathy thinks it's time they started saving for Bob's retirement.

They already have an adequate emergency fund, and are buying their home with a mortgage. They follow the Route Map to the question: Are you in a firm's pension scheme? Since Bob is self-employed, he isn't – but neither is he contributing to a personal pension scheme. He sees from the table on p. 202 that he'll get tax relief on the premiums he pays, and decides to put £20 a month into such a scheme.

Cathy and Bob decide they'd like to save a bit more than this for their retirement – they reckon they could manage another £5 a month, and then bits and pieces less regularly. For their £5 a month, they're prepared to commit themselves for a long time, and consider the shortlist this leads them to: with-profits endowment policies, unit-linked savings plans and index-linked Save-As-You-Earn. They decide to go for a unit-linked savings plan (a high-investment one) – they realize that it's the riskiest of the three – but they're hoping it may be worth the risk. They decide to add odd savings to their building society ordinary share account (where they've got their emergency fund). When they've built up a big enough lump sum, they'll go through the lump-sum Route Map.

18 Investment facts

The hard work in planning your investment strategy starts now – there's really no sensible alternative to sifting through at some stage the facts and figures collected in this chapter.

A summary of the main types of investment open to you starts on p. 198. Within the space available, it isn't possible to give full details of every investment. However, the most important points are picked out in the table (▷ p. 197 for why each column in the table is important) and there is also a reference to the most recent *Money Which?* report on the subject.

Details of the main taxes investors need to bear in mind are also given. The information was correct at the time of going to press. However, tax rules and rates tend to change with each new Budget. When they do, you need to look carefully at your current investments, to see if they need updating.

Income tax
Income from most types of investments is taxed. But with a few investments, the return is tax-free (▷ the table on pp. 198–203 for details).

Some income is taxed at the basic rate before you get it (eg share dividends and unit trust distributions, interest from local authority loans). If you don't pay tax – or pay less tax than has been deducted – you can claim back some or all of the tax deducted. But if you pay tax at higher rates, or the investment income surcharge, you'll have to pay extra tax.

Note that with building society interest you can't claim back the basic rate tax that's deemed to have been deducted from it, even if you pay no tax. And the *grossed-up* amount of building society interest (▷ p. 219) is added to your income to work out any higher rate tax or investment income surcharge.

Investment income surcharge
People who have a lot of investment income may have to pay the investment income surcharge. For the 80/81 tax year, you started paying this if your investment income (after deducting certain outgoings, such as mortgage interest) came to more than £5,500. The rate of surcharge on investment income over this level is 15 per cent.

A warning for the elderly
If you are 65 or over, you may qualify for *age allowance* (a special income tax allowance for the over-65s with modest income). For details. ▷ p. 220. Note that if your 'total income' (▷ p. 216) is above a certain level, age allowance is reduced. This might make investments where the return is not taxable (eg National Savings Certificates) worth considering.

Investments treated especially favourably for income tax purposes
With a few investments, the return is tax-free. This may make them particularly worth considering if you pay tax at higher rates or the investment income surcharge. We've indicated which of these investments are in the table under Points about tax.

With some other investments, the tax relief on payments makes them more attractive the higher the rate of tax you pay.

This applies to people who:
● make payments into an employer's pension scheme (▷ p. 55)
● make payments into personal pension schemes (for the self-employed or those not in their employer's pension scheme ▷ p. 46)
● borrow money to buy their own home, or certain other homes (▷ p. 223).

Generally speaking, for each £ you pay on which you get tax relief, you escape tax on the most heavily taxed £ of your income. Pension payments (whether to an employer's scheme or a personal pension scheme) can be set off only against the earnings to which they relate.

So, for the 80/81 tax year, if you pay tax at the basic rate, each extra £ on which you get tax relief saves you 30p in tax. And if, for example, you pay higher rate tax at 60 per cent plus the 15 per cent investment income surcharge, and are buying your home with a mortgage, each extra £ you pay in interest saves you 75p in tax.

Note that with life insurance premiums which qualify for tax relief you get a subsidy of 17½ per cent of your premium (15 per cent from 6 April 81) – irrespective of the rate of tax you pay, and even if you pay no tax at all (▷ p. 222). But if you surrender your policy within 4 years of taking it out, you have to pay back some of the subsidy, on a sliding scale related to the length of time you have paid your premiums.

Capital transfer tax
You obviously need to bear this tax in mind when you are working out how much you'll be able to pass on to your family and other heirs. Take advantage of ways of cutting your CTT bill — eg by making use of tax-free ways of giving things away during your lifetime, having the proceeds of life insurance policies go straight to your children instead of to your husband or wife. CTT is discussed in detail in chapter 15.

Capital gains tax
You may have to pay this tax (CGT) on the capital gain you make on investments — eg shares, a second home.

What is a capital gain? You may make a capital gain (or loss) whenever you *dispose* of an *asset*, no matter how you came to own it. But you won't always be taxed on such a gain.

Anything you own (whether in the UK or not) counts as an asset — for example, houses, jewellery, shares.

You dispose of an asset not only if you sell it, but also if you give it away, exchange it, or lose it. You also dispose of an asset if it's destroyed or becomes worthless, if you sell rights to it (eg grant a lease), or if you get compensation for damage to it (eg insurance money) and don't spend all the money on restoring the damage. But a transfer of an asset between husband and wife who are not separated doesn't count as a disposal. Nor does the transfer of an asset you leave when you die.

Tax-free gains
You aren't normally liable for CGT on:
● your own home
● an additional home lived in rent-free by a dependent relative
● private cars
● British money (including post-1836 gold sovereigns)
● foreign currency which you got for personal or family expenditure (eg for a holiday abroad or for keeping a home abroad)
● British government stock held for a year or more, or inherited
● National Savings Certificates, British Savings Bonds, Save-As-You-Earn
● personal belongings, antiques, jewellery and other tangible movable objects, provided the value of each object *at*

the time of disposal is below a certain limit (£2,000 in the 80/81 tax year). A set — eg a silver tea service — is looked upon as one object, unless separate parts of it are sold to unconnected people
● animals, boats and other tangible movable objects which are *wasting assets* (assets with a predictable life of 50 years or less). But business assets are usually liable for capital gains tax, and so is an interest in a lease
● life insurance policies, if you are the original owner or if they were given to you (but you may be liable for income tax on the gain)
● betting winnings (including football pool dividends and premium bond prizes)
● gifts of assets liable for capital gains tax which you make during the tax year provided their total market value is not above a certain limit (£100 in the 80/81 tax year)
● gifts to charities
● gifts to certain national institutions — eg the British Museum, National Trust
● Treasury-approved gifts of outstanding interest (eg works of art, historic buildings, collections) — and sales of such assets to certain national institutions
● compensation or damages for wrongs or injuries you have suffered.

Working our your gain (or loss)
A gain you make on an asset is normally a *taxable gain* (and a loss is an *allowable loss*), unless the asset appears in the list of tax-free gains left.

In general, your gain (or loss) is *the amount you get when disposing of the asset* (or its market value at the time, if you give it away) less *any cost of the asset to you* (or its market value at the time you came to own*

it, if it was given to you or you inherited it).

But if you owned the asset before 6 April 65 there are special rules, which could mean less tax to pay — check with your tax office for details.

You can deduct from a gain, or add to a loss, all the allowable expenditure you have incurred, including:
● any cost of acquiring and disposing of the asset (eg commission, conveyancing)
● capital expenditure which has increased the value of the asset (eg improvements to property, but not ordinary maintenance).

Shares
If you buy several lots of the *same* share at different times, they are put into what is called a *pool* and the cost of each share is taken to be the average cost of buying the shares.

So, for example, if you pay £700 for 250 shares in a company, and later pay £300 for another 250, your total holding of 500 shares has cost you: £700+£300=£1,000. This works out at an average cost of £2 a share.

If you then sell some of the shares, the calculation of your gain or loss will be based on this *average* cost.

But the rules for working out the gain or loss are more complicated if:
● you bought some or all of the shares before 6 April 65
● you have had a scrip or rights issue
● you have had shares or cash from a take-over bid for the company.

If this applies to you, it's worth getting more detailed help with your calculations (try your tax office)

How gains are taxed
Capital gains tax is worked out on your *net capital gains* for the tax

year. In general, your net capital gains will be the *taxable gains* you made on any assets disposed of during the tax year *less* any *allowable losses*. But the detailed rules for setting losses off against gains can be complicated (▷ p. 196).

For the 80/81 tax year, if you make net capital gains of £3,000 or less, there'll be no capital gains tax to pay. If you make net capital gains of over £3,000, the first £3,000 of gains you make will be free of tax, anything over £3,000 will be taxed at 30 per cent.

Charles Harvey made a taxable gain of £7,000 by disposing of his second home in August 80. If this had been his only disposal during the 80/81 tax year, and if he had no allowable losses left over from earlier years, his capital gains tax bill for 80/81 would have been:
● on the first £3,000, no tax
● 30 per cent on the remaining £4,000, ie £1,200 tax.

Capital gains tax
(cont.)

Setting losses against gains
To arrive at your net capital gains for the year:

Step 1 Subtract your allowable capital losses on assets disposed of during the year from your taxable capital gains for the year

Step 2 If the answer to Step 1 is:
● *a minus number* (ie your losses for the year exceed your gains). Your net capital gains for the year are zero and there's no tax to pay. You can carry forward the balance of your losses (together with any losses left from previous years) to future years
● *between £0 and £3,000*. This figure is your net capital gains for the year and there's no tax to pay. You can't carry forward any of this year's allowable losses. But any losses left over from previous years *can* be carried forward
● *more than £3,000*. Any allowable capital losses you have left over from previous years will be used to reduce your net capital gains further. But your net gains won't be reduced to below £3,000 (as £3,000 of gains would be tax-free anyway). If you still have allowable losses left after reducing your net capital gains to £3,000, the balance is carried forward to future years.

When you have to pay
Capital gains tax is due on 1 December after the end of the tax year in which you made the gain – or within 30 days of the date on the Notice of Assessment the taxman sends you, if this is later.

Charles Harvey realizes he can set some losses off against the £7,000 gain he made on his second home. In the 80/81 tax year he made a loss of £2,000 on some shares he sold. And he has £5,500 of allowable losses carried forward from previous years – from a disastrous investment in Nogood Enterprises. He works out his net capital gains for the year:

Step 1 Subtracting his allowable loss for the year from his taxable gain for the year leaves £7,000−£2,000 =£5,000

Step 2 This is more than £3,000, so the allowable losses brought forward from earlier years will be used to reduce his net capital gains to £3,000. This means using up £5,000−£3,000 =£2,000 of his carried-forward losses. This leaves him with £5,500−£2,000=£3,500 of losses to carry forward to the 81/82 tax year.

Charles also works out what his tax situation would have been if his loss on Nogood Enterprises had been made in 80/81:

Step 1 His allowable losses for the year would have been: £5,500+£2,000 =£7,500
Subtracting this from his gain for the year would have left £7,000−£7,500, ie a *net loss* of £500.

Step 2 His net capital gains for the year would have been zero. But he would have had only £500 of losses to carry forward to 81/82.

Capital gains and marriage
In the tax year they get married (unless they happen to marry on 6 April) a couple's capital gains are taxed as if they were still single – though transfers of assets between them do not count as disposals.

But from the following year, the couple's gains are taxed jointly – ie the husband's losses are set off against the wife's gains and vice versa: if the couple's joint gains for the 80/81 tax year exceed £3,000 they pay CGT.

A couple can elect to have their capital gains *separately assessed*. This won't, on its own, affect a couple's overall tax bill – it simply means that the wife will be responsible for paying her share of the bill.

To be separately assessed for CGT, apply on form CG11S within 3 months of the end of the tax year. You will remain separately assessed until you ask to be taxed jointly again (by filling in form CG 11S−1).

Whether or not a couple have their capital gains separately assessed, either can ask for his or her own losses for any year to be set off against his or her gains only. This *can* affect the couple's tax bill.

To apply to have your own losses for a particular tax year set against your own gains only, write and ask the taxman within 3 months of the end of the tax year in which you made the losses. You have to apply each year.

Paul Plantin made a taxable capital gain of £1,600 in the 80/81 tax year. His wife, Sheila, made an allowable loss of £1,200.

Paul and Sheila talk it over and realize that if they are taxed in the normal way, Sheila's loss will be set off against Paul's gain. They'll have no tax to pay – but will have no losses to carry forward.

If Sheila asks to have her own losses for the year set against her own gains only, however, there will still be no tax to pay (because their joint gains, ignoring Sheila's losses, are less than £3,000). And Sheila will be able to carry her £1,200 loss over to set against her future gains.

How to avoid paying more CGT than necessary
● be sure to deduct from a gain, or add to a loss, all the allowable expenses you have had to pay
● if you have things which have increased in value and on which you will have to pay CGT when you sell them, you can avoid tax by keeping the gains you make each year below £3,000. It's worth making use of this £3,000 allowance each year if you can – it can't be carried forward to use the next year
● if you have shares which have increased in value and which you want to keep, you may

be able to avoid a large tax bill when you finally sell them by, each year, selling enough to make net gains of up to £3,000, and then buying the shares back next day. But bear in mind the cost of buying and selling shares – this could outweigh the CGT saving
● if your losses for the year add up to more than your gains, you can carry forward the balance of the losses to set against gains you would have to pay tax on in later years. So keep a careful record of your losses
● if either husband or wife has made net losses during the year, while the other has made net gains of less than £3,000, the one who made the losses should ask for them to be carried forward and set against future gains. There'll still be no tax to pay that year, and there may be a tax saving in later years.

The columns in Figure 18.1

For regular saving or lump sum?
Some investments are very flexible. The minimum amount you can invest is fairly low — so they can be used as homes for lump sums, regular savings and odd bits of spare cash.

But some investments are open only to people who have a fair-sized lump sum of money to invest, and others only to people who want to save a regular amount, each month or year, say. Of course, if you've a lump sum, you can invest it bit by bit on a regular basis, if you like.

Minimum investment
This column tells you the minimum sensible amount you can invest. This isn't necessarily the same thing as the minimum amount you're *allowed* to invest. For example, with an NSB ordinary account, you can invest as little as 25p — but your money doesn't earn interest unless you have at least £1 in your account.

Does it pay a regular income?
Some investments pay income direct to you at regular intervals. With others, the income is added to the value of what you first invested.

Of course, with some investments which don't pay an income out to you (eg property bonds, index-linked National Savings Certificates), you may still be able to give yourself a regular 'income' by cashing part of your investment at regular intervals — indeed, with some investments (such as property bonds) there are often standard schemes to allow you to do this.

With some investments which pay out a regular income, the income is fixed when you take out the investment (eg local authority loans). With other investments (eg building societies) the income can vary after you've invested your money.

If you need to be sure of getting a regular number of £££ from your investment each year, go for one that pays out a fixed income — but ▷ Keeping up with inflation, p. 181.

Note that if you go for a fixed income, you may regret your decision if interest rates in general rise — investments with interest rates which vary may turn out to have been better bets. On the other hand, if interest rates in general fall, you will feel pleased with yourself for putting your money in a fixed income investment.

How long is the investment meant to be for?
This column tells you how long you should expect to have to leave your money invested in order to get the best return.

How quickly can you get your money back?
In some cases, the answer is you can't. So don't put your money in one of these investments unless you're certain you'll be able to leave it there for the agreed period.

With other investments, you may be able to cash in early but not get back (or not be sure of getting back) what you paid in. So, if you want a certain amount of money at a certain time — eg to go on holiday in 2 years' time — you'd be wise to steer clear of these investments too.

Does value of capital fluctuate?
Investments can be divided into two types:
● the value of the capital you invest stays the same (but ▷ Keeping up with inflation, p. 181)
● the value may fluctuate.

Unit trusts, single-premium investment bonds and Krugerrands are examples of investments where the value of the capital invested will fluctuate. With investments like these, you stand a chance of making a capital gain, but also run the risk of losing some of your money.

And because the value of the capital fluctuates, the success of your investment depends very much on *when* you invest and *when* you cash your investment. For more about how to reduce the risk of doing very badly, ▷ p. 182.

Points about tax
This column gives basic information about tax treatment. Certain investments are more suitable for taxpayers than for those who don't pay tax — so non-taxpayers should beware of investments in the Route Maps which have ● next to them. Other investments, where the return is tax-free, look more attractive the higher your rate of tax — marked with ● on the Route Maps.

Where you can get the investment
This column tells you where to go to put your money in these investments.

Other comments
This gives snippets of information about how some of the investments work, who might find it worthwhile to consider or avoid a particular investment, and so on.

Figure 18.1 The investments compared

Type of investment (and latest *Money Which?* report to look at)	For regular saving or lump sum?	Minimum investment (1)	Does it pay a regular income?	How long is investment meant to be for?	How quickly can you get your money back?
Annuities (*Money Which?*, June 75, p. 123)	Lump sum	(2)	Yes, normally arranged at time you buy the annuity. The older you are at that time, the higher the income – see also Other comments	Until you die	You can't – once you've made investment you can't cash it in
Bank deposit accounts	Either	None	No – but interest is added to capital at regular intervals and can be withdrawn. Interest can vary	Any period – a home for emergency funds and a temporary home for other funds	In practice, with most banks at once – but may lose some interest
British government stocks (*Money Which?*, September 75, p. 142)	Lump sum	None (3)	Yes – income fixed at the time you buy the stock (except with a few stocks (4))	Until stock due to be redeemed (paid back) by government – but some stocks can also be short-term speculation (14)	Can sell stock at any time. Can take a day or two to get money if sold through stockbroker, a week or so otherwise
British Savings Bonds	Either	£5 (maximum £10,000)	Yes – income is fixed and is paid out every 6 months	5 years gives best return (because get bonus of 4% of original investment at end of 5 years)	1 month (but no interest paid if cash in before held for 6 months)
Building societies – Ordinary shares (*Money Which?*, September 80)	Either	£1	Yes – can choose to have interest paid out to you. Interest can vary	Any period – a home for emergency funds and a temporary home for other funds	In theory, with most societies, a month, in practice, on the spot or in a few days
– Subscription shares (*Money Which?*, September 80)	Regular saving	£1 a month (maximum often £50 a month)	Normally, no	Any period	▷ **Ordinary shares** above
– Term shares (*Money Which?*, September 80)	Lump sum	Often £500 or £1,000	Yes – can normally choose to have interest paid out to you. Interest can vary	Generally, 2, 3 or 4 years	Normally can't, until end of period you've agreed to invest for (though your heirs can get it if you die)
– Life insurance linked to building societies (*Money Which?*, September 79, p. 510)	Regular saving	£3 to £8 a month	No	Best return under 80/81 tax rules after 4 years	Can cash in any time. But if cash in within first 4 years, may have to pay some of premium subsidy (▷ opposite) back
Cashing in on your home when retired (*Money Which?*, December 79.)	Lump sum (5)	(6)	Yes – income arranged at the time you take out the scheme (depends on age and sex)	Until you die	You can't
Commodities – Direct investment (*Money Which?*, December 76, p. 157)	Lump sum	(8)	No	In the main, short-term speculation	Can sell at any time

For footnotes ▷ **p. 202**

Does value of capital fluctuate?	Points about tax	Where can you get investment?	Other comments	
Not applicable – can't get capital back	Income made up of 2 parts – interest on capital and return of part of capital. Only interest part is taxable – normally paid after deduction of basic rate tax	Life insurance company or broker	Only worth considering for older people (over 65, say). Man gets higher income than woman of same age. Can also get temporary and deferred annuities	**Annuities**
No	Interest is taxable – but paid without deduction of tax	High-Street bank, National Girobank	You don't need a current account at the bank to open a deposit account – except with National Girobank	**Bank deposit accounts**
Yes – but if you hold stock until redemption, you know for certain what you'll get back	Interest is taxable – paid without deduction of tax if bought through National Savings Stock Register, normally after deduction of basic rate tax if bought through stockbroker. May be liable for capital gains tax if stock held for less than a year.	Stockbroker, post office, High-Street bank	Best stock for you depends, to large extent, on rate of tax you pay. Get advice on which stock to choose – eg from stockbroker, T S B, other bank. Buying and selling costs less for small investments if made through National Savings Stock Register	**British government stocks**
No	Interest is taxable – but final bonus is tax-free	Post office, High-Street bank		**British Savings Bonds**
No	Building society pays tax on interest before it's paid out to you. If you pay tax at higher rates, or investment income surcharge, have to pay extra tax. If pay no tax, can't claim tax back	Building society	Also ▷ Building up your interest *Money Which?*, June 79, p. 332.	**Building societies – Ordinary shares**
No	▷ **Ordinary shares** above	Building society	Normally pays 1¼% more interest than building society ordinary shares	**– Subscription shares**
No	▷ **Ordinary shares** above	Building society	Normally pays higher rate of interest than building society ordinary shares – say, 1% higher for a 3-year term. Also ▷ Building up your interest in *Money Which?*, June 79, p. 332.	**– Term shares**
No	Return tax-free so long as pay tax at no more than the basic rate – always tax-free if keep policy going for at least 10 years, or three-quarters of its term, whichever is less	Life insurance company, building society	Government subsidizes premiums (currently you pay only 82½% of full premium, 85% from 6 April 81) – so more is invested in building society for you than premium costs you. But policy is less worthwhile if you are 65 or more, or in poor health	**– Life insurance linked to building societies**
(7)	Get tax relief on mortgage interest. For how annuity taxed ▷ **Annuities** above	Hambro Life, Save & Prosper, Home Reversions or insurance broker	For how schemes work, see footnote (5). Only worth considering for older people (over 70, say). Not recommended for non-taxpayers	**Cashing in on your home when retired**
Yes	Gain may be liable for income tax (including investment income surcharge) or CGT	Commodity broker	Investing directly in commodities not sensible for most people. Very risky	**Commodities – Direct investment**

Figure 18.1 The investments compared

Type of investment (and latest *Money Which?* report to look at)	For regular saving or lump sum?	Minimum investment (1)	Does it pay a regular income?	How long is investment meant to be for?	How quickly can you get your money back?
— Commodity funds (*Money Which?*, December 76, p. 157)	Lump sum	£1,000, say	Varies with fund. Some pay an income — with others you can get income by cashing units	Long-term investment or short-term speculation	Varies with fund — a few days or a month
Diamonds (*Money Which?*, September 74, p. 160 and September 78, p. 498)	Lump sum	Varies	No — in fact, you have to pay for insurance, etc.	Long term	Can sell at any time — but may find selling difficult, and unlikely to get back as much as you paid for a few years
Endowment policies (*Money Which?*, December 77, p. 672)	In the main, regular saving	£3 to £5 a month	No	10 years or more — period usually agreed when take out policy	Can cash in policy at any time but what you get back is normally at discretion of company (and in first year or two may get little or nothing)
Finance company deposits	Lump sum	(10)	Yes — can choose to have interest paid out to you. Interest usually fixed if invest for agreed period. Otherwise can vary	(10)	With deposits made for agreed period, you can't (though your heirs normally can if you die). With other deposits, varies
Gold (Coins, bullion) (*Money Which?*, June 75, p. 102)	Lump sum	Varies (1 Krugerrand around £530 April 80)	No — in fact, you have to pay for insurance, etc.	Long-term investment or short-term speculation	Can sell coin or bullion at any time
Home (*Mortgages, Money Which?*, December 77, p. 656)	Either	Normally at least 10% of price of home	No (unless you let it out)	Any period	May take several months to sell your home
Income and growth bonds (*Money Which?*, June 78, p. 348)	Lump sum	£500	Income bonds — yes; growth bonds — no	Fixed period, often 5 years or more	With some companies, at end of agreed period only. With others, can cash in early — but return up to company
Index-linked investments — National Savings Certificates (Retirement Issue) (*Money Which?* September 77; June 80)	Either	£10 (maximum £1,200)	No — but can cash certificates to get an income	Initially for 5 years (get bonus of 4% of original investment at end of 5 years). Can keep money invested longer	Around a couple of weeks (but certificates not index-linked if cashed in before held for 12 months)
— Save-As-You-Earn (Third Issue) (*Money Which?*, September 77; June 80)	Regular saving	£4 a month (maximum £20 a month)	No	5 years of saving — can leave money invested for further 2 years (taking out new scheme at same time)	Around a couple of weeks (but if cash in before 5 years are up, no index-linking — get interest at 6% instead)
Local authority investments — Local authority loans (often called **bonds**) (*Money Which?* September 76, p. 128)	Lump sum	Often £100 to £500	Yes — interest fixed at the time you invest	Agreed period — normally between 1 and 7 years	You normally can't (though your heirs may be able to if you die)
— Yearling bonds and **Local authority stocks** (*Money Which?* September 76, p. 128)	Lump sum	(15)	Yes — income fixed at the time you invest (except with a few stocks (4))	As for British government stocks (but are redeemed by local authority)	Can sell on Stock Exchange at any time; takes a day or two to get your money

For footnotes ▷ p. 202

Does value of capital fluctuate?	Points about tax	Where can you get investment?	Other comments	
Yes	▷ *Money Which?* report	Direct from fund, or through insurance broker, stockbroker, etc	For legal and tax reasons, funds based offshore – Isle of Man or Channel Islands, say	**– Commodity funds**
Yes	Gain may be liable for capital gains tax	Diamond merchant or investment company, jeweller	Need expert knowledge for direct investment. New investment schemes (including a diamond fund) have sprung up since last full *Money Which?* report	**Diamonds**
Get at least a guaranteed amount at end of policy (or if you die) – more if policy is a with-profits one	Return tax-free so long as pay tax at no more than the basic rate – always tax-free if keep policy going for at least 10 years, or three-quarters of its term, whichever is less	Life insurance company or broker	Government subsidizes premiums on most regular-premium policies (currently you pay only 82½% of full premium, 85% from 6 April 81). Non-profit policies not recommended. With-profits policies better value	**Endowment policies**
No	Interest is taxable. If finance company technically classed as a bank, paid without deduction of tax	Finance company	Often considered a somewhat riskier investment than bank deposit accounts, say – and so may pay a higher rate of interest (9)	**Finance company deposits**
Yes	Liable for capital gains tax (possibly income tax if count as gold trader). May have to pay VAT when buy gold bullion in UK	Stockbroker, High-Street bank, coin dealer, London Gold Market	Most convenient way to invest directly is to buy gold coins. Can now invest indirectly through insurance-linked gold bond (may cash part for income)	**Gold** (Coins, bullion)
Yes	For tax relief rules ▷ p. 223. No CGT on main home	For how to raise the money ▷ ch. 5, p. 73	Proved a very good investment in the past – ▷ Fig. 16.1, p. 182	**Home**
No	Tax treatment depends on how bond works – can work in one of several ways. Check with company before investing	Life insurance company or broker		**Income and growth bonds**
Yes – but won't get back less than you invested	Return tax-free	Post office, Trustee Savings Bank	Commonly known as *granny bonds.* Value goes up in line with Retail Price Index – even after initial 5-year term is up. Only for women aged 60 or over, men aged 65 or over	**Index-linked investments – National Savings Certificates** (Retirement Issue)
Yes	Return tax-free	Post office, High-Street bank, your employer	At end of 5 years, value of each payment increased in line with increase in Retail Price Index since payment made – continues to be index-linked for further 2 years (at end of which you get a bonus of 2 monthly payments)	**Save-As-You-Earn** (Third Issue)
No	Interest is taxable – normally paid after deduction of basic rate tax	Local authority	Doesn't have to be your own local authority that you invest in	**Local authority investments – Local authority loans** (often called **bonds**)
As for British government stocks	Interest is taxable – paid after deduction of basic rate tax. Liable for CGT on any capital gain (or income tax in certain circumstances)	Stockbroker (or local authority for stocks when stock first issued)	Local authority stocks are alternative to British government stocks – but normally give slightly higher return.	**– Yearling bonds** and **Local authority stocks**

Figure 18.1 The investments compared

Types of investment (and latest *Money Which?* report to look at)	For regular saving or lump sum?	Minimum investment (1)	Does it pay a regular income?	How long is investment meant to be for?	How quickly can you get your money back?
National Savings Bank – Ordinary accounts	Either	£1 (maximum £10,000)	No – but interest can be withdrawn. Interest can vary	Any period – a home for emergency funds, a temporary home for other funds	£100 at once (about a week to withdraw all money)
– Investment accounts	Either	£1 (maximum £50,000)	No – but interest can be withdrawn. Interest can vary	Any period over a month	1 month
National Savings Certificates (19th issue) (for Retirement Issue ▷ Index-linked investments)	Either	£10 (maximum £1,500)	No	Best return 5 years	Around a couple of weeks (but return lower if cash in within first 5 years)
Personal pension schemes (11) (12)	Either	Varies – often £100 a year	Yes – normally from any age between 60 and 75	You make payments until income starts (income carries on for life)	You can't cash investment in
Premium bonds (*Which?*, February 78, p. 106)	Either	£5 (maximum £10,000)	No – but might win prizes	Any period – but can't win prize until bond held for 3 months	Around a couple of weeks
Shares (*Money Which?*, December 73, p. 184)	Lump sum	£700, say, in each company	Yes – most companies pay dividends. These can vary	In the main, long-term investment. But can also be short-term speculation	Can sell shares and get money in 2 to 4 weeks – but may get less than you invested
Single-premium investment bonds (eg managed bonds, property bonds) (*Money Which?*, September 78, p. 514)	Lump sum	Varies – normally between £250 and £1,000	No – but most companies have schemes which let you cash in part of investment regularly (can cash up to 5% a year without paying tax at the time)	In the main, long-term investment	Varies – often a week or so to sell. May get back less than invested
Things (eg antiques, stamps, oriental rugs . . .) (*Money Which?*, December 79)	Lump sum	Varies	No – in fact you have to pay for insurance, etc.	In the main, long-term investment	As quickly as you can find a buyer
Unit-linked savings plans (*Money Which?*, December 78, p. 678)	Regular saving	Varies – normally between £5 and £25 a month	No	At least 10 years	Can cash at any time – but may get back less than you invested (and in first year or two, may get little or nothing)
Unit trusts (*Money Which?*, June 74, p. 100)	Either	Varies (13)	Yes – amount can vary	In the main, long-term investment	Varies between trusts – can normally sell each day (but you may get back less than you invested)

1. Gives an idea of the minimum it's sensible to invest.
2. Depends on age and minimum income company will pay out – but £1,000 or more, say.
3. If you buy stock on National Savings Stock Register (through post office or TSB). With a stockbroker, buying and selling costs make buying less than £400 or so less worthwhile.

4. The interest paid on a few stocks varies.
5. Which you get by mortgaging your home (or in the case of two of the Home Reversions schemes, selling part or all of it) to insurance company – ▷ p. 49.
6. With Hambro Life and Home Reversions, min. value of home £10,000; with Save & Prosper, £13,500.

7. With Hambro Life, Save & Prosper and one of the Home Reversions schemes, you still benefit in full from increase in value of home. With one of the Home Reversions schemes where you sell your home to the company all the increase in value of the home goes to the company and with the other, half the increase does.
8. You need several thousand £££

Does value of capital fluctuate?	Points about tax	Where can you get investment?	Other comments	
No	First £70 interest each year is tax-free — all interest paid without deduction of tax	Post office	No interest if invest for less than a month	**Nat. Savings Bank** — **Ordinary accounts**
No	Interest is taxable — paid without deduction of tax	Post office	Worth considering if you don't pay tax	— **Investment accounts**
No	Return is tax-free	Post office, High-Street bank		**National Savings Certificates** (19th Issue)
With some schemes — yes; with others — no	Get tax relief on payments — ▷ pp. 221-2. Income paid to you taxed as earnings *not* investment income	Life insurance company or broker	Don't need to be self-employed to invest in one — ▷ pp. 46-7. Can choose to have lump sum on retirement instead of part of pension	**Personal pension schemes**
No	Prizes are tax-free	Post office, High-Street bank	Prizes worked out to give return of 7% on all bonds held for 3 months or more. Chance of winning a prize in any year if hold £10 of bonds is around 1 in 150	**Premium bonds**
Yes	Dividends are taxable — paid after deduction of basic rate tax. Liable for CGT on any gain	Stockbroker, High-Street bank, or other agent (eg accountant)	Buying shares of just one or a few companies is very risky. For how to spread risks ▷ pp. 182-3	**Shares**
Yes	When you cash in bond, you'll have to pay some tax on the gain you've made (including any amounts you got earlier on, not taxed at the time) if you pay tax at higher rates or the investment income surcharge	Life insurance company or broker	Value of investment depends on performance of fund of investments normally run by insurance company — eg property fund, equity fund, managed fund. Can switch between funds. Only way to invest small sum in property	**Single-premium investment bonds** (eg managed bonds, property bonds)
Yes	No capital gains tax unless value of item at time of disposal more than £2,000	Auctions, dealers, other collectors	Need expert knowledge. Potentially a good hedge against inflation. Watch out for the dealer's mark-up	**Things** (eg antiques, stamps, oriental rugs . . .)
Yes	Return tax-free so long as pay tax at no more than the basic rate — always tax-free if keep policy going for at least 10 years, or three-quarters of its term, whichever is less	Life insurance company or broker	Government subsidizes premiums (currently you pay only 82½% of full premiums, 85% from 6 April 81). Money is invested in unit trust or insurance company fund (as for single-premium investment bonds). Go for high-investment plan — ▷ report	**Unit-linked savings plans**
Yes	Income is taxable — paid after deduction of basic rate tax. Liable for capital gains tax on any gain (but until 5 April 80 got tax credit of 10% of gain)	Direct from unit trust company or via insurance broker, stockbroker, High-Street bank	Most units are authorized by the Department of Trade — this means, for example, the Department can lay down rules about how prices of units are worked out and so on	**Unit trusts**

9. Under the Banking Act, companies will need to be licensed by Bank of England to accept deposits. A Deposit Protection Fund will be set up — this will guarantee to pay 75% of deposit up to £10,000, if company fails. In April 80, Act not yet in full operation.
10. Usually two types of deposits. With one type you invest for an agreed period (often 1, 2 or 3 years); minimum investment is often £1,000.

With other, you invest for any period but have to give notice to withdraw money; min. investment often £100.
11. Can also make *additional voluntary contributions* to firm's pension scheme — ▷ p. 46.
12. See *Handbook to self-employed pensions*, available from Fundex Ltd, Freepost, London EC4B 4QJ.

13. For lump sums often between £100 and £500; for regular savings, often £10 a month.
14. Stock prices tend to go up if interest rates in general fall, and to go down if interest rates, in general, rise.
15. £1,000 for yearling bonds. For buying local authority stock through a stockbroker, buying and selling costs make buying less than £400 or so less worthwhile.

19 Borrowing

Borrowing money to buy or improve your home — the largest debt most people ever take .on — is covered in ch. 5. Here we deal with borrowing on a smaller scale, and usually for a shorter term.

'Neither a borrower nor a lender be' is a saying we all hear some time in our lives. But borrowing (like lending) can make a lot of sense as part of your financial strategy. This is because, when prices are rising, it can be to your advantage to borrow to buy goods straight away rather than save to buy them later.

Borrowing in times of inflation can mean that:

● you save £££ by buying at today's prices – what you save could cover the interest you have to pay on the loan

● the buying power of what you pay in interest and in repaying the loan decreases as time passes.

For example, suppose you borrow £100 and agree to pay the £100 back at the end of the year, together with interest of £10. At the end of the year, you'll hand over £110. Suppose also that inflation runs at 10 per cent over that year. Then the buying power of the £110 you pay back is only £100 – so that in real terms the loan has cost you nothing. Generally the real cost of borrowing is the difference between the **APR** (▷ opposite) and the rate of inflation.

If you save up for whatever you want to buy, you should earn interest on your money – but the savings above could still more than compensate for this, as our example (▷ opposite) shows.

How much will you have to pay to borrow?

It may pay to buy now, instead of saving to buy later. But whether it does or not depends heavily on what *you* have to pay (in interest and other charges) for the money you borrow.

The cost (in terms of the interest you pay) of loans from various sources varies widely. Forms of credit which tend to be expensive (eg some hire purchase and trading checks, say) might cost 2 or 3 times as much as a bank overdraft – or even more.

In the past, it was difficult to compare the cost of borrowing from different lenders as they were able to quote their charges in a number of different ways. But from 6 October 80, most advertisements or other literature which offer credit must quote the *annual percentage rate of change (APR)* for the loan. The APR puts the costs for different methods of borrowing on a comparable basis – so can be used as a guide to the cost of the credit being offered. The example below shows how much easier it is to choose the cheapest type of loan when the APR is quoted.

Example

Jane wants to buy a refrigerator costing £200. The rates in the advertising material she looks through are:

	Terms	APR
Hire purchase, through shop	20% deposit; low monthly payments of £9 for 2 years	35.4%
Personal loan from bank	19.5% true rate of interest	19.5%
Trading voucher	No deposit; low weekly payments of £2.90 for 94 weeks	43.1%
Personal loan from finance company	14% flat rate of interest; pay back loan in monthly instalments over 1 year	27.9%

In our example, Jane can easily see that the personal loan from her bank is her cheapest source of credit.

If the APR for a loan isn't quoted by the lender, ask for a written quotation which shows it.

Annual percentage rate of charge (APR)

The annual percentage rate of charge takes into account not only what you pay in interest, but also the following:

● any service charge you have to pay in order to get the loan (eg an arrangement or acceptance fee)

● any payments you have to make for a compulsory maintenance contract or premiums for certain compulsory insurance policies.

● the extra cost you incur if you buy on credit from a shop which normally gives a cash discount.

The APR also takes into account how much you actually owe at different times during the loan. With any loan which you repay in instalments, the amount you owe gets less each time you make a payment. For example, if Jane took out the finance company personal loan above, she would owe £200 for only 1 month. At the end of a month, her first instalment would reduce the amount she owes. She gradually pays off more and more of the loan each month, until at the end of the 12 payments she owes nothing. On average over the year, she would owe just over £100 – just over half the amount of the total loan. But, for this loan, Jane still pays interest of 14 per cent of £200 – ie £28. The APR (which takes into account Jane's diminishing debt) works out at just under 28 per cent.

Jack and Sid both want to buy a motorbike. At the moment it costs £250, which neither of them has. Both can afford to put about £22 a month towards buying the bike.

Jack decides to put £22.50 a month into a building society account until he has saved enough to buy the bike. He gets 8 per cent interest on his savings (with no further tax to pay).

Sid borrows the £250 from the bank on a one-year personal loan. He pays £22.78 each month in interest and repayment of the loan (ie almost the same as the amount Jack saves each month).

Here is how Jack's savings build up:

By November, Jack has saved £250.65 (including the interest on his savings at 8 per cent after tax). But the price of the bike has risen meanwhile (to a staggering £320) so Jack will have to go on saving. By the time he has saved £320 (which will take him 3 months more) the price of the bike may have risen again. Total cost of bike to Jack: at least £320.

Sid gets a personal loan of £250 from his bank, and pays back £22.78 a month. After a year he is clear of the debt and he has the use of the bike all year too. Of course, if he hadn't bought the bike, he could have saved the £22.78 a month instead – earning interest of around £11. So the total cost of the bike to Sid is: £273.36 for the loan plus £11 for the lost interest – ie £284.36 in all.

Sid has come off well from the deal, because the swift rise in the bike's price, and the relatively low cost of his loan favoured him. In different circumstances, Jack might have ended up better off – if Sid had had to pay more for the loan, say, or the price of the bike had risen less dramatically over the year.

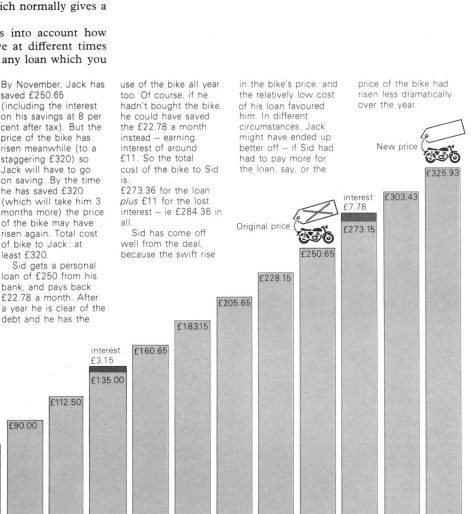

Tax relief

One of the factors to take into account when you work out the cost of borrowing is whether or not you can get tax relief on the interest you pay for the loan.

What can you get tax relief on?

Broadly speaking, you can get tax relief on loans of up to £25,000 in all to buy or improve the following:
● your *only* home, or if you have more than one home, your *main* one (normally the one you and your family live in most of the time)
● the home of your former or separated wife or husband
● the home of a dependent relative who doesn't pay rent (▷ p. 221 for what counts as a dependent relative – but there's no set limit on the amount of income that the relative can have).

What counts as improving a home?

A loan for improving your home can qualify for tax relief only if it is used for altering the home *permanently*. Ordinary repairs and decoration don't count as permanent – but converting your loft or insulating your home, building an extension or a swimming pool, or putting fitted units into your kitchen do count. So does restoring a house bought in a dilapidated condition, converting your home into flats, landscaping your garden or improving the street outside your home. A loan to install central heating or double-glazing qualifies for tax relief – but not one to buy portable radiators or night storage heaters, which aren't fixed.

You may also be able to get tax relief on the interest you pay on other loans (▷ p. 223 for details). If you're in doubt whether or not the interest on a loan qualifies for tax relief, check with your tax inspector.

How tax relief works

For each £ you pay out in interest which qualifies for tax relief, you escape tax on the most heavily taxed £ of your income – including investment income surcharge, if you pay it. So, for example, if you pay tax at 40 per cent on at least as much of your income as you pay in interest, each £ of interest costs you no more than £1 minus 40p – ie 60p.
● Take advantage of tax relief
Plan your borrowing to take full advantage of tax relief, and keep the interest you pay to a minimum. Suppose, for example, you want to install central heating in your main home and buy a car, but can afford to pay cash for only one of these things. In this case, you'd be better off borrowing for the central heating (which counts as improving your home) and paying cash for the car. That way you'd get tax relief on the interest.

Warning Interest on bank overdrafts and on credit cards doesn't qualify for tax relief, whatever the money is spent on.

What you should bear in mind – apart from cost – when choosing a loan

Loans differ from each other in more ways than simply what they cost you in interest. Some are tied to specific goods; with others you borrow cash. Some loans are relatively long term (up to 5 or 10 years, say), and some are short. And your financial track record will have a lot of impact on the cost and availability of loans from some sources, but less on loans from other sources.

Below we take a brief look at why you should keep these differences in mind when deciding how to arrange your borrowing.

Cash or goods?

Some types of loan are inextricably tied to the goods you're buying – and you wouldn't consider this type of loan unless you wanted the goods in question. HP-type agreements are examples of this type of loan.

With other loans, you get cash in your hand, and you can use the money to spend on anything you decide to. Overdrafts and insurance policy loans tend to be like this – they generally have no conditions tied to them.

In between these two extremes of complete flexibility or inflexibility, there's a wide range of loans to choose from. In the summaries of the different types of loan starting on p. 210, we've indicated what strings are attached.

The fact that you're borrowing cash doesn't *necessarily* mean that the loan is entirely flexible. With an ordinary loan from the bank, for example, the bank manager will probably want to know what you intend to use the money for – and with a personal loan, he certainly will. And credit cards and store credit, although obviously linked to the purchase of goods, aren't inflexible in the way that HP and credit sale agreements are. If you buy goods with them that you'd ordinarily pay cash for, they can be just as flexible as borrowing money.

In general, you'll find it's normally cheaper to borrow cash (eg from your bank) to finance your purchases rather than to take a loan connected specifically to the thing you want to buy (eg HP to buy a car).

Your rights
● Extortionate rates Under the Consumer Credit Act, you can take a lender to the county court (sheriff court if you live in Scotland) if you feel you've been charged an extortionate amount for credit. The court can order the lender to reduce his charges. However, what counts as extortionate isn't yet clear – it will emerge from court cases, and will depend on many factors. So don't take this course until you have exhausted all others. If you think you have cause for complaint, and can't get satisfaction from the lender, start off with the local trading standards officer (sometimes called a consumer protection officer). For address see the phone book, under the name of your local council. Other places to try for help are your local Citizens' Advice Bureau, consumer advice centre, or your solicitor.

Your rights
● Doorstep loans
If anyone approaches you in the street or calls at your home with an offer to lend you money, he is breaking the law unless you have asked him in writing to do so (and he has a licence to lend money). It isn't illegal, however, if the offer of credit is in connection with something the person is selling. See also cooling-off period on p. 209.

● Fees to credit brokers
If you go to a broker — a mortgage broker, for example — to try to arrange a loan, he isn't allowed to charge you a fee of more than £1 unless he fixes you up with a loan. Even if he manages to find someone willing to lend you the money, he isn't allowed to charge you more than £1 unless you take up the offer within six months.

A credit broker can ask for a deposit when you first approach him. You are entitled to all except £1 of this deposit back unless you take out a loan arranged by him.

Length of loan

Here it's important that you take a good look at your overall financial position. Drawing up a budget, like the one we show on p. 164, may be a valuable first move.

Ask yourself how long you need to spread repayments over. Generally speaking, the longer the period of the loan, the lower the instalments. But if your need for a loan is very short-term (just a couple of weeks, say) then you could use a credit card to tide you over. Provided you pay off the debt within 25 days of getting the account from the credit card company, the loan won't cost you a penny.

As well as the length of loan, give some thought to the timing of your repayments. Try to work out how they'll fit in with your overall budget. If your income comes in at irregular intervals (which is possible if you are a freelance worker, say) then you might find it easier to repay capital and interest in one lump sum at the end of the loan, rather than in regular instalments every month.

With a loan that's going to last more than a year or so, ask yourself too how well you'd be able to manage if for some reason (eg sickness, redundancy, unforeseen emergencies) your financial situation took a turn for the worse.

Where your overall budget is concerned, the timing of repayments and the number of years they'll continue for can matter almost as much as their size.

Your financial standing

Anyone who lends money wants to be repaid sooner or later — so they won't give you a loan in the first place unless they're reasonably sure they'll get their money back. Things a lender is likely to bear in mind are your past track record, your income, and what security you can offer for the loan.

● Your past track record
If you've blotted your credit copybook in the past — particularly if you've had a court order made against you for debt and haven't paid it off within a month or so — you'll probably be on the files of a *credit reference agency*. A lender will almost certainly contact this kind of agency to check your creditworthiness. If you're in their files, you may find it difficult to get the loan you want.

A lender is also likely to ask for the name and address of your employer, building society manager, bank manager, landlord — and he might write to any of these, stating the amount you want to borrow, and asking for references about you.

● Your income
You're almost certain to be asked for details of your income when you apply for most forms of credit. You are also likely to have to provide details of your regular financial commitments – eg your mortgage, rates, HP payments and so on.

● Security
It's sometimes easier to get a loan (or you may be able to borrow more, or at a lower rate of interest) if you can offer security for the loan – ie you give the lender rights to assets which he can sell if you don't pay all you owe. When you've paid off the loan, he returns the security to you.

The kind of assets the lender would be interested in are:
● your house
● an insurance policy with a cash-in value (preferably higher than the value of the loan)
● investments – stocks, shares, National Savings Certificates, and so on.

If you don't have such assets yourself, you may still be able to get credit if you can find someone (like a friend or relative) to guarantee to pay back the loan if you default. But, of course, if you run into financial trouble, and can't pay the debt, your guarantor may have to instead.

Your rights
● Credit reference agencies
If you're refused credit, you have the right to know the name and address of any credit reference agency contacted, if you ask for it in writing within a month of being refused credit.

Whether you've been refused credit or not, you have the right to ask any credit reference agency for a copy of their file on you (you must enclose a small fee). If you find their information is wrong, you have the right to insist it be corrected. Copies of any corrections must be sent to you and to anyone who has been given a reference on you in the previous 6 months.

Note that this right of access only applies to outside agencies — not to the internal files of, say, banks and finance companies.

The two largest agencies are:
Credit Data Ltd, Markham House, Markham Rd, Chesterfield, Derbyshire, S40 1SQ.

UAPT, 145–149 London Rd, Croydon, Surrey, CR9 2SY

HP or cash?

People often talk about getting 'discounts for cash'. Others claim that HP prices can be cheaper because the dealer gets a cut from the finance company. This debate is particularly common in the case of cars, especially when you're offering your old one in part exchange. The picture has become even more complicated with the advent of 'free' or 'cheap' HP, offered by some garages and department stores and most mail order companies.

If you have a choice between buying on HP and paying cash (borrowing the money from somewhere else if need be), use the Route Map below to find out which is likely to be cheaper.

Example

Bill Bright is thinking of buying a new car – a Sierra with a list price of £3,600. He finds he could get a discount of £300 if he paid cash – but no discount if he takes up the 24-month cheap HP being offered through the dealer. With the HP deal, he has to pay a deposit of a third of the cost price (ie £1,200) and monthly instalments of £115 – a total HP price of £3,960. Bill uses the Route Map to help him decide which way of paying for the car would prove cheaper:

- cheapest cash price is list price less discount for cash, ie £3,600 − £300 = £3,300.
- HP deposit is £1,200.
- so the amount effectively borrowed is £3,300 − £1,200 = £2,100.

If Bill had this amount of cash, he could earn interest on it by investing it in, say, a building society at $10\frac{1}{2}$ per cent. He could earn roughly:

$$\frac{£2,100}{2} \times 2 \times 10\tfrac{1}{2}\% = £220.50$$

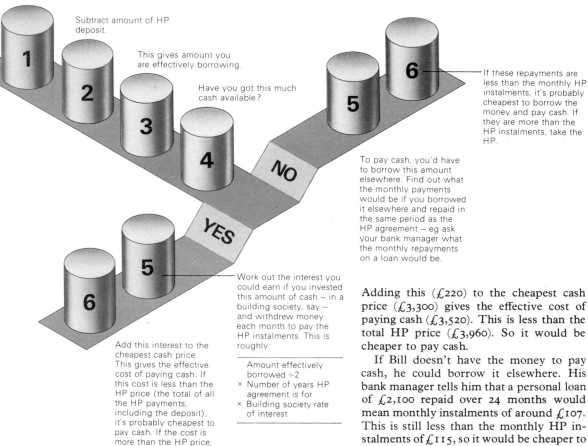

Should you go for 'free' or 'cheap' HP?

Find out cheapest cash price, taking account of any discount.

Subtract amount of HP deposit.

This gives amount you are effectively borrowing.

Have you got this much cash available?

NO

To pay cash, you'd have to borrow this amount elsewhere. Find out what the monthly payments would be if you borrowed it elsewhere and repaid in the same period as the HP agreement – eg ask your bank manager what the monthly repayments on a loan would be.

If these repayments are less than the monthly HP instalments, it's probably cheapest to borrow the money and pay cash. If they are more than the HP instalments, take the HP.

YES

Work out the interest you could earn if you invested this amount of cash – in a building society, say – and withdrew money each month to pay the HP instalments. This is roughly:

Amount effectively borrowed ÷2
× Number of years HP agreement is for
× Building society rate of interest

Add this interest to the cheapest cash price. This gives the effective cost of paying cash. If this cost is less than the HP price (the total of all the HP payments, including the deposit), it's probably cheapest to pay cash. If the cost is more than the HP price, take the HP.

Adding this (£220) to the cheapest cash price (£3,300) gives the effective cost of paying cash (£3,520). This is less than the total HP price (£3,960). So it would be cheaper to pay cash.

If Bill doesn't have the money to pay cash, he could borrow it elsewhere. His bank manager tells him that a personal loan of £2,100 repaid over 24 months would mean monthly instalments of around £107. This is still less than the monthly HP instalments of £115, so it would be cheaper to get a personal loan and pay cash.

Which method of borrowing for you?

The best way for you to borrow depends on several things – eg how much you need, how long for, what you want to buy with the money, and so on. There's no one solution that's best for everyone. On this page we give you a series of tips aimed at keeping the cost of your borrowing to a minimum. Starting on p. 210 we go through each of the main ways of borrowing.

Your borrowing checklist

● Try to get a free or cheap loan – eg from your employer

Many employers give free or cheap loans to enable employees to buy season tickets for public transport. But some give loans for other purposes – eg for buying a house or car. You may be able to get a cheap loan from some other source – eg through your union or professional association. You might also see whether you could pay regular suppliers (eg of oil for central heating) in regular instalments rather than in one lump sum.

● Take advantage of the tax relief available on loans to buy or improve your home. For details ▷ p. 206.

● Want to borrow a lot (over £750, say)?

If you can't get a cheap loan from some source, try the following in this order: an insurance policy loan, or, if the loan is for home improvement, an increased mortgage; a bank ordinary loan; a bank personal loan; a finance company loan, second mortgage, or HP (but shop around to compare charges).

● Want to borrow a smaller amount and spread repayments over a year or more?

Try the following: an insurance policy loan; a bank ordinary or personal loan; a finance company loan, HP or shop account (but shop around to compare charges).

● Want to pay back fairly fast?

Try the following: a credit card; a bank overdraft; another type of bank loan; HP, option account, or mail order (but shop around to compare prices).

What if .. ?

However carefully you plan your borrowing, and investigate the possibilities available, the story may not end there. Don't just give up: you may be able to do something to put the situation right. See below for what your rights are.

Your rights

● Cooling-off period
A cooling-off period gives you time to have second thoughts about credit agreements which you sign in your own home – as a result of persuasive sales talk by a door-to-door salesman, for example. You already get a cooling-off period with HP and credit sale agreements. The Consumer Credit Act extends the idea to all types of credit except mortgages, loans for less than £30, and loans which you arrange entirely by post or telephone. With all other types of credit agreement which you sign at home, you'll be able to back out within 5 days of signing and receiving a copy of the agreement which has been signed by the lender.

● Faulty goods
If you buy goods which turn out to be faulty, you can make a claim against the seller under the Sale of Goods Act 1980. But under the Consumer Credit Act 1974, for goods bought on credit on or after 1 July 77 you can also make a claim against anyone who lent you the money to buy those goods – provided that
● the seller arranged the loan (eg a garage arranging to sell you a car on hire purchase)
● the goods in question cost more than £30 *but not more than* £10,000.
● you borrowed £5,000 or less.
You can claim against Access, Barclaycard and Trustcard, but not Diners and American Express (because they

don't offer extended credit – you have to pay your account in full at the end of the month).
Suppose, for example, that you buy double-glazing from a door-to-door salesman who arranges for you to pay for it with a personal loan from a finance company. If the double-glazing subsequently turns out to be faulty you can claim against:
● the firm which sold you the double-glazing *or*
● the finance company.
It would probably be best to contact the seller first. If he's unhelpful, try the lender.

● Want to pay off early?
The Consumer Credit Act gave the government the power to introduce rules about how much lenders can charge you if you decide to pay off a loan early. Until the government does this, however, you'll have to pay whatever early repayment fee the agreement states – even if it says you have to pay all the interest that would have been due over the whole period of the loan. So check the small print of your agreement carefully before signing, and make sure you know what early repayment penalties you may incur later on. And check too whether or not the government has brought out its own rules – try your local Citizens' Advice Bureau for information.

● Can't pay?
If you take out credit and then find you can't keep up the payments, bear in mind that goods bought under hire purchase or conditional sale agreements (▷ p. 213) *belong to the lender* until you've finished paying for

With all other forms of credit, the goods bought belong to you – but the money belongs to the lender, and he can take you to court to get it back. If you are taken to court and have a court order made against you for the debt – and you don't pay it off within a month or so – you could well end up on the files of a credit reference agency (▷ p. 207), and that may seriously hamper your chances of getting credit in future.

If you do find yourself in difficulties, let the lender know – he won't be as irritated as if he suddenly discovers you are months behind on your repayments. Try to keep on paying something, rather than stopping altogether. And if you live in England or Wales try not to get more than £200 in arrears – that way you won't have to pay the lender's costs if he takes you to court and wins.

Bank overdraft

Anyone with a bank account can ask his bank manager for an overdraft. He'll probably ask what you want the money for and how you intend to pay it back. If he agrees, he'll let you overdraw on your current account up to an agreed limit. You can use as much or as little of the facility as you need — and you pay interest only on the amount by which you're overdrawn, *not* on the overdraft limit. The amount of your overdraft will vary as money is paid into your account and drawn out again.
● How much can you borrow?
Not more than your bank manager reckons you can afford to repay.
● For how long?
Usually a matter of months, though you can ask for longer.
● For what purpose?
No restrictions, but your bank manager may be interested. If you want the money for something specific, he may prefer you to have a loan.
● Security required?
Not normally, unless the amount is large or your bank manager has doubts about you. Providing security could mean you pay a slightly lower rate of interest.
● Cost
Interest is worked out on what you owe each day, and is charged at between 2 and 5 per cent above the bank's base rate — which will vary from time to time. The bank may charge an *arrangement fee* for making the overdraft facility available (eg 1 per cent of your overdraft limit, or, perhaps, a flat sum of £5, say). With some banks, having an overdraft may increase your bank charges.
● Other points
If you go over your agreed overdraft limit,

you're likely to get a warning letter and, if your bank manager doesn't agree to a higher limit, your cheques may be bounced.
Don't overdraw without first asking your bank manager.
You can't get tax relief on the interest you pay on an overdraft, no matter what you spend it on.

Verdict
Cheap and very flexible.

Bank ordinary loan account

Anyone with a bank account can ask for an ordinary loan. Your bank manager will want to know what you want it for, and will have to be satisfied that you can pay it back. If you get one, a loan account is opened in your name and the amount you've agreed to borrow is transferred from it into your current account. You agree to make regular fixed repayments (usually by standing order) from your current account to pay off the loan (or you may agree to pay it off in a lump sum on an agreed date). Interest may be included in the repayments or charged to your current account. You pay the interest even if your current account is in credit.
● How much can you borrow?
Not more than your bank manager reckons you can afford to repay.
● For how long?
Typically up to 5 years, sometimes longer.
● For what purpose?
No restrictions, but your bank manager will normally want to know. You may be able to use an ordinary loan to pay off a more expensive credit agreement if your bank manager agrees.
● Security required?
May be asked for if you borrow a large sum or you're paying back over several years. Providing security could mean you pay a slightly lower rate of interest.
● Cost
Interest is normally worked out on what you owe each day — at much the same rate as would be charged for an overdraft. But an ordinary loan will work out more expensive, because money paid into your current account won't temporarily reduce the amount you owe.

There's likely to be an *arrangement fee* (around 1 per cent of the amount you borrow) for the work involved in setting up the loan.
● Other points
Most banks don't advertise ordinary loans at all — so don't assume your bank doesn't make them. Much of time they're slightly cheaper than personal loans (which the banks *do* advertise).
Your bank may insist you have a loan account if you're overdrawn considerably on your current account and haven't shown any signs of paying it off.

Verdict
Can be cheaper than a personal loan — but interest rate not fixed.

Bank personal loan

You choose (within limits) how much you want to borrow and how quickly you want to pay it off. You repay by equal monthly instalments, normally by standing order from your current account. The rate of interest is fixed for the whole period of the loan, and interest is included in the repayments. Some banks will give personal loans to people who don't have current accounts with them. Access Loan and Barclaycard Master loan are also like a personal loan.
If you're under a certain age (60 or 65, say) when you take out the loan, it normally comes with life insurance which pays off what you owe if you die, provided you've kept your repayments up to date.
To get an Access Loan or Barclaycard Masterloan you send in an application form; other types of personal loan are normally arranged through your bank manager.
● How much can you borrow?
Most banks offer loans of up to £5,000 for home improvements, less for other reasons. But you may be able to borrow more. You can normally choose any multiple of £10. Your bank manager won't let you borrow more than he reckons you can afford to pay back.
● For how long?
Normally up to 5 years for home improvements, 2 years for cars, 3 years for other purposes. You can normally choose any multiple of 6 months.
● For what purpose?
Normally no restrictions, but the bank will want to know — and personal loans are most frequently given for buying specific things.
● Security required?

Not usually, but you may be able to borrow more if you provide security (especially for home improvement loans).
● Cost
Most banks currently work out the total interest charge as a fixed percentage of the amount you originally borrowed for each year of your loan. The rate of interest is normally fixed for the length of the loan (which may work out a bit more expensive than an overdraft or ordinary loan). There's normally no arrangement fee.
● Other points
If you're off work sick, or because of an accident, some banks may agree to extend the repayment period by up to 6 months without charging extra interest.

Verdict
Fairly cheap and easy to arrange. Interest rate fixed — so you know where you stand.

Bank budget account
A budget account is a way of spreading the cost of household bills and other lump sum payments over the year
You add up your estimate of all the bills you want to include in the scheme and agree the total with your bank. You then divide the total by 12, and make out a monthly standing order for that amount to your budget account. You then pay all the bills on your list out of the budget account — usually with a special cheque book. Sometimes this account will be in credit, sometimes overdrawn — but by the end of the year what you've paid in should roughly equal what you've paid out, and you settle the balance with the bank.
● For how long?
An account normally lasts 1 year. You then open a new one if you want to.
● For what purpose?
All your regular bills (eg electricity, insurance, road tax and so on) can be included, as well as other payments — holidays, Christmas shopping, for example.
● Security required?
No.
● Cost
Different banks work out their charges in different ways. Most charge interest when your account is overdrawn. Some also charge for each cheque you write. And some make a charge based on the total estimate of your bills (eg £4 a year for £600 total bills).
● Other points
It's not worth including in the scheme any payments that you can spread without extra cost — eg your rates, which your local authority lets you pay in 10 or 12 instalments at no extra cost.

Verdict
May be useful if your bills tend to come in droves. But could be an expensive way of forcing yourself to budget.

Credit cards
Anyone over 18 can apply for an Access card, Barclaycard or Trustcard. Application forms ask for details of your job, income, financial commitments and if you own or rent your home. You'll be given a *credit limit* (£300, say). You can then spend up to that amount in shops, restaurants and so on which accept the card (or draw cash at a bank in the scheme) just by producing the card and signing a *sales voucher* (or cash advance voucher).
Each month you get a detailed statement showing what you've spent and the minimum you must pay (in mid-80, £5 or 5 per cent of what you owe, whichever is more). You can pay more if you want to, and if you pay the whole amount within 25 days of the statement date and you haven't made any cash withdrawals, there are no interest charges. This means you might have up to 8 weeks' or more interest-free credit.
● How much can you borrow?
Any amount up to your credit limit — if you want this increased, ask. In practice, the card company is likely to up the limit from time to time.
● For how long?
You can pay off what you owe as quickly or slowly as you like — so long as you pay at least the minimum amount due each month.
● For what purpose?
Each of the cards is accepted at numerous shops, restaurants, travel agents, garages and so on in the UK and abroad. Most of these will accept the card in payment for anything they sell. And you can get cash from any UK bank and, with Barclaycard and Trustcard, certain banks

in the Visa system abroad.
● Security required?
No.
● Cost
Free if you always settle your bills within 25 days of the statement date and don't withdraw any cash. Otherwise, a fixed charge is made each month on what you owe — which can work out fairly pricey if you let your debt run for a long time. It's generally more expensive to get a cash withdrawal.
● Other points:
You can't get tax relief on the interest you pay on a credit card debt, no matter what you spent the money on.
Diners Club and American Express don't work the same way as Access, Barclaycard or Trustcard; you're supposed to pay the full amount you owe each month.
A number of shops and department stores have recently started issuing their own credit cards (▷ Shop accounts, p. 166).

Verdict
Convenient and flexible. Cheap if you repay within a few months and don't borrow cash, but quite expensive if you let the debt run.

Revolving loan
Some banks and finance companies offer revolving loans, which work much the same way as shop budget accounts (▷ p. 166). but you can spend the money where you like. You agree to make a regular monthly payment (£10, say) into a special account, and in return you can draw out up to a multiple of that amount (30 times it, say). There may be a minimum monthly payment and a maximum amount you can borrow (say £1,000).
● For how long?
Lasts indefinitely. You can close the account at any time by stopping your payments and paying off what you owe (or withdrawing your money if you're in credit).
● For what purpose? Anything you like.
● Security required? No.
● Cost
Interest is normally worked out on what you owe each day. Finance companies generally quote a monthly rate, while banks quote an annual rate. The rates work out somewhat higher than on overdrafts or personal loans, and could change during the term of your loan. Some lenders pay you interest when your account is in credit.
Remember that you're obliged to keep paying even when you don't owe anthing (unless you close the account). This can effectively increase the cost of your borrowing quite considerably.

Verdict
A credit card or an overdraft would be more flexible (and could be cheaper).

Insurance policy loan
If you have a life insurance policy with a high enough cash-in value, you can apply to the company to borrow money on the strength of it. Most insurance companies give loans against their *endowment* and *whole life* policies. And a few give them against unit-linked policies too. But you can't normally borrow against *home service* (*industrial*) policies.
If you get a loan you just pay interest on it; the amount you borrow is deducted from the proceeds of the policy when it comes to an end.
● How much can you borrow?
Most companies will lend up to 90 per cent of the current cash-in value (less with unit-linked policies).
● For how long?
The loan normally runs until the end of the policy, but you can pay it off earlier.
● For what purpose? Any. The companies don't normally ask.
● Security required?
Yes – you deposit the policy with the company.
● Cost
There are normally no charges apart from interest – which may vary from time to time. Interest rates tend to be lower than for an overdraft, say. As you're only paying interest, the actual amount you pay out (each month or year, say) is low too.
● Other points
If the cash-in value of your policy increases you may be able to borrow more after a year or two, if the insurance company agrees.

Verdict
A cheap way of borrowing. But don't take out life insurance just to get a cheap loan.

Finance company personal loans
These work in much the same way as personal loans from a bank. You can say how quickly you want to pay the loan off (though there may be a minimum monthly payment) and you agree this and the amount of your monthly payments at the outset. Interest is included in the payments and, with most companies, the rate of interest is fixed for the whole period of the loan.
● How much can you borrow?
From £100 up to £5,000 (often more).
● For how long?
Generally up to 5 years – but perhaps less for smaller amounts.
● For what purpose?
No restrictions, but the company will almost certainly want to know.
● Security required?
Not normally. But some loans are in fact *second mortgages* on your home (▷ opposite).
● Cost
The cost is somewhat higher than for bank loans – but there's no arrangement fee.
● Other points
Application forms for these loans tend to ask for information about your home, job, income, bank, outgoings and other commitments – and the company may ask for references about you from the people you name.
Insurance policies sometimes offered with the loans (covering repayments if you're off work through sickness, say) can be very expensive. Check elsewhere before you take out the cover.

Verdict ·
Rather expensive. Try your bank first.

Increasing your mortgage
If you own your own home and have a mortgage with a building society or local authority, you may be able to increase the amount of your mortgage to pay for any improvements or repairs you want to carry out. The society or authority will probably want details of what you intend to do – you'll probably have to send plans and builder's estimates with your application. They may want to revalue your home before agreeing to give you a loan (and you'll have to pay for this, whether or not you get a loan).
● How much can you borrow?
You may be able to borrow the full cost of the improvements, as long as the amount, added to your mortgage, doesn't come to more than a certain percentage (80 per cent, say) of the lender's estimate of the value of your home when the improvements are completed.
● For how long?
The further advance is normally repaid over the remaining period of your mortgage – but the society may consider extending the whole mortgage by a few years, to reduce your monthly payments.
● For what purpose?
Most improvements to your home, though many societies won't lend for redecoration only, or for expensive luxuries like swimming pools. You may also be able to borrow money in this way to buy the freehold of a leasehold house, or to buy the share of the home owned by your separated or divorced husband or wife.
● Security required?
Yes – your home.
● Cost
Most societies charge for revaluing your home (unless they've valued it very recently) and there'll be the lender's solicitor's fee to pay. These may total around £40 for a £4,000 loan. The interest rate will be the same as for your mortgage. Because the loan is likely to be spread over a long period, the actual monthly payments will be relatively low. And you'll usually get tax relief on the interest you pay (▷ p. 206).
You may have to increase the cover given by any life insurance policy linked to your mortgage – an endowment policy if you have an endowment morgtgage, a mortgage protection policy if you have a repayment mortgage. And don't forget that improving your home is likely to mean you'll need more house buildings insurance cover (▷ pp. 84–9).

Verdict
Normally the cheapest way of paying for home improvements. But not worth it for small amounts, as the costs of setting up the loan outweigh the advantage of low interest rates.

Bridging loan
For details ▷ p. 75.

Second mortgage

A second mortgage is a loan which, though not used to buy your home, is made against the security of part of the value of your home. So if your home is currently worth a lot more than you owe on any first mortgage, you may be able to get a second morgage from a bank, finance company or insurance company.

Apart from being secured on your home in this way, a second mortgage is likely to be very much like a bank ordinary loan, a bank personal loan or a finance company personal loan. Although you may be charged a slightly lower rate of interest on one of these loans if it's a second mortgage — because of the security you're providing — it may be more complicated and more expensive to arrange (there may, for example, be legal costs and a valuation fee).

● How much?
Most banks and companies don't fix a maximum loan, but they're not likely to lend more than they think you can pay back, and may not let the loan *plus* any other mortgage come to more than a certain percentage (90 per cent, say) of the estimated value of your home.

● For how long?
Generally up to 7 or 10 years — less if you're borrowing under £10,000.

● For what purpose?
No restriction, but the company will want to know.

● Security required
Yes — your home.

● Cost
Interest charges work out about the same as for an overdraft (for a bank second mortgage) or finance company personal loan (if you go to a finance company).

● Other points
If the loan is for home improvements, you may be able to get tax relief on the interest you pay (▷ p. 206). If you already have a mortgage, try asking the lender for an additional loan first.

If you've got an endowment mortgage, you could ask your insurance company to consider giving you a second mortgage. Though the interest rate would be lower than a bank or finance company, you'd probably have to take out another endowment policy too.

A second mortgage may have to be paid off if you sell your house; so make sure that should you want to pay off the loan early, the terms are reasonable.

If you can't keep up the payments, your home might have to be sold to pay off the loan.

Verdict
Can be useful for borrowing large amounts. Try your bank before a finance company or mortgage broker.

HP

The term HP is often used to cover three different types of credit, all normally arranged by the person who sells you the goods — hire purchase, credit sale and conditional sale. Finance company personal loans may also be thought to be HP, as they are often offered with specific purchases. But there are important differences between all these.

Hire purchase

With hire-purchase agreements, you don't actually own the goods until you've finished paying for them. Until that time — when you also have to make a payment (£3, say) for the 'option' to purchase — you are, technically, *hiring* them, either from the retailer or (more likely) from a finance company which has bought them from the retailer. So you can't sell the goods until you've paid the full HP price.

● How much can you borrow?
Normally the value of the goods you're buying less a deposit — which may be controlled by government regulations.

● For how long?
You normally pay in monthly instalments for periods of up to 3 years.

● For what purpose?
For anything on which HP is offered. It's not normally available on things which have a low resale value (like clothes).

● Security required?
As the things you're buying belong to the shop or finance company, they can repossess them if you don't pay up, though once you've paid a third of the HP price (including the deposit) they can do so only with a court order (so long as the HP price is £5,000 or less).

● Cost
Varies widely, from 'free' HP to an APR of over 60 per cent. And with 'free' credit you may be missing out on substantial discounts (▷ p. 208).

● Other points
As you're technically hiring the goods, you have the right to end the agreement and return the goods but you'll have to pay any overdue instalments — and if you haven't paid half the total price you might have to make up the difference. What's more, if you haven't looked after the goods properly, you'll have to pay compensation to the lender (or put the goods right).

If the shop or finance company points out any defects in the things you're buying *and* the defects are stated in the HP agreement, you can't return the goods, and the lender can escape any responsibility for these defects. The same applies if the goods are stated as being second-hand.

Verdict
Readily available but often expensive. Shop around and check on APR. Often cheaper to borrow the money and pay cash.

Credit sale

Credit sale may seem much like HP, because the shop normally arranges for you to pay for what you're buying by instalments. But the goods are yours from the start, so you can't send them back just because you've changed your mind, and the lender can't repossess them if you don't keep up the payments. Even so, the agreement may say that if you sell the goods before you have paid in full, you have to pay all future instalments right away — though you'd normally get some reduction in the interest charged if you repaid early.

Conditional sale

With conditional sale, the seller owns the goods until you have fulfilled certain conditions — in particular you must have paid all the instalments. Apart from the fact that you're not technically hiring the goods (the seller is letting you use them while you pay) and so there is no 'option' to purchase, the terms are much the same as for hire purchase.

Moneylenders and credit brokers

Moneylenders and credit brokers may lend their own money, but more often they are brokers who arrange loans and second mortgages from other lenders — such as finance companies or merchant banks. They may charge for finding you a loan, and may get commission from the lender.

Most of these lenders are quite choosy who they lend money to and they'll probably want to know what you want it for. They'll normally want a lot of information about your home, job, income, bank, your other commitments; they may ask for references about you from people you name; and they may want to visit you in your home.

● How much can you borrow?
Generally up to £1,000, though they may be able to arrange larger loans (if you mortgage your home, say).

● For how long?
Anything from a few days to a few years — longer for larger amounts.

● For what purpose?
Normally no restrictions.

● Security required?
Not for smaller amounts (up to £1,000, say). Larger loans will generally be easier to get and slightly cheaper if you provide security.

● Cost
Interest rates and charges vary widely.

● Other points
Make sure you know all the terms of the deal and that the APR is filled in on the contract *before* you sign; and check what happens if you repay early.

Verdict
Try other sources first.

Shop accounts

Many shops run credit accounts of various types.

With a *monthly account* you get a monthly statement and have to pay off the full amount you owe each month. With some shops, interest may be charged if you break the rules and don't pay up on time.

With an *option account* you get a monthly statement and can choose to pay off all your debt, or just part of it (there's usually a minimum payment of £5 or 5 per cent of what you owe, whichever is more). You're charged interest on the amount outstanding when your statement is issued.

With a *budget account* you agree to pay a certain amount (£10, say) each month — but there's nothing to stop you paying more some months (to reduce or pay off what you owe). You're allowed to borrow up to some multiple of your agreed monthly payment (24 times it, say). The minimum regular payment is generally £5 — and there may be a set maximum.

Many chain stores issue their own plastic identity cards to people who have one of these accounts.

● How much?
Usually no limit on monthly accounts and option accounts. With budget accounts the limit is the multiple of your monthly payment.

● For how long?
Option accounts and budget accounts can run indefinitely — or you can pay them off at any time.

● For what purpose?
Any of the goods or services available in that shop. But some shops have restrictions on the type of purchase or amount you can spend.

● Security required?
No.

● Cost
Monthly accounts and option accounts cost nothing if you pay off the whole of what you owe each month. But if you pay only the minimum payment each month it can work out pricey. And a budget account could effectively cost even more if you let it get into credit — only a few pay you interest when this happens.

● Other points
With some budget accounts, you get a statement only at 3- or 4-monthly intervals — so you could lose track of how much you owe.

Verdict
Don't shop at a pricey store just because you have a credit account there. An option account is more flexible than a budget account.

Trading checks and vouchers

You buy a check from a trading check company and pay for it in instalments — usually collected by an agent who calls at your home once a week. You can use the check to buy things at any of a long list of shops.
Some shops issue their own trading checks for use only in shops in their group. *Paybonds* work in a similar way but are generally cheaper (and available only in the Midlands).

● How much?
Most checks are for £30 or less, vouchers for up to £500.

● For how long?
With checks, you normally make 21 weekly payments, each of $\frac{1}{20}$ of the face value of the cheque. But long-term vouchers are usually paid off over 1 2 or 3 years.

● For what purpose?
For buying anything from the shops on the list you get. This can range from bootlaces to such things as holidays and car insurance.

● Security required?
No. But if you haven't had a check before, you'll be asked lots of questions about your finances and may have to provide references.

● Cost
Varies according to the exact terms. APR is normally very high (somewhat less for long-term vouchers).

● Other points
If you don't spend all the check almost straight away, you're paying the same amount of interest for less credit — so the APR can be much higher.

The shops on the company's list may not be the cheapest.

Verdict
Can be very expensive — try to borrow elsewhere first. Vouchers are cheaper than checks.

Mail order catalogues

Mail order catalogues offer a wide range of goods, nearly all available on credit. Most companies operate through local part-time agents. You choose what you want sign the forms which the agent fills up and sends off, and you can normally pay in equal instalments over 20 weeks — longer for higher amounts. With most companies, the credit price is the same as the cash price — so the credit is 'free'.

● Cost
For some things, mail order prices compete quite well with shop prices. But for others it may work out more expensive than buying at a good value for money shop with a credit card.

Verdict
May be worth it if you can't get to the shops easily. May be worth becoming a mail-order agent — you get a commission on sales, including to yourself.

PART FIVE

The State and you

20 Income tax

One way the government raises money is by taxing people's money and possessions – through income tax, capital gains tax (CGT), and capital transfer tax (CTT), for example. We deal with CGT in chapter 18, p. 195, and with CTT in chapter 15, pp. 168–73. In this chapter we concentrate on how much *income tax* you have to pay.

Income tax is a tax on income from earnings, pensions, investments and so on. But you aren't likely to have to pay tax on the whole of your income: part of it is likely to be free of tax because you can:

● claim *outgoings* – the taxman's term for certain payments you have to make, such as mortgage interest and expenses in your job

● claim *allowances* – what you get for, say, being married, looking after children, supporting a needy relative, and so on. Broadly, this is how it works:

All your income is added together to arrive at your **gross income**	say, £5,500
From this you deduct your **outgoings**	say, £924
This leaves what the taxman calls your **'total income'**	£4,576
From this you deduct **allowances**	say, £1,815
This leaves your **taxable income**	£2,761

What you pay in income tax is based on your *taxable income* for a 12-month period from 6 April of one year to 5 April of the next. This is known as a *tax year* – for example, the period from 6 April 1980 to 5 April 1981 is the 80/81 tax year.

What you pay in income tax depends not just on how much taxable income you have, but also on the rates of tax and rules that apply for that tax year.

Tax law and tax changes

Each year, usually in March or April, the Chancellor of the Exchequer makes his main *Budget speech*, proposing the rates of tax and amounts of allowances for the coming tax year, and any changes he wants to make in tax law.

These proposals are set out in detail in a *Finance Bill*. They are then discussed in Parliament and may be amended before becoming law as a *Finance Act*.

In recent years, the Chancellor has tended to propose further tax changes during the tax year – in *mini-Budgets*.

In the rest of this chapter we give the tax rules and rates that applied in the 80/81 tax year. For more details, and information on changes in the rules, see the *Money Which? Tax Saving Guide*, published in March each year.

Rates of income tax

Tax is charged at increasing rates on successive slices of your taxable income. Fig. 20.1 shows the tax rates for the 80/81 tax year.

The first £11,250 was taxed at the *basic rate* of 30 per cent. Anything more than £11,250 of taxable income was taxed at a series of higher rates (ranging from 40 per cent to 60 per cent).

Investment income surcharge

If you have more than a certain amount of investment income, you will have to pay additional tax – called the *investment income surcharge*. For the 80/81 tax year, the surcharge is 15 per cent on investment income over £5,500 (after deducting certain outgoings but not normally any allowances).

Figure 20.1   Tax rates for 1980/81

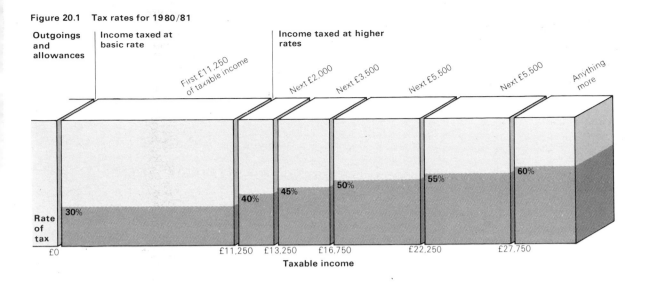

| Outgoings and allowances | Income taxed at basic rate | | Income taxed at higher rates | | | |

First £11,250 of taxable income · Next £2,000 · Next £3,500 · Next £5,500 · Next £5,500 · Anything more

Rate of tax: 30% 40% 45% 50% 55% 60%

£0 · £11,250 · £13,250 · £16,750 · £22,250 · £27,750

Taxable income

How tax is collected

If you get wages, or a salary, or a pension from an ex-employer, the tax is collected under the PAYE system. If you pay tax in this way, the PAYE system may also be used to collect tax on income not taxed before you get it (like bank deposit account interest, small-scale freelance income and, currently, State retirement pension). It may also be used to collect any higher rate tax due on investment income which was taxed only at the basic rate before you got it (like dividends and building society interest). For more details on PAYE ▷ p. 10.

If you have any sources of income not taxed under PAYE, the taxman may send you what is known as a *Notice of Assessment*. This is the form the taxman uses to tell you how the tax you have to pay on your income from different sources has been worked out. It states the type and amount of income being taxed, deductions for allowances and outgoings, if any, and the amount of tax payable.

Most people taxed under PAYE will not be sent a Notice of Assessment, but those with high earnings or complicated circumstances may be sent what the taxman calls a *Schedule E Notice of Assessment*. A *Schedule A and D Notice of Assessment* – normally accompanied by a demand to pay any tax due – is sent to the self-employed, to those who rent out property, or to those who have investment income on which they pay a higher rate of tax or the investment income surcharge.

If you get a Notice of Assessment, check it at once – and appeal against it within 30 days of the date on it if you don't agree with it (▷ p. 224 for more details).

If you have a number of sources of income, you may get several Notices of Assessment (eg one for your earnings, one for your income from renting) – check each one carefully.

When is tax due, and which year's income is your tax bill based on?

For most people, who work for an employer, tax for any tax year is based on their earnings for that year – called *current year basis*. The tax is collected under PAYE – your employer deducts the tax due from your earnings before he pays you. But with some types of income, your tax bill for a particular tax year *won't* be based on the income you got in that tax year. For example, with interest paid to you without tax being deducted (like interest on a bank deposit account) the tax for any tax year will normally be based on your income in the previous tax year – called *preceding year basis*. This also applies with income from being self-employed. With this type of income, you normally pay the tax that's due in one, or two, lump sums on fixed dates in the year. See Fig. 20.2, p. 218, for when tax is due.

With some investment income (eg share dividends, interest on local authority loans) tax is deducted (or deemed to have been deducted) before the income is paid to you. If you owe further tax on this income, it will be collected later – again, ▷ Fig. 20.2 for details.

Tax schedules
Tax law divides income into a number of different categories called *schedules*, which may in turn be subdivided into *cases*. The taxman may refer to these in correspondence with you. The schedules most likely to concern you are:
● Schedule A: income from unfurnished property
● Schedule D: *cases I and II* income from being self-employed; *case III* income from investments and annuities; *cases IV and V* income from abroad; *case VI* miscellaneous income (including investment income from furnished accommodation and income from occasional freelance work)
● Schedule E: income from a job where you are employed or are a director of a company. Also most pensions.

How the taxman knows what to charge

Many taxpayers receive an annual Tax Return on which they have to fill in details of their income, outgoings and allowances. The taxman uses this information to work out their tax bill.

If you have straightforward tax affairs (eg you are single, wth no claim to allowances or outgoings other than the single person's allowance and your only income comes from a job in which you are taxed under PAYE) you may only be sent a Tax Return every few years. However, if you get income that isn't taxed, or not fully taxed, before you get it the onus is on you to obtain a Tax Return from the taxman if you have not automatically been sent one. It is certainly in your interest to ask for one if there are allowances or outgoings you could claim but have not.

The Tax Return

There are several different types of Tax Return including:

- form 11P – intended for people with above-average incomes who work for an employer
- form P1 – sent to those with fairly simple tax affairs
- form 11 – in the main for the self-employed.

Whichever type of form you receive, you should complete it as soon as possible, take a copy for your own records (there's space on the Inland Revenue notes which come with your Return), and send the original to the taxman.

One confusing point about the Tax Return is that, although its heading indicates one tax year, it does in fact cover two years. In the 1981/82 Tax Return, for example, you must enter your income, outgoings and capital gains, for the *past* year ending on 5 April 81, but the personal allowances you claim will be for the year *ahead*, ending on 5 April 82.

Whether or not a married woman has to complete her own Tax Return depends on the circumstances. If husband and wife are living together, the general rule is that the wife's income – and any claim she may have for outgoings and allowances – must be shown on her husband's form. Separate columns are shown for 'Self' and 'Wife'.

There are two exceptions. If husband and wife get married *during* a tax year (ie after 6 April) each will have to complete a separate Tax Return for the first tax year of their marriage (assuming they get sent a Return). Also where either husband or wife has claimed separate assessment ($\triangleright$ p. 128) each may if they choose complete their own Tax Return.

A women who is single has, of course, to fill in her own form. And so do women who are separated from their husbands (unless it is only a temporary separation) or divorced or widowed. She should enter her income and outgoings in the 'Self' column, leaving the 'Wife' column blank.

Figure 20.2 Tax calendar for 80/81 tax year

Type of income	1980/81 tax bill normally based on income you get between :	Date tax due (1)
Wages or salary	6 April 80 and 5 April 81	Tax at basic and higher rates deducted when you get the income (ie monthly, weekly) under PAYE
Investment income already taxed (eg interest on loans to local authorities). Share dividends and unit trust distributions. Building society interest	6 April 80 and 5 April 81	Tax at basic rate deducted (or deemed to have been deducted) before you get the income. If you pay tax at higher rates, or the investment income surcharge, this extra tax due on 1 December 81 (2)
Investment income not taxed before you get it (eg interest from bank deposit account)	6 April 79 and 5 April 80(3)	Tax at basic and higher rates, and investment income surcharge, due on 1 January 81 (2)
Rents which count as investment income(4)	6 April 80 and 5 April 81	Tax at basic and higher rates, and investment income surcharge, due on 1 January 81 (2)
Profits from being self-employed	For your accounting year ending between 6 April 79 and 5 April 80(3)	Tax at basic and higher rates normally paid in two equal lump sums: 1 January 81 (2) and 1 July 81

1. If most of your income comes from employment, any tax due on income from other sources – provided it doesn't vary much from year to year – may in practice be deducted under PAYE from your earnings, so you will not be paying tax at the dates shown in this column.
2. Or 30 days after the date on the Notice of Assessment, whichever is later.
3. But special rules apply to early and closing years.
4. For how rents from property are taxed $\triangleright$ p. 219.

Income

Different types of income are taxed in different ways – we give brief details of the most important types of income below.

Pay from your job

You will be taxed on your earnings from your job under PAYE. Your tax bill for a tax year is based on your earnings for the same tax year (*current year basis*). Most people can get details of the earnings on which they pay tax from their P60 form (given to them by their employer at the end of each tax year).

Certain *fringe benefits* you get (eg a company car, a cheap loan) may be taxed too. The taxman has special, fairly complicated rules about how fringe benefits are valued for tax purposes.

Pay when you leave a job

Earnings your employer owes you, paid when (or after) you leave your job – eg normal wages, pay in lieu of holiday, and commission – are taxed in the normal way.

But certain payments are generally tax-free – eg, pay in lieu of notice and redundancy money up to a certain limit (£10,000 in the 80/81 tax year) or lump sum payments for an injury which ended your job (▷ p. 23 for more details).

Social security benefits

Most social security benefits are tax-free under the present rules. The taxable ones currently are: widow's or widowed mother's allowance, industrial death benefit for widows, invalid care allowance, mobility allowance, and invalidity allowance paid to pensioners. The Government has announced that from April 82 (at the earliest) it intends to tax sickness, unemployment and invalidity benefit and supplementary benefits paid to the unemployed or strikers, maternity allowance and industrial injury benefit.

Pensions

Most pensions are taxable, and count as earned income. A *State retirement pension*, a *widow's pension*, or an *old person's pension* (paid to the over-80s) is currently paid without tax being deducted (from April 82, it's proposed that these pensions should be taxed before being paid). A *pension from your former employer* generally has tax deducted from it under PAYE (▷ p. 44).

Certain pensions are tax-free – the list includes social security supplementary pensions, industrial injuries disablement pensions, war widow's pension and war disablement pension.

Rent you get

If the accommodation you let out is furnished *and* the rent covers services such as cleaning, laundry and meals, the rent may be treated as earned income. You will be taxed on the rent *less* expenses (like the cost of the services you provide, rates, repairs and decorations) and *less* an allowance for depreciation of any fixtures, furniture and furnishings. The income will be taxed in the same way as income from being self-employed (▷ p. 33).

If the accommodation is unfurnished, or if it is furnished but you don't provide services, the rent will be treated as investment income – which may mean more tax. You can deduct expenses from the rent, and something for depreciation of any fixtures, furniture and furnishings.

Interest not taxed before you get it

Examples of interest paid in this way are:
- National Savings Bank (NSB) ordinary accounts (but first £70 of interest is tax-free)
- Trustee Savings Bank (TSB) savings accounts
- NSB and TSB investment accounts
- High-street bank deposit accounts
- British Government stocks bought on the National Savings Stock Register – eg through a Post Office.

Your tax bill for the 80/81 tax year will normally be based on the amount of interest you got in the 79/80 tax year (*preceding year basis*). Special rules apply to the first 3 and last 2 years in which you get interest of this type from each source – check with the taxman for details.

Building society interest

Building societies pay tax to the Inland Revenue before they pay out interest.

Because tax has already been paid in this way, you don't have to pay basic rate tax on the interest you get from a building society. But if you aren't liable to tax you can't claim back the tax the building society has already paid.

If you pay tax at higher rates, or the investment income surcharge, you will have to pay extra tax. When working out your tax bill, the taxman includes the grossed-up amount of building society interest as part of your income – ie the amount which after deduction of tax at the basic rate would leave the interest you actually got. To work

Checklist of tax-free income

- many grants and scholarships for education
- grants for improving your home (▷ p. 82)
- rate rebates, rent rebates and allowances
- tax-free pensions (▷ left)
- tax-free social security benefits (▷ left for those which are taxable)
- annuities and pension addition paid to people holding certain gallantry awards – eg Victoria Cross, George Cross, Distinguished Conduct Medal
- luncheon vouchers up to 15p a working day
- gifts, eg from generous relatives
- personal gifts from employer
- redundancy money and certain other payments when you leave a job – up to £10,000 (▷ p. 23)
- proceeds from Save-As-You-Earn, National Savings Certificates, Ulster Savings Certificates, premium bond prizes
- final 4 per cent bonus from British Savings Bonds
- first £70 interest from ordinary account with National Savings Bank
- part of the income from many annuities
- income from family income benefit life insurance policy (▷ p. 140)
- betting winnings, lottery prizes
- strike pay
- interest on a tax rebate (▷ p. 225)

out the grossed-up amount, do the following sum: divide the interest you get by

$$\frac{100 - \text{basic rate of tax}}{100}$$

ie for the 80/81 tax year, divide by

$$\frac{100 - 30}{100} = 0.7$$

You are liable to tax on this grossed-up amount at the highest rate of tax you pay (including the investment income surcharge if you pay it). But you are treated as having already paid basic rate tax on the interest – so you only have to hand over the difference.

Income from stocks, shares, etc

Share dividends from UK companies (and distributions from unit trusts) are accompanied by what is called a *tax credit* – which is set against the tax you have to pay on this income.

Your gross (before-tax) income is taken to be the dividend *plus* the tax credit. The amount of tax credit for the 80/81 tax year is 30 per cent of this gross income. So, for example, if the dividend is £70, the tax credit is £30 and your gross income is £100.

A similar system applies with interest or other investment income taxed at the basic rate before being paid to you (eg interest on a local authority loan, or interest from most British government stocks bought through a stockbroker). You get a *tax voucher* or other document saying how much tax has been deducted, and the gross income from the investment is interest you get paid *plus* the tax deducted during the year.

If you get income of this type and don't pay tax you may well be able to claim tax back from the taxman. If you are liable for basic rate tax (but no more) on the whole of your income of this type, your liability for tax on this income is automatically met by the tax credited or deducted – so you have nothing more to pay.

If you pay tax at higher rates, or the investment income surcharge, you will have to pay extra tax.

Allowances

Here we describe briefly the allowances (sometimes called reliefs) that can be claimed. In most cases, an allowance of, say, £100 means that you are let off paying tax on the most heavily taxed £100 of your income. But allowances won't normally reduce your investment income surcharge bill.

When you are filling in your 81/82 Tax Return you are claiming allowances for the coming tax year – from 6 April 81 to 5 April 82. In Fig. 20.3, p. 222 we give the amounts of these allowances for the 80/81 tax year (which you will need for checking your last year's tax bill). Any changes for 81/82 will be announced in the 1981 Budget speech.

Single, married, elderly

Single taxpayers get the *single man's or woman's personal allowance* (unless they qualify for age allowance – ▷ below. A 'single' person includes a widow; a widower; someone who is divorced; a woman in the year she gets married (unless she gets married on 6 April); a husband and wife who are separated, if the husband isn't entitled to the married man's personal allowance; and a couple who have chosen to have the wife's earnings taxed separately (▷ p. 127).

A married man will get the full *married man's personal allowance* if he is already married at the start of a tax year, or if he gets married between 6 April and 5 May of that year. He gets a reduced amount for that tax year if he gets married on 6 May or later (▷ p. 128). If the husband or wife is 64 or over before the start of the tax year, the husband may qualify for *age allowance*.

Wife's earned income allowance can be claimed by any woman who was married at the beginning of the tax year, who has earned income of her own (from a job, business or pension), and who has not chosen to have these earnings taxed separately. This allowance can be claimed only against the wife's *earned* income.

Elderly people may benefit by claiming *age allowance* rather than single person's or married man's allowance. Full age allowance can be claimed by anyone who is 64 or over before the first day of the tax year (ie 6 April), and whose 'total income' (▷ p. 216) for the tax year is not more than a certain amount – for 80/81, this was £5,900.

Your age allowance is reduced by £2 for each £3 by which your 'total income' exceeds £5,900. But note that the allowance will not be reduced below the amount of the ordinary single person's or married man's allowance – so you can't lose by claiming.

People with special needs

Dependent relative allowance is for people who help needy relatives. You can claim it if, at your own expense, you look after or help to support:
● any of your or your wife's relatives who cannot look after themselves because of infirmity or old age ('old' means being 64 or over before the start of the tax year)
● your mother or mother-in-law (whether or not she is old or infirm) if she is a widow, separated or divorced.

You can get an allowance for each dependent relative you support.

To get the full allowance the relative must live with you, or you must contribute at least £75 a year towards his or her keep. If you pay out less, your allowance will be reduced to the amount of your contribution. In addition, the relative's 'total income' (▷ p. 216) must not be more than the single person's basic State retirement pension – for the 80/81 tax year, this was £1,284. If the relative's 'total income' is more than this, your allowance is reduced by £1 for each £1 of income over the limit.

Widow's bereavement allowance can be claimed by a widow in the year her husband dies. The amount depends on when in the tax year her husband dies – ▷ p. 130.

A housekeeper allowance can be claimed by a widow or widower who has a relative or employee *living in the home* and acting as housekeeper. However, if your housekeeper is a relative, you cannot claim this allowance if someone else is claiming any other allowance for them (including married man's personal allowance). A widower can't claim it for the tax year his wife dies. And you can't claim housekeeper allowance at all if you are claiming the additional personal allowance for children (▷ right).

Son's or daughter's services allowance can be claimed by anyone who is 64 or over before the start of the tax year or infirm (or whose wife is) *and* has to depend on the services of a son or daughter who they live with and maintain. A married man, even if 64 or infirm will not normally get the allowance if his wife is under 64 and in good health.

Blind person's allowance can be claimed by anyone registered with a local authority as a blind person. You get the full allowance even if you're registered as blind for only part of the year. Note that registration as *blind* doesn't mean that you have to be totally without sight.

Anyone who gets tax-free blindness disability payments has their allowance reduced by the amount of these payments.

Children

Child allowances are being phased out, but in two exceptional circumstances it is still possible to get one.

You can claim child allowance for the 80/81 and 81/82 tax years, but not after, if *all* the following apply:
● your child lives outside the UK for the whole of the tax year (apart from not more than 30 days visiting the UK). But to qualify, the child must *not* live in one of a number of specified countries – ie Australia, Austria, Canada, Finland, Gibraltar, Israel, Norway, Spain, Sweden, Jersey, Isle of Man, New Zealand, and the countries of the EEC
● the child will be under 19 at the end of the tax year
● you are not eligible for child benefit for the tax year.

You can claim child allowance for a child who is a student for the 80/81 tax year, but not after, if *all* the following apply:
● the child was in full-time education on 31 December 76
● on that date, he or she was either 19 or over, or on an 'advanced' course
● he or she follows a full-time course in the academic year which starts during the appropriate tax year, and *either* gets no grant at all from public funds, *or* gets a grant which is liable to be reduced on account of the parents' income, but isn't (because the parents' income is too low).

Additional personal allowance for children is intended for people who have no husband or wife to help with bringing up children. A single person, or a married man whose wife is totally incapacitated for the whole tax year, is entitled to this allowance. For who the taxman counts as 'single' ▷ opposite page – but note that a husband and wife who have chosen to have the wife's earnings taxed separately *can't* claim this allowance.

You can claim this allowance if you have living with you a child who is your legitimate (or legitimated) child, stepchild, or legally adopted child, or any other child you maintain at your own expense. If the child is 16 or over at the start of the tax year, you get it only if the child is in full-time education or training.

Personal pension payments

You can get tax relief if you are self-employed – or have a job where you are not a member of your employer's pension scheme – and pay premiums to a personal pension scheme (or contribute to a trust scheme).

Personal pension payments are treated for tax purposes as *outgoings*, and so are deducted from your gross income in order to arrive at your 'total income' (▷ p. 216). But they can be set off only against the earnings to which they relate.

You get tax relief on the full amount of your payments, up to a maximum of $17\frac{1}{2}$ per cent of your own *non-pensionable earnings* for the year. Non-pensionable earnings are your earnings from being self-employed, or your earnings from jobs in which you don't belong to a pension scheme. If you don't use up your full allowance one year, you can carry it forward to a future year, and make payments over the normal limit. Note that if the main or sole object of the scheme is to give a pension or lump sum to your widow, widower or dependants, you can't get tax relief on the amount by which your payments exceed 5 per cent of your non-pensionable earnings, or £1,000, whichever is less.

Death and superannuation benefits
You get tax relief on the part of your trade union subscription which goes towards superannuation (ie pension), funeral or life insurance benefits. And with certain combined sickness and life insurance policies issued by friendly societies, you get tax relief on the part of your premiums that covers the life insurance.

You may also get some tax relief on compulsory payments you have to make (eg by the terms of your job) for an annuity which pays out on your death to your wife and children.

With trade union subscriptions, or this type of friendly society premiums, you get tax relief at your top rate of tax on half the amount you pay towards superannuation, funeral or life insurance benefits. With compulsory annuities, how much tax relief you get depends on your income – again, check with your employer.

Life insurance
Your insurance company automatically gives you the tax relief you are entitled to by reducing your life insurance premiums. For the 80/81 tax year, the premium subsidy is $17\frac{1}{2}$ per cent of your premiums (15 per cent for 81/82).

You get the benefit of this $17\frac{1}{2}$ per cent subsidy even if you don't pay tax. And you get the subsidy on premiums you pay on your husband's or wife's life, or on your joint lives, even if you choose to have the wife's earnings taxed separately. But you don't get any subsidy on premiums in excess of £1,500 a year – or $\frac{1}{6}$ of your 'total income' ($\triangleright$ p. 216), if this is greater. A married couple won't get any subsidy on premiums in excess of £1,500 a year – or $\frac{1}{6}$ of their *joint* 'total income' if this is greater.

Figure 20.3   Allowances for 1980/81

Single man's or woman's personal allowance	£1,375
Married man's personal allowance	£2,145
Wife's earned income allowance	up to £1,375
Age allowance Single man or woman	up to £1,820
Married man	up to £2,895
Child allowance ($\triangleright$ p. 221) For each child, 16 or over on 6 April 80	£365
For each child, 11 or over but under 16 on 6 April 80	£335
For each younger child	£300
Additional personal allowance for children	£770
Housekeeper or person looking after children	£100
Dependent relative allowance Single woman (or wife who has earnings taxed separately)	£145
Other person claiming	£100
Widow's bereavement allowance	up to £770
Son's or daughter's services allowances	£55
Blind person's allowance	£180
Superannuation and death benefits	Commonly half the amount you pay towards superannuation, funeral, life insurance
Personal pension payments	What you pay, but not more than $17\frac{1}{2}$ per cent of non-pensionable earnings

Outgoings

With most *outgoings* (mortgage interest payments, for example), for each £ you pay out, you escape tax on the most heavily taxed £ of your income – including the investment income surcharge, if you pay it. With *expenses to do with your job* you can get tax relief only on your *earnings from that job* – so claiming these expenses can't reduce your investment income surcharge bill, say.

Expenses in your job

If you are an employee, and you pay for something to do with your job, you may be able to get tax relief on the amount you pay – but there are a number of conditions which have to be met.

The expense must be *necessary* for your job – and not simply necessary to you as an employee. For example, feeling you need a briefcase, say, to do your job properly wouldn't be enough. And you can only claim tax relief for the part of the expense which is *wholly* and *exclusively* to do with your job – so with a car, for example, it is only the business use which can be claimed.

The expense must be incurred *in carrying out your job*. For example, the cost of travelling to work will not be allowed – because you are not considered to start carrying out the duties of your job until you get there.

Expenses you should claim for – bearing all these conditions in mind – include:
● fees and subscriptions to professional societies relevant to your job, and which are recognized by the Inland Revenue
● cost of replacing, cleaning and repairing special protective clothing (eg overalls, boots) necessary for your job and which you are required to provide
● cost of reference books necessary for your job, which you are required to provide
● upkeep and replacement of tools, etc, which you are required to provide
● proportion of cost of running home if part of home is used exclusively for business, and you are required to work there
● travelling expenses (including hotel expenses) incurred strictly in the course of carrying out your job. Does not include cost of travel between home and work. Running cost of own car: whole cost if used *wholly* and *necessarily* for your job, proportion of cost if used privately as well
● reasonable hotel and meal expenses when travelling in the course of your job (as long as you keep up a permanent home).

You may have some expenses – such as travelling or entertaining expenses – where your employer has paid you back what you

spent. Employees earning at a certain rate (£8,500 a year or more in the 80/81 tax year), and directors (whatever they earn), may have to claim in their Tax Return for these expenses. This is because, for these people, the expenses may have been included in their income – and would be taxed, unless deducted as an outgoing.

Interest payments

You can get tax relief on the interest you pay on certain loans known as *qualifying loans* (▷ below). And, until 5 April 82, you can also get tax relief on some or all of the interest you pay on most other loans taken out before 27 March 74.
● Qualifying loans
Bank overdrafts and credit card debts – whatever the money is spent on – can't be qualifying loans; nor can any loan which has to be paid back within 12 months (unless the interest is paid in the UK to a bank, stockbroker or discount house).

For most people, the most important qualifying loan is likely to be a mortgage to buy (or improve in a permanent way) their only or main home. You can get tax relief on the interest you pay on up to £25,000 of such loans (married couples can have only the one £25,000 limit between them). For details of tax relief on different types of mortgage ▷ pp. 72–3.

Other loans which might count as qualifying ones include loans for:
● buying or improving (subject to your overall £25,000 limit) the only or main home of your former or separated wife or husband, and/or of a dependent relative
● buying or improving property you intend to rent out
● buying an annuity, if you are 65 or over, and the loan is secured on your only or main home (subject to a limit on that loan of £25,000)
● paying estate duty or capital transfer tax.

Covenants

A deed of covenant is a legally binding agreement under which one person promises to make a series of payments to another person or a charity. Payments you make under a covenant may qualify for tax relief at the basic rate and, from the 81/82 tax year, at higher rates if the covenant is to be to a charity – ▷ p. 129 for details.

Alimony and maintenance

You normally get tax relief on any enforceable payments you make, but not on voluntary payments (▷ p. 130 for details).

Self-employed? There are different rules about the expenses you can get tax relief on (▷ p. 33 for details).

Challenging the taxman

Here we tell you what you should do if:
- your PAYE code is wrong
- you've just had a tax bill you don't agree with
- you discover that, for years, you've not been claiming an allowance or outgoing you've been entitled to.

Step 1

Check that your first impression is correct. If necessary, use past *Money Which?* Tax Saving Guides to help you.

Step 2

Challenge the taxman if you find there really is an error. Depending on what's amiss you'll have to:
- ask to have your PAYE code changed
- appeal against a Notice of Assessment
- claim tax back.

If you and the taxman can't agree, you can take your case to the General or Special Commissioners – ▷ opposite. Be sure to keep copies of *all* your correspondence with the taxman. And if you talk to him over the phone, or discuss your tax problems at a local PAYE enquiry office, keep notes of what is said. When you contact the taxman, quote the tax reference number which is on all forms and letters you get from him.

Changing your PAYE code

If your circumstances change during the tax year – eg if you become entitled to a new allowance or outgoing – tell the taxman straight away and ask him to change your code.

If your PAYE code is not correct at the end of the tax year you will pay the wrong amount of tax under PAYE – and either have to claim a rebate, or be faced with more tax to pay, in a later year.

To get your code changed, write to the taxman straight away and tell him what change you want made – enclose your most recent Notice of Coding, if you've still got it.

How long it takes to get your new code depends on what changes you ask for, how busy your tax office is, and whether the taxman needs any more information from you. If you don't get your new code, or an acknowledgement, or some sort of request for information (eg a Tax Return) within a month, phone your tax office. If your tax office is a long-distance call away, you can instead ask your local PAYE enquiry office (address in phone book, under *Inland Revenue*) to contact your tax office.

Appealing to the taxman against a Notice of Assessment

If you think any of the figures on a Notice of Assessment sent to you are wrong, and to your disadvantage, appeal within 30 days of the date on it.

Note that if you appeal against a Schedule A and D Notice of Assessment you still have to pay the tax demanded – unless you also, within 30 days, apply for a postponement of part or all of the tax. Be particularly careful to appeal on time if the assessment is based on an estimate of your business profits for the year. If the estimate has been made because you have failed to provide information the taxman needs – eg your business accounts for the year – *and* if you don't appeal within 30 days, you won't normally be able to appeal later, even if your actual profits turn out to be much lower.

If you don't appeal within 30 days, a late appeal may, however, be accepted if you have got a good excuse – eg you were away on holiday when the assessment arrived.

But if you don't appeal, you can still claim tax back if you discover later that the assessment was wrong because you made a mistake in filling in your Tax Return – eg you forgot to enter an outgoing, or claim an allowance to which you were entitled.

If you receive a large tax bill which you can't afford to pay in one go, the taxman may agree, in cases of hardship, to let you pay off the tax you owe in monthly or weekly instalments. You'll probably have to pay interest on what you owe – ▷ right.

Note that if the taxman is after you for tax you owe due to a mistake on *his* part from tax years further back than the previous one, you don't have to pay it if your gross (before-tax) income is less than a certain amount (£4,000 a year from 7 November 1979). And you don't have to pay in full if your income is somewhat higher – ask your tax office for details. The mistake may have been, for example, that the taxman had overlooked part of your income which you had told him about.

Claiming tax back

You may have paid too much tax for a number of reasons. We look at the most important below.

Your PAYE code was too low

During the tax year you may, for example, have taken out a new or larger mortgage, or you may have started to look after a dependent relative for whom you can claim an allowance. Until your PAYE code is

Tax paid late
If you don't pay the tax when it's due, interest starts to be charged on what you owe, at a rate of 12 per cent a year (9 per cent for the period before 1 January 1980). You won't be asked to pay this interest unless it is over £30.

Tax overpaid
If you have paid too much tax, the taxman may have to pay *you* interest, at a rate of 12 per cent, tax-free (9 per cent for periods before 1 January 1980). He has to do so if the tax overpaid was more than £25. But your over-paid tax does not start earning interest until 12 months after the end of the tax year for which it is due, or until the end of the tax year in which you actually paid the tax – whichever is later.

adjusted you will have been paying too much tax ($\triangleright$ p. 10 for how the PAYE system works). If your code is increased before the end of the tax year, you'll get a repayment of tax through the PAYE system in the same tax year. But if your code number has not been increased by the end of the tax year, you'll have to claim a rebate from the taxman. You could ask the taxman for a Schedule E Notice of Assessment, which will show the amount of the overpayment. A refund should swiftly follow. For how to get your PAYE code changed $\triangleright$ opposite.

You had a gap between jobs
If you are employed and have a gap between leaving one job and taking up another, any tax refund will be paid to you by your new employer through the PAYE system, provided you had both jobs in the same tax year. If the gap overlaps into the next tax year, or you do not take up a new job at all, or you go abroad to work for another employer, send your form P45 ($\triangleright$ p. 12) to the taxman and ask for a repayment.

If you are out of work for more than 4 weeks, and you want your overpaid tax back before you start work again, apply to your tax office for a tax rebate (ask for form P50).

Error or mistake in past years
If you discover that you have been given insufficient allowances in past tax years or you have failed to claim outgoings you were entitled to, then, whether it is your or the taxman's mistake, you can claim a repayment. You can go back for all or any of the last 6 complete tax years. This means that if you find a mistake or something you failed to claim – and tell the taxman about it before, say, 6 April 81 – you can go right back to 6 April 74 with your claim for tax rebates. Send full details to the taxman.

You have income that is taxed before you get it
With many types of investment income (eg interest on local authority loans, alimony and maintenance payments, trust income) tax at the basic rate is deducted from the income before you get it. And you get tax credits with share dividends and unit trust distributions ($\triangleright$ p. 220). If you pay no tax, or should pay less tax than has already been deducted (plus any tax credits) you may well be able to claim a tax rebate. If you are in a situation like this (as many retired people may be) you will probably get a special Tax Claim Form (R40) instead of the normal Tax Return.

Fill it in and send it to your tax office with your tax vouchers (which give details of tax deducted and tax credits). You don't need to wait until the end of the tax year to do this – claim as soon as you have received all your investment income of this type. You can arrange to have repayments made in instalments during the year, rather than wait until the tax year ends.

If you have to claim tax back regularly and don't get form R40, ask your tax office to send it to you.

Appealing to the General or Special Commissioners
If you and the taxman cannot agree on what tax you should pay, you can appeal to either the General Commissioners or the Special Commissioners.

The General Commissioners are unpaid local people who hear appeals informally in your area. There is a paid clerk who gives them advice on tax laws. Special Commissioners are experts on tax and are paid. Unless you choose otherwise (or there's no choice – $\triangleright$ below), your case will go to the General Commissioners. You may want to consider the Special Commissioners instead if your case involves a fine point of law, but you would be wise to take professional advice on this. And you will have no choice in certain circumstances. For example, the Special Commissioners must consider your appeal if you have made a mistake filling in the *income* section of the Tax Return.

On the other hand, the General Commissioners must consider your case if:
● you are appealing against a PAYE code
● you are claiming tax back because you have failed to claim an allowance.

Note that in Northern Ireland there are no General Commissioners. Appeals can be taken to the County Court instead.

If your appeal is about a point of fact – eg what your business takings are – the Commissioners' decision is normally final, and you can't appeal against it. On a point of law (eg what expenses you are able to claim) the loser can appeal to the high court and so on up to the House of Lords. But note that there's no right of appeal to the high court if you're appealing against your PAYE code.

At the Commissioners' hearing, each party pays his own costs – so if you handle your own case, it will cost you nothing but your time. If the case is taken further, the loser has to pay – and the legal costs can be heavy.

2I Social security

Many people who could get social security benefits never claim them. Accurate figures on the number who could claim them but don't are hard to come by. But an estimate, using figures from government surveys of family spending, is that over a million people miss out on supplementary benefit alone. The same figures suggest that as many as 2 million people who could claim rate rebates, rent rebates or rent allowances fail to do so.

It isn't altogether surprising that benefits often fail to reach the people who need them. There's a bewildering array of benefits offered by various government departments and local authorities – more than 60 separate benefits are listed in the Department of Health and Social Security leaflet *Which benefit?* The rules about who qualifies for the different benefits – and the amounts payable – can be extremely complicated. Valiant efforts have been made to make many claim forms and explanatory leaflets simpler and easier to read, but the sheer complexity of the system makes this a Herculean task.

Much of the problem stems from the way in which the social security system grew up. Until the twentieth century, virtually the only publicly provided welfare scheme was the help for 'paupers' offered under the Elizabethan Poor Laws. Successive twentieth-century governments spliced on an old age pension, unemployment benefit, sickness benefit, widow's pension and so on. But as this was, by and large, done piecemeal, the resulting system was something of a hotch-potch.

The Beveridge Report, produced at the height of World War II as a blueprint for social security after the war, is often taken as the starting point of the modern Welfare State. Yet many of the features of the earlier social insurance system survived, while successive governments have added more benefits to the system or changed the rules laid down by Lord Beveridge in his report.

The present system is one nobody would deliberately have built up from scratch, but it would be difficult and expensive to rationalize it without cutting the amounts of benefits which some people now get. The end result is that it can be hard work sifting through all the information available to sort out whether or not you're getting all the benefits you can claim.

How this chapter is arranged

We have already described quite a few benefits elsewhere in this book – benefits for those off sick, unemployed, or bringing up children, for example. In this chapter, we give some general advice about how to get help and information about claiming benefits, how to appeal against an adverse decision on a benefit, and so on. And there are details of some benefits not mentioned elsewhere in the book. At the end of the chapter, we look in more detail at the National Insurance contribution conditions which have to be satisfied to claim many benefits.

We have gone into supplementary benefit in some detail in this chapter: this is the basic benefit designed to make sure that nobody has too little to live on, and therefore is important to a wide range of people with low incomes.

Opposite, there is a guide to where to turn in the book to find details of benefits which you might claim in a number of situations. When you use the checklist, be sure to look at *all* the possible situations which might apply to you.

Northern Ireland
Most benefits are the same as in the rest of the UK, but forms, leaflets, and where to go may be different. For details of benefits in Northern Ireland, get *Family benefits and pensions in N. Ireland* from the DHSS, Room 111, Dundonald House, Stormont, Belfast BT4 3SF.

Where you can find details of different benefits

How you qualify

Broadly, benefits fall into two categories: those which are *contributory*, and those which are *non-contributory*.

With *contributory* benefits, your National Insurance (NI) contribution record (or, occasionally, that of your husband or wife) determines whether or not you can get the benefit – and often how much you get. The rules about the amount and type of contributions vary according to the benefit. With some benefits, for example, only Class 1 NI contributions qualify – so that the self-employed (who pay Class 2 and, perhaps, Class 4 contributions) can't normally claim such benefits. And certain married women and widows who pay reduced rate NI contributions may not qualify for *any* of these benefits in their own right. For more details about NI contributions ▷ p. 235.

Non-contributory benefits do not depend on your NI contribution record. But you may have to meet *residence qualifications* instead – ie have been living in the UK for a certain time. And if the amount of benefit payable depends on the income, savings and so on of the person claiming, you may have to satisfy a *means test* to determine your resources. The income rules differ for different benefits – so you might qualify for one means-tested benefit but not another.

Whether the benefit is contributory or non-contributory, there may be other stringent conditions attached – medical tests, periods off work before a claim is made, and so on. But try not to be dismayed by the array of conditions attached to many benefits – the golden rule is

● if in doubt, read the appropriate DHSS leaflet or get advice (eg from your local social security office or any of the other sources listed below). **If you think you might qualify, claim.**

How much?

With most benefits, the amounts that are paid change each year (normally in November, but sometimes in April). Throughout this book, we've given the latest available rates of benefit, to give you some idea of the scale of benefit payable. When we say, for example, that 'in November 80, the amount paid was ...' we are giving the rates that apply for the year starting in November 1980 – ie until November 1981. For the most up-to-date rates, see leaflet NI 196 *Social security benefit rates* (available from social security offices).

With a limited range of contributory benefits, you may currently get an *earnings-related* amount on top of the basic benefit – this amount is based on your earnings from an employer in previous tax years (or, in some circumstances, the earnings of your husband or wife). And with certain benefits (contributory and non-contributory), you may get an extra amount for each child you support (▷ Child increases, below) and for one of certain adult dependants (▷ Wife/adult dependant increases, overleaf).

Child increases

Many benefits include increases for each child supported by the person claiming. The conditions for qualifying for child increases vary from benefit to benefit (see appropriate DHSS leaflet). But in general, child benefit must be being paid for the child. A married woman living with her husband can get child increases only if her husband is unable to support himself because of a physical or mental disability.

Even if the amount of the social security benefit you get is reduced because you haven't paid enough NI contributions, you should still get the full rate of child increase. But you can't normally get more than *one* child increase for each child – even if you qualify for two benefits which pay child increases. Child increases are tax-free.

The amount of child increase depends on which benefit you are getting:

● with widow's benefit, invalidity pension, retirement pension, invalid care allowance – child increase in November 80 was £7.50 a week

● with maternity allowance, sickness, unemployment and industrial injury benefits – child increase in November 80 was £1.25 a week.

Wife/adult dependant increases

With some benefits, you get an additional amount for:

● your wife

● your husband – if he can't support himself because of a physical or mental disability

● a close relative who normally lives with you

● a woman looking after a child for whom you are entitled to a child increase (▷ previous page).

But you can get only *one* wife/adult dependant increase – even if you support more than one such dependant or qualify for more than one benefit which pays this increase.

The rules about the amount of increase you get and how the dependant's income affects the increase vary from benefit to benefit – for details see the leaflet on that benefit and NI 196 *Social security benefit rates*.

Eligible for more than one benefit?

There are fairly complicated rules about which other benefits you can get if you are already getting a particular benefit. In general, you can't get more than one benefit for the same reason – for example, if you're off work because of an injury and are entitled to get both sickness benefit and industrial injury benefit, you can't get both. Normally, the higher of the benefits will be paid – in this case, industrial injury benefit is likely to be the higher one.

However, *child benefit* (▷ p. 155) is normally payable to people getting other social security benefits. And some *supplementary benefit* may often be paid in addition to whatever other benefits are payable (▷ opposite).

Where to go for help and information

Where possible we list, at the end of the details about each benefit, useful leaflets, giving their title, number and where to get them (these leaflets should also be available from main post offices). But below are some other sources of general information. The list is necessarily limited in scope – we can't possibly include every book, leaflet or organization which might be useful. But the following are good places to start:

● your local social security office: this is not only a source of leaflets describing the benefits – it should also be able to give help and information to people who need it (for address, see phone book under *Health and Social Security, Dept. of*)

● a Citizens' Advice Bureau – address in phone book. If your area has a Law Centre, this might be able to offer similar help

● a welfare rights officer. These days, some local authorities are employing people to help those in need to find their way round the social security system – ask at the town hall if your local authority offers this service

● a claimants' union: these are locally organized and often fairly ephemeral – you might have to ask around to find out if there is one in your area. Try the phone book

● the Citizens' Rights Office: this is a free advisory service on claiming benefits run by the Child Poverty Action Group (who publish some useful leaflets about the different benefits). The address is 1 Macklin Street, London WC2 5NH

● your trade union: this might be able to help you, particularly with claims to do with your work.

If these organizations can't help, try your local councillor – especially for benefits administered by local authorities (eg rate and rent rebates). You can contact him through the local council offices. As a last resort, you could try to get help from your MP (for name, ask at your local library, and write to House of Commons, London SW1A 0AA).

Note that the disabled might get help on benefits from the Disability Alliance (1 Cambridge Terrace, London NW1 4JL), or from the Disablement Income Group (28 Commercial Street, London E1 6LR) – they both offer free advisory services. And organizations set up for particular disabilities (eg blindness, multiple sclerosis) might be able to help. For addresses, see *Annual Charities Digest* in your local library.

War pensions
Anyone who is disabled or bereaved as a result of war or armed service (and their children, parents and other dependants) might qualify for a pension or lump sum under the *war pension scheme*. The rates of pension are normally higher than ordinary social security pensions – and they are tax-free. There is also a back-up welfare service offering extra help and advice to war pensioners.

If you think you might qualify (the description of war service is broad, and includes service in the Armed Forces since 1939 and civilian service in World War II) contact the War Pensions Office. Write, giving full details, to: Controller, Central Office (War Pensions), Department of Health and Social Security, Norcross, Blackpool FY5 3TA.

Supplementary benefit
This is currently tax-free, but there are proposals to tax supplementary benefit paid to the unemployed and families of strikers as from April 1982 onwards (▷ p. 28).

Supplementary benefit

This is the basic social security benefit designed to prevent anyone having too little to live on. You can claim it even if you are getting other benefits, if these leave you with inadequate resources. But you don't get it if:
● you are in paid full-time work
● you are under 19 and in full-time education, in a school or college.

A married woman living with her husband (or a woman living with a man as his wife) can't usually claim – the man must claim. And strikers, or people involved in a trade dispute, can normally claim only for their dependants (▷ p. 28).

There are two different types of supplementary benefit:
● supplementary pension – paid to people over pension age (65 for men, 60 for women)
● supplementary allowance – paid to people aged 16 or over, but under pension age. Anyone getting supplementary allowance must register for work and be available for work – this will exclude, for example, students during term-time. But single parents, some blind and chronically sick people, and certain other groups may be excused from signing on.
● How much?
There is no fixed amount of supplementary benefit – what you get depends on the result of a means test. This test is designed to discover your *resources*, and supplementary benefit is paid to bring these resources up to your *requirements*. Both resources and requirements are measured using official definitions.

Broadly, *resources* include almost all forms of income of the person claiming, and of his wife if he is a married man (or of a woman he lives with). Any earnings are included after deduction of tax, NI contributions, pension contributions and necessary work expenses (like travelling costs, trade union subscriptions and child-minding expenses). Small amounts of certain types of income can be subtracted from this total – these amounts are known as *disregards*. For example, from November 80 a man registered as unemployed could subtract the first £4 a week of his own earnings *plus* the first £4 a week of his wife's net earnings, *plus* up to £4 a week of any other income (eg industrial disablement benefit or war disablement pension – but not most other social security benefits nor a pension from a former employer).

Income from savings and investments is left out of resources. But anyone with more than £2,000 of savings and investments (excluding the value of an owner-occupied home) is not entitled to get supplementary benefit. This means people will have to live off their capital until it falls below £2,000, before they can get supplementary benefit.

Requirements are calculated in three parts. First, there is an allowance for housing costs: this covers rates and water rates; rent for a tenant (only part in certain circumstances – eg if there is a subtenant, or the rent is unreasonably high). House owners get their mortgage interest payments counted in, ground rent or feu duty, and a sum towards repairs and insurance. People who live in someone else's house (eg with relatives) usually get a fixed allowance for housing costs – £2.15 a week in November 80.

Second, there is a living allowance (known as the *scale rate*): an amount to cover the expenses of day-to-day living. The amount depends on the size of the family and the ages of any children in the family (▷ Fig. 21.1 for the amounts payable in November 80). The long-term scale is for people over pension age, and for people who have been getting supplementary benefit for a continuous period of one year or more and have not been required to register for work during that time. People aged 80 or over get 25p a week extra (50p if both of couple over 80). And blind people get a blindness addition of £1.25 a week. Anyone who voluntarily left their last job without good reason – or who was dismissed because of misconduct – may get lower-than-normal rates.

Figure 21.1 Supplementary benefit living allowances in November 80

	Ordinary scale £ a week	Long-term scale £ a week
Couples living together	34.60	43.45
Single people living in their own home, or a home they pay rent or rates for	21.30	27.15
Single people living in someone else's home		
Aged 18 or over	17.05	21.70
Aged 16 or 17	13.10	16.65
Plus, for each dependent child		
Aged under 10	7.30	7.30
Aged 11 to 15	10.90	10.90

Third, there is an allowance for unavoidably high day-to-day expenses, called *additional requirements*. These additional payments are given, for example, to people who must follow a special diet, or who have abnormally high laundry bills because of illness. A *heating addition* of £1.40 a week is made automatically to a supplementary pensioner over 70, or to a family on supplementary benefit with a child (or children) under 5. In both cases, they must be householders – ie not living in someone else's home. Additions are sometimes paid to people with central heating, and people who need to spend a lot on heating because of their health.

You can also claim one-off lump sum payments to cover essential one-off expenses which, if you paid them yourself, would leave you with less than £300 of capital. You may be able to get one of these *exceptional needs payments* for new bedding or furniture, or special tools or clothing for work. And, in certain very exceptional circumstances, you can get help to pay off HP debts.

See the example in last column for how this works in practice.

● How to claim

If you have to register for work and claim unemployment benefit, claim on form B1, available from unemployment benefit offices. If not, claim on form SB1 from a social security office or post office.

● Further information

SB 1 *Cash help: How to claim supplementary benefit*
SB 2 *Supplementary benefits and trade disputes*
SB 7 *Living together as man and wife*
SB 8 *After you've claimed supplementary benefit*
SB 9 *After you've claimed supplementary benefit when you're unemployed*
(All available from social security offices.) *Supplementary benefits handbook* is a more comprehensive guide – details of cost and availability from HMSO.

Cash help in emergencies

People who wouldn't normally qualify for supplementary benefit – because, for example, they're in full-time work – may be able to get a cash grant or loan if they are in *urgent need*. Urgent need is yet to be defined in regulations, but might include emergencies like becoming homeless because of fire.

People who start full-time work can claim supplementary benefit for up to 15 days to tide them over until their first pay day.

Is your income low?

People who qualify for supplementary benefit also get the welfare benefits dealt with on the opposite page. But people who are in full-time work (and therefore don't qualify for supplementary benefits) can get these welfare benefits free or cheap if their *resources* are less than their *requirements* (as defined for supplementary benefit). And people whose income is a few £££ over the level at which supplementary benefit is paid – whether or not they are in full-time work – may also qualify for help with the cost of these welfare benefits.

To get an idea if your income might count as *low*, get leaflet M11 *Free Milk and vitamins, glasses, dental treatment and prescriptions* from a post office or social security office.

Dan and Tessa Taylor have 2 children, aged 4 and 11, and pay £12.50 a week in rent and rates. They have the following *requirements* (using the weekly figures for November 80):
£34.60 for their living allowance
£7.30 for their 4-year-old
£10.90 for their 11-year-old
£12.50 to cover their rent and rates

£1.40 heating addition
This adds up to £66.70. The Taylors can get supplementary benefit if their *resources* are less than this total (provided they meet the other qualifications for getting benefit).

Help with the cost of housing

Rate rebates
This is a benefit administered by local authorities (not the Department of Health and Social Security) to help with the burden of rates.

People on supplementary benefit can't get rate rebates — they get help with their rates as part of their benefit. So if you might qualify for both supplementary benefit and a rate rebate, ask your local social security office for help with deciding which to go for.
● Who qualifies?
Anyone paying rates on their home — which includes tenants, whose rates are often hidden in their rent — provided their income is below a certain level. The level to qualify for a rebate depends on the size of the family of the person claiming, and the amount paid in rates. The levels will go up in November 80 — details not finalized when this book went to press. In November 79, a couple with 2 children on a before-tax income of £4,000 a year would have got a rate rebate if their rates had come to around £61 a year or more.
● How much?
This depends mainly on the income of the person claiming, the size of their family and the amount they pay in rates. For example, in November 79, the couple in the example above could have got around £116 rebate on a yearly bill of £250. Disabled people qualify for somewhat larger-than-normal rebates, and also ▷ p. 99. The maximum rebate for November 79 was £166 a year (£234 in London GLC area). Maximum amounts in 1980 are to be £249.60 a year (£351 in London GLC area). This benefit is tax-free.

● How to claim
If you pay rates directly to the council, apply to your local authority treasurer's office; if you pay rates as part of your rent, apply to your local authority housing department. The addresses of both these departments are in the phone book, normally under the name of your local district council or London borough.
Note that you can't get a rebate for water rates, nor, except in Scotland, for sewerage charges.

● Further information
How to pay less rates (in Scotland, Rate rebates — latest), available from local authorities and Citizens' Advice Bureaux.

Rent rebates and allowances
These are benefits administered by local authorities (not the Department of Health and Social Security) to help with paying the rent. Council tenants get a rebate in the form of reduced rent; private tenants get a cash amount called an allowance.

People on supplementary benefit can't get rent rebates (or allowances) — they get help with the rent as part of their benefit. So if you might qualify for both supplementary benefit and a rent rebate (or allowance), ask your local social security office for help with deciding which to go for.
● Who qualifies?
Anyone paying rent for their home — provided their income is below a certain level. The level to qualify for a rebate (or allowance) depends on the size of the family of the person claiming, and the amount paid in rent. The levels will go up in November 80 — details not finalized

when this book went to press. In November 79, a couple with 2 children on a before-tax income of £4,000 a year could have got a rent rebate (or allowance) if their rent had come to around £3.45 a week or more.
● How much?
The amount of rebate (or allowance) depends mainly on the income of the person claiming, the size of their family and the amount they pay in rent. In November 79, the couple in the example above could have got about £7 a week rent rebate (or allowance) if their rent was £15 a week. Disabled people qualify for larger-than-normal rent rebates/ allowances. The maximum rebate in November 79 was £10 a week (£13 in London GLC area). Maximum amounts from 1 July 80 are £23 a week (£25 in London GLC area). This benefit is tax-free.
● How to claim
Apply to your local authority housing department (address in phone book, normally under the name of your local district council or London borough).
Note that you won't get a rebate (or allowance) for any part of your rent which goes to pay for heating, lighting, furniture or services.

● Further information
There's money off rent (in Scotland, Rent rebates — read all about it) available from local authorities and Citizens' Advice Bureaux.

Welfare benefits

Free prescriptions
● Who qualifies?
Any of the following:
● children under the age of 16
● anyone over pension age (men aged 65 or over, women aged 60 or over)
● families getting family income supplement (▷ p. 156)
● people who qualify for welfare benefits because their income is low (for what this means ▷ opposite)
● expectant mothers and women who have had a baby in the past 12 months
● people with certain medical conditions (eg diabetes, colostomy); for a full list, see leaflet FP91/EC91 (▷ below)
● war service disablement pensioners for treatment for their war services disability.
● How to claim
If you're under 16, over pension age, a war service disablement pensioner, or receiving supplementary benefit or family income supplement, simply fill in the back of the prescription form before going to the chemist. Expectant mothers should ask their doctor, midwife or health visitor for a form to claim exemption. Mothers with a child under 12 months and people with certain medical conditions must apply for an exemption certificate — see leaflet FP91/EC91 for details. If you're claiming because your income is low, claim on leaflet M11.
● Further information
FP91/EC91 NHS prescription charges — exemptions and refunds (available from post offices and social security offices).

Cheap prescriptions
For a fixed charge, you can buy a prepayment certificate which entitles you to all NHS

prescriptions free of charge for the period of the certificate. Prescription charges will be 70p each from April 80 to December 80, and a prepayment certificate will work out cheaper for that period if you need more than 6 items in 4 months or more than 17 items in a year. From December 80, prescription charges go up to £1 — prepayment certificates are likely to be worthwhile for similar numbers of prescriptions.
You can get a prepayment certificate by filling in form FP95/ EC95 (available from post offices and social security offices).

Free or cheap NHS dental treatment and glasses
● Who qualifies?
Any of the following:
● children under 16, and children over 16 still at school. Until April 81, all young people under 21 can get free dental treatment (but not free false teeth if aged 16 or over and not at school)
● anyone getting family income supplement (▷ p. 156)
● people who qualify for welfare benefits because their income is low (▷ opposite)
● expectant mothers and women who have had a baby in the last 12 months can claim free dental treatment
● How to claim
The dentist or optician can give you the right form — so ask, if you think you qualify.

● Further information
M11 Free milk and vitamins, glasses, dental treatment and prescriptions.
NHS 4 Your teeth and the NHS
NHS 6 Your sight and the NHS (all available from post offices and social security offices).

Welfare benefits
(cont)

Free milk and vitamins
● Who qualifies?
Any family getting supplementary benefit or family income supplement — or a family which qualifies for welfare benefits because their income is *low* (▷ p. 230) — can get one pint of milk a day and vitamins A, C and D for an expectant mother and each child under school age.

Handicapped children between the ages of 5 and 16, who aren't at school, can get free milk, and so can children at an approved nursery or play-group or with a registered childminder.
● How to claim
If you're claiming because your income is low, claim on leaflet M11 (▷ below). If you're on supplementary benefit or family income supplement, you should automatically get tokens for free milk and vitamins — contact your local social security office if not. For handicapped children, claim on form FW20 (available at social security offices).

● Further information
MV1 *Milk and vitamins for you and your children* (available from health centres and clinics).
M11 *Free milk and vitamins, glasses, dental treatment and prescriptions* (available from post offices and social security offices).

Refund of fares to travel to hospital
● Who qualifies?
The following people can get a refund of their fares (and the fares of their dependants) to go to an NHS hospital for treatment — including the fares of an escort if necessary:
● people on supplementary benefit

(▷ p. 229)
● people on family income supplement (▷ p. 156)
● people who qualify for welfare benefits because their income is *low* (▷ p. 230).
● people getting war pensions
● How to claim
If you're on supplementary benefit or family income supplement, get a refund of your fares at the hospital — you'll need to show your benefit order book.

If your income is low, claim on leaflet H11 (▷ below). If you're a war pensioner, ask at your local social security office.

● Further information
H11 *Help with travelling expenses for hospital patients* (available from hospitals and social security offices).

Free NHS hearing aids
● Who qualifies
Anyone with impaired hearing for whom a hearing aid is prescribed. The aid will be supplied and fitted, serviced, maintained and supplied with batteries, free of charge.
● How to claim
First see your family doctor, who will, if necessary, send you to a special clinic in the local hospital for examination. If the clinic prescribes a hearing aid, they will refer you to a hearing aid centre, who will supply and fit the aid.

Benefits for the disabled

None of these benefits depends on your NI contribution record.

Attendance allowance
This is a weekly payment for people who are severely disabled (physically or mentally) and need a lot of looking after.
● Who qualifies?
The person claiming must:
● need constant supervision or frequent attention because of a physical or mental disability — and this need must have lasted at least 6 months (including any periods spent in hospital)
● be aged 2 or over. If under 16, the person claiming must need substantially more supervision or attention than a normal child of the same age
● normally live in the UK, be present in the UK, and have been present there for 26 weeks out of the last 12 months.

Anyone who is not of British nationality or who was born outside the UK must meet extra residence conditions — ▷ leaflet in next column for details.
● How much?
The amount of the allowance depends on the extent to which the person has to be looked after. In November 80 the rate of allowance was £21.65 a week for a person needing care *both* day *and* night; £14.45 a week for a person needing care *either* day *or* night. This benefit is tax-free.
● How to claim
Claim on the form in leaflet NI 205 (▷ next column). Attendance allowance can't be paid for any period before it has been claimed, so claim it as soon as you meet all the conditions. If you haven't yet needed care for 6 months, you

can claim after 4 months of needing care — so you will get the allowance as soon as the 6 months are up. For a child approaching the age of 2, claim when 22 months old.

After you have sent your claim form to the local social security office, you will be visited by a doctor who will examine you and make a report on your health and the attendance you need. The actual decision on your claim will be made by the Attendance Allowance Board (or a doctor delegated to act for it). This board is an independent body of doctors and lay-people.

● Further information
NI 205 *Attendance allowance* (available from social security offices).

Invalid care allowance
This is a weekly payment for people who can't work because they have to stay at home to care for a severely disabled relative — but a married woman (or a woman living with a man as his wife) cannot normally claim.
● Who qualifies?
The person claiming must:
● be of working age (16 to 65 for men, 16 to 60 for women)
● not be doing any work which pays more than £6 a week
● not be attending a course of full-time education
● normally live in the UK, be present in the UK and have been present here for at least 26 weeks out of the last 12 months.

The person claiming must also spend at least 35 hours a week caring for a severely disabled close relative (▷ leaflet below for which relatives count as close). To count as severely disabled, the

relative must be getting attendance allowance (▷ left), or a similar allowance payable with war pensions or pensions for disablement at work.

A married woman can get this allowance only if she is separated from her husband, and he contributes less than the amount of invalid care allowance towards her maintenance.

Anyone getting sickness or invalidity benefit, unemployment benefit, retirement pension, non-contributory invalidity benefit and certain other social security benefits cannot normally get invalid care allowance — but if the amount of these benefits is less than the amount of invalid care allowance, the difference will be paid on top of the other benefits. Anyone getting supplementary benefit, can get invalid care allowance — but the amount of allowance counts as a resource in working out the amount of benefit payable (▷ p. 229).
● How much?
The allowance was £16.30 a week in November 80. Increases for children or for an adult dependant (▷ p. 227) may be paid with this benefit. For example, a married man getting an increase for his wife and for 2 children got £41.10 a week in November 80. This benefit is taxable (but increases for children are tax-free).
● How to claim
Claim on the form included in leaflet NI 212 as soon as you think you qualify. Send the form to the Invalid Care Allowance Unit (address in the leaflet).

● Further information
NI 212 *Invalid care allowance* (available from social security offices).

Legal help

Mobility allowance
This is a weekly payment for people who are so severely disabled that they are unable (or virtually unable) to walk.
● Who qualifies?
The person claiming must:
● be aged 5 or over,
● be unable (or virtually unable) to walk, likely to remain so for at least a year, and be able to benefit from greater mobility
● normally live in the UK, be present in the UK and have been present in the UK for a total of 12 out of the last 18 months.
Anyone whose health would be made much worse by the exertion of walking, or whose life would be in danger, counts as virtually unable to walk. And disabled people who qualified for help under the pre-1976 vehicle scheme for the disabled automatically qualify
● How much?
The amount of the allowance was £14.50 a week in November 80 This benefit is taxable.
People getting mobility allowance can lease a car on favourable terms, or buy one on HP, under the *Motability scheme* – details from Motability, State House, High Holborn, London WC1R 4SX.
● How to claim
Claim on the form in leaflet NI 211. Send the claim forms to DHSS Mobility Allowance Unit, Norcross, Blackpool FY5 3TA.
After you have sent back your claim form, a medical examination will be arranged, unless you're claiming another allowance which provides the DHSS with evidence of your inability to walk.

● Further information
NI 211 *Mobility allowance* (available from social security offices).

Non-contributory invalidity pension
NCIP is a weekly payment for people who have not been able to work for some time and who don't qualify for the full flat rate of sickness or invalidity benefit because they haven't paid enough NI contributions.
● Who qualifies?
The person claiming must:
● be aged 16 or over, and under pension age (65 for men, 60 for women). But NCIP is not normally payable to anyone aged under 19 if still at school or college full-time (unless the course is specially arranged for physically or mentally handicapped people)
● have been incapable of work for a continuous period of at least 28 weeks. NCIP is not payable for any period within these 28 weeks. But once qualified, if NCIP is claimed again after a break of not more than 13 weeks, the benefit can start again as soon as the break ends – without waiting another 28 weeks
● not get as much as (or more than) the weekly amount of NCIP in sickness benefit, invalidity benefit, injury benefit and certain other social security benefits
● live in the UK, and have been present in the UK for at least 26 weeks out of the last 12 months, *and* have lived in the UK for a total of at least 10 years during the past 20 years.
But a married woman living with her husband, or separated from her husband and getting maintenance

from him of at least as much as the weekly amount of NCIP, or a woman living with a man as his wife, has to meet extra conditions. She can't get NCIP unless as well as meeting the other conditions, she is incapable of doing her normal household duties for a continuous period of at least 28 weeks.
● How much?
The amount of the benefit was £16.30 a week in November 80. Increases for children or for an adult dependant (▷ p. 227) may be paid with this benefit. For example, a married man getting an increase for his wife and for 2 children got £41.10 a week in November 80. This benefit is tax-free.
● How to claim
Claim on the form in leaflet NI 210 (leaflet NI 214 for married women). Claim as soon as you think you qualify (or if you think you will qualify within 6 weeks). You will have to supply evidence that you are unable to work, usually in the form of a doctor's statement.
If you go or intend to go back to work of any kind, or plan to go abroad, notify your local social security office. The same applies if you are a woman getting NCIP and get married, or begin to live with a man as his wife. If you (or your wife) go into hospital, NCIP won't normally be reduced unless the stay lasts for more than 8 weeks.

● Further information
NI 210 *Non-contributory invalidity pension*
NI 214 *Non-contributory invalidity pension for married women*
(Both available from social security offices.)

There are two kinds available: *legal advice* (for people who need help from a solicitor) and *legal aid* (for those involved – or who might be involved – in civil or criminal court proceedings).
● Who qualifies?
People whose resources are low in relation to their needs. Anyone getting supplementary benefit or family income supplement normally qualifies automatically.
● What for?
Legal advice covers help from a solicitor up to a value of £25, £55 if you're filing a petition for a divorce. Court proceedings and representation at tribunals are not covered (▷ Legal aid)
Legal aid covers all the work done by a solicitor before going to court. It also covers the cost of a barrister to represent you in court. For civil cases, this help can be claimed either if you are being sued, or if you want to sue someone else. For criminal cases, the help is available only if you are being charged. You may have to pay towards the cost of legal aid if you are well off enough.
● How to claim
Legal advice: Get the name of a solicitor who does this kind of work (Citizens' Advice Bureaux have a list).
Legal aid: For *civil* proceedings, consult a solicitor and make it clear that you want legal aid. For *criminal* offences, contact a solicitor as soon as you are charged or else in court.
For both legal advice and legal aid, you will have to give details of your income and capital.

● Further information
A guide to legal aid
Legal aid, financial limits
Legal aid could help you
Guide to legal aid in Scotland
(All these should be available from local Citizens' Advice Bureaux and public libraries.)
Ask for current leaflet titles from Law Society Press Office, (01–242–1222). In Scotland, try the Scottish Law Society (031–226–7411).

Criminal injuries compensation
● Who qualifies?
People injured as a result of a crime of violence or when trying (or helping police) to prevent a crime or arrest a suspected criminal. Dependants of those killed as a result of a violent crime may also qualify. Doesn't depend on NI contribution record.
● How much?
Depends on the amount of pain or suffering caused by the injury; and on any loss of earnings or out-of-pocket expenses. You won't qualify if all these items are assessed to add up to less than the lower compensation limit – £150 in mid-79. This benefit is tax-free.
● How to claim
Get application form CICB 2, from the Criminal Injuries Compensation Board, 10–12, Russell Square, London WC1B 5EN.

● Further information
Leaflet *Crimes of violence – a guide to the compensation scheme*, available from address above.

Help from local authorities

Local authorities have the power to offer many forms of help if they wish. But they aren't obliged to provide many of the benefits described here, so the provision of these *discretionary benefits* can vary considerably from one local authority to another. With some types of help, you might have to pay some or all of the cost – the amount depends on how well off you are and which local authority area you are in.

The following types of help may be available for the sick, convalescent, elderly, disabled, or mentally handicapped:

● help with the housework – a home help may help out with the housework. There may be a laundry service for the incontinent, or for people who are too ill to do their own laundry

● meals on wheels – a midday meal delivered to the house, or available at a day centre (▷ below)

● day centres – somewhere to go during the day, normally providing handicraft facilities, educational and social activities

● cheap or free travel – for example, low fares on buses, recuperative holidays and outings

● day nurseries and playgroups – for children under school age

● special aids and equipment for the home – for example, wheelchair ramps, special bathroom fittings for the infirm. Help with the cost of installing a telephone may be available, and help with the quarterly rental charge

● nursing at home – where the person concerned is capable of living at home, nursing equipment (for example, special beds) and visits by nurses and health visitors can be organized

● visits by health visitors and social workers – to advise you and make sure you get all the help you need

● residential homes – for people who can't cope in their own home, temporarily or permanently. Some local authorities offer sheltered housing – homes grouped around facilities for the old and disabled, often with a warden on hand.

Most of these forms of help are available from local authority social services departments (address in phone book, usually under name of local county or district council or London borough). But help with adapting the home is normally provided by local authority housing departments (address in phone book, under name of local district council or London borough). And nursing in the home is provided by local health authorities – doctors can normally make the arrangements.

Claiming benefits

If, after reading this book, you think you might qualify for one of the benefits described, get the explanatory leaflet we refer you to for further information (the names of these leaflets may change, but you should get the right leaflet if you ask for the title and number we give). Then, if you aren't sure whether to claim, talk to the people at the local social security office too.

Once you have satisfied yourself that you appear to qualify for a benefit, put in a claim.

**Don't put off claiming:
you could lose out if
you delay.**

Make sure you follow any instructions on the claim form and relevant leaflet. With some benefits, you must produce documents (for example, birth or marriage certificate, recent pay slips) – but don't delay putting in a claim if some of these are missing – you can supply them later.

Appeals

If you decide to appeal against a decision on a benefit you have claimed, act quickly – you normally have to appeal within a certain time of the decision (commonly within 21 days). Details of how to appeal (which depends on the benefit) will normally be sent to you at the same time as the decision.

With many benefits (for example, supplementary benefit, sickness benefit and unemployment benefit) you can appeal to an independent tribunal. But even when there is no formal appeal procedure, you might be able to change a decision by insisting that a mistake has been made – supplying documents you had mislaid or other evidence could help.

With formal appeals, you can argue your own case or be represented (which might increase your chances of success). But whether or not you are represented, it makes sense to attend the appeal – or to send someone along if you can't go yourself.

The organizations mentioned on p. 228 may be able to help you organize your appeal, and might even send along someone to represent you. You might qualify for free or cheap legal advice (▷ p. 233) – ask at your local Citizens' Advice Bureau.

Your contribution record and the benefits you can get

To get many social security benefits, you have to have paid the right amount in the right sort of NI contributions at the right time. Any deficiency in your contribution record may reduce the amount of benefit you're entitled to.

This won't always happen: in some situations you can get credits to make up a deficiency (▷ p. 236) and there are special rules to help out those off work to care for children or invalids (▷ p. 236).

Contribution classes
You won't pay any contributions at all if you are
● under 16
● over pension age (65 for men, 60 for women).

Otherwise, what you pay and what you can claim depend on what class of contribution you pay.

Class 1 contributions are paid by anyone who is employed and earns more than the lower earnings limit (the equivalent of £23 a week, £99.67 a month in the 80/81 tax year). Class 1 are paid as a percentage of all earnings up to the upper earnings limit (£165 in the 80/81 tax year). They are usually deducted at source in the same way as tax under PAYE.

The employer also has to pay a contribution – again, a percentage of the employee's earnings.

How much you both pay depends on
● how much you earn
● whether or not you are contracted out of the State pension scheme (▷ p. 54) – less if you are.

On p. 52, we give the rates of Class 1 contributions that are paid.
Some married women and widows can pay a reduced rate of Class 1 contributions (▷ p. 237).

Class 2 contributions are paid by the self-employed. They are paid at a flat rate (£2.50 a week for the 80/81 tax year), and are compulsory unless your earnings are very small (£1,250 a year for the 80/81 tax year).

The self-employed may also have to pay *Class 4* contributions (▷ next column).

Some married women and widows may have chosen not to pay Class 2 contributions at all (▷ p. 237).

Class 3 contributions are voluntary. They may be paid by those not liable for Class 1 or 2 contributions (ie mainly those who are not working) and who aren't entitled to credits to fill gaps in their contribution record (▷ p. 236). Class 3 contributions are a fixed amount – £2.40 a week for the 80/81 tax year). See p. 236 for whether or not it's worth choosing to pay Class 3 contributions.

Class 4 contributions

are compulsory for the self-employed whose profits are above a certain level. In the 80/81 tax year they were 5 per cent of profits between £2,650 and £8,300.

Foreign contributions may also count towards benefit. Ask at your social security office.

Credited contributions are awarded in some situations (▷ p. 236).

How the system works
Since April 75, *contribution years* have been the same as tax years – beginning on 6 April. For each year, there is a lower earnings limit (below which Class 1 contributions don't need to be paid) and an upper earnings limit (beyond which no further Class 1 contribution has to be made).

Most NI benefits have one or more contribution conditions which you have to satisfy to get the particular benefit. It is important for married women and widows to remember that whether they qualify for benefit may depend not on their own contribution record, but on their husband's.

It is also important to remember that Class 2 and 3 contributions don't count for all benefits. And neither Class 4 contributions nor the reduced rate Class 1 contributions which some married

women and widows can pay (▷ p. 237) count towards any of the benefits.

Figure 21.4 overleaf gives details of the social security benefits which depend on your NI contribution record. It shows the classes of contribution which count towards qualifying for each benefit, and gives a brief outline of the contribution conditions which you have to meet in order to qualify.

To get the full basic benefit you usually have to have paid a certain amount in contributions – the amount is set in terms of what you would pay in Class 1 contributions if your earnings were at the lower earnings limit. Where other classes of contribution also count towards qualifying, each contribution is counted as the equivalent of a Class 1 contribution at the lower earnings limit.

Full Class 1 contributions paid on earnings above the lower earnings limit count towards earnings related amounts which may be paid on top of basic benefit. This currently applies to unemployment benefit, sickness benefit, maternity allowance, widow's allowance and industrial injury benefit. The extra contributions also count towards increases in retirement pension and invalidity pension.

With some benefits (ie unemployment and sickness benefit, maternity allowance and grant, and the earnings-related supplement of industrial injury benefit), you have to have paid (or been credited with) a particular amount in contributions in what is called the *relevant tax year* (running from 6 April).

This year is *not* the same as the benefit year (broadly, the calendar year) in which you are claiming. The relevant tax year is usually the last tax year which ends before the start of the benefit year for which you are claiming. Figure 21.2 below shows how this works out in practice. (But note that for maternity allowance you add about 3 months to the dates shown on the left-hand side.) You can see that your claim this year could be based on your contribution record in a year which started over 2½ years ago.

With widowed mother's allowance, retirement pension and widow's pension, you must have clocked up a minimum number of what are known as *qualifying years* to get the full amount of benefit. A qualifying year is one in which you have paid (or been credited with) an amount in Class 1 contributions of at least as much as 52 contributions at the

Figure 21.2 What is the relevant tax year?

Claim arising between:	Relevant tax year
6 Jan 80 to 3 Jan 81	6 Apr 78 to 5 Apr 79
4 Jan 81 to 2 Jan 82	6 Apr 79 to 5 Apr 80
3 Jan 82 to 1 Jan 83	6 Apr 80 to 5 Apr 81
2 Jan 83 to 6 Jan 84	6 Apr 81 to 5 Apr 82

Fig. 21.3 How many qualifying years needed?

Length of working life	Number of qualifying years needed
10 years or less	Length of working life, minus 1
11–20 years	Length of working life, minus 2
21–30 years	Length of working life, minus 3
31–40 years	Length of working life, minus 4
41 years or more	Length of working life, minus 5

lower earnings limit. Each Class 2 or 3 contribution counts as a Class 1 contribution at the weekly lower earnings limit.

The number of qualifying years needed compared with your working life is shown in Figure 21.3, p. 235. Your *working life* is the number of complete tax years from the one in which you were 16, and ending with the one before you reach pension age (65 for men, 60 for women), or die – whichever is earlier.

To work out your *qualifying years* for contributions made before 6 April 75, add up all your contributions and divide by 50 – rounding up in your favour.

Should you pay Class 3 contributions? Class 3 contributions count towards some benefits (▷ Fig. 21.4). They are rarely worth paying unless you need just a few to plug up gaps in your record.

The people who should perhaps consider paying them are young married men, who want to protect their wife's entitlement to widow's benefit or child's special allowance (▷ p. 157). So they may be particularly important for married male students, low-paid apprentices, or prisoners. In general, the younger the contributor the more difference Class 3 contributions will make.

The home responsibilities rules (▷ next coloumn) have made Class 3 contributions much less important for those at home looking after children or invalids.

Home responsibilities Since 6 April 78, special rules apply to people who are unable to work regularly because they have to stay at home to look after someone. These new rules make it easier to qualify for a retirement pension (or widow's benefit, for widows).

These special rules apply if during a whole tax year:
● you receive child benefit for a child under 16
or
● you look after an invalid regularly – at least 35 hours a week – who receives either

attendance allowance or constant attendance allowance
or
● you receive supplementary benefit so that you can look after an elderly or sick person at home.

The rules mean that the qualifying years (▷ above) you need to qualify for full benefits are reduced by each year you have to spend at home. But the number of years you need can't be reduced to below 20 – so you could still end up with reduced benefit if you fail to clock up at least 20 qualifying years.

When credits are awarded With all contributory benefits, you must have acutally *paid* some contributions to qualify. Credits alone don't qualify you for anything.

In general, the following people can get credits towards some benefits:
● those between the ages of 16 and 18, who stay on at school
● those receiving or eligible for sickness, invalidity or unemployment benefit, or invalid care allowance
● those who have recently stopped

studying, training or an apprenticeship
● those taking Manpower Services Commission training courses, provided they and the courses meet certain conditions.

If you're in doubt about whether or not you will get credits to fill a gap in your contribution record, ask at your local social security office.

Figure 21.4   Contribution conditions for contributory benefits

Benefit	Which class of contributions	Normal conditions for full amount
Unemployment benefit (flat rate)	Full Class 1	● Equivalent of 25 contributions at the *lower earnings limit* paid in any tax year (1) AND ● Equivalent of 50 contributions at the *lower earnings limit* paid or credited in *relevant tax year* (▷ p. 235)
Earnings-related supplement (4)	Full Class 1	● Drawing full flat-rate benefit AND ● Paid full Class 1 contributions in *relevant tax year* on earnings amounting to more than 50 times the *lower earnings limit* (▷ p. 235)
Sickness benefit (flat rate)	Full Class 1, Class 2	● As for unemployment benefit
Earnings-related supplement (4)	Full Class 1	● As for unemployment benefit
Maternity grant (It's proposed that, from April 82, no contributions should be needed for this benefit – rules given will end if proposal becomes law)	Full Class 1, Class 2 Class 3	● Equivalent of 25 contributions at the *lower earnings limit* paid in any tax year (1) AND ● Equivalent of 25 contributions at *lower earnings limit* paid or credited in the *relevant tax year* (▷ p. 235) (1)
Industrial injury and death benefit	None needed	● Full amount paid irrespective of contribution record
Earnings-related supplement (4)	Full Class 1	● As for unemployment benefit
Maternity allowance (flat rate)	Full Class 1, Class 2	● As for unemployment benefit
Earnings-related supplement (4)	Full Class 1	● As for unemployment benefit
Death grant	Full Class 1, Class 2, Class 3	● Equivalent of 25 contributions at the *lower earnings limit* paid in any tax year before year of death (1)
Widow's allowance (2) (flat rate)	Full Class 1, Class 2, Class 3	● As for death grant
Earnings related addition (2) (4)	Full Class 1	● As for unemployment benefit

Married women and widows

Some women (broadly, those married before 6 April 77) were able to choose to pay a lower rate of Class 1 NI contribution (or no Class 2 contribution at all, if they were self-employed). Women who made this choice can continue to go on paying the reduced rate (or no contribution at all) — but ▷ right.

Unless they notify their local social security office that they want to pay the full rate of contribution, they won't be able to claim any of the contributory benefits

(▷ Fig. 21.4) on their own contributions record.

They can still get a pension, on their husband's record of contributions, but it will be lower than the regular State pension, and not payable until the husband (rather than the wife) retires. Maternity grant and death grant may also be paid on their husband's contributions.

Should you choose to pay the full Class 1 (or Class 2) contribution? It is tricky to weigh the pros and cons of changing your mind

and opting to pay the full stamp. A young married woman who intends to take some years off work to raise a family might well be advised to stump up the full Class 1 contribution while she's still working. This will make her eligible for a pension in her own right — and the home responsibility scheme (▷ opposite) will protect this pension if she decides to stay at home for some time to look after children. Paying full Class 1 contributions will also let her qualify for maternity allowance, if she works for long

enough before leaving to have a child. And when at work she would also qualify for unemployment benefit, sickness benefit and invalidity benefit.

Self-employed married women are in a more tricky position. Class 2 contributions (which don't count towards some benefits. ▷ Fig. 21.4) are a flat-rate, no matter what you earn.

If your earnings are likely to fluctuate, it may be sensible to be cautious about committing yourself (when you're feeling fairly well off) to paying out a sum that

may well be a burden if your earnings start to plummet.

Because the self-employed don't qualify for the additional State pension on retirement, they need to look particularly carefully at what income they'll get when they retire. And because they won't have sick pay insurance provided by an employer (as some employed people do — ▷ p. 142) they should consider taking out this type of insurance themselves. If you are self-employed, and have chosen to pay no NI stamps at all (and therefore don't qualify for even the basic benefit) looking at these two factors could be even more vital for you than for others.

Even if you've chosen to pay lower Class 1 contributions or no Class 2. contributions, you'll automatically have to pay the full Class 1 or Class 2 contributions if you don't work for an employer, nor are self-employed, during any 2 consecutive tax years after April 78. And if your marriage ends in divorce or annulment, you also have to start paying full Class 1 or Class 2 contributions.

Benefit	Which class of contributions	Normal conditions for full amount
Child's special allowance (2)	Full Class 1, Class 2, Class 3	● Equivalent of 50 contributions at *lower earnings limit* paid in any tax year before year of death of former husband
Widowed mother's allowance (2)	Full Class 1, Class 2, Class 3	● Must have *paid* enough contributions in any tax year before year of death for that year to be a *qualifying year* (1) AND ● Adequate number of *qualifying years* (▷ p. 235)
Additional pension (2) (3)	Full Class 1	● Drawing basic benefit AND ● Paid full Class 1 contributions on earnings above *lower earnings limit* since 6 April 78
Widow's pension (2)	Full Class 1, Class 2 Class 3	● As for widowed mother's allowance
Additional pension (2) (3)	Full Class 1	● As for widowed mother's allowance
Invalidity benefit (flat rate)	Full Class 1, Class 2	● Must have been entitled to sickness benefit for 28 weeks. Sickness benefit will then be replaced by invalidity benefit automatically
Additional pension	Full Class 1	● As for widowed mother's allowance
Basic retirement pension	Full Class 1, Class 2, Class 3	● Must have *paid* enough contributions in any tax year for that year to be a *qualifying* year AND ● Adequate number of *qualifying years* (▷ p. 235)
Additional pension (3)	Full Class 1	● Drawing basic retirement pension AND ● Paid full Class 1 contributions on earnings above *lower earnings limit* since 6 April 78 (▷ p. 235)

1. This condition must be satisfied before *any* benefit can be paid.
2. Only late husband's contributions count.
3. If you (or your late husband, for widow's benefits) belonged to a contracted-out employer's pension scheme after April 78, the employer's scheme will effectively pay some or all of your additional pension.
4. To be reduced from January 81, and abolished by January 82. This will probably apply to industrial injury and death benefit.

Index